Library of
Davidson College

T. E. Brown

FO'C'S'LE YARNS
an uncensored edition
of four Manx narratives
in verse

Edited by

Max Keith Sutton

Maureen E. Godman

Nicholas L. Shimmin

University Press of America, ®Inc.
Lanham • New York • Oxford

Copyright © 1998
University Press of America,® Inc.
4720 Boston Way
Lanham, Maryland 20706

12 Hid's Copse Rd.
Cummor Hill, Oxford OX2 9JJ

All rights reserved
Printed in the United States of America
British Library Cataloging in Publication Information Available

Library of Congress Cataloging-in-Publication Data

Brown, T. E. (Thomas Edward), 1830-1897.
Fo'c's'le yarns: an uncensored edition of four Manx narratives in verse / T.E. Brown ; edited by Max Keith Sutton, Maureen E. Godman, Nicholas L. Shimmin.
p. cm.
Partial Contents: Betsy Lee—Christmas Rose—Captain Tom and Captain High—Tommy Big-eyes.
Includes Bibliographical references.
1. Narrative poetry, English—Isle of Man. 2. Dialect poetry, English —Isle of Man. 3. Isle of Man—poetry. I. Title
PR4175.B5F63 1998   821'.8—dc21   98-29733 CIP

ISBN 0-7618-1215-6 (cloth: alk. ppr.)

The paper used in this publication meets the minimum requirements of American National Standard for Information Sciences—Permanence of Paper for Printed Library Materials, ANSI Z39.48—1984

To Richard Eversole and Dollin Kelly, and in memory of

Geoffrey Crellin

T. E. Brown at Clifton College
Manx National Heritage

Contents

Abbreviations	vii
Acknowledgments	ix
Introduction	xi
A Note on the Gloss	xxv
Brown's Preface	xxvii
Betsy Lee	1
Christmas Rose	45
Captain Tom and Captain Hugh	109
Tommy Big-Eyes	145
Explanatory Notes	237
Betsy Lee	237
Christmas Rose	245
Captain Tom and Captain Hugh	253
Tommy Big-Eyes	257
Textual Notes: Copy Texts, Treatment of Variants, and Editions Cited	265
Betsy Lee	269
Christmas Rose	277
Captain Tom and Captain Hugh	285
Tommy Big-Eyes	289
Selected Bibliography	295

Fo'c's'le Yarns

Fishing Boats, Port Erin
Manx National Heritage

Abbreviations

The following abbreviations are used in the gloss and the explanatory notes:

CP	*The Complete Poems of T. E. Brown.* Introduction by W. E. Henley. London: Macmillan, 1901.
Cregeen	Archibald Cregeen. *A Dictionary of the Manks Language.* 1835. Ilkley: Moxon Press, 1984.
Killip	Margaret Killip. *The Folklore of the Isle of Man.* London: Batsford, 1975.
Kimbrough	Joseph Conrad. *The Nigger of the "Narcissuss."* Ed. Robert Kimbrough. New York: W. W. Norton, 1979.
Kneen	J. J. Kneen. *The Place-Names of the Isle of Man, with their Origins and History.* Douglas: The Manx Society, 1925-6.
Letters	*Letters of Thomas Edward Brown.* Edited with an Introductory Memoir by Sidney T. Irwin. 2 vols. Westminster: Constable, 1900.
Moore	A. W. Moore, with Sophia Morrison and Edmund Goodwin. *A Vocabulary of the Anglo-Manx Dialect.* London: Oxford University Press, 1924.
OED	*Oxford English Dictionary.* 2nd ed. Prepared by J. A. Simpson and E. S. C. Weiner. 20 vols. Oxford: Clarendon Press, 1989.
Paton	C. I. Paton. *Manx Calendar Customs.* Publications of the Folk-Lore Society 110. London: W. Glaisher, 1939.
Teignmouth	Charles John Shore, Lord Teignmouth. *Sketches of the Coasts and Islands of Scotland and of the Isle of Man.* 2 vols. London: Parker, 1836.
Tobias	Richard Tobias. *T. E. Brown.* Boston: Twayne Publishers, 1978.
Wright	Joseph Wright. *The English Dialect Dictionary.* 6 vols. 1898-1905. London: Oxford University Press, 1961.

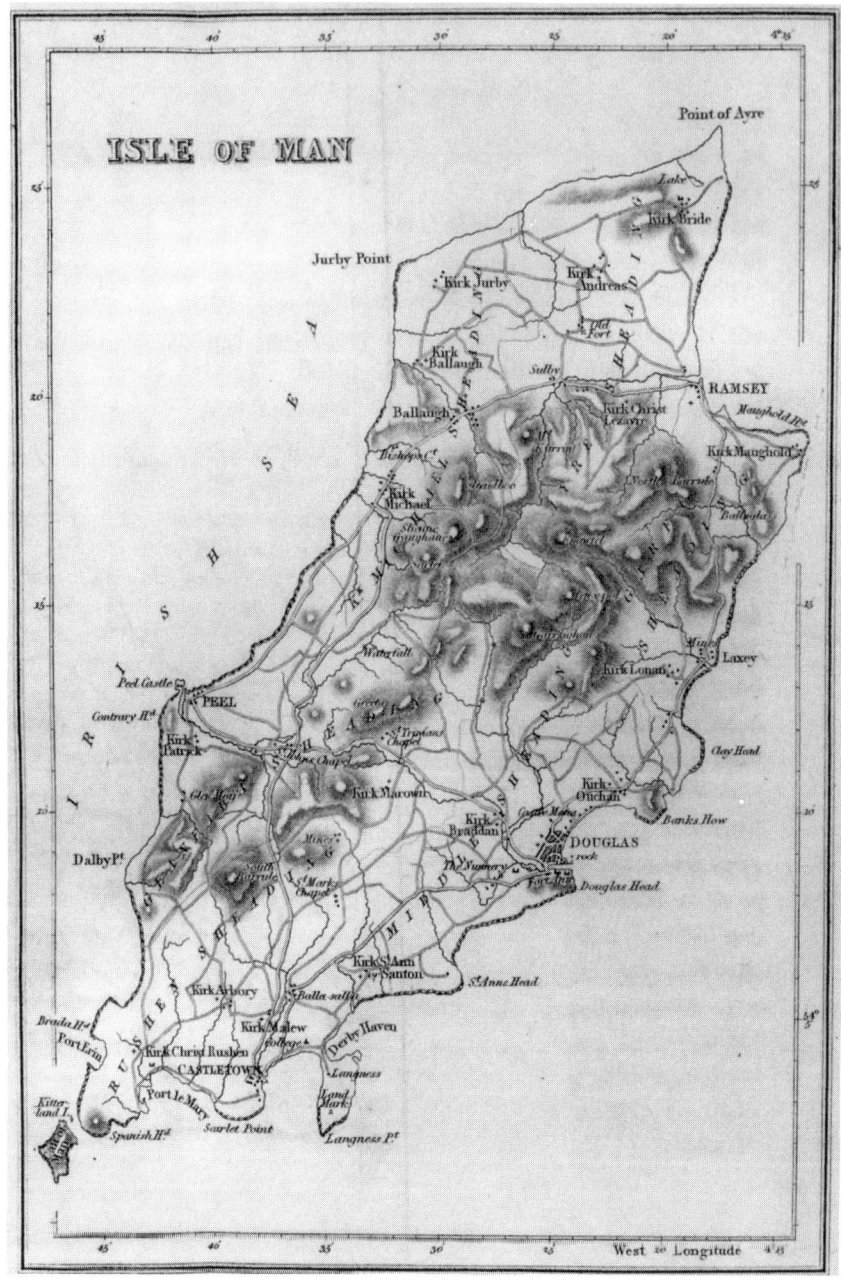

Map from Lord Teignmouth's *Sketches of the Coasts and Islands of Scotland and of the Isle of Man*, vol. 2 (1836)

Acknowledgments

Funding for the publication of this edition has been provided by the Manx Heritage Foundation and by the Joyce and Elizabeth Hall Center for the Humanities at the University of Kansas. The University provided two grants from the General Research Fund and a sabbatical to support work on the project. The Manx National Heritage gave permission to use photographs from the Manx Museum; the Manx Heritage Foundation permitted the use of drawings from *Manx Sea Fishing,* and the Manx Experience gave permission for the use of illustrations from *Here is the News: An Illustrated Manx History.* Special thanks are due to librarians at the University of Kansas, the University of Illinois, the British Library, the Bodleian Library, and the Manx Museum Library where particular help has come from Ann Harrison before her retirement and more recently from Roger M. C. Sims, Librarian Archivist. Additional help came from the folklorist and song collector Roy Palmer, who kindly identified an obscure song in *Tommy Big-Eyes,* and from Les Quilliam, an expert on Manx place names. At Clifton College, special information was provided by Derek Winterbottom, head of the History Department. Of the many helpful individuals on the Isle of Man Dollin Kelly and the late Geoffrey Crellin provided readings, recitations and tapes in dialect, guidance to places that figure in the Yarns, and the hospitality that made research a joy.

More thanks go to Claire Sutton for help with editing, to James Helyar for aid in designing the book, to many helpful colleagues, including James Hartman, Harold Orel, Elizabeth Schultz, Haskell Springer, Chester Sullivan, and George Worth, to Paul Jefferson, and to the staff of the College Word-Processing Center, especially Pam LeRow, Lynn Porter, and Paula Courtney, who worked for years preparing the texts for publication. The three editors gratefully acknowledge a debt to Richard Tobias, whose book on Brown in 1978 demonstrated the importance of the uncensored texts that are presented in this edition.

Old Kirk Braddan
The Manx Experience

Introduction

> Have you read T. E. B.'s poems? It was a pity he was a parson, as it compelled him to write parsonically.
>
> —Thomas Hardy to Florence Henniker

Thomas Hardy must have missed some unparsonical lines by T. E. Brown (1830-1897), the clergyman and schoolmaster who became the national poet of the Isle of Man.[1] In the originally printed texts that were revised and collected in *Fo'c's'le Yarns* (1881), the storyteller swears, describes prostitutes, and asks if his shipmates were ever "in love with a boy." In other passages that were later deleted, he comments on the size of a woman's breasts, gives details of rustic courtship in a cattle-barn and a straw-rick, and reports his mother's defense of his alleged "bychild." He tells how a parson's wife accused her adopted daughter of stealing her husband's affections, how a young woman apparently fell in love with her uncle while she was engaged to his son, and how a Methodist preacher abused his wife because she would not have sex with him. Hardy's ignorance of these matters was not exactly his fault, although he might have known about the parson's jealous wife from reading *Christmas Rose* in Macmillan's *Collected Poems of T. E. Brown* in 1900. This edition included versions of the four yarns that Brown himself had bowdlerized for Macmillan in 1880, omitting "coarse" passages to suit a cautious publisher. Unless Hardy had seen *Betsy Lee* in *Macmillan's Magazine* in 1873 or in booklet form, the earthier side of Brown's writing would have been as hidden from him as it is from most readers today. To restore what was lost, the uncensored versions of *Betsy Lee* (1872, 1873), *Christmas Rose* (1873), *Captain Tom and Captain Hugh* (1878), and *Tommy Big-Eyes* (1880) are presented in this edition.

Being a clergyman was not what compelled Thomas Edward Brown to bowdlerize his poetry, even though by his upbringing he seemed destined for a career in the Manx church. Born in Douglas on the Isle of Man in 1830, he grew up outside the town at Kirk Braddan with eight siblings in the household of

---

[1]Hardy went on to pity William Barnes for the same reason in this letter of 22 October 1900, *The Collected Letters of Thomas Hardy*, ed. Richard L. Purdy and Michael Millgate, 2 (Oxford: Clarendon Press, 1978): 270.

a poor vicar, Robert Brown, whose poetry won a compliment from Wordsworth. After attending King William's College as a day pupil, Thomas left the Island for Oxford in 1849 to become a "Servitor" (a charity scholar) at Christ Church, perhaps the most aristocratic of Oxford colleges. The experience confirmed him in the role of an outsider, set apart from other undergraduates by an untasseled cap, by "a kind of horse-box railed off"[2] for Servitors at chapel, and by exclusion from the Oxford Union and all clubs and athletic teams. Full of resentment and hurt pride, he worked hard to earn a rare Double First, only to be denied a fellowship at Christ Church on the grounds that no previous Servitor had become a "Student" (fellow) of the college. The whole ordeal, he claimed, left him with a lack of "social strength" and a tendency toward "isolation."[3] A friend added that it left him "ever in an attitude of protest against the tyrannies of privilege," pointing him even then toward his role as the voice of the Manx folk, but not as a poet of social protest. His revolt, said the friend, was "interior."[4]

His professional role as a teacher and clergyman suggests a certain lack of social strength in accepting and handling public responsibilities. Made a fellow of Oriel in 1854, he was ordained a deacon the following year, but he put off being priested until 1884 and never became a parson in full charge of a parish. He returned to the Island in 1855 as vice-principal of King William's College and married his second cousin, Amelia Stowell, in 1857, but he did not keep his roots in native soil. Returning to England in 1861 as headmaster of the Crypt School in Gloucester, he soon clashed with the Board of Governors, the parents, and the students, while making a friend of one pupil, W. E. Henley, the future poet, editor, and pugnacious champion of Brown's verse. From 1864 until 1892 he served as master of the Modern Side at Clifton College, Bristol. There in the late 1860s he began the long cycle of *Fo'c's'le Yarns*, ten in Anglo-Manx and two in standard English. By this time poetry was making a stronger call upon his inner life than the public duties of the Anglican priesthood.

The inhibiting force that compelled Brown to censor the first series of *Yarns* came not from his religion but from the respectability of a London publisher. Hardy should have guessed it, given his own problems and compromises in publishing serial fiction. As an outsider to the literary world, Brown had no idea of the troubles that lay ahead when he began negotiating with Alexander Macmillan in November 1880. His first two narratives, *Betsy Lee* and *Christmas Rose*, had been privately printed. Revised for *Macmillan's Magazine* in 1873, *Betsy Lee* met with little editorial disapproval, although Brown did remove the word w—-e that rhymed with *door*, and at Macmillan's suggestion he took out four lines that read like a parody of the talking flowers in Tennyson's "Come into the Garden, Maud." Otherwise uncensored, *Betsy Lee* pleased

---

[2][T. E. Brown], "Christ Church Servitors in 1852: By One of Them," *Macmillan's Magazine* 19 (November 1868): 50.

[3]Ibid., p. 53.

[4][The Rev. John Quine's Address at St. Matthew's Church, Douglas], *Isle of Man Daily Times*, quoted by Max Keith Sutton in *The Drama of Storytelling in T. E. Brown's Manx Yarns* (Newark: University of Delaware Press, 1991), p. 29.

Macmillan, who received from George Eliot a letter conveying her "hearty and frankly expressed admiration" and even one from Mrs. Tennyson that he thought might reflect her husband's cautious approval.[5] The laureate's views went unrecorded, but she and their nineteen-year-old younger son were enthusiastic: "Lionel fell in love with 'Betsy Lee' and made her known to me," Mrs. Tennyson wrote to Brown's colleague at Clifton, H. G. Dakyns, "and I like her very much, and I doubt not that we shall both like the Christmas rose, and that Mr. Tennyson will take courage and make acquaintance with both."[6]

Brown's friends at Clifton had long been supportive—and apparently unembarrassed by anything in *Betsy Lee*. After hearing the poet read it at a dinner party in 1870, John Addington Symonds wrote of being "so carried away by his mimetic force that I see every incident with photographic distinctness.... If Brown would only hire a Hall and recite his poem he would draw crowds."[7] Soon readings of *Betsy Lee* actually were drawing crowds in lecture halls at Rugby and on the Isle of Man. Newspaper reports of these events mention no complaints about coarseness. Nor apparently did Brown receive any when *Captain Tom and Captain Hugh* and *Tommy Big-Eyes* appeared in the *Isle of Man Times*. With no warning of any problem, the poet approached Macmillan in 1880 with the price of the book, not propriety, foremost in his mind. He wanted a cheap edition to attract readers in the north of England but went ahead with the project when the publisher insisted on a higher price.[8]

The shock came when Macmillan's partner, George Lillie Craik, reported that he had read *Tommy Big-Eyes* "with some pain to a company"—which might have included his wife, Dinah Mulock, the author of *John Halifax, Gentleman* (1856). The pain was caused by "certain coarsenesses" that "are humourous and spirited, but are they not bordering on the offensive?" Craik objected also to "the length & number of digressions," these being mainly the storyteller's clashes with his listeners, whom he sometimes stops to chastise for rudeness and stupidity. Craik warned that in the poem's present state, "Readers

---

[5] Alexander Macmillan to Brown, 10 May 1873, Macmillan Letter Book, vol. 608, British Library.

[6] 15 May 1873, *Letters to a Tutor: The Tennyson Family Letters to Henry Graham Dakyns*, Robert Peters, ed., with Janine Dakyns (Metuchen, N. J.: Scarecrow Press, Inc., 1988), p. 111.

[7] Letter to H. G. Dakyns, 30 November 1870, *The Letters of John Addington Symonds*, ed. Herbert M. Schueller and Robert L. Peters, 2 (Detroit: Wayne State University Press, 1968): 119-20.

[8] The 1881 edition of *Fo'c's'le Yarns* sold for seven shillings, sixpence a copy, which was three shillings more than the price of Arnold's edition of Wordsworth in Macmillan's Golden Treasury series. Macmillan agreed in 1886 to publish the somewhat smaller second series of *Yarns* for only three shillings, sixpence a copy, the price of *Betsy Lee* in 1873. See Sutton, p. 122, and the letter from Macmillan of 27 October 1886, MS in Macmillan Letter Book, vol. 608, British Library. Despite the lower price, Brown chose another publisher for the second series.

would throw it aside[,] some for its length & others for matters of taste which offended them."9

Brown wrote at once asking Craik to mark the objectionable passages but received no reply. Instead of waiting, he set to work bowdlerizing not only *Tommy Big-Eyes* but also the three other poems in the projected volume. "I have been cutting out at a great rate," he wrote Macmillan at the end of December 1880. In the process he was changing the voice and the nature of his Manx persona, Tom Baynes, the yarnspinner in the forecastle:

> My poor Tom Baynes will now appear in the character of a castrato, more musical, I hope, certainly less formidable, less vigorous. Somehow I don't seem to care much about him. Tom ought to swear, and that hugely—I have not left him a single oath: he ought to handle scripture with a fine freedom—I have stopped 'his allowance' of texts.10

In less than a month, Brown had censored his work with a thoroughness that the most prudish editor might have commended.

The neutering of his persona subverted his goal of affirming Manx identity through the voice of a genuine Manxman. By making this figure "less formidable, less vigorous," Brown weakened a key image of the life that he hoped to "fix upon the page," as he wrote in the dedicatory poem for *Tommy Big-Eyes* in 1880. Here he spoke of preserving some record of Manx manners and speech so that future readers might "see, as in a glass," what their forefathers "held dear" and how they lived. The poems were to be an "anchor" for the "Keltic souls" of coming Manx generations whose outward lives would be "lost in the empire's mass." Already the sense of national identity was fragile upon an island dominated for centuries by foreign powers and invaded each summer by thousands of English tourists. The native tongue was dying, the dialect that Brown mastered was starting to sound quaint, and the country still lacked a distinct literary tradition, although it did have an oral tradition of ballads and songs in the Manx language. To let a London publisher determine the tone of the *Yarns* was one more surrender to an outside force.

With a limited literary heritage to draw from, Brown was trying to write the first long narratives of Manx life told from a Manxman's viewpoint in the Manx dialect. Through Macmillan he hoped to go beyond his immediate audience and reach English readers who had no literary reason to care about the Island. Previous volumes of poetry in standard English by Brown's father in 1826 and by William Kennish in 1844 had done little to put the Isle of Man on the cultural map of Britain. Kennish emphasized Manx folklore, as did Esther Nelson in her best-known poem about the demonic men of Carrasdoo in *The Island Minstrelsy* (1839). In a highly romantic vein, Elizabeth Cookson dealt with Manx legends in *Poems from Manxland* (1868), as if bidding to make the

---

[9] December 1880, MS in Macmillan Letter Book, vol. 608, British Library; for the full text, see Sutton, p. 124.

[10] 29 December 1880, *Letters to Macmillan*, ed. Simon Nowell-Smith (London: 1967), p. 182.

Island seem as haunted and picturesque as any place in Ireland or Scotland. Despite these efforts and the summer tourists swarming in from Manchester and Liverpool, some reviewers in 1881 thought the *Yarns* might be set in Ireland, so little did they know of the dialect and the topography. Aside from Scott's *Peveril of the Peak* (1822) and parts of Wilkie Collins's *Armadale* (1866), few popular novels dealt with the Island, and native characters in fiction were as inconspicuous as the taciturn Manxman in *Moby Dick* (1851). Unlike Scottish or Irish writers in dialect—or the popular novelist Hall Caine who borrowed extensively from the *Yarns* in such works as *The Deemster* (1887) and *The Manxman* (1894)—Brown "could not assume any knowledge of local character" among his English readers or count on anyone beyond the Island to recognize Tom Baynes as a "familiar type."[11] The poet had to create him from life, knowing that most readers would see him as a stranger.

The model for his yarnspinner, Brown said, was a Manx sailor whom he had known and sailed with in the 1850s. "Bob Lucas is the prototype of my Tom Baynes," he told an audience at Peel in 1893, forgetting for the moment that he had also said that he was Tom Baynes himself. Hot-tempered like both the poet and his persona, Bob Lucas was physically powerful like Tom Baynes, sometimes "fierce" yet basically good-natured, nervous but "only from worrying about other people getting into danger." As a storyteller he apparently inspired the style but not the plots of the *Yarns*, although Brown did claim that a short one, "The Indiaman," was told "almost word for word by Bob Lucas, as a personal experience."[12] Telling stories in the first person was in itself a typical Manx trait, the poet believed.[13] With virtually no tradition of native written narration, Manx culture depended upon oral storytelling, as he noted after a visit in 1886: ". . . the whole Island was quivering and trembling all over with *stories*—they are like leaves on a tree. The people are always telling them to one another. . . . They are a marvellously *narrational* community."[14] As Richard Tobias notes, stories were ways of trying to preserve a people's sense of cultural identity.[15] By telling of his early life on the Island, Brown's yarnspinner takes on the role of a representative Manxman, keeping the past alive through the ancient art of oral narration.

His mastery of this art is somewhat problematic. Digressing, Tom Baynes often loses the thread of the narrative; taunted by his listeners, he stops to scold them or to argue, and sometimes his memories overwhelm him with emotion. His "genius for parenthesis" falls short of an old Manx preacher's ability to "tell

---

[11]N. L. Shimmin, "The Making of a Manx Literature: Regional Identity in the Writings of Hall Caine and T. E. Brown" (Ph.D. diss., University of Lancaster, 1988), p. 18.

[12]Quoted in Sutton, p. 36.

[13]See Sutton, p. 40.

[14]Letter to A. M. Worthington, 18 October 1886, quoted in Richard Tobias, *T. E. Brown* (Boston: Twayne Publishers, 1978), p. 147.

[15]See Tobias, p. 147.

four stories concurrently";[16] nor does he always measure up to the Manxmen of earlier days who exercised their right to defend themselves in a court of law, sometimes speaking for an hour or more with "considerable eloquence."[17] At his worst, Brown's persona is more like an inept West Indian storyteller who kept losing his place and was "interrupted constantly."[18] But his blunders turn out to be ways of arousing his audience, and in the forecastle he makes a point of gauging their responses, as when he insists that the lamp be properly lit at the start of *Christmas Rose*:

> it puts me out
> If I can't see what you chaps is about. . . .   (37-8)

He draws strength from "the look of a man" and encouragement

> when Bill says aw!
> and Tommy says aye! and Harry says hem!   (44-5)

Such signals guide him along the "two-way street" of oral narration.[19]

Even more crucial in actual storytelling is the dramatic presence of the speaker. Although the look and sound of Tom Baynes may be imagined from reading, the *Yarns* need someone to enact the narrator's role, as Brown himself did in public performances. Like William Barnes in Dorset, the Manx poet dramatized his verse not only with his voice but also with "face-play" and gestures. Reading *Betsy Lee* in 1873 on the Isle of Man, the poet became his persona, transforming his schoolmasterly self into the "rough simple big-hearted sailor spinning his yarns between decks. . . ."[20] Later reviewers wished for a phonograph and "instantaneous photography" to suggest what eluded "cold type." Along with the shifting dynamics of his voice came "the play of his countenance," his gestures, and his pauses, which "were frequently more mirth-provoking than any of his utterances."[21] Following Brown's example, later Manx performers such as Dollin Kelly have turned the written texts into scripts to be enacted. Memorizing the c.1600 bowdlerized lines of *Betsy Lee*, Mr. Kelly

---

[16]A. J. Costain, "The Manx Poems," in *Thomas Edward Brown: A Memorial Volume, 1830-1930*, intro. by Ramsey B. Moore (Cambridge: at the University Press on behalf of The Isle of Man Centenary Committee, 1930), p. 155.

[17]Charles John Shore, Lord Teignmouth, *Sketches of the Coasts and Islands of Scotland and of the Isle of Man,* 2 (London: John W. Parker, 1836): 235; quoted in Maureen E. Godman, "An Edition of *Christmas Rose*: The Second of T. E. Brown's *Fo'c's'le Yarns*" (M.A. thesis, University of Kansas, 1990), p. 10.

[18]Roger D. Abrahams, *The Man-of-Words in the West Indies* (Baltimore: Johns Hopkins University Press, 1983), p. 184.

[19]Walter J. Ong, *Interfaces of the Word: Studies in the Evolution of Consciousness and Culture* (Ithaca: Cornell University Press, 1977), p. 69.

[20]"Besty Lee, Read by the Author," *Isle of Man Times*, 16 August 1873, quoted in Sutton, p. 42.

[21]"Manx Characters, Lecture at Peel by the Rev. T. E. Brown," *Isle of Man Examiner*, 1 June 1894, quoted in Sutton, p. 43.

has made a monodrama out of the poem for performance on the Isle of Man and in Edinburgh. On tapes available at the Manx Museum in Douglas, he speaks with dramatic changes in tempo and volume, and gives the characters distinctive voices as Brown himself had done a century before.

The recording lets one hear the sounds of the Anglo-Manx dialect, although *Betsy Lee* reflects it to a lesser degree than the yarns that came after. The dialect emerged as Manx Gaelic began dying out, serving as a transitional mode of speech that was moving closer to standard English by the late nineteenth century. As spoken by the narrator, it mixes sounds from Scotland, Ireland, and northwestern England.[22] *Ould* in the yarns approximates Scottish *auld*; the same dipthong (as in *now* in the south of England) appears in *soul* or *sowl*, *hould*, and *bould*. The northern *oo* resembling the vowel in the received British pronunciation of *book* is heard in such words as *up*, *come*, *tongue*, *gud*, *blud*, and *courtin*; in northern speech, "words like *blood* and *good*, *mud* and *hood*, are prefect rhymes."[23] The longer *oo* as in *food* is heard in *hook*, *crook*, *look*, and *book*—while *buck* has the sound of southern *book*.[24] Hearing the same vowel, Brown rhymes *door* with *sure*, the final *r* sounding like *uh* in both words. London reviewers who guessed that the poems were set in Ireland would have noticed a thin sprinkling of Manx terms such as *ma chree* (my heart) that marked Irish speech, as well as the spellings of *misthress* or *craythur*, the softened *t* in this position being common to both dialects. Brown avoided another parallel by not writing *thing* as *ting* or *thief* as *teef* as these words might have been pronounced by Manx as well as Irish speakers, and only rarely does he use *the* or *th* to indicate a Manx pronunciation of *to*.[25] The final *r* that would be strongly sounded in Ireland was heard at mid-century only in the northern and western parts of the Isle of Man, according to Brown; in the south at Castletown, near his yarnspinner's point of origin, *where* and *there* were pronounced "theeaw" and "wheeaw," he told a lecture audience in 1894.[26] As in many varieties of English, a final *g*, *d*, or *t* is frequently dropped, allowing Manx speakers to run words together in phrasal units as they would have done in their mother tongue.

The influence of the Manx language upon the dialect may also be seen in such spellings as *mayve* and *tervil* (*maybe* and *terrible*) where the shift from *b* to *v* suggests the Manx system of mutable initial consonants. Manx spelling was understandably erratic, and Tom Baynes does not always pronounce the same word the same way in the forecastle. His syntax often reflects the lack of a verb to show possession in Manx (as in other Celtic languages), so that "A dog is at

---

[22] George Saintsbury called Brown's version of it "a jargon of broken down Celtic and vulgarist English" : *Cambridge History of English Literature*, ed. A. W. Ward and A. R. Waller, 13 (Cambridge: Cambridge University Press, 1916): 196.

[23] Arthur Hughes and Peter Trudgill, *English Accents and Dialects* (Second edition; London: Edward Arnold, 1987), p. 28.

[24] See Hughes and Trudgill, p. 29.

[25] For pronunciations of Anglo-Manx words, see A. W. Moore, with Sophia Morrison and Edmund Goodwin, *A Vocabulary of the Anglo-Manx Dialect* (London: Oxford University Press, 1924).

[26] See Sutton, p. 45.

me" does duty for "I have a dog." For passive constructions, Tom follows the Manx option of using *going* (Mx. *goll*) when he says that a woman "was goin a heisin at them," meaning that she was being lifted (hoisted) by them.27 To intensify an adjective he uses an article—"the happy"—instead of *how* or *so*. His use of verbs bothered English critics partly because the subject is often left to be understood (Manx verbs normally precede the subject) and also because his reliance upon participles and progressive tenses can make it difficult to sort out the exact sequence of events. Expressed in quick four-beat couplets, the narrator's Celtic sensibility and linguistic habits challenged Victorian readers who were accustomed to slower-paced verse in standard English.

Understandably, Macmillan wanted to make the *Yarns* accessible to people in the south of England, so Brown anglicized many spellings and changed such forms as "gorrit" and "aburrit" to "got it" and "about it," adding a gloss as well. Even this was a surrender, for he once wrote that his aim in *Christmas Rose* was, within "the strictest possible limitations of a very rugged dialect, to make the old sailor convey the most delicate nuances of thought and emotion that he can, however gropingly attain to."28 Altering Tom's words further compromised the image of an actual Manxman, the sailor Bob Lucas, to suit a publisher's notion of English tastes.

The grooming of Tom Baynes to meet Victorian standards did not consist only of simplifying the dialect and changing his expletives from "d——" and "by gough" to "dear me" and "bless me." To make him "one of nature's gentlemen," as *The Times* called him in 1881,29 and to win approval of his language ("racy without being vulgar"),30 Brown even deleted his more graphic accounts of eating and digestion. Farmhands no longer belch in the revised *Tommy Big-Eyes*; the old miser in *Betsy Lee* now has no "guts" and can no longer "groan in his innards, and retch and hawk" when he comes to visit. Prettified for Macmillan, the little boys in *Christmas Rose* have "big round eyes" instead of "snotty noses" (332). Sexual squeamishness changes "stallions" to "hosses" and stops Tom from saying that he came "out of" his mother. That formidable woman can no longer cuss in the scene from *Betsy Lee* that especially pleased George Eliot; she cannot say "bychild" or affirm the significance of the act of begetting one: "A man's own flesh, and the love and the life / Was in it" (1110-11). The original Tom Baynes accepts the flesh as part of the love and the life that he celebrates; the gentleman in the revision suffers from Victorian reticence about it.

Some of the alleged coarseness appeared in what Craik called the digressions, the passages showing the interplay between the storyteller and his shipmates. The sailors express their natural interests in women and sex,

---

27See George Broderick, "Manx," in *The Celtic Languages*, ed. Martin J. Ball with James Fife (London: Routledge, 1993), p. 272, on passive constructions.

28Letter to Macmillan, 26 February 1873, MS in Macmillan Collection, British Library.

29"Fo'c's'le Yarns," *The Times*, 21 September 1881, p. 4.

30"New Books and New Editions," *Pall Mall Gazette* 33 (4 June 1881): 21; see also Sutton, pp. 129-32.

wanting to hear all about Tom and Betsy in the hay, grinning knowingly until he disappoints them by reporting only that she spoke loving words and sang a hymn while wrapped in his arms. The men have similar expectations in *Tommy Big-Eyes* when he tells how farm boys and girls court communally on winter nights in the stackyard, where a sound like a sigh coming out of the straw makes him think "these stacks is allis breathin." When the sailors laugh, Tom grows both defensive and nationalistic, insisting that Manx youths are "dacent" and "a chap is a fool / That thinks the country is like Liverpool." By deleting the whole passage (1442-83), Brown streamlined the story at the expense of the drama in the forecastle where Tom struggles to assert his authority and defend his positive view of Manx life.

The intrusive listeners pose a constant threat to his vision. Young and impertinent, coming in some cases from outside the Isle of Man, the troublemakers represent a "new order" that opposes the yarnspinner's nostalgia.[31] If his is the garrulous voice of Manx tradition, theirs are the impatient, undercutting countertones of modern skepticism about the virtues of the rural past. Romanticism in any form can stir their cynicism. They tease him about telling so many love stories: "Love again?" someone says near the start of the third yarn in the series; later, after a long lyrical passage on falling in love, Tom thinks he hears a snore. In *Betsy Lee* he is so touchy about this sort of needling that he threatens to shove his boot down Bob's throat, yet the offenders keep puncturing the nostalgic mood after each evocation of childhood innocence. These disruptions of the main narrative were cut from *Betsy Lee* along with a long tirade against Bob for wanting the heroine to be like a prostitute. Without the rough counterpoint of the sailors' responses, the story goes more smoothly, but the storyteller's nostalgia meets no opposition, and the conflicts between old and new ways of seeing vanish from the poem. The result is a less polyphonic text that simplifies Brown's regionalism, his perspective on the past, and his representation of romantic love.

The revision also simplifies his remarkable imitation of the give-and-take of oral storytelling. The interplay in the forecastle provides vivid reminders of how an audience can influence narration. By voicing their opinions, Tom's unruly shipmates create an observable model for the reader's private acts of resistance and projection in responding to a story. When not resisting the narrator, the sailors may act out the reader's desire for clarification, as in Tom's account of his youthful feelings for the parson's adolescent sons:

> *Fond* was it I said I was? chit-chit!
> Fond's not the word, no not a bit—
> I was mad after them two boys, I was.

Naturally, the sailors ask questions (shown in italics):

---

[31]N. L. Shimmin, "Nostalgia and Cultural Development--Manx Identity in T. E. Brown's Fo'c's'le Yarns," *Literature of Region and Nation* 1 (July 1989): 8.

> Ware ye navar in love with a boy? *What way?*
> Well that's a thing I cannot say—
> *Like a brother or that?* No! no! no! no!
> *What do I mean?* Well wait then, Joe!
> Wait my lad! What I mean is willin
> To die for them two in a minute, a-spilling
> My last drop of blood, if so be it was wanted
> For the gud of them; and haunted lek, haunted
> With their look and their laugh—do ye follow the thing? (386-99)

In this passage, storytelling becomes dialogue, with the listeners' questions prodding the narrator to clarify a feeling that still bewilders him as he seeks a name for it. Probably because the feeling might be construed as homoerotic, Brown deleted these lines and toned down the rest of the passage for fear of offending Macmillan. Cuts such as this took away much of what gives the poems special relevance to the study of readers' responses. Questions of narrative authority, of interpretation, of the role of an audience in shaping a discourse keep emerging in the forecastle, as Tom struggles with his intrusive listeners. The (rare) reader of the original texts can feel the clash of conflicting viewpoints while looking in vain for any final word from the poet himself. Brown's is the silent voice in these polyphonic narratives—a blank that may be filled in but only by an inference that remains open to further questioning.

In trying to make sense of people and events, no single voice has all the answers. The bullying narrator often thinks he has them, but the limitations of a single viewpoint are especially apparent when this middle-aged bachelor tries to tell the younger sailors what he knows about women. In *Betsy Lee*, he wants the men to accept the conventional image of an innocent woman who dies of a broken heart; the skeptics resist, but eventually everyone seems to share Tom's view of the heroine. At least the skeptics grow silent. In the next poem his task is harder because Christmas Rose fails to match any familiar stereotype. In a cancelled early passage, a sailor tries to make her fit one when he wrests control of the story and says she was "*a tight little armfull. . . kissing again / When a chap kissed her*" (537-8). Tom reacts furiously, and not just because someone has usurped his authority. He knows her as the exact opposite of the sailor's fantasy—a woman who never showed sexual feeling for any man in her life. Drawing from Manx folk-beliefs in witches, ghosts, fairies, and other orders of beings, he even suggests that she comes from another world and therefore cannot be expected to respond to human passion. Defending her mystery challenges both the sailors' attitudes and certain conventions in Victorian society. A critic wrote in 1898 that Rose was responsible for "the death of one brave boy and the ruin of another"—as if her duty were to marry in spite of her feelings.[32] The blame she incurs for wanting to stay single and find freedom in the world outdoors suggests a possible prototype, the shepherdess Marcela in *Don Quixote* (Book I, Chapters 12-14), a work described briefly in

---

[32] "Poems of Thomas Edward Brown," *Quarterly Review* 187 (1898): 385. The reviewer was Brown's old friend, J. R. Mozley; see Godman, pp. 11-12.

the poem. Blamed for her lover's death, Marcela defends herself and preserves her freedom; Rose, on the other hand, escapes "deep blame" only by dying: for the critic, this act alone "absolves her in the reader's mind." Her sexual independence has violated a Victorian taboo, felt in the forecastle and tacitly assumed by the man reviewing the poem.

In the next two yarns, women who stray from convention create additional problems—first for the storyteller and then for the poet in trying to please his publisher. In *Captain Tom and Captain Hugh,* young Annie starts out as the most conventional of heroines but becomes problematic once her feelings turn from her cousin to his gloomy father. The question of just what she feels for her uncle vanishes from the revision, after Brown deleted every sign that she fell under the spell of this older man. The result makes her a completely colorless but safely conventional heroine.[33] In the last and longest poem in the series, *Tommy Big-Eyes,* a Methodist preacher's wife refuses to have sex with him, and as in *Christmas Rose* the narrator faces the task of defending a woman who frustrates masculine desire. In the original text, Tom tries to make the men see Cain as a monster physically and verbally abusing his wife, firing bits of scripture at her to make her submit. The sailors resist the narrator's viewpoint as long as they can, sympathizing with the aggrieved husband and blaming the wife for driving him toward adultery. The deleted passages slow down the story and risk sounding coarse to Victorian ears, but they are integral to the depiction of oral storytelling. By resisting and trying to learn more, the listeners become models for readers, not in their sexist biases but in their engagement in the narrative act. The deletions virtually destroy the model.

If the drama—the element of conflict—in the act of storytelling depends upon Tom's interplay with his audience, the tonal complexity of these four poems depends upon it also and upon the language that Craik found offensive. In Brown's original design, the rough talk in the forecastle frames Tom's stories of lost childhood, romantic love, and women who elude men's understanding. His poetic themes must find expression in a prosaic context and in a dialect that has the ring of actual rustic speech. Brown's imitation of people talking should give his work a special place among poems of the late nineteenth century. As dialect verse, the *Yarns* represent a subcurrent in the colloquial tradition in British poetry, revived in standard English by Byron in *Don Juan* and by Browning and Clough[34] (although neither Victorian poet used such low diction as Brown's). Clough's unfinished final work, "Mari Magno or Tales on Board" (1862, 1863), might have given Brown the idea for a series of stories told at sea. The narrators of these tales are well-bred passengers, not common sailors like

---

[33]See Tobias, p. 123. His study was the first to deal critically with the deletions, although Selwyn G. Simpson pointed out some of them in *Thomas Edward Brown, the Manx Poet: An Appreciation* (London: Walter Scott Publishing Company, 1906).

[34]On the "colloquial tradition" in nineteenth-century British verse, see Bernard Arthur Richards, *English Poetry of the Victorian Period* (London: Longman, 1988), pp. 37-52. Richards treats dialect poetry separately and ignores Brown, but he notes that a poet using dialect "opens a door that provides an exit from the narrowing effects of standard English" (p. 59).

Tom Baynes and his mates, and they speak in formal couplets, not ragged ones in rustic dialect; yet they do comment—politely—upon each other's stories, and by agreeing to tell tales of "love and marriage" they focus upon a topic that is central to the *Yarns*. Clough's is by far the more stylized way of depicting spoken narration. Even when writing tetrameter couplets, as Brown does, he offers an elegantly patterned version of educated speech, with inverted syntax and other reminders of neoclassical verse. The Manxman's repetitions, looser phrasing, and skippier rhythms come closer to suggesting the eddies and crosscurrents of oral storytelling.

Through a former pupil Brown may have had some influence upon later developments in the colloquial tradition. In January 1876, W. E. Henley showed him an experiment in free verse, apparently believing that Brown would be receptive, as he was, although he told the young poet that current tastes would prefer the more "objective" and "well carved" version in sonnet form.[35] From Henley to Ford Madox Ford (who cited Henley in general terms as "a considerable and fine Influence")[36] to Ezra Pound (who praised Ford extravagantly as a pioneer in writing verse that really talks), the colloquial tradition moved on toward eventual dominance in twentieth-century poetry. Through Henley, Brown might have played a part in this movement if the young innovator had read *Betsy Lee* by 1875 and caught the spoken quality of the verse:

> *you thought there was love*
> *In the case*—did you, Bob? So help me I'll shove
> This boot down your throat, if you don't stop laughin. . . .   (19-21)

Tom's stories always rhyme, but the shifting rhythms, the phrasing, and the diction keep so close to common speech that at moments reading becomes hearing:

> I suppose then, Billy, you knew the gel?
> *You didn!* No! I knew you didn!
> (*Christmas Rose*, 1791-2)

Brown imitated Manx English so well that even in the 1980s a visitor on the Island had trouble distinguishing the "quick, tinny, musical Manx voice" that "came ringing off the page" from the voices in the street: "Was I reading this, or was this just Mrs. Quillin talking to Terry Kelly beyond the window?"[37] Jonathan Raban found that at the least mention of their poet men and women would "recite whole passages at a time":

---

[35] Quoted in Edward H. Cohen, "The Evolution of Henley's *In Hospital*," *Victorian Authors and Their Works: Revision Motivations and Modes*, ed. Judith Kennedy (Athens: Ohio University Press, 1991), p. 66.

[36] *Memories and Impressions*, intro. by Michael Killigrew, vol. 5 of *The Bodley Head Ford Madox Ford* (London: Bodley Head, 1971), p. 137.

[37] Jonathan Raban, *Coasting* (New York: Simon and Schuster, 1989), p. 69.

xxiii   *Introduction*

> I had T. E. Brown coming out of my ears. He was a national institution. The Bristol schoolmaster had managed to find a voice which embodied all of Man's insular pride and all its insular sense of grievance and slight. Listening to his verse, with its nostalgia for old days and folk ways, its foursquare localness, its constant undercurrent of xenophobia, I thought that T. E. Brown. . . might be just the poet for Britain at large in the late twentieth century.[38]

Although the sardonic analogy between Brown's desire to preserve Manx identity and British fears of losing theirs in a united Europe hardly flatters the poet, Raban does show that at least on the Island, the yarnspinner's voice survived bowdlerization. Brown needed the original coarseness, however, to bring out the full flavor of the Manxman's speech, and he needed the younger sailors' rude interruptions to counter the nostalgia that Raban finds dominant in the Macmillan texts. Only through contrasts could he emulate his idol, Robert Burns, who mixed things gross with things beautiful, with the "juxta-position heightening the effect," Brown believed, "not of the grossness, but of the beauty."[39]

To the degree that Victorian and later readers wanted the beauty without the grossness, Brown's revisions achieved the desired end. While English reviewers were expressing horror at French naturalism, the *Yarns* won praise for presenting "rough fisher lads and lasses with perfect fidelity to fact, and yet without a single touch of coarseness."[40] Another critic, possibly Henley himself, praised the poet for deleting everything from the 1873 text of *Betsy Lee* that might "jar the reader."[41] By 1900, when Brown's *Collected Poems* appeared along with two volumes of his letters, one might refer to "T. E. B." as Hardy did and expect to be understood. Unlike Henley, however, the greater writer saw a problem in poetry that sounded too much like a parson's for his own tastes. Although more careful attention to *The Doctor* and *Roman Women* might have modified Hardy's impression, his note of ill-omen was prophetic. By 1952, a critic in *TLS* observed that Brown had "receded to the very fringes of literature and memory." The *Yarns* now seemed too conventionally Victorian, too "idealized" to be "more than of antiquarian interest today."[42] In their uncut form, they might have fared no better, given the general aversion to any dialect but one's own and the complaint that they were far too long. Yet one thing should have been apparent: as first printed, these poems were not conventionally Victorian. Had they been, they would not have alarmed a Victorian publisher and provoked such a massive act of self-censorship.

Brown's truer self recognized his mistake. In 1886 he wrote Macmillan, "I should indeed like to try rather another public than that of Drawing rooms and

---

[38]Raban, p. 71.
[39]Letter to his sister Margaret, 10 February 1895, MS in Manx Museum Library.
[40]Walter Whyte, "Thomas Edward Brown," in *Charles Kingsley to James Thomson*, in *The Poets and Poetry of the Nineteenth Century*, ed. Alfred H. Miles, 5 (1891; London, George Routledge & Son, 1905): 522.
[41]"Reviews," *Scots Observer* 2 (15 June 1889): 102. Henley edited this journal.
[42]"Manxman on the Modern Side," *TLS* no. 2,627 (6 June 1952): 370.

swell people. 'Fo'c's'le Yarns' was emasculated with a view to the Drawing-room table as the apotheosis of publication; the apotheosis has turned out something of a euthanasia, and now I am minded to publish cheaply and for the 'vulgar.' . . . The essential thing with me now is to get at a different public."[43] He lived up to his resolution by switching publishers for his next collection. When *The Doctor* appeared in 1887, there were only minor alterations of the 1876 text—even though Tom Baynes swears occasionally and one character sells his willing sister to an army officer and ends up as a pimp in Liverpool. Whether Brown gained a "different public" by temporarily abandoning Macmillan is unclear, but already the poem had won the admiration of the philologist Max Müller, the Crown Princess of Germany, and—according to one unverified report—Robert Browning.[44] With such backing, Brown could ask Macmillan for some restorations in the new edition of *Fo'c's'le Yarns*, which came out in 1889 along with the volume containing the third series, *The Manx Witch and Other Poems*. Yet aside from several restored pages of *Tommy Big-Eyes*, the only other changes were minor—a few lines reinserted in *Betsy Lee* (728-42, 746-9). No new edition of *Fo'c's'le Yarns* appeared in Brown's lifetime, and the *Collected Poems* of 1900 followed the bowdlerized 1881 and 1889 texts; the 1900 version has been reprinted ever since. If the poet wanted major restorations, he did too little, too late.

He did complain, however. A few months before his death in 1897, he encouraged an Australian correspondent to compare the original yarns published in the *Isle of Man Times* with the revised versions:

> I should be glad if you would note the differences. In "Tommy Big-Eyes," more especially, these differences are important. They chiefly proceed from omissions. And these omissions were intended to pacify one of Macmillan's partners, and also to avert the anger of the Methodists in this Island. But I wish them restored. They are strongly, perhaps too strongly, expressed. But on the maxim, "Call a spade a spade," they seem to me, on reflection, quite justifiable.[45]

This edition restores the omissions.

---

[43]13 October 1886, Macmillan Collection Add. 55006, British Library.
[44]See Tobias, p. 135, and Sutton, p. 194, n. 31.
[45]Letter to Thomas Harrison, 26 February 1897, in William Cubbon, "Thomas Edward Brown," *A Bibliographical Account of Works Relating to the Isle of Man*, 2 (Oxford: Oxford University Press, 1939): 909.

A Note on the Gloss

Brown supplied no gloss for the original editions. Initially reluctant, he complied with Macmillan's request and added footnotes for the 1881 edition, as he did for the next two volumes in the series. He worried about having too many notes; some have been omitted for this edition and some have been added, especially for the deleted passages, which had no gloss. His notes are the ones left unidentified. His footnote numbers are omitted as intrusive for those readers who have no need to check a word. The only superscript is the degree sign indicating an explanatory note in the back of the volume. Omissions in 1881 of five or more consecutive lines are cited with the poems as well as in the Textual Notes.

The dedicatory poem for the 1881 edition was first printed with the title "Preface" in the 1878 edition of *Captain Tom and Captain Hugh.*

Herring

Fisherman's Home
Manx National Heritage

Preface

To sing a song shall please my countrymen,
    To unlock the treasures of the Island heart;
With loving feet to trace each hill and glen,
    And find the ore that is not for the mart
Of commerce: this is all I ask.
No task,
        But joy, God wot!
        Wherewith "the stranger" intermeddles not—

Who, if perchance
    He lend his ear
As caught by mere romance
    Of nature, traversing
    On viewless wing
    All parallels of sect,
    And race, and dialect,
Then shall he be to me most dear.

Natheless, for mine own people do I sing,
    And use the old familiar speech,
    Happy if I shall reach
    Their inmost consciousness.
One thing
    They will confess—
I never did them wrong:
And so accept the singer and the song.

        Clifton, Nov. 19, 1877.

Life in the Forecastle, from J. Ross Browne, *Etchings of a Whaling Cruise* (1846)

Betsy Lee

I SAID I would? Well, I hardly know,
But a yarn's a yarn; so here we go.
It's along of me and a Lawyer's Clerk,°
You've seen mayhap that sort of spark!
As neat and as pert, and as sharp as a pin,
With a mossel of hair on the tip of his chin;
With his face so fine, and his tongue so glib,
And a saucy cock in the set of his jib;
With his rings and his studs and all the rest,
10 And half a chain cable paid out on his breast.
Now there's different divils ashore and at sea,
And a divil's a divil° wherever he be;
But if you want the rael ould mark,
The divil of divils is the Lawyer's Clerk.
Well—out it must come, though it be with a wrench,
And I must tell you about a wench
That I was a courtin of, yes me!
Aye, and her name it was Betsy Lee.
Betsy Lee—*you thought there was love*
20 *In the case* —did you, Bob? So help me I'll shove
This boot down your throat, if you don't stop laughin;
It's a regular stopper that snigglin and chaffin.
When a man has a yarn to spin, d'ye see,
He must spin it away, and spin it free,
Or else—well perhaps—*there isn no call —*
But just don't do it again, that's all!

    Now most of you lads has had a spell
Of courtin and that, and it's hard to tell
How ever a youngster comes to fancy
30 That of all the gels it's Jinny or Nancy,
Or Mary or Betsy that must be hisn.
I don't know how it is or it isn,
But some time or other it comes to us all,

19-26   *Omitted.*

Just like a clap of shoot or a squall,
Or a snake or a viper, or some such dirt,
Creep—creep—creepin under your shirt,
And slidin and slippin right into your breast,
And makin you as you can't get rest:
And it works and it works till you feel your heart risin—
40 God knows what it is if it isn pisin.
You've bathed in a dub that had seaweed in it,
And just dropt your legs to rest for a minute,
And let them go lazily dingle—dangle,
And felt them caught by the twistin tangle—
That's somethin like the kind of job;
But ah, I loved Betsy, I did—now, Bob!

You see—we're a roughish set of chaps,
That's brought up rough on our mammies' laps;
And we grow and we run about shoutin and foolin
50 Till we gets to be lumps, and fit for the schoolin.
Then we gets to know the marks and the signs,
And we leaves the school, and we sticks to the lines,
Baitin and settin and haulin and that,
Till we know every fish from a whale to a sprat;
And we gets big and strong, for it do make you stronger
To row a big boat, and to pull at a conger.
Then what with a cobblin up of the yawl,
And a patchin and mendin the nets for the trawl,
And a risin early and a goin to bed late,
60 And a dramin of scollops as big as a plate,
And the hooks and the creels and the oars and the gut,
You'd say there's no room for a little slut.
But howsomdever it's not the case,
And a pretty face is a pretty face;
And through the whole coil, as bright as a star,

34	shoot: sudden fall of soot in the chimney.
41-6	*Omitted.*
50	lumps: good-sized lads.
51	the marks and the signs: of the fishing grounds.°
56	conger: a large eel (ed.).
57	cobblin up of the yawl: repairing the yawl (ed.)°

Conger Eel

A gel slips in, and there you are!

    Well, that was just the way with me
And the gel I'm speakin of—Betsy Lee.
Ah, mates! it's wonderful too—the years
70 You may live dead-on-end with your eyes and your ears
Right alongside of the lass that's goin
To be your sweetheart, and you never knowin!
Her father and mine used to hob-and-nob,
Being next-door neighbours—avast that Bob!
You didn laugh?—you lubberly skunk!
It's div'lish nice for a fool in his bunk
To be lyin and laughin, and me goin on
And a tellin such things—now isn it, John?
Eh, Bill? He says he—*meant nothin by it?*—
80 Well, I only want the chap to be quiet.
For there's wounds, my mates, that won't take healins,
And if a man's a man, he's got his feelins.
All right! I thank you, William my lad,
I *will* just taste it—it's not so bad.

    Well—as I was a sayin, her father and mine
Was neighbours, and both in the fisherman line;
And their cottages stood on the open beach,
With a nice bit of garden aback of them each.
You know the way them houses is fixed,
90 With the pigs and the hens and the childher mixed;
And the mothers go round when the nights begin,
And whips up their own, and takes them in.
Her father was terrible fond of flowers,
And his garden was twice as handsome as ours—
A mortal keen eye he had for the varmin,
And his talk was always of plantin and farmin.
He had roses hangin above his door,
Uncommon fine roses they was to be sure,
And the joy of my heart was to pull them there,
100 And break them in pieces on Betsy's hair.
Not that Betsy was much of a size
At the time I mean, but she had big eyes,
So big and so blue, and so far asunder,
And she looked so sollum I used to wonder.
That was all—just baby play,
Knockin about the boats all day,
And sometimes a lot of us takin hands
And racin like mad things over the sands.

73-84   *Omitted.*

Ah! it wouldn be bad for some of us
110 If we'd never gone furder, and never fared wuss;
If we'd never grown up, and never got big,
If we'd never took the brandy swig,
If we were skippin and scamp'rin and cap'rin still
On the sand that lies below the hill,
Crunchin its grey ribs with the beat
Of our little patterin naked feet;
If we'd just kep childher upon the shore
For ever and ever and ever more.
There's Bob again, and also Dick!
120 Now the question is, which am I goin to lick,
Though it's an ugly sort of a thing to lather
A lad, when you was shipmates with his father.
You—*ast my pardon?*—well, there let it end,
For a son is a son, and a friend is a friend.

Now the beauty of the thing when childher plays is
The terrible wonderful length the days is.
Up you jumps, and out in the sun,
And you fancy the day will never be done:
And you're chasin the bumbees hummin so cross
130 In the hot sweet air among the goss,
Or gath'rin blue-bells, or lookin for eggs,
Or peltin the ducks with their yalla legs,
Or a climbin, and nearly breakin your skulls,
Or a shoutin for divilment after the gulls,
Or a thinkin of nothin, but down at the tide,
Singin out for the happy you feel inside.
That's the way with the kids, you know,
And the years do come and the years do go,
And when you look back it's all like a puff,
140 Happy and over and short enough.
Now, Bob! are you at it again? all right!
Just somebody give the fellow a light!

Well, I never took notions on Betsy Lee,
Nor no more did she, I suppose, on me,
Till one day diggin upon the sand—

---

110   wuss: worse.
119-24   *Omitted.*
130   goss: gorse.
142   a light: a light for his pipe (ed.).

Gibbins, of course you'll understand,
A lad as was always a cheeky young sprout,
Began a pullin of Betsy about;
And he worried the wench till her shoulders were bare,
150 And he slipped the knot of her beautiful hair,
And down it come, as you may say,
Just like a shower of golden spray,
Blown this way and that by a gamesome breeze,
And a rip-rip-ripplin down to her knees.
I looked at Betsy—my gough! how she stood!
A quiv'rin all over, and her face like blood!
And her eyes, all wet with tears, like fire,
And her breast a swellin higher and higher;
And she gripped her sickle with a twitchy feel,
160 And her thumb started out like a coil of steel,
And a cloud seemed to pass from my eyes, and a glory°
Like them you'll see painted sometimes in a story,
Breathed out from her skin; and I saw her no more
The child I had always thought her before,
But wrapped in the glory, and wrapped in the hair,
Every inch of a woman stood pantin there.
So I ups with my fist, as I was bound,
And I d----s his eyes, and I knocks him down,
But from that day by land and sea,
170 I loved her! oh, I loved her! my Betsy Lee!

It's a terrible thing is love—did you say?
Well, Edward, my lad, I'll not say nay.
But you don't think of that when the young heart blows
Leaf by leaf, comin out like a rose,
And your sheets is slacked off, and your blood is a prancin,
And the world seems a floor for you to dance on.
Terrible—eh? yes, yes! you're right,
But all the same, it's God's own light.
Aw, there was somethin worth lovin in her—
180 As neat as a bird and as straight as a fir;

---

146   Gibbins: sand-eels.
155   my gough [*gh* as in Scot. *loch* but rhymed later with *cough*]: or *gogh*, "used in expletives as a softened form of 'God'" (Moore).
175   sheets: ropes used to adjust the sails (ed.).

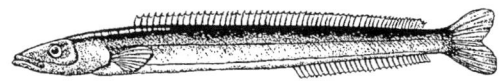

Gibbin

And I've heard them say, as she passed by,
It was like another sun slipped into the sky—
Kind to the old and kind to the young,
With a smile on her lip, and a laugh on her tongue,
With a heart to feel, and a head to choose,
And she stood just five feet four in her shoes.
Oh, I've seen her look—well, well, I'll stop it!
Oh, I've seen her turn—well, well, then! drop it!
Seen, seen! What, what! All under the sod
190   The darlin lies now—my God! my God!

    All right, my lads! I shipped that sea;
I couldn help it! Let be! let be!
Aw them courtin times!° Well it's no use tryin
To tell what they were, and time is flyin.
But you know how it is—the father pretendin
He never sees nothin, and the mother mendin,
Or a grippin the Bible, and spellin a tex,
And a eyin us now-and-then over her specs.
Aw they were a decent pair enough them two!
200   If it was only with them I'd had to do.
Bless me! the larned he was in the flowers!
And how he would talk for hours and hours
About diggin and dungin, and weedin and seedin,
And sometimes a bit of a spell at the readin;
And Betsy and me sittin back in the chimley,
And her a clickin her needles so nimbly,
And me lookin straight in ould Anthony's face,
And a stealin my arm round Betsy's wais'.
Aw the shy she was! But when Anthony said
210   "Now, childher! it's time to be goin to bed"—
Then Betsy would say, as we all of us riz,
"I wonder what sort of a night it is;"
Or—"Never mind, father! I'll shut the door;"
And shut it she did, you may be sure;
Only the way she done it, d'ye see?
I was outside, but so was she!

    Ah, then was the time! just a minute! a minute!
But bless me the sight of love we put in it!
Ah, the claspin arms! ah, the stoopin head!
220   Ah, the kisses in showers! ah, the things that we said!
And when—now, Bob, I know what you're at—
Oh, God in heaven! not that! not that!

---

211   riz: rose.
221-44 *Omitted.*

I know what you're thinkin! I know your surt,
Your trollopin madams, and all that dirt.
I know the lot with their cheeks so pink,
And their eyes a swimmin and blazin with drink,
With blackguard talk for whoever they meet,
And a squealin and scuttlin about the street:
I know their laugh too—aw I know it well—
230 The sort of a laugh you might laugh in hell.
Oh yes! they can laugh, but just you mind them,
And you'll see the divil that's grinnin behind them.
Now listen, Bob! and listen you, Jem!
Did you think that Betsy was like one of them?
Like one of *them!* why that's what you'd wish!
Well there's chaps that's straight like a cuttle-fish:
For though the water be clear and blue
As the heaven above, they'll manage to brew
Some stuff in their brains, or their lights, or their gall,
240 Or the Divil knows where that'd muddy it all.
No, no! my lads! that's not what I meant—
Innocent! Innocent! Innocent!
Aw, I'll say it; aw, I'll swear it, and swear it again
For ever and ever and ever—Amen.

    Now avast, my lads, with chaffin and smut,
And I'll tell you my notion of an innocent fut.
For it's no use the whole world talkin to me,
If I'd never seen nothin of Betsy Lee
Except her foot, I was bound to know
250 That she was as pure as the driven snow.
For there's feet that houlds on like a cat on a roof,
And there's feet that thumps like an elephant's hoof;
There's feet that goes trundlin on like a barra,
And some that's crooky, some as straight as an arra;
There's feet that's thick, and feet that's thin,
And some turnin out, and some turnin in;
And there's feet that can run, and feet that can walk,
Aye, feet that can laugh, and feet that can talk—
But an innocent fut—it's got the spring
260 That you feel when you tread on the mountain ling;
And it's tied to the heart, and not to the hip,
And it moves with the eye, and it moves with the lip.
I suppose it's God that makes when He wills
Them beautiful things—with the lift of His hills,
And the waft of His winds, and His calms and His storms,

---

253   barra: barrow.
260   ling: a variety of heather (ed.).

Fo'c's'le Yarns 8

    And His work and His rest; and that's how He forms
    A simple wench to be true and free,
    And to move like a piece of poethry.

    Well, a lass is a lass, and a lad is a lad;
270 But now for the luck ould Anthony had.
    For one ev'rin, as I was makin the beach,
    I heard such a hollabaloo and a screetch
    That I left the boat there as she was, and I ran
    Straight up to the houses, and saw the whole clan
    Of neighbours a crowdin at Anthony's door,
    For most of the boats was landed before,
    And some pressin in, and some pressin out;
    So I axed a woman what it was all about;
    And "Didn ye hear the news?" says she;
280 "It's a fortin that's come to ould Anthony Lee."
    Then she tould me about the Lawyer chap,
    That was in with them there, and his horse and his trap,
    And his papers "with seals as big as a skate"—
    Bless me! how them women loves to prate!
    And "a good-lookin man he was," she said,
    "As you might see! and a gentleman bred;
    And he's talkin that nice, and that kind, and that free!
    And it's a fortin he's got for ould Anthony Lee!"

    So I said—"All right!" but I felt all wrong;
290 And I turned away, and I walked along
    To a part of the shore, where the wreck of a mast
    Stuck half of it out, and half of it fast.
    And a knife inside of me seemed to cut
    My heart from its moorins, and heaven shut
    And locked, and barred, like the door of a dungeon,
    And me in the trough of the sea a plungin,
    With the only land that I knew behind me,
    And a driftin where God himself couldn find me.
    So I made for the mast, but before I got at it
300 I saw Betsy a standin as straight as a stattit,
    With her back to the mast, and her face to the water,
    And the strain of her eyes gettin tauter and tauter,
    As if with the strength of her look she'd try
    To draw a soul from the dull dead sky.
    Then I went to her, but what could I say?
    For she never took her eyes away:

---

271   ev'rin: evening.
280   fortin: fortune.
283   skate: ray fish (ed.).
300   stattit: statue.

Only she put her hand on my cheek,
And I tried, and I tried hard enough to speak,
But I couldn—then all of a sudden she turned,
310 And the far-off look was gone, and she yearned
To my heart, and she said—"You doubted me;"
And I said—"I didn then, Betsy Lee!"

    So her and me sat down on the mast,
And we talked and talked, and the time went fast,
When I heard a step close by, and—behould ye!
There was the Lawyer chap I tould ye
Had come with the papers (confound the pup!),
And says he—"I'm sorry to interrup',"
He says, "such a pleasant têtertête;
320 But you'll pardon me; it's gettin late,
And I couldn think of returnin to town
Without payin my respects, as I feel bound,
To the lovely heiress, and off'rin her——,"
And cetterer, and cetterer—
You know how they rattles on. So we rose,
And all the three of us homeward goes.
But blest if he didn buck up, and says he,
With a smirk, "Will you take my arm, Miss Lee?"
And Betsy didn know what to do,
330 So she catched a hould, and there them two
Goes linkin along. Aw, I thought I'd split
With laughin, and then I cussed a bit.
And when we come up to the houses—the rushin
There was to the doors, and Betsy blushin,
And him lookin grand, and me lookin queer,
And the women sayin—"What a beautiful pair!"
Now it mattered little to me that night
What stuff they talked, for I knew I was right
With Betsy; but still, you see, of a rule,
340 A fellow doesn like to look like a fool.
And the more I thought of the chap and his beauin,
The madder I got; so when he was goin,
And I held the horse, and gave him the reins,
And—"There's a sixpence," says he, "for your pains—
A sixpence, my man!" I couldn hould in,
And once I began I did begin,
And I let him have it *hot*, as they say;
But he only laughed, and druv away.

---

327   buck up: play the *buck*, act pretentiously.
331   linkin: arm-in-arm
339   of: as.

And they all of them laughed to hear me swear;
350 But Betsy—of course she wasn there.

Now heave ahead, my lads, with me!
For the weeks rolled on, and ould Anthony Lee
Did just what he always wanted to do,
For he took a farm they called the *Brew*,
In a hollow that lay at the foot of a hill,
Where the blessed ould craythur might have his fill
Of stockin and rearin and grassin and tillage,
And only about a mile from the village.
And a stream ran right through the orchard, and then
360 Went dancin and glancin down the glen,
And soaked through the shilly, and out to the bay,
But never forgot, as it passed, to say,
With the ringin laugh of its silv'ry flow—
"She's thinkin of you, and she tould me so."
Laugh on, my hearties! you'll do no harm;
But I've stood when the wind blew straight from the farm,
And I've felt her spirit draw nigher and nigher,
Till it shivered into my veins like fire,
And every ripple and every rock
370 Seemed swep' with the hem of Betsy's frock.

A blessed ould fool? very well! very well!
But a blessed ould fool's got a story to tell,
And a blessed ould fool must have his own way,
For a song is a song, and a say is a say.
But maybe there's none of you wants any more!
Oh yes! Bob Williams! I heard you snore!
Or was it a pig with a twist in his snout?
Take a rope's-end, Bill! and hit him a clout!
But—of coorse! of coorse!—Ah little Sim!°
380 Is he off? little lad! just fist us the glim!
Ah, beauty! beauty! no matter for him!
No matter for him! Aw, isn he gud?
With his nose like a shell, and his mouth like a bud!
There's sauce enough in that there lip
To aggravate ever a man in the ship.
Did ye hear him to-day agate of his chaff?
Well! how he made the skipper laugh!

354	*Brew*:	hill-slope (Moore).
361	shilly:	fine gravel.
371-8	*Omitted.*	
380	fist us the glim:	hand us the light (ed.).
382	gud:	good.
386	agate:	busy with (ed.).

Just come here and look at him, mates!
Isn he like them things up the Straits?
Them picthurs the Romans has got in their chapels?
Brave little chaps, with their cheeks like apples!
Holdin on to their mawthers' petticoats,
And lookin as spunky and bould as goats!
Bless me! the body them craythurs has got!
Clean! without a speck or a spot!
And they calls the little boy Jesus, and her
With her head wrapped up in a handkecher
They calls the Vargin, and all them starts
And patterin-nostrin, and—bless their hearts!
What is he dreaming of now, little lad!
Brother and sister and mother and dad?
And lobsters a creepin about the creel,
And granny hummin her spinnin-wheel?
Or him in the parlour a lyin in bed,
And a twiggin the spiders over-head?
"Hushee-bow-babby upon the tree-top!
And when the wind blows the cradle will rock—"
Ah Simmy my boy, I've done my best—
Somethin like that—but as for the rest——
Leave the hammock alone now, Dick, and be civil!
But he raely is a purty young divil.

"Go on! go on!" Is that your shout?
Well, what is this I was thinkin about?
I'm in for it now, and it's no use bilkin—
Oh, aye! the milkin! ould Anthony's milkin!
I never thought on for the whys or the hows,
But I was always terrible fond of cows.
Now aren't they innocent things—them bas'es?
And havn they got ould innocent faces?
A strooghin their legs that lazy way,
Or a standin as if they meant to pray—
They're that sollum and lovin and studdy and wise,
And the butter meltin in their big eyes!
Eh? what do you think about it, John?
Is it the stuff they're feedin on—
The clover and meadow-grass and rushes,
And them goin pickin among the bushes,
And sniffin the dew when it's fresh and fine,

389	Straits: up the Mediterranean.
405	a twiggin: observing (ed.).
418	bas'es: beasts.
420	strooghin: stroking, trailing.
422	studdy: steady.

The sweetest brew of God's own wine!
430 And the smell of the harbs gets into their sowls,
And works and works, and rowls and rowls,
Till it tightens their tits and drabs their muzzle—
Well, it's no use o' talkin—it's a regular puzzle:
But you'll notice the very people that's got to atten'
To the like, is generally very aisy men.

Aw ould Anthony knew about them pat,
Alderney, Ayreshire, and all to that!
And strippin and rearin, and profit and loss—
Aw, he was a clever ould chap, ould Anthony was.
440 More by token that's the for
Him and me had our first war.
You see, I was sittin there one night
When who should come in but ould Tommy Tite?°
Tight he was by name and by nathur,
A dirty ould herpocrite of a craythur,
With a mouth that shut with a snick and a snap—
Tight for sure like the Divil's own trap;
And his hair brushed up behind and before—
Straight like the bristles that's on a boar.
450 Well, that man was thin! I never saw thinner,
A lean, ould, hungry, mangy sinner!
Hitched up all taut on the edge of his chair—
And his guts stowed away with him—well, God knows where.
And he'd sit and he'd talk! well, the way he'd talk!
And he'd groan in his innards, and retch and hawk—
And—"Scuse me!" he'd say, "it's my stemmick, marm!"
And wasn it him that owned the farm?
And of coorse ould Anthony made a fuss
About him, but I didn care a cuss.

460 Well, there they were talkin and talkin away
About carrots and turmits, and oats and hay—
And stock and lock and barrel, bless ye!
The big words they had was enough to distress ye!
With their pipes in each other's faces smookin,
And me lookin and longin, and longin and lookin—
Lookin for Betsy's little signs—
The way them pretty craythurs finds
To talk without talkin, is raely grand—
A tap of the fut, a twitch of the hand!

---

432   drabs: makes wet.
440   the for: the reason.
449   Straight: just.

470 A heise of the neck, a heave of the breast!
A stoop like a bird upon its nest!
A look at father, a look at mawther!
A one knee swingin over the other!
A lookin lower, and a lookin higher!
A long, long straight look into the fire!
A look of joy, and a look of pain!
But bless ye! you understand what I mean.
So on they talked till all the fun
In her darlin little face begun
480 To work—and I couldn hould it in,
And I laughed, and I laughed like anythin'.
My goodness! the mad ould Anthony got,
With his eyes so wide, and his cheeks as hot,
And as red as a coal; and the other fellow
Was turnin green and turnin yellow;
And the ould woman bucked up as proud as you plaze,
But ould Anthony spoke, and says he, he says—
"It's most unfortnit—I hope you will—
I mean it's most disrespectable——
490 But I hopes, Misther Tite, as you'll excuse—"
And so he went on with his parley-voos—
"Just a young man from the shore," says he,
"As drops in in the ev'rin for company!
A umble neighbour as don't know batther,
You see, Misther Tite, I knew his father."
Well I choked that down, but I says to myself—
Pretendin to stare at the plates on the shelf—
"You've got me, ould man! but I'll owe you one
For that, before the stakes is drawn."
500 But it's my belief, that from that day,
He never liked me anyway.

"But about the milkin?" all right! all right!
I'm nearly as bad as ould Tommy Tite!
Spinnin round and round and round,
And never a knowin where am I bound.
Well, mostly every ev'rin, you see,
I was up at the milkin, with Betsy Lee.
For when she was milkin, she was always singin;
I don't know what was it—may be the ringin
510 Of the milk comin tearin into the can,
With a swilsh and a swelsh and a tantaran,

---

470   heise: hoist, lift.
486   bucked up: drew herself up.
494   batther: better.

A makin what the Lawyer gent
Was callin a sort of *accumpliment*.
But the look of a cow is enough to do it,
And her breath, and her neck, and the way she'll slew it—
As if she was sayin, the patient she stud,
"Milk away! it's doin me gud."
And the sun goin down, and the moon comin up,
And maybe you takin a little sup,
520 And the steam of the hay, and your forehead pressin
Agin her round side! but for all it's a blessin
When they're nice and quiet, for there's some of them rough,
And kicky and pushy and bould enough.

Now Betsy would sing and I would hear,
And away I'd be like a hound or a deer,
Up the glen and through the sedges,
And bless me the way I took the hedges!
For I'd be wantin to get in time to the place
To see the last sunlight on Betsy's face.
530 And when I'd be gettin a-top of the brew
Where ould Anthony's house was full in view,
Then I'd stop and listen till I'd got it right,
And answer it back with all my might.
And when I come down, she'd say—"I heard!
You're for all the world like a mockin-bird."
She had her fun! aw, she had her fun!
And I'd say—"Well, Betsy, are you nearly done?"
And I'd kiss her, and then she'd say—"What bother!"
And the cow lookin round like a kind ould mawther.
540 One cow they had—well of all the sense
That ever I saw, and the imperence!
God bless me! the lek of yandhar ould mailie!
A brown cow she was—well raely! raely!
She's made me laugh till I abslit shoutit—
Pretendin to know all about it.

Well, one ev'rin I'd been laughin like a fool,
And Betsy nearly fallin off the stool—
In the orchard we were, and the apple blossom
Was shreddin down into Betsy's bosom,

513	*accumpliment*:	accompaniment.
515	slew:	turn.
516	the patient she stud:	she stood so patiently.
521	agin:	against.
	for all:	indeed (Moore).
530	brew:	hill.
542	mailie:	cow without horns.

550 And I was pickin them out, d'ye see?
And the cow was lookin and smilin at me,
When—creak went the gate, and who should appear
But Misther Richard Taylor, Esqueer!
That's the Lawyer chap—and says he,
"Plasantly engaged, Miss Lee!"
So Betsy was all of a twitter lek,
And she catched her handkecher round her neck,
And straightened her hair, and smoothed her brat,
And says—"Good everin!" just like that.

560 Well, I hardly knew what to do or to say,
So I just sat down, and milked away.
But Betsy stood up to him like a man,
Goodness! how that girl's tongue ran!
Like the tick of a watch, or the buzz of a reel,
And hoity-toity! and quite genteel—
Rittle-rattle—the talk it kem,
Oh, hoky-poky! Jerusalem!
Now I didn mind her bein civil,
But she seemed so pleased to see the divil.
570 Aw, I might have been a thousand miles away—
Of coorse! of coorse! I know what you'll say—
But I couldn stand it—so I watched my chance,
And I turned the tit, and I gave it him once,
A right good skute betwix the eyes—
Aw, murder! murder! what a rise!
With the milk all streamin down his breast,
And his shirt and his pins and all the rest,
And a bran new waistcoat spoiled, and him splutt'rin,
And a wipin his face, and mutt'rin—mutt'rin—
580 And at last he says—"I shall go," says he,
"And kermoonicate this to Misther Lee."
"Aw, Tom!" says Betsy; "Aw, Betsy!" says I;
"Whatever!" says she, and she begun to cry.
"Well," I says, "it's no wonder o' me,
With your ransy-tansy-tissimitee."

But we soon made it up, and it was gettin late,
And again I heard the garden gate.
"There!" says I, "he's goin: so now, little missis!"
And kisses, kisses, kisses, kisses!

---

558   brat: apron.
567   *hoky-poky*: from *hocus pocus*, deception, trickery (*OED*).
574   skute: squirt (ed.).
585   ransy-tansy-tissimitee: burden of a song sung by children dancing: *Here comes three Dukes a ridin.*

"Take care!" says she; "Never fear!" I said;
Yes, a fool! an ould fool! but she loved me, Ned.
So I cleared the fence, and the stream, and the pebbles
Chimin all night with their little trebles,
And tenors and bassers down at the fall,
Answerin back with a kindly call
(She used to tell me it sent her to sleep)
(Just at the dam it was middlin deep);
And I crossed the glen, and I took a short cut,
And all at once I heard a fut.
I guessed it was him, and I was right,
With his boots goin winkin through the night.
"Good night!" says I. "Good night!" says he.
"And what did you tell ould Anthony Lee?"
Aw, then he begun, and he cussed and he swore,
The divil behind, and the divil before—
And all what he'd do—and he'd have the law—
And "if it hadn been—" "Come, stop that jaw!
Have it out! have it out, Misther Taylor!" says I;
"Here we are under God's own sky.
Have it out like a man, if it's a man you are!
Have it out! have it out, my lad! if you dare;
And don't stand there like a blue baboon
With your long teeth chatterin in the moon!"
"Not if I knows it!" says he, "Tom Baynes.
No! no!" says he, "I've other means."
"Have ye?" says I, and I grips the seat
Of his trousis, and sends him over a gate.
I didn know what he meant—good Lord!
But he kep' his word! he kep' his word!

    This was in spring, and the summer come,
And, behould ye! my gentleman still was dumb,
For he maybe thought about that spree
The less said the better for he.
For he's one of them chaps that works in the dark,
And creeps and crawls—is a Lawyer's clerk;
And digs and digs, and gives no sign,
Spreadin sods and flowers at the mouth of his mine;°
And he'll lay his train, and he'll hould his match,
And he'll wait and he'll wait, and he'll watch and he'll watch,
Till the minute comes, and before you sneezes
You're up to heaven in a hundred pieces.
Aw, it's a bitter poison—that black art,
The lie that eats into your heart;

---

601   winkin: creaking.

A thing gath'rin round you like a seine
Round the fish, and them never feelin the strain;
A squall comin tippytoe off the land,
And houldin its breath till it's close at hand,
And whisp'rin to the winds to keep still
Till all is ready—and then with a will,
640 With a rush and a roar they sweeps your deck,
And there you lies a shiv'rin wreck.

    Well, winter come, and then the cows
Was goin a milkin in the house.
And if you want peace and quietness,
It's in a cow-house you'll get it the best.
For the place is so warm, and their breath is so sweet,
And the nice straw bedding about their feet,
And hardly any light at all,
But just a dip stuck on to the wall,
650 And them yocked in the dark as quiet as ghos'es,
And a feelin for each other's noses.
And, bless me! sometimes you'd hardly be knowin
It was them, excep' for their chewin and blowin.
Aw, many a time I've felt quite queer
To see them standin so orderly there.
Is it the Lord that makes them so still?
Aw, I like them craythurs terrible!
Aye, aye! the sea for the leks of us!
It's God's own work (though treacherous!);
660 But for peace and rest and that—d'ye see?
Among the cows is the place for me.
And *lastly*, as the Pazons is sayin, it's there
You'll have your gel, if anywhere—
All your own among the hay,°
Wrapped in your arms! and the things that she'll say,
And the things that she'll do, you could hardly tell
Before that she loved you half as well.

    At least lek that's what Betsy done—
(Ah, no! my lads, avast your fun!)—
670 Speakin so soft and speakin so low,
Or speakin nothin at all, you know;
Or singin hymns, no matter what,
"Gentle Jesus," and the like o' that.°
And that's the way she was one night,

---

650   yocked: [yoked by a] plank sliding in a groove and confining the cow's neck.
662-9 *Omitted.*

Pressed to my heart as tight as tight—
"Sing *Glory be!*"° the darlin said,
"And then it'll be time to be goin to bed"—
When all of a sudden at the door
Come a clatt'rin of clogs, and there for sure
680 Stood Peggy, the sarvant, all out o' breath,
And, "You're wanted," says she, "Miss Elizabeth!"
So I got up, and I was goin too;
"Aw, no!" says Peggy, "that'll never do!"
And she went—and she went—and my heart gev a shever—
And I never saw her again! no never! never!

Well! well! well! well!—What ails the ship?
Hold on! hold on! I got a grip.
Who's at the helm? Is it Juan Cronin?
With all this criss-crossin and herrin-bonin!
690 My patience! or is it Tommy Teare?
That's a tervil onasy fellow to steer!
Have another pipe? Why, thank you, Eddart,
You're a feelin lad, and I allis said it.
Yes, give me the can! I'll just take a swipe—
Aye! another pipe—another pipe—
And, Eddart my lad, was that a letter
You got from home? Is your father better?
Is your mother hearty? I knew her well,
A nice little sthuggha of a gel!
700 And, Eddart, whenever you'll be goin to write,
Tell them I was axin (I've got a light)
How were they. And, Eddart, mind you'll put in
If ould Tommy Tite's lookin after the tin,
And if the herrins was plenty this year,
And is the gaery drained, d'ye hear?
And have ould Higgison rose the rent?
Aw, Eddart and me is well acquent.

Well, well! I didn know what was up,
Nor whether to go, nor whether to stop.
710 So I waited a bit, and I took off my shoes,
And, thinks I, the ould people's gone to roos';
And maybe she's waitin all alone,

---

691   onasy: uneasy.
694   swipe: a scoop of tobacco.
699   sthuggha: thick-set, but well-proportioned (Mx. *stuggey*, a stoutling—Cregeen).
703   tin: money (ed.).
705   gaery: piece of waste-land (Mx. *garee*, a sour piece of land—Cregeen).

And wond'rin and wond'rin am I gone.
And I looked and I looked, and I crossed the street
As quiet as a mouse in my stocking-feet,
And I crep' in among the honey-suckles
At the porch, and I gave a tap with my knuckles,
Just this way, when the door gave a flirt,
And there stood ould Anthony in his shirt—
720 Hard and keen, and his ould bald head
Like Sammil when he was riz from the dead—°
In the Bible, you know, yes! just the sem,
Isaac and Peter and the like of them,
That's allis got conks like turkey's eggs,
And the wind blowin free round their blessed ould legs,
Enough to frecken you in the night,
He was so awful and big and white.
And says he, "I thought it was you that was knockin—
Oh it's very shockin! it's very shockin!"
730 "What's shockin?" I says; "Oh" he says, "it's no use
Pretendin, young man!" "Well why the deuce,"
Says I, "can't you give the thing a name?"
"Oh raely," says he, "for shame! for shame!"
And "it's could," he says, "and I think I'll go in—
Oh it's an awful sin! an awful sin!"
"Sin," says I, "well, whatever it is,
Who tould you this! who tould you this?"
"Misther Taylor," he says; "Misther Taylor!" says I,
"Oh indeed!" then he tould me why,
740 And all about it, how Jenny Magee
Had come home, and laid a child to me—
And "Nice purseedins," he says, "indeed!"
And—*who was I?* and the beggarly breed
The lot of us was, and—*how dar I*, says he,
How dar I look up to Betsy Lee?
"Is he here?" I says; "No! no!" "That's well!
Thank God! thank God! for by heaven and hell,
If I had caught him in the wud,
The sun would have risen upon his blud."
750 "Oh!" says he, quite freckened lek,
"What shockin feelins!" and — *Could I expec'?*—
And—*did I raely mean?*—and before I could say
This or that, he was in, and turned the key.

---

714 street: road (ed.).
724 conks: heads.
726 frecken: frighten (ed.).
728-42 *Omitted 1881; restored 1889.*
734 could [rhymes with Scot. *auld*]: cold (ed.)

Aw, up to that I was proud enough,
Bould as a lion, and middlin rough;
But left there alone, that sore distressed,
All the strength of the night come upon me and pressed
And forced me down till I fell on my knees,
And I heard the moan of the long dead seas
760 Far away rollin in on the shore,
And I called to ould Anthony through the door—
"Aw, listen to me! aw, listen to me!
Aw, Misther Lee! aw, Misther Lee!
He's bought that woman," I said, "he's bought her
To swear that lie; and it's after your daughter
He is himself! aw, listen to me!
Aw, Misther Lee! aw, Misther Lee!"
Not a word! not a word!—"It's a lie," I cried,
"It's a lie, if on the spot I died;
770 So help me God, sir, it is a lie!"
Never a word or a sound of reply!
"Aw, Misther Lee!" I says, "can I see her?
Aw, Misthress Lee! are *you* up there?
Let me see Betsy! she'll belave me!
Let me see Betsy! Save me! save me!
She hears me now, and her heart is broke!"
I said, and I listened, but no one spoke.
"She's dyin! you're stoppin her mouth!" I said;
"You're houldin her down upon the bed!
780 Aw, you'll answer for this at the day of doom!
You're smotherin her there in the little room!
Betsy! Betsy! my darlin love!
Betsy! Betsy! oh Father above!"

And then I fell right forrid, and lay
Quite stupid, how long I cannot say;
But the first thing I felt when I tried to stand
Was something soft a slickin my hand.
And what do ye think it was but Sweep!
The ould black coly that minded the sheep!
790 "God bless ye!" says I, "I've a friend in you!"
And he was a middlin sulky craythur too.
So I dragged myself up, and picked a bit
Of the honey-suckle, and buried it
In my breast, and I wandered round and round,
But not a mossel of light could be found.
I was like a drunken man the way I staggered,
And across the street, and through the haggard,

---

797   haggard: stackyard.

And into the fields, and I know nothing more
Till they found me in the mornin upon the shore.

800 *Well, he was a villyan anyway?*
He was a villyan — did you say?
A villyan! —Will you cuss him, Bill?
Aye, cuss your fill, boy, cuss your fill!
A villyan—eh? but before I'm done
You'll know something more about him, my son.
Now, men, what was I to do? can ye tell?
Just leave it alone? aye—maybe as well!
But I never would strike my flag to a lie
Before I knew good reason why.
810 No, no! my lads! it's not in my blud—
I never did, and I never wud.
But ye see I was only a youngster then,
And didn know much of the ways of men.
Beside the shame! God bless ye! the shamed
I was to think that the lek should be named.
For that's the worst of a divil still —
You'll be ashamed, but he never will;
And you'll be in the doldrums under his lee,
With the breeze took out of your sails, but he!
820 Aw, he'll hould his luff, and lay his head well
To the wind, and look in the eye of hell.

Well, I thought and I thought till at last a plan
Come into my head, and—"That's the man!"
I says—"The Pazon!—I'll go to him,
And I'll know the worst of it, sink or swim."
So I claned myself, and I had a draw
Of the pipe, and I went, but middlin slaw,
For my head was workin uncommon hard
All the way, and I didn regard
830 For nothing at all, and the boats comin round
The Stack,° a beatin up for the ground,
And a Rantipike schooner° caught in the tide,

---

808   strike my flag: lower my flag, surrender (ed.).
812-21   Omitted.
818   in the doldrums under his lee: cut off from the wind by his ship; immobilized by him (ed.).
820   hould his luff: sail close to the wind; here, confidently pursue his goals (ed.).
827   slaw: slow.
831   beatin up for the ground: heading into the wind for the fishing ground (ed.).

And a nice little whole-sail breeze outside,
Not much matter to me you'd 'spec—
No! but you'll allis be noticin lek.

Now the grandest ould pazon, I'll be bail,
That ever was, was ould Pazon Gale.°
Aw, of all the kind and the good and the true!
And the aisy and free, and—"How do you do?
840 And how's your mother, Tom, and—the fishin?"
Spakin that nice, and allis wishin
Good luck to the boats, and—"How's the take?"
And blessin us there for Jesus' sake.
And many a time he'd come out and try
A line, and the keen he was, and the spry!
And he'd sit in the stern, and he'd tuck his tails,
And well he knew how to handle the sails.
And sometimes, if we were smookin, he'd ax
For a pipe, and then we'd be turnin our backs,
850 Lettin on never to see him, and lookin
This way and that way, and him a smookin
Twis' as strong and as black as tar,
And terrible sollum and regular.
Bless me! the sperrit that was in him too,
Houldin on till all was blue!
And only a little man, but staunch,
With a main big heart aback of his paunch!
Just a little round man—but you should ha' seen him agate
Of a good-sized conger or a skate:
860 His arms as stiff, and his eye afire,
And every muscle of him like wire.

But avast this talk! What! what did you say?
Tell us more about the Pazon—eh?
Well, well! he was a pazon—yis!
But there's odds of pazons, that's the way it is.
For there's pazons now that's mortal proud,
And some middlin humble, that's allowed.
And there's pazons partikler about their clothes,
And rings on their fingers, and bells on their toes:°
870 And there's pazons that doesn know your names,

833	whole-sail breeze: enough wind to justify raising all the sails (ed.).
834	'spec: expect.
836	I'll be bail: I'll be bound—I'll swear (ed.).
850	Lettin on: pretending.
865	odds: different types (ed.).
866	mortal: very.

"Shut the gate, my man!" and all them games.
And there's pazons *too* free—I've heard one cuss
As hard and as hearty as one of us.
But Pazon Gale—now I'll give you his size,
He was a simple pazon, and lovin and wise.
That's what he was, and quiet uncommon,
And never said much to man nor woman;
Only the little he said was meat
For a hungry heart, and soft and sweet,
880 The way he said it: and often talkin
To hisself, and lookin down, and walkin.
Now there's some of them pazons they're allis shoutin,
And tearin at you, and ravin and routin,
And they gets you pinned with a lot of others
In a coop, and they calls you sisthers and brothers;
And you can't get out, so the beggars raises
Their vice, and gives it you like blazes.
What's the good of all that surt!
Sweatin and actin and bustin their shirt;
890 Shiverin the verry roof to splanthers—
I never liked them roaring ranthers.°
Yes! our pazon was quiet, but, mind ye! don't doubt
But the same man knew well what was he about.
Aye, many a time I've seen his face
All slushed with tears, and him tellin of *grace*
And *mercy* and that, and his vice so low,
But trimblin aw, we liked him though!

    And he wasn livin above the bay
Where I was livin,° but a bit away,
900 Over the next, and betwix the two
The land ran out to a point, and a screw
Of the tide set in on the rocks, and there
He'd stand in the mornin, and listen to hear
The dip of our oars comin out, and the jealous
We were of the Derbyhaven fellows!
And the way we'd pull to try which would be fuss!
And "Pazon!" we'd say, "are you comin with us?"
And the Derbyhaven chaps would call—
And the way he'd smile and say nothing at all!
910 Well, that's the Pazon, you'll understand,
Aye, the very man, the very man.
Aw, if I once get agate of him—

882-91   *Omitted.*
906   fuss: first.
912   get agate of him: start talking about him.

But some night again, if I'll be in the trim,
I'll maybe be tellin you more, if so be
You'll be carin to listen, and all agree.

Well, the Pazon was walkin on the gravel—
My conscience! the slow that man did travel!
Backwards and forrards, and stoppin and thinkin,
And a talkin away to hisself like winkin;
920 And a pickin a flower, or a kickin a stone,
There he was anyway all alone.
And I felt like a reglar blund'rin blockit,
And I stowed the quid in my waistcoat pocket,
And I said, "Here goes! I don't care a fardin,"
And I opened the gate, and into the garden.
And—"Pazon!" I says, "I've come to you."
"Is it true, Tom Baynes?" he says, "is it true?"
And he looked—"No it isn!" I said, quite pale;
"So you needn look that way, Pazon Gale!
930 It isn true!" So the ould man smiled,
And says he, "Well, don't be angry, child!"
Child he called me—d'ye see? d'ye see?
Child!—and he takes my hand, and says he,
"I suppose you've got a yarn to spin:
Come in, Tom Baynes, come in, come in!"
So in we went, and him smilin like fun,
Into the parlour; but the Misthress run
Quite shamed lek, a whiskin through the door,
And droppin her things upon the floor.
940 And the sarvant keeked over the landin-top—
A dirty trouss, with her head like a mop—
And she gurned like a cat, but I didn care,
Though they're middlin spiteful them craythurs are.

So I tould the Pazon all that I had,
And he says, "God bless ye! God bless ye! my lad!"
Aw, it's himself that knew my very soul,
And me so young, and him so oul'.
And all the good talk! and never fear—
And leave it to him, and he'd bring me clear—
950 And Anthony wanted talkin to—
And on with the hat—and away he'd go—
And *young Misther Taylor (a son of ould Dan!)*

---

922   blockit: blockhead.
923   quid: chewing tobacco (ed.).
940   keeked: peeped.
941   trouss: slut.
942   gurned: grinned.

Was a very *intelligent* young man.
"Aisy! Pazon," says I, and he went;
And all the road home—"*in-tel-li-gent*"—
I said, "what's that?" some pretty name
For a —— deng it! these pazons just like crame,
They're talkin that smooth—aw, it's well to be civil—
"A son of ould Dan's!" and Dan was a divil.

960 That was a Monday; a Thursday night
The Pazon come, and bless me the fright
The ould woman was in, and wipin the chair,
And nudgin and winkin—"Is Thomas there?"
He says—"Can I see him?" So up I got,
And out at the door, and I put a knot
On my heart, like one of you, when he takes
A turn and belays, and houlds on till it breaks.
And—"Well?" I says—then he looked at me,
And "Have you your pipe, Thomas?" says he;
970 "Maybe you'd better light it," he said,
"It's terrible good to study the head."
And he wouldn't take rest till I had it lit;
And he twisses, and twisses, and—"Wait a bit!"
He says, and he feels, and "We're all alone,"
Says he, and behould ye! a pipe of his own.
And "I'll smook too," he says; and he charges,
And puffs away like Boanarges.°
I never knew the like was at him afore:
And so we walked along the shore.
980 And if he didn behove to spin a yarn
About the stars—and Aldebarn,
And Orion°—and just to consedher
The grand way God had put them together,
And wasn it a good world after all,
And—what was man°—and the Bible—and Paul—
Till I got quite mad, and I says—"That'll do!
Were you at the Brew, Pazon? were you at the Brew?"
Aw, then it all come out, and the jaw
Ould Anthony had, and the coorts, and the law;
990 And—*Jane Magee and her mother both*—
He had gone there twice, but she stuck to her oath—
And—*what could he do?* "I'm going," says I—
"Keep up your heart now!" "I'll try, I'll try."
"Good night, and mind you'll go straight to bed!

---

967   belays: tightens or secures a rope (ed.).
971   study: steady.
973   twisses: twists, figets.
978   the like was at him: that he had such a thing.

"God bless ye, Tom!" "And you, sir!" I said.
"Come up in the mornin! Good night! good night!
Now mind you'll come!" "All right! all right!"

And it's into the house, and "Mawther," I says,
"I'm off." "What's off?" says she, "if you plaze!
1000 Off! what off!" says she, "you slink!"
And she was sharplin a knife upon the sink,
And she flung it down, and she looked that way—
Straight and stiff; and "What did you say?
Off! off where?" and the sting of a light
Snapped quick in her eye—"All right! all right!"
I says, and away to the chiss I goes—
"Stand by!" I cried, "I want my clothes;"
And I hauled them out—aw, she gev a leap,
And "Lave them alone!" she says, "you creep!"
1010 And she skutched them up, and she whisked about
As lithe as an eel, and still lookin out
Over her shouldher, and eyein me,
Like a flint, or some dead thing—"Let be,
Mawther," I says, "let go! you'd batther!"
Aw, then if she didn begin no matther!
And she threw the things upon the floor,
And she stamped them, and down on her knees, and she toor,
And ripped, and ragged, and scrunched away,
Aw, hands and teeth,—I'll be bound to say
1020 Them shirts was eighteen pence the yard!
Rael good shirts! aw, the woman was hard.
Hard she was, and lusty, and strong—
I've heard them say when she was young,
She could lift a hundred-weight and more,
And there wasn a man in the parish could throw her.
And as for shearin and pickin potatoes—
Aw, well, she bet all, and always as nate as
A pin, and takin a pride in it—
For there's some ould women, they're hardly fit,
1030 They're that dirty and stupid, and messin and muddin,
I wudn live with the like—No! I wudn!
But yandhar woman—asleep or awake—

1000   slink: sneak.
1001   sink: sink-stone.
1006   chiss: chest.
1009   creep: creeping creature—very common term of contempt.
1010   skutched: caught (ed.).
1026   shearin: reaping with a sickle (*OED*).
1027   bet: beat (ed.).
1032   yandhar: yonder—that.

Was a clane ould craythur and no mistake.
But hard—aw hard! for the ould man died,
And she looked, and she looked, but she never cried—
And him laid out, as sweet as bran,
And everything white,—like a gentleman.
And brass nails—bless ye! and none of your 'sterrits,
But proud in herself, and sarvin the sperrits.
1040 And "Misthress Baynes now! was he prepared?"
"God knows!" says she—aw, the woman was hard.
But if you could have prised the hatches
Of that strong sowl, you would have seen the catches
She made at her heart, choked up to the brim,
And you'd ha' knew she was as dead as him.
But mind me! from that very day
The woman's-juice, as you may say,
Was clean dried out of her, and she got
As tough and as dry, and as hard as a knot.
1050 Hard—but handy, and goin still,
Not troublin much for good or ill;
Like the moon and the stars God only touched
Once long ago, and away they scutched;
And now He never minds them a bit,
But they keep goin on, for they're used of it.

Goin on! Well she did go on that night,
And up from the floor, and her back to the light
Of the fire (it was burnin middlin low),
And the candle capsized, and she looked to grow
1060 That big in the dark, and never a breath,
But standin there like the shadda of death—
Never a breath—for maybe a minute,
Just like a cloud with the thunder in it
Dark and still, till its powder-bags
Burst—and the world is blown to rags.
Aw, she gave it them with a taste—she did,
"And was it that flippity-flappity flid
Of a Betsy Lee? and she knew well enough
What I'd come to at last with my milkin and stuff,
1070 And sniffin about where I hadn no call,
And the lines hangin rottin upon the wall,
And the boat never moored, and grindin her bones
To sawdust upon the cobblin stones—

1038	'sterrits:	hysterics.
1039	sarvin the sperrits:	serving out the spirits.
1053	scutched:	whisked (Moore).
1055	of:	to.
1073	cobblin stones:	large stones on the beach.

And the people talkin—And who were the Lees?
Who were they now after all, if you please?
Who were they to cock their nose?
And Lee's ould wife with her strings and her bows,
And her streamers and trimmins, and pippin and poppin
Her d——d ould head like a hen with a toppin!"
1080 *Did she cuss?* aye, she cussed, and it's a rael bad hearin,
Mind ye! a woman cussin *or* swearin—
Partikler your mawther—still for all it's true,
There's differin sorts of cussin too.
For there's cussin that comes down like fire from heaven
Fierce and strong—like the blast that's driven
From the mouth of a seven-times heated furnace;°
That's you see, when a man's in earnes'.
And there's cussin that's no use whataver,
Slibberin slobberin slushin slaver—
1090 A fool's lips runnin with brimstone froth,
The muckin skum of the Divil's own broth.

"And had they forgot when they lived next door?
A lazy lot, and as poor as poor—
And—*Misses Baynes! the beautiful tay
You've got—and I raely think I'll stay—*
And—*could you lend me a shillin till to-morrow?*
And borrow, borrow, borrow, borrow.
Aye, and starvin, and him doin nothin for hours
But pokin about with his harbs and his flowers—
1100 The lig-y-ma-treih! the dirty ould bough!
And now it was *Misther Lee!* my gough!
Misther and Misthress Lee in the gig—
Make way, good people!—aw, terrible big!
And would I demean myself to them?
You silly-billy! for shame! for shame!"
And at it again—"And what she would rather—
And me the very spit of my father!
And what *was* a bychild, if you come to that?
It wasn a dog, and it wasn a cat;
1110 But a man's own flesh, and the love and the life

1079 toppin: crest.
1080-91 *Omitted.*
1100 lig-y-ma-treih [[pronounced approximtely as *lyi´guh muh thrai*; *th* almost like *t, ai* as in *air*]: taking time, dilatory (Mx. *lhiggym y hraa*, "Letting the time [pass]"—Moore).
  bough [*gh* as in Scot. *loch*]: poor (creature).
1107 spit: exact likeness. Cf. spit and image (ed.).
1108 bychild: illegitimate child (ed.).
1108-13 *Omitted.*

Was in it—let be she wasn your wife—
And after all why shouldn she be?
She was a strappin wench was Jinny Magee,
And good at the work, and worth a hundred
Of your Betsy things—and why should we be sundered?
And Jinny and her would agree, never fear her!"
Aw, she was despard though to hear her.

"Hush! mawther!" I says, "aw, mawther, hush!"
And she turned to the fire, and I saw her brush
1120 The tears from her eyes, and I saw the workin
Of her back, and her body jerkin, jerkin:
And I went, and I never said nothin lek,
But I put my arm around her neck,
And I looked in her face, and the shape and the strent',
And the very face itself had went
All into one, like a sudden thaw,
Slished and slushed, or the way you've saw
The water bubblin and swirlin around
The place where a strong man have gone down.

1130 And I took her and put her upon the bed
Like a little child, and her poor ould head
On my breast, and I hushed her, and stroked her cheek,
Talkin little talk—the way they speak
To babies—I did! and d—— the shame!
Wasn it out of her I came?
And I began to think of Absalun,°
And David cryin "My son, my son!"
And the moon come round, and the light shone in,
And crep' on her face, and I saw the thin
1140 She was, and the wore, and her neck all dried
And shrivelled up like strips of hide:
And I thought of the time it was as warm
And as soft as Betsy's, and her husband's arm
Around it strong and lovin, and me
A cuddled up, and a suckin free.
And I cried like Peter in the Testament,°
When Jesus looked at him, and out he went,
And cried like a fool, and the cock a crowin,
But what there was in his heart there's no knowin.
1150 And I swore by the livin God above
I'd pay her back, and love for love,

1117   despard: desperate.
1124   strent': strength.

And keep for keep, and the wages checked,
And her with a note, and all correct.
Then I kissed her, and she never stirred;
And I took my clothes, and, without a word,
I snicked the door, and by break o' the day
I was standing alone on Douglas quay.

I shipped foreign of coorse, and a fine ship too,
China bound,° the *Waterloo*—°
1160 Captain Davis—the time I joined her—
"Carry-on Davis?" aye, I thought you'd mind her.
A tight little ship, and a tight little skipper—
Hadn we a race with the Liverpool clipper,
The *Marco Polo*,° that very trip?
And it's my opinion that if that ship—
But never mind! she done her duty,
And the *Marco Polo was* a beauty—
But still—close-hauled, d'ye see? Well! well!
There's odds of ships, and who can tell?
1170 That was my ship anyway,
And I was aboard her two years to a day,
And back though for all, and her a dischargin,
And the hands paid off, so you'll aisy imargine
The keen I was for home, and the tracks
I made right away, and no one to ax,
Nor nothing—"And surely hadn I heard
From nobody?" Bless ye! divil a word!

It was dark when I come upon the street,
And my heart hung heavy on my feet,
1180 And—all turned in, but in the ould spot
A light was burnin still, and the hot
I felt, and the chokin, and over the midden,
And up to the pane—and her face half-hidden,
And her sure enough, and the ould arm-cheer,
And as straight as a reed, and terrible speer!
And the needles twinklin cheerily,
And a brave big book spread out on her knee,
The Bible—thinks I—and I was raely plased,
For it's a great thing to get ould people aised

1152   checked: stopped at the owner's.
1153   note: wage note left at home by a seaman.
1156   snicked: clicked (*OED*).
1168   close-hauled: with sails flat in order to sail as close to the wind as possible (ed.).
1172   dischargin: unloading (ed.).
1185   speer: spare, thin.

1190 In their minds with the lek o' yandhar, and tracks,
And hymns—it studdies them though, and slacks
Their sowls, and softens their tempers, and stops
Their coughin as good as any drops.
And if they don't understand what they're readin—
The poor ould things—it's a sort of feedin—
Chewin or suction—what's the odds?
One way's man's, and the other God's!

"But how about Betsy?" well, wait a bit!
How about her? aye that was it—
1200 And what a man knows, you see he knows,
So I lifts the latch, and in I goes,
"Mawther!" I says—my God! the spring
She gev, and says she—"It's a scandalous thing,"
She says, "Comin back in their very closes!
And it's bad enough, but I'll have no ghoses!°
Be aff!" says she, "be aff! be aff!"
Well, I raely couldn help but laugh.
"I'm Thomas Baynes, your son!" I said;
"I'm not a ghost." "And aren't you dead?"
1210 "No!" I says, and I tuk and gev her a kiss:
"Is that like a ghost?" "Well, I can't say it is."
"And—Betsy, mawther?" Aw, Christ, the look!
"Betsy, mawther?"—the woman shook;
And she spread her arms, and I staggered to her,
And I fell upon my knees on the floor;
And she wrapped my head in her brat—d'ye hear?
For to see a man cryin is middlin queer:
And then, my mates, then—then I knew
What a man that's backed by the Divil can do.
1220 For hadn this Taylor come one day,
And tould them I was drowned at sea?
And ould Anthony Lee, that might have knew better,
Never axed to see the letter
Nor nothin, but talked about "Providence;"
And the men at the shore they hadn the sense;
And the Pazon as simple as a child,
And that's the way the villian beguiled
The lot of them, for they didn know
What to do or where to go,
1230 As if there wasn no owners nor agent,

1190	the lek o' yandhar: things like that; tracks: tracts.
1204	closes: clothes (ed.).
1206	aff: off.
1216	brat: apron.

Nor Lloyd's,° where they might have heard immadient.

    And Betsy, be sure, heard all before long,
They took care of that, and then ding-dong,
Night and day the ould people was at her—
And would she marry Taylor?° and chitter-chatter!
And never a word from Betsy Lee
But "It cannot be! it cannot be!"
And thinner and thinner every day,
And paler and paler, I've heard them say;
1240 And always doin the work and goin,
And early and late, and them never knowin,
For all they thought theirselves so wise,
That the gel was dyin under their eyes.
And—"Take advice, and marry him now!
A rael good husband anyhow."
And allis the one against the three—
And "It cannot be! it cannot be!"

    One night he was there, and words ran high—
Ould Peggy was tellin—and "Let me die!"
1250 She says—"let me die! let me die!" she said,
And they tuk her upstairs, and put her to bed,
And the Doctor come—I knew him well,
And he knew me—ould Doctor Bell°—
A nice ould man, but hard on the drink,
And the fond of Betsy you wouldn think!
He used to say, but he'd never say more,
Her face was like one he'd seen afore.
Aw, that's the man that had supped his fill
Of troubles, mind! but cheerful still.
1260 And a big strong man; and he'd often say
"Well, Thomas, my lad, and when's the day?"
And "would I be axin him up to the feed?"
The day indeed! the day indeed!
So he went up all alone to see her,
For Betsy wouldn have nobody there,
Excep himself: and them that was standin
And houldin their breaths upon the landin
Could hear her talkin very quick,
And the Doctor's vice uncommon thick—
1270 But what was said betwix them two
That time, there was none of them ever knew:
God knows, and *him;* but the nither will tell;
Aw, he was safe to trust was Doctor Bell.

1272   the nither: neither of them.

But when he come down—"Is she raely dyin?"
Ould Anthony said; but the Doctor was cryin.
And—"Doctor! Doctor! what can it be?"
"It's only a broken heart," says he;
And—*he'd come again another day*—
And he tuk his glass and went away.

1280 And when the winter time come round,
And the snow lyin deep upon the ground,
One mornin early the mother got up
To see how was she, and give her a sup
Of tea or the like—and—mates—hould on!
Betsy was gone! aye, Betsy was gone!
"Gentle Jesus, meek and mild!
Look upon a little child!
Pity my simplicity!
Suffer me to come to thee!"
1290 That's the words I've heard her sing
When she was just a little prattlin thing—
And I raely don't think in my heart that ever
She was different from that—no never!
Aw, He'd pity her simplicity!
A child to God! a woman to me!
"Gentle Jesus!" the sound is sweet,
Like you'll hear the little lammies bleat!
Gentle Jesus! well, well, well!
And oncc I thought—but who can tell!
1300 Come! give us a drop of drink! the stuff
A man will put out when he's dry! that's enough!
To hear me talkin religion——eh?
You must have thought it strange?—*You didn*—ye say?
You didn!—no!—d——n it! you didn—*you!*
Well, that'll do, my lads; that'll do, that'll do.

Well, of coorse the buryin—terrible grand,
And all in the papers you'll understand—
"Elizabeth, daughter of Anthony Lee
And Mary his wife—and twenty-three."
1310 But bless me! you've seen the lek afore—
And the Doctor waitin at the door,
And wantin somethin—and "Could I see her?"
And "Yes! aw, yes!" and up the steer—
And he looked, and he looked—I've heard them say—
Like a man that's lookin far away;
And he kissed her cheek, and he shut the lid,

1313   steer: stair.

That's what they tould me the Doctor did.

    But, however, you musn suppose, my men,
That all this was tould me there and then—
1320 Aw, I thought I'd somethin to tell ye, mind!
That wasn much in the spoony line—
No! no! the words ould mawther said
Was—"Betsy is dead, Tom; Betsy is dead!
And it's Taylor has kilt her anyway,
For didn he tell you were lost at sea!"
Nothin more—and up I sprung
To my feet, like a craythur that had been stung,
And I couldn see nothin but fire and blood,
And I reeled like a bullock that's got the thud
1330 Of the slaughterer's hammer betwix his hurns,
And claps of light and dark by turns,
Fire and blood! fire and blood!
And round and round, till the blindin scud
Got thinner and thinner, and then I seen
The ould woman had hitched herself between
My arms, and her arms around my neck,
And waitin, waitin, and wond'rin lek.
Aw, I flung her off—"He'll die! he'll die!
This night, this very night," says I:
1340 "He'll die before I'm one day ouldher;"
And I stripped my arm right up to the shouldher—
"Look here!" I says, "hesn God given
The strength?" I says, "and by Him in heaven,
And by her that's with him—hip and thigh!°
He'll die this night, by G—— he'll die!"
"No! no!" says she, "no, Thomas, no!"
For I was at the door intarmined to go.
And she coaxed and coaxed, and "wouldn it be better
To speak to him fuss, or to write a letter,
1350 Or to wait my chance?" and all that stuff!
"And then I could kill him aisy enough."
"Aisy! that's not what I want at all,"
I says—"I'll stand on his body, and call
The people, and let them know right well
It's me that sent the villian to hell."
"And then you'll be hung," says she, and I laughed—
"Will you go to the Pazon?" "It's not his craft,"
I says; "the work I've got to do

1321   spoony: sentimental, romantic (ed.).
1330   hurns: horns.
1347   intarmined: determined.
1350-6 *Omitted.*

Is no Pazon's work." "Would I go to the Brew?"
1360 Aw, when she said that I made a run—
But she held me, and—"Oh my son! my son!"
And cryin and houldin on to me still—
"Will you go to the Pazon?" "Yes! I will,
If that'll give you any content."
Not another word, but away we went—
And her in the dark, a keepin a grip
Of my jacket for fear I'd give her the slip,
And a peggin away with her poor old bones,
And stumblin and knockin agin the stones—
1370 And neither the good nor the bad was said,
And the one of us hadn a thing on our head—
And the rain it rained, and the wind it blew—
Aw, the woman was hard, but the woman was true.

"Missis Baynes!" says the Pazon, "Missis Baynes! Missis Baynes!
Will you plase to tell me what this means?"
And white as a sheet, and he cuts a caper,
And he drops the specs, and he drops the paper,
And backs and gets under the lee of a chair—
I'm blest if the Pazon didn look queer!
1380 I raely thought he was goin to fall—
And says mawther—"He isn dead at all!
Don't be freckened!" and—holy Moses!
Wasn he paid to look after ghos'es?°
Aw, then the joy he took of me!
"And the only one saved from the wreck!" says he;
"There wasn no wreck—God d—— his eyes!
No wreck at all, but Taylor's lies!"
"For shame then! Thomas!" and up she stud.
"Let him cuss!" says the Pazon, "it'll do him gud."
1390 And the look he gev, and the sigh, and the sob!
And he saw in a minute the whole of the job.
And he tried to speak, but he wasn able,
And I laid my head upon the table—
Quite stupid lek, and then them two
Began to talk, and I hardly knew
What was it they said, but "the little drop!"
I heard, and "you'll 'scuse him," and "Woman, stop!
The lad is drunk with grief," he said,
And he come and put his hand on my head;
1400 And the poor old fingers as dry as chips!
And the pity a tricklin off their tips—
And makin me all as peaceable—

1371   the one of us: neither of us.

Aw, the Pazon was kind and lovin still!
Full of wisdom and love, and blessin,
Aw, it's kind and lovin was the Pazon!

So at last, ye see, whatever they had,
I didn say nothin, good or bad;
And they settled betwix them what would I do,
And neither to go to the town nor the Brew,
1410 "But off to sea again, aye straight!
And, if I could, that very night."
So they roused me up, and "Me and your mawther"—
The Pazon says—"Aw, ye needn bother,"
Says I, "all right!" and then I'll be bail
I took it grand out of Pazon Gale—
"Now, Pazon," I says, "you know your man—
And a son of ould Dan's too! a son of ould Dan!"
We were at the door just ready to go—
Aw, the Pazon couldn help smilin though—
1420 *A son of ould Dan's!*—aye, just that way—
A son of ould Dan's!—eh? Billy! eh?

Well, I kept my word, and off at once,
And shipped on a coaster, owned in Penzance;
But it was foreign I wanted, so very soon
I joined the *Hector* bound for Rangoon.
Ah, mates! it's well for flesh and blood
To stick to a lass that's sweet and good,
Leastways if she sticks to you, ye know;
For then, my lads, blow high, blow low,
1430 On the stormiest sea, in the darkest night,
Her love is a star° that'll keep you right.
But there wasn no sun nor star for me—
Drinkin and tearin and every spree—
And if I couldn keep the divil under,
I don't think there's many of you will wonder.

Well, Divil or no, the *Hector* come home;
We raced that trip with the *Flying Foam*,°
And up the river the very same tide,
And the two of them berthed there side by side;
1440 A tight run that, and the whole of it stuck
In the paper—logs and all—good luck!
And the captain as proud, and me like a fool
Spreein away in Liverpool°—

1415 took it grand out of Pazon Gale: taunted, took the wind out of his sails (ed.).

And lodgins of coorse, for I never could stand
Them Sailors' Homes,° for a man is a man,
And a bell for dinner and a bell for tay,
And a bell to sing and a bell to pray,
And a bell for this and a bell for that,
And "Wipe your feet upon the mat!"
1450 And the rules hung up; and fined if you're late,
And a chap like a bobby shuttin the gate—
It isn raisonable, it isn:
They calls it a Home, I calls it a Prison.
Let a man go wherever he chooses!
Ould mawther Higgins' the house that I uses—
Jem Higgins' widda—you'll be bound to know *her*—
Clane, but not partickiler.
There's Quiggin's too, next door but one,
Not Andrew, of coorse! but Rumpy John—
1460 She's a dacent woman enough is Nancy,
But Higginses allis tuk my fancy.
There's some comfort there, for you just goes in,
And down with the watch and down with the tin,
And sleepin and wakin, and eatin and drinkin—
And out and in, and never thinkin—
And carryin on till all is blue,
And your jacket is gone and your waistcoat too.
Then of coorse you must cut your stick,
For the woman must live, however thick
1470 You may be with her: and I'm tould there's houses
Where the people 'll let ye drink your trousis;
But Higginses! never! and it isn right!
Shirt and trousis! honour bright!

But mostly afore it come to the spout
I'd ask if the money was all run out,
And she'd allis tell me whether or no,
And I'd lave my chiss, and away I'd go.
And so this time I took the street,
And I walked along till I chanced to meet
1480 A shipmate, somewhere down in Wappin'°—
And "What was I doin? and where was I stoppin?"
And "Blow it all! here goes the last copper!"
And into a house to get a cropper.

1468   cut your stick: be off (*OED*).
1471   drink your trousis: drink so much on credit that you have to sell your trousers to pay the bill (ed.).
1474   come to the spout: reached the point where you had to pawn things (pawn shops had a fixture called a "spout"—ed.).
1483   cropper: crupper, a small measure of spirits.

It was one of them dirty stinkin places,
Where the people is not a bit better than bases,
And long-shore lubbers a shammin to fight,
And Jack in his glory, and Jack's delight°—
With her elbers stickin outside of her shawl
Like the ribs of a wreck—and the divil and all!
1490 And her childer cussin and suckin the gin—
God help them craythurs! the white and the thin!
But what took my eye was an ouldish woman
In and out, and goin and comin,
And heavy feet on the floor overhead,
And "She's long a dyin," there's some of them said.
"Dyin!" says I; "Yes, dying!" says they;
"Well, it's a rum place to choose to die in—eh?"
Aw, the ould woman was up, and she cussed very bad—
And—"Choosin! there's not much choosin, my lad!"
1500 "And what's her name?" says I; says she,
"If ye want to know, it's Jinny Magee."
Aw, never believe me but I took the stair!
And "Where have you got her? where? where? where?"
"Turn to the right!" says she, "ye muff!"
And there was poor Jinny, sure enough!
There she was lyin on a wisp of straw—
And the dirt and the rags—you never saw—
And her eyes—aw them eyes! and her face—well! well!
And her that had been such a handsome gel!

1510   "Tom Baynes! Tom Baynes! is it you? is it you?
Oh can it be? can it be? can it be true?"
Well I cudn speak, but just a nod—
"Oh it's God that's sent you—it's God, it's God!"
And she gasped and gasped—"Oh I wronged you, Thomas!
I wronged you, I did, but he made me promise—
And here I'm now, and I know I'll not live—
Oh Thomas, forgive me, oh Tom, forgive!
Oh reach me your hand, Tom, reach me your hand!"
And she stretched out hers, and—I think I'm a man,
1520 But I shivered all over, and down by the bed,
And "Hush! hush! Jinny! hush! hush!" I said;
"*Forgive ye!*—Yes!" and I took and pressed
Her poor weak hand against my breast.
"Look, Tom," she said, "look there! look there!"
And a little bundle beside a chair—

1485   bases: beasts.
1486   long-shore lubbers: dock workers (ed.).

And the little arms and the little legs—
And the round round eyes as big as eggs,
And full of wondher—and "That's the child!"
She says, and, my God! the woman smiled!
1530 So I took him up, and I says—quite low—
"Is it Taylor's?" I says: "Oh no! no! no!"
"All right!" I says; "and his name?" "It's Simmy:"
And the little frock and the little chimmy!
And starved to the bones—so "Listen to me!
Listen now! listen! Jinny Magee!
By Him that made me, Jinny ven!
This child is mine for ever—Amen!"
And "Simmy!" I says, "remember this!"
And I put him to her for her to kiss;
1540 And then I kissed him; but the little chap
Of coorse he didn understand a rap.
And I turned to Jinny, and she tried to rise,
And I saw the death-light in her eyes—
Clasped hands! clenched teeth! and back with the head—
Aye, Jinny was dead, boys! Jinny was dead.

"Come here," I says, and I stamped on the floor,
And up the old woman come to be sure.
"See after her!" I says, "ould Sukee!"
And "All very well!" she says, "but lookee!
1550 You gives yourself terrible airs, young man!
Come now! what are you going to stand?"
But I took the child, and says I, "I'm goin:"
"Indeed!" she says, "and money owin!
And the people'll be 'spectin a drop of drink,"
And cussin, *and who was she, did I think?*
And the buryin too, for the matter of that!
"Out of the way!" says I, "you cat!"
And down the stair, and out at the front,
And the loblollyboys shoutin "Down with the blunt!"
1560 And a squarin up, and a lookin big,
And "hould him! down with him! here's a rig!"
"Stand back, you Irish curs!° stand back!"
Says I, for there wasn a man in the pack:
"Stand back, you cowards; or I'll soon let ye see!"
So off we went—little Simmy and me.

1533   chimmy: chemise, shirt.
1536   ven: dear.
1548   ould Sukee: tea-kettle (Wright). Sukee=Susan (ed.).
1559   loblollyboys: "loafers" about the docks.
         blunt: money.
1561   rig: some fun (ed.).

Is that him there asleep? did you ax?
Aye, the very same, and them's the fac's.
And now, my lads, you'll hardly miss
To know what poor little Simmy is.
1570 Bless me! it's almost like a dream,
But the very same! the very same!
Grew of coorse, and growin, understand ye!
But you can't keep them small agin nathur, can ye?
Look at him, John! the quiet he lies!
And the fringes combin over his eyes!
I know I'm a fool—but—feel that curl!
Aw, he's the only thing I have in all the world.

Well, on we marched, and the little thing
Wasn so heavy as a swaller's wing—
1580 A poor little bag of bones, that's all,
He'd have bruk in two if I'd let him fall.
And I tried all the little words I knew,
And actin the way that women do.
But bless ye! he wouldn take no rest,
But shovin his little head in my breast,
For though I had lived so long ashore,
I never had carried a child before.
And not a farlin at me; so the only plan
Was to make tracks straight off for Whitehaven,°
1590 And chance a logger loadin there—
Aw, heaps of them yandhar—never fear!
And the first time ever I begged was then,
And the women is raely wuss till the men—
"Be off!" says my lady, "be off! you scamp!
I never give nothin to a tramp!"
So I made her a bow, for I learnt with my letters,
To "ordher myself to all my betters."°
But when the sun got low in the sky,
Little Simmy began to cry.
1600 Hungry! I says, and over a gate
And into a field, and "Wait then, wait!"
And I put him sitting upon the grass—
Dear o' me! the green it was—
And the daisies and buttercups that was in,
And him grabbin at them astonishin!
So I milked a cow, and I held my cap,

1588   not a farlin at me: not a farthing in my possession.
1590   logger: lugger, a small vessel, decked and rigged with lugsails normally on two masts (ed.).
1593   wuss till: worse than.

And I gave it to the little chap;
And he supped it hearty enough, the sweep!
And stretched hisself, and off to sleep—
1610 And a deuced good supper and nothin to pay,
And "Over the hills and far away."°

So by hook, or by crook, or however it was,
I got down to Whitehaven at last;
And a Ramsey logger they call the *Map*—
Jemmy Corkhill—I knew the chap.
"Hullo!" says I—"Hullo!" says he;
"It's yourself that's been on the divil's spree,
And a baby at ye—well! well! good Lord!"
"All right!" says I, and heaves him aboard—
1620 And—*Bless his soul the fun! and a chile in!*
So that's the way I got to the Islan'.
I landed at Ramsey and started off
The soonest I could, and past Ballaugh,
And Kirk Michael, and the Ballacraine—°
I hadn been there I couldn tell ye the when.
And you may think how he wasn much of a load,
But I was checked when I come on the mountain road;
And I found a spot where the ling was high,
And terrible thick and soft and dry—
1630 And a big rock standin Nor-east by East—
The way of the wind—aw, a beautiful place!

So I laid me down, and the child in my arms,
And the quick little breath, and the dogs at the farms,
And the curlews whistlin, passin by—
And the noise of the river below, and the sigh
Of the mountain breeze—I kept awake,
And a star come out like a swan on a lake,
White and lonely; and a sort of amazement
Got hould on me, and the leads of a casement
1640 Crissed-crossed on the sky like a window-frame,
And the long, long look! and the far it came!
Aw dear! I thought it was Jinny Magee
In heaven makin signs to me.°
And sleep at last, and when I awoke,
The stars was gone, and the day was broke,
And the bees beginnin to think of the honey,
And who was there but little sonny?

1608   sweep: good-for-nothing (Moore).
1620   *a chile in*: a child in the case.
1627   checked: tired.

Loosed from my arms, and catchin my hair,
And laughin, and I laughed too, I'll swear.
1650 And says I—"Come, Simmy, my little buffer!
You're small, but what is it sayin?—*Suffer
The little children to come to me*—°
So here goes! Simmy;" and "Glory be,"°
I said, and "Our Father," and two or three
Little hymns I remembered—"Let dogs delight,"°
The first two verses middling right—
And "Little boy with cheerful eye,
Bright and blue as yandhar sky;"
And down, and takin the road to the Lhen,°
1660 And the clear the sun was shinin then,
And the little church that white; and below—
The stones—and—well, you know! you know!

But at last I come to the shore, and I ran,
For though it was early I saw a man
Diggin lug on the beach, and I didn want
To meet the like, so I made a slant,
And back and in by the Claddagh° lane,
And round by the gable—Ned knows what I mean;
And in at the door; and "Mawther!" I said,
1670 "Mawther!" but she was still in bed.
"Mawther! look here! look here!" I cried;
And I tould her all how Jinny had died,
And this was the youngster, and what I intended,
And she heard me till my story was ended,
And just like a stone—aw, never a word!
And me gettin angry, till this little bird
Chirrups up with a crow and a leap—
And—"Mammy seepy! Mammy as'eep"—
Just that baby way—aw, then the flood
1680 Of the woman's-life come into her blood;
And she stretched her arms, and I gave him to her,
And she cried till she couldn cry no more.
And she took to him grand, though of coorse at fuss
Her hand was out, ye see, to nuss.
But after dinner she had him as nice—
And a singin, bless ye, with her poor ould vice.

The sun was down when I left them awhile,
And up the Claddagh, and over the stile,

1665   lug: sand worms for bait.
1667   Claddagh [*dd* as *th* in *then*; *gh* as *ch* in Scot. *loch*]: marsh, low land along rivers (Moore).
1683   fuss: first.

And into the ould churchyard, and tryin
1690 To find the place where Betsy was lyin.
It was nearly dark, but I wasn alone,
For I seen a man bending over a stone—
And the look, and the heave of the breast—I could see
It *was* a man—in his agony.
And nearer! nearer! the head! the hair!
My God! it was Taylor! Taylor—*there*!
Aw, then it all come back again,
All the throuble and all the pain,
And the one thought in my head—*him there at her grave!*
1700 And I stopped, and I said, "May Jesus save
His soul! for his life is in my hand—
Life for life! it's God's command,
Life for life!" and I measured my step—
"So long he shall live!" and I crep and crep—
Aw, the murderer's creep—"God give him grace!"
Thinks I—then to him, and looked in his face.
Aw, that face! he raised it—it wasn surprise,
It wasn fear that was in his eyes;
But the look of a man that's fairly done
1710 With everythin that's under the sun.
Ah, mates! however it was with me,
He had loved her, he *loved* her—my Betsy Lee!
"Taylor!" I said; but he never spoke:
"You loved her," I said, "and your heart is broke."
And he looked—aw, the look—"Come, give us your hand!"
I says—"*Forgive you?* I can! I can!
For the love that was so terrible strong,
For the love that made you do the wrong."
And, with them words, I saw the star
1720 I tould you of, but brighter far:
It wasn Jinny, but Betsy now!
"Misther Taylor," I says, "we cannot tell how,
But it was love—yes! yes! it was love! it was love!
And He's taken her to Hisself above;
And it's Him that'll see that nothin annoys her,
And—" "Watch below! turn up!" "Aye, aye, sir!"

Fishing Boats, Port St. Mary
Manx National Heritage

Christmas Rose

"THE PAZON! the Pazon! the Pazon!" says you—
All right—but avast with your hollabaloo!
It is the Pazon, sure enough;
But what's the use of all that stuff?
My patience! if it's the Pazon you're at,
What's the good of shoutin like that?
"The Pazon! the Pazon!" well go ahead,
And take your fill, as the Scotchman said!
No! that won't do! I won't hev it! no!
10 I saw you kinkin and winkin though,
And laughin and actin—things that's theer!
Is it me to talk, or you to hear
That's wantin? come now! that's fair play—
Now what did I say now, what did I say?
Do you think I want—well that's a spree!
Me want! oh father! me! yes me!
That's gud though, yes! it's gud, it's gud!
I like it I do—but—rot your blood!
It's your look-out, not mine, eh Sam?
20 Oh I'm all right, my hearties, I am.

    Well that's a bit better! aye! aye! aye!
That's more decent-like certainly—
Keep her at that, and mayve we'll do.
Will I touch a drop? thank you! thank you!
And look ye! youngster, take that lamp,
And fix it a bit—what—what! you scamp!
Is it a rope's end eh? be swivel!
Or here's your physick—a cheeky young divil!

2-51	*Omitted.*	
10	kinkin: [*Sc. and N. dial.*] having a fit of laughter or coughing (*OED*).	
15	spree: a piece of fun (Wright).	
23	mayve: maybe (ed.)	
27	rope's end: a lashing with a rope (ed.).	
	swivel: quick (ed.).	

Oil! man—won't it burn brighter than that?
30 Blast yandhar cook with his stinkin fat,
And his skimmins and scummins and scrapins and dirt!
Cooks and cabbage! I know the surt—
And I wish them skippers—bother the light!
I'm terrible onaisy to start to-night—
Terrible in the world—but howsomedever,
Once I'll get way I'll be workin it clever—
Aw never you fear! but it puts me out
If I can't see what you chaps is about—
And not only that—why bless your sowls!
40 Aren't we done in the same mowls?
And isn there strength in the look of a man,
And power in his eye, you understand,
Sittin and lookin that way to draw
The stuff in your head, when Billy says *aw!*
And Tommy says *aye!* and Harry says *hem!*
Aw it's then I'm in the proper trem—
When you lifts me up like a wave of the sea,
And off I goes bowling fair and free.
Aye, aye! the lads is gud thallure—
50 But of coorse! of coorse! why *to* be sure.

But where to begin—stop, stop a bit!
Where to begin—Is that lamp lit?
I've gorrit, I've gorrit! It's lek you'll mind
The big storm in hunder-thirty-nine—°
You do? at least some does—then think of your sins!
For that's the time my story begins.

It was Christmas time, if I remember,
Or at any rate well in the month of December—
They were up at the School that night practisin
60 (And even then the wind was risin),
Ould Hughie the clerk, and Jem—Jemmy—Jem;°
Aw well there was a pair of them—
And Dicky-Dick-beg agate of the fiddle,
And the son and the daughter, and him in the middle—
Carvels—of coorse—again the Ail Varey—°

40	mowls [*ow* as in *how*]:	moulds (ed.).
49	thallure:	Mx. *dy liooar*, enough, galore (Moore).
53	gorrit:	got it (ed.).
63	Dicky-Dick-beg = Dicky son of Little Dick (ed.).	
	agate: at work at.	
65	Carvels: Carols.	
	again: against, in preparation for (ed.).	

Christmas Rose

You'll mind it, Ned! you and me and Mary,
And all the gels and the lads from the shore
Carryin on outside of the door.°
It was blowin hard when they went to bed,
70　And "There'll be jeel to-night!" the ould man° said.
But childher sleep sound; and the fust I knew
Was mawther shoutin for any two—
And I jumped, and I looked, and there was the wall,
But the divil a roof there was at us at all—
Divil a straw; but the bits of spars,
And the sand and the spray, and the scud and the stars:
And all the houses stript° the same,
Hardly a rafter, hardly a bame—
And the tearin and callin one to another,
80　And "Jenny! where are ye?" and "Mawther! mawther!"
And all the lot of them comin flyin
Out on the street—and the shoutin and cryin,
And the ould women catchin a bit of close
And stickin a pin in it—where God knows!
And cuttin like mad; and the pullin and hawlin
And "Give us that rope!" "Make fast that tarpaulin!"
Bless my heart! the confusion though!
But the ould man took for the beach, you know—
Aw a right ould sea-dog! keen on the scent—
90　Sniffin and snuffin away he went,
And round the gable, and out on the strand,
And crouchin and slouchin a-back of his hand,
And a-layin his head to the wind like a bullet,
And a-edgin out to the side of the gullet—
Wasn I after him straight? and just
When I caught his arm the blazin bust
Of a rocket went up, and "Studdy!" he said
"There's a ship ashore on Conisthar head."°
And a gun come boomin through the roar
100　Of the waves, and "A ship! a ship ashore!"
The both of us shouted, and we ran like mad—
Aw it's the wonderful wind the ould man had!
And "Here! all hands!" he says "just as ye are!
There's a ship ashore on Conisthar!"

　　　　　Ail [pronounced *eel* as in Mx. *oie'l*] Varey: Eve of Mary,
　　　　　Christmas Eve.
　70　　　jeel: damage.
　85　　　cuttin: running (ed.)
　94　　　gullet: gulley (ed.).
　97　　　Studdy: Steady.

What does Billy say? *He knows what that means?*
Aye—aye? then look ye? it's Thomas Baynes,
A. B., that gives you the lie to your face,
You son of a sea-cook out of place!
Just look at me now! and take it hot!
110 The lie in your throat—eh? the lie in your throat!
You know what it means? aye! aye! perhaps
You do—I've heard of your divil's traps,
You East-coast lubbers, and seen them too—
D—— it! let him come on! hurroo! hurroo!
His blood is up? is it? how much by the pound?
Easy up and easy down—
I'm thinkin—eh Billy? you'd better sit quite,
And tell us about the Whitby light—°
Eh Billy! who trims it? a man or a woman?
120 A mortal fine light, and studdy uncommon!
And the Pazons, Billy—is it really facs
They prays in the Church for God to send wracks?
"Ho! ho! gud news! a ship on the stones!
Praise God from whom°——and pick her bones!"
You'll get lave,° my lad; but the ouldest men
Navar heard of the like of that at the Lhen.°
Of coorse, if a ship is goin to pieces
In pieces she'll go, and them bl—— Poleeses,
And custom-house sharks, and the coastguard force—°
130 And Lloyds and Droits°—why—equal of coorse!
You're not goin to leave her to that d—— lot,
With their pokin and chalkin and touch-me-not.
Aw I'll not deny it—we've made a lef
Of the ship and the cargo both—we hef—
Watchin our chances—navar fear!
And stowin them here and stowin them there,
And the Derby Haven fellows was wuss,
For they took to the graves,° and I wouldn trus'
But the Church itself: for I've heard the ould people
140 Tell how the coastguards searched the steeple,
And even the pulpit, and all they were able;
But the things was under the C'mmunion table.

Well, well, well! that'll do! that'll do!
The same to me, the same to you!

105-48	*Omitted.*	
107	A.B.:	Able Bodied Seaman (ed.).
117	quite:	quiet (ed.).
125	get lave:	may do what you like (ed.).
133	made a lef:	made a lift, plundered (ed.).
137	wuss:	worse (ed.).

And there's not much luck in it anyway—
Aye, aye! who knows? well all I'll say
Is just what happened lek and no more—
You'll understand the ship was ashore,
Not on the point,° where we might have got at her,
150 You'll mind, but out in shoaly water—
The Scranes they calls it, and deep inside;
But the Scranes shoals bad, and a ten-knot tide
Rakes them, and at Spring ebbs you'll get
About a fathom—eh Ned? that's it?
Well that's where she was; *And could you see
The people aboard?* aye, aye! let be!
My lads, let's drop it! let's drop it, however!
Could a boat have lived? tut! bless ye! navar!
Navar! no life-boats, nor apperaturs,°
160 Nor nothin them times! Lord help the craythurs!
D——ye! drop it now! do! It was light,
Broad day, when she parted amidships—*All right!*
Was the word, and *Steady! all hands look out!*
Then navar a word till one gev a shout
And another, and hands was gript in a minute,
And I looked at the trough, and what was there in it
But a nigger swimmin strong and hard
On his back; and a bundle—I didn regard
What, but somethin white, and the lef'
170 Of the sea curled round him, and swep' it adref';
And he turned on his face, and he made a bite
With his teeth, and he caught it, and held it as tight
As tight; and struck out, but rather slow,
Aw a pluckier nigger I navar saw;
Nor nobody else—and pluck is pluck;
But whether it was his heart was bruck
With the strength of the sea, I cannot tell;
But when they got hould of him he fell
In their arms; and, sure enough, he was dead!
180 Poor fellow! But what d'ye think he had
Clenched in his teeth that they had to cut
The tapes with a knife, they were that tight shut—
What but a little child?° a gel!
And livin too! aw well, well, well!
If you'd ha' heard the cheer, and the women crying,
And runnin, and taking their turn and tryin
To warm it at their bresses, and rockin,

---

168   regard: notice.
169   lef': lift
176   bruck: broken.

And doublin themselves over it—well it was shockin!
And *go and tell the Pazon!* such squealin;
190 But the Pazon was there already kneelin
By the black man's side: and he'd got a book,
And workin the rules; and he wouldn' look
At the baby a bit, for he said, and he smiled,
"The women 'll be sure to look after the child."
But all the rules of the Royal Human—
Tryin and tryin—they wouldn do man!
Aw he worked them well, and they all of them worked,
And lifted and shook him, and rolled him and jerked,
And rubbed him and all; and a fine man, look'ee!
200 Of his limbs, though his legs was a little crooky—
As big as me, or mayve bigger—
And the Pazon manoeuvering over the nigger—
And some of the men fit enough to cry
To think that a man like that should die,
And him in their hands! But they had to give in
At last, and the Pazon tied up his chin
With his own handkercher, and strooked
His arms by his side; and he looked and looked,
And then he kissed him! aye, aye! he ded!
210 He ded though! and these is the words he said—
And all with the hats off, holdin ther breath—
"Thou hast been faithful unto death—
I will give thee a crown of life"—°
Them's the words, and turns to the wife;
"And now let's see the baby!" says he,
And took it and nussed it as nice as could be.
And of every sowl aboard that wreck
That's all that hed a chance, I espec',
To reach the shore; for a ship that catches
220 On the Scranes is very soon turned into matches.
Some of the cargo was got to land—
Not much—no divers, you'll understand,
Convanient to yandhar place; but her name
Was found on a bit of plankin that came
In the trawl one day: but no manifess
Nor log, nor list of passengess,
Nor nothin—only the name, d'ye see?
The Hidalgar—so it's a Spaniard she'd be.

---

195   Royal Human: Royal Humane Society.
203   fit enough to cry: very nearly crying.
207   strooked: straightened—to stroke can mean to "lay out a dead body for burial" (Wright).
225   manifess: ship's manifest.

        Well the little gel was took home at the Pazon,
230   And nest day he was down at the Village as'in
      For a nuss, and an aunt of mine bedad!
      Bless me the diddy that woman had!
      Went up every day to give it the bress—
      And no writin on it, the way of address,
      Nor sign, nor marks, except on its sheff
      A I. and a D., and a thing like as eff
      A haythen God or some of these charrims,
      I think they called it a cut of arrims;
      But, howsomedever, that's the why
240   They thought the child was terrible high.

        And the nigger was buried as grand as you plaze,
      In the Pazon's ground, just a bit of a raise
      At the top of the churchyard; and a mortal sight
      Of people, and sarvice, and everything right;
      And *dust to dust*, and the clerk with the muck
      On the point of the spade—and the nate he shuck
      And the sollum—a-makin believe that way
      They were all agate of a Christian—eh?
      And a stone! aye, a stone, and the very vess°
250   The Pazon said over him at fess—
      I know the man that cut it, and he tould me
      In the teens of pounds! in the teens, behould ye!
      And a fust-rate job at Jemmy Bluitt—
      Aw the man could do it! the man could do it!

        And the little gel did thrive for all—
      Aw man-alive! and straight, and tall,
      And strong on her feet; and every faythur
      Like a child twice her age—the little craythur!
      Dark though, and keen, and soopil still,
260   And the Pazon loved her terrible.
      I've seen him with her beside him a-settin
      On the darkie's grave, and her a-gettin

---

231   bedad: Irish, "By Dad" or "By God" (*OED*).
232   diddy: breast (ed.).
235   sheff: shift (ed.).
236   eff: if (ed.).
238   cut: coat (ed.).
246   the nate he shuck: how neatly he shook [the spade] (ed.).
248   agate of: dealing with (ed.).
250   fess: first (ed.)
253   at: by.
257   faythur: feature.
259   soopil: supple, lithe.

Daisies and that, and a-pokin them straight
In his face, and him with the love and the light
And the strength and the strain of his soul's desire
All round the child like a glory of fire.
Aw it's truth I tell ye—but I've heard them say
The misthress wasn much that way.
She'd look middlin sharp now and then at the pair,
270 And bite her thread with a wrench, and stare;
But quite—aw quite! just hemmin and hummin
A bit—she was hard to make out—that woman;
At least I'm tould so—I was middlin young
Them times, and the misthress was close o' the tongue,
A dry sort of woman, and no-ways free,
But allis civil enough to me.
What did they call the child? eh, Dan?
Wasn I goin to tell you man?
My patience! there's chaps—but I knows what I knows—
280 Well—they called her the Christmas Rose.°
In the Church? in the Church! *God bless your sowl!*
Indeed! and, if I may make so bowld,
Ler him bless it, says I—what then?
Hould him, boys! he's took again!
*And was the water hove in her face
On a name like that?* Just so if you plaze—
And have you any objections parteglar?
Well a d—— fool is a d—— fool reglar.
A name like that! Now, if I chose—
290 But blast ye! take it! Christmas Rose!
Christmas Rose—d'ye hear? d'ye hear?
Christmas Rose. Now then what cheer?
Christmas Rose! you'll 'scuse me, mates.
But I like to chastise these runagates.

Yes—Christmas Rose; and all around,
And the Pazon standin in his white gown;
And me up the steeple, or some of them places,
In the bight of a rope a-swinging like blazes;
And I saw it all, though they didn see me,
300 A swingin strong and a swinging free.
And when the preachin come to an end
It was me that sung out *Amen! Amen!*
Aw the Pazon looked; but bless ye! I cut,
And they navar knew it was me: but chut!

---

283   ler: let (ed.).
285   *hove*: thrown in her face; was she baptized?
295-306 *Omitted.*

What stuff I'm talkin! and me that's got
To make a short run of it, whether or not.

Now the Pazon had childher, George and James,
Sons the both, and that's the names;
And that's the lot that ever they had;
310 And such times as they come, I've heard it said,
The wife and himself was middlin ould.
And the woman was dry—upon my sowl
I believe she was, and bony uncommon,
Aw it's dry and bony was the woman.
I've raelly thought many a time she was jus'
Like yandhar Sarah in Genesus,°
The time she took owld Abram's whore
By the shouldhers, and put her to the door.
Only the misthress, whatever annoyed her,
320 Had a way to keep the divil inside her:
Like them burnin mountains seems done their burning,
But the fire is in them churnin and churnin
The brimstone—aw d—— such women! I say—
They'd brek the heart of Methusaleh.
Now the time I'm tellin the boys, you know,
Was little things just beginnin to go—
George was the ouldest, a tidy bit;
I don't know was James in perricuts yit—
Just little things with the little bare pelt
330 Of their legs and their arms, and navar a belt,
But a runnin string, and a blue check brat,
And snotty noses, and all to that.
I don't believe that ever the mother
Herself was used to take much bother
About them—middlin fond of the bed
She was; and, as for the Pazon, he said
To my aunt when she spoke to him aburrit,
"Now Tildhar," he says, "you musn worrit
About the lek; for, harkee! Tildhar—
340 I'll hev my childher like other childher."
I don't know was it because he got
No pride in him; or mayve he thought
It was gud for childher to be together,
And out in the muck, and out in the weather;

---

325   Now the time I'm tellin: at the time I'm telling about, (ed.).
329   pelt: skin (ed.)
331   brat: apron.
332   all to that: that sort of thing.
337   aburrit: about it (ed.).
339   About the lek: that sort of thing.

And sweatin and tearin and fightin away;
And a-gettin strong as you may say:
And hard, and apt to take their part,
And hand with hand, and heart with heart;
And free and bould in the talk, and givin
350 And takin, and laughin and lovin and livin
With the rest: and rough, if you like, but ready,
With the stuff in them that when they'd get steady,
And 'd know their place, them's the boys, by jing,
That 'd have spunk in them for anything.
Like trees that grows in the open air,
Eh lads? and chances it, rain or fair,
Blow high, blow low, they've got the grain
In their heart that'll polish and polish again.
Now did he do right, or did he do wrong?—
360 Is it me? chut! capers! ger along!

Bless me the emps they got, and the pluck!
But that was long after the Pazon took
The strange child home; for then they were jus'
Soft innocent baby things, I suppuss:
And terrible fond it's lek they'd be
Of the little sister that come from the sea.
But when they come to be lumps the fond
They got of me, you'll understand,
And me of them—aw down on the shore
370 Reglar mos'ly—I tould ye before
That light 'd go out if you didn take care!
D—— it! who's that laughin there?
Laugh then laugh! while you have the chance—
Mayve the fool would like to dance—
Aw if I'd just—but navar mind!
Laugh! laugh! laugh! we'll all of us jine
Turn about, wheel about! heel and toe!
He-he-he! and ho-ho-ho!
Now for the light! It's Tommy the Reef!
380 I seen it in your face, you thief!
Look at him now! the sollum! my gough!
Aye and ye must give a nice little cough—
Must ye? quite genteel! my sonny!
Aw it's terrible funny! it's partiklar funny!
Navar fear, Tommy! my blessin upon ye!

---

360   ger: get (ed.)
361   emps: imps (ed.)
367   lumps: good-sized urchins.
369-400 *Omitted along with* 407-9 *and* 413-6.
376   jine: join (ed.).

You'll get fool's pardon, and so G—— d—— ye!

Fond was it I said I was? chit-chit!
Fond's not the word, no nor a bit—
I was mad after them two boys, I was—
390 Mad—d'ye hear? why then Doodoss!°
Ware ye navar in love with a boy? *What way?*
Well that's the thing I cannot say—
Like a brother or that?° No! no! no! no!
What do I mean? Well wait then, Joe!
Wait my lad! What I mean is willin
To die for them two in a minute, a-spillin
My last drop of blood, if so be it was wanted
For the gud of them; and haunted lek, haunted
With their look and their laugh—do ye follow the thing?
400 Worshipin! worshipin! worshipin!
That's it—aye! and the heads like wool—
That curly, and all of them beautiful!
And when they got big and took sense they begun
To take a pride in theirselves, and done
Theirselves that nice, and their clothes that fine
And soft and differin lek from mine
That I loved to touch them: and the brave sweet smell
That come off them—aye straight like a gel—
And the cut of them; and when they were rowin
410 In the boat with me all stripped and showin
Their arms that white and strong for all,
And their neck like a tree and their back like a wall—
Aw I've seen them bathin, and I don't care
But I've felt that shamed and confused, d'ye hear?
That I've looked (you may laugh, but what's the odds?)
To see were they men or a sort of gods.
And mawther was allis scouldin of coorse,
She was the woman that could, and never got hoorse—
And who was I, and what was the gud?
420 *And place was place, and blood was blood.*
But let them grow a bit and I'd see
They wouldn take up with the leks of me.
But the Pazon was terrible wise, you know,
And he saw at once which way the wind blow.
Aw I hev him now with the ould blue eyes—
The tender, the lovin, and the wise.
So with her it was allis "babby!" and "fool!"
And *when was I goin to begin to cool?*
But there wasn a thing goin under the sun
430 But the Pazon knew the way it was done:
For his heart was just four pieces joined,

A man and a woman and a child, and a kind
Of a sort of Holy Ghos' or another—
So he knew what was at me better than mawther;
Just a fit that was on me lek
That 'd hev its time and then it 'd brek
Like a spell of weather, and I'd be waking
Swivel enough and no gud to be shaking
A poor craythur that's draemin, but all the same
440 If he's draemin, his drame is a happy drame.
And I believe there was more till that;
I believe the Pazon knew what he was at:
I believe he knew it was good for us
For me and for them, for better for wuss,
That all we had in us should have fair play,
And all give account at the judgement day.
Aw the heat of young blood is a terrible thing,
And it swims in your head, and makes it sing
Queer songs enough—but doesn it loose
450 Your soul like a bud that's sticky with juice,
Till it creaks, and it cracks, and it opens free
In the eye of the sun most gloriously?
Anyway—look at the other surt,
A steppin their tippytoes over the dirt!
And kep' that stric', and watched that close
That is their guts at them God only knows!
And bless ye! keeping no company
But only with the top of the tree;
And no spunk in them, and no chance if they had it,
460 And—*marry a fortin, and be a credit!*

    Aw well but the Pazon was kind and he'd say—
"Come up man, Thomas!" or "Stay la', stay!"
Aw as free as free! and the servant tould
To give me my dinner, bless your soul—
In the kitchen of coorse; and them comin creepin
Across from the parlour, the divils! and peepin;
And her with a clout a-hitting them sudden,
And me lookin foolish and workin the puddin.
And he'd play with us too, would the Pazon, yis!
470 Tops and marbles, and not amiss,
Not him—and laughin at all their jokes,
And knuckle down, and take his canokes—°

---

434   at me: what ailed me.
438   Swivel: quickly.
441   till: than.
462   la': interjection; Mx. *lah*, lad (Moore).

Duckstone—no! nor Hommer-the-let—°
Well—no! I don't think it would hardly be fet
For a Pazon to run with his shirt all a-muck
Of sweat, and singin out "Double the Duck!"
And eyein and creepin just the same 's
An ould black cat; besides them games—
They doesn do—of coorse they doesn—
480 Without a little bit of cussin.
But out with the ferrets agate of the warren,
Or in the haggard playin But-thorran,
And them two boys with their imprince mockin,
And trippin the Pazon up most shockin;
And floorin him, and rollin him over,
And tryin to bury him in the clover,
Or straw, or the lek; and him a strugglin
Pretendin lek, and his ould throat gugglin
And splutterin out the stuff; and me
490 As shamed as ever I could be—
Aw the hat flyin here and the stick flyin there—
Well the shy and the shamed—aw navar fear!
"A blessed ould fool!" you'll be thinkin? not him!
But a sort of a blessed ould Cherubim,
If you like: and who can tell the sorras
He was working out of him with them sporras—?
Lyin and kickin—and if he had thought
The limb I was, and the way I taught
Them boys to cuss, it isn't there
500 I'd 'a been, it's lek; aw dear! aw dear!
Childher is strange; for nearly the fuss
I knew them I axed them could they cuss.
And they said "No"; and I wouldn take rest
But they must learn—and the words—"Say thes!"
I said, and "Say that!" and to it we went,
Bless my heart though the innocent!
And I don't know—but Him that's above,
Which they say His name is Love,
He'll be knowin all the same
510 Was I as innocent as them.
Aw I taught them though; and the ouldest was clever;
Well he could work it for sure, however;

482		haggard: stackyard.
		But-thorran: hide-and-seek round the stacks.
496		sporras: sparrows (ed.).
498		limb: a mischievous person; a young imp or rascal (*OED*).
501		fuss: first.
503		take rest: would not be satisfied.
512		for sure: really.

But James was quiet over it still,
Noways hearty, though comfible.

But *the gel*—did you say? I know! I know!
The gel! the gel! just so! just so!
Gels! gels! gels! and sorrow and sin
They're in everythin, in everythin.
And *what was she lek?* yes! yes! I hear—
520 *What was she lek?* aye—never fear!
The little gel that was took from the wreck?
What was she lek eh? what was she lek?
Is it what was she lek? stop! stop a bit!—
The way she'd stand, the way she'd sit!
And George and her, and takin an oar,—
And up in the church—and down on the shore—
And the turn, and the spring, and the lookin behin'
And the eye all full like a cup with wine—
And—what was I sayin? let's see! let's see!—
530 I can't! I can't! the leks o' me
Draw a picthur of her! come! that's a rig!
But *was she little or was she big?*
Little or big? What's in my head?
Little or big I think you said?
Thank ye, Billy; and *handsome?* eh—
Handsome, says you—fair play! fair play!
*And a tight little armfull, and kissing again
When a chap kissed her*—Now then! now then!
Is it down your throat you want that pipe?
540 Now is it! you sniggling yard of tripe!
Do you know now what are you talkin about?
Do you know anything, you clout?
Me that never looked at her
But almost trimblin, mind ye—there!
Trimblin! aye! I know what you're at—
No! I couldn ha' thought o' her like that—
Lord bless your sowl! you iggorant noddy!
Wasn there fire come out of her body—
Aye all over her a blaze
550 That beat you back, like the Bible says
The sword of fire afore now at the door
Of the garden of Eden though to be sure—
And burnin and burnin,

---

531   rig: joke.
535-42   *Omitted.*
540   sniggling: snickering, unimportant (Wright).
547   noddy: ignorant blockhead.

     And turnin and turnin
Every art that no base of a divil
With his cuts and his capers, no matter how swivel,
And dirt in his heart, and mowin and mockin,
Could enter the place where God was walkin!
Now then you'll understand mayhap—
560   Aw Juan, Juan! you're a poor sort o' chap!

     Well they were wonderful them three—
To see them together was something to see.
Well they were scandalous though for all!
And the whole of the three o' them middlin tall;
And her in the middle, and them ither side,
And the strength, and the step of them, and the pride!
George was the biggest a goodish lot,
And the curley yellow hair he got!
And the eyes as blue and as a soft as a wenches,
570   But a splendid strappin lad of his inches.
And bould he looked, and keen, defyin
The world, like a lump of a bull or a lion.
He was middlin red in the face was George;
And so was James, but not that large
In the shouldhers and back like the ouldest, but rather
Stoopin lek, and favourin the father.
But pluck! aw bless ye! there wasn a patch
Betwix them—I navar saw their match—
Game to the heels—aw make your bet!
580   The true breed them! and navar fret!
But if they were red then she was white—
The way I tould ye—with the sheets of light
Comin off her skin, and dazzlin tarble,
Jest lek she'd been cut out of marble,
Or the way the Bible says about Moses—°
With the fire on his face and all his closes.
But what's the use of me? I shudn
Be tryin the lek, and I said I wudn.
But just one thing, and that's her hair—
590   Well it wasn't right—no! no! I'll swear
It wasn—some charm or the lek no doubt
Was put on it—aye! Says you "Ger out!"

---

555   art: way.
557   mowin: grimacing, making faces (ed.).
563   scandalous: marvellous.
572   lump of a bull: a big bull.
576   favourin: resembling.
577   patch: the slightest difference.
583   tarble: terrible (ed.).

Aisy all! Some witch or another
Must have spun that stuff; neither father nor mother
Done that, my lads! It was black as nubs,
But streaks of red like you'll see in the dubs
Where they're cutting the turf; or down in the river,
Where it's deeper and darker and redder than ever—
And all like a cloud around her scutched—
600 Aw she must have been wutched! she must have been wutched!
The three of them—the three of them!
I see them now, and it's like a drem;
A drem it's like—and it's strange to a man,
But I'm allis seein things that's gone.
She was proud, 'deed she was uncommon proud—
Aw that's what the Pazon himself allowed!
Aye many's the time I've seen the ould man
At the door, and houldin the hat in his hand;
And her on the step, and him that narvous,
610 And backin and fillin,° and at-your-sarvice!
And bowin and bowin; and her on the step
With the sit of her head and the curl of her lep—
Sweet, but proud; and her foot like a queen's,
And her only just comin into her teens!
Aw I'll never forget the time—no never!
One day she was coming across the river,
Not far from the shore, where the stones is high
And far betwix—and to see her fly
Like a bird all colours! bless your hearts!
620 The way they gets them in foreign parts—
And a jumpin delicate lek, and lettin
On a stone like a feather; and then she'd be gettin
Her perricuts round her, and balancing
Like a image set on a fine hair spring.°
And I got aback of the bushes below,
The way she wouldn see me, you know;
And my heart in my mouth—when jig-a-maree!°
Her hair got caught in the branch of a tree—
Nuts, or trammon, or—navar mind!
630 But there she was, clane caught behind;
And whatever she'd do! and took that sudden—
It wudn let go! it wudn! it wudn!

---

595 nubs: coals.
596 dubs: pools (ed.).
599 scutched: caught.
600 wutched: bewitched.
605 'deed: indeed.
621 lettin: lighting (ed.).
629 trammon: elder.

Christmas Rose 61

    So in I goes, nearly up to my wase—
No stones for me! aw it was a race!
And a plunge and a kick and a scramblin through—
And up to her before she knew,
It's lek with the noise of the water thund'rin
In her ears, and me with my hand asund'rin
The hair—aw she turned! and believe it or not!
640 She made a leap, and she cleared the lot,
And she stood all shiverin! and the flashes
Of her eyes was awful, reglar splashes
Of fire they was—and "It's not afraid—"
Says she—"but how dar ye? how dar ye?" she said—
"How dar ye?" Lord bless me! I didn stand
To think, I can tell ye, but away I ran,
And never stopped, I went that slicks,
Till the best of a mile was put betwix.
But that same night I crep and crep
650 Back to the place, and I made a grep
Overhead on the chance, and I caught the hair
That was hangin still on the trammon there—
Aw the tingly it felt in the dark, and the queck
It run up aroun' my finger lek!
You'd ha' thought it was steel—the coil it had,
And the spring—but am I goin mad?
Eh boys? aw laugh! laugh hearty! I say;
For that's d—— nonsense anyway!

    But the very next mornin I'll engage
660 Down come George in a terrible rage;
And him and James in their Sunday clothes,
And says they "You've 'sulted Christmas Rose."
" 'Sulted her?" "Yes! 'sulted her!" they says;
"And it's up to the church you must go and confess
On your bended knees this minute!" they said,
"And apologize!" that's the word they hed.
Aw they wouldn take rest but up I stud;°
So I claned myself the quickest I cud,
And away with them; and as stiff as may be,
670 Talking together, but not to me.
I didn like it a bit, mind you!
And I didn hardly know what to do,
Nor whether to go nor whether to stay,
But I felt like a d—— fool anyway.
"And what must I say?" says I, "when I'm there;"
"Aw it's all put down in the paper here,"
Says James, and whips it out of his pocket—
"Listen to this!" he says, "you blockit!"

And sure enough they had it as grand
680 As any lawyer in the land—
Aw the terrible big words that was in,
And the *wicked* and *imprint* I'd been;
And *inasmuch*, and *seein how far*,
And *the court*, and *the prisoner at the bar*—
My gough! and they stopped in the highroad twice
For to make me ply it to say it nice.
And when we got up—aw cheeagh voddie!°
You'd ha' wondered the soul was left in my body.
And *wasn I ouldher?* I don't say nay;
690 But they come over me that way—
Ouldher of coorse; but it's no use o' talkin,
The art that was at them boys was shockin—
Aw they'd work it, bless ye! and, whether or no,
They said the word, and you had to go.

Well behould ye! there she was
Out in the garden, and a chair on the grass,
The Pazon's chair, with its arms like a gig,
Took out of the study o' purpose, and big
Enough to hold half the parish with aise—
700 And—cock her up with a stool, if you plaze,
Under her feet! and if she hedn
A scarf or the lek, with yallar and red in,
Twisted through her hair to gev her
A look like a crown on her head, did you ever?
Aw a reglar queen; and behould ye! a fan
And tippin it this way and that in her hand;
And frownin and frownin—and "Let him come forrit!"
Says she, and I tried, but I hadn gor it—
No not a bit—but middlin handy
710 Down on my knees like a jack-o-dandy,
Or a play-actor, or the lek, and a mixture
At them and at me°—that's the way I fixed her—
Humblin—bumblin—and "no offence!"—
And up's with her chin, and "Take him hence!"
She says, and she gives a bit of a nod,

---

682   *imprint*: impudent.
686   ply: work at (ed.)
692   that was at them boys: those boys had.
707   forrit: forward (ed.).
708   gor: got (ed.).
710   jack-o-dandy: a little pert, conceited fellow (*OED*).
712   At...at: Of...of (ed.).
          fixed: placated (ed).
714   up's: possibly "up [it] is"—see also 805 (ed.).

"He has his pardon"—his pardon! My God!
I'm laughin now, but I didn laugh then;
And the boys at me straight, and all hearty again,
And shakin hands, and "*Navar mind!*"
720 *But it was nacassary*, and tervil kind;
And—*Just be careful lek! I'd bathar!*
And—*the same friends as ever!* and coaxin rather.
But she got up, and she took a sweep
Of the grass with her frock, and I felt like a creep—
And the swing of her waist, and the ribbons flyin—
Aw a creep! a creep! there's no denyin—
And the pick and the peck, and in with a taste—
And " 'Scuse me, marm!" and "I ast your grace!"
And the way and the look—"He hev his pardon!"
730 If ever there was a fool in that garden,
It was me that was in—but, right or wrong,
She houldt me, she did though, uncommon strong—
Her vice of coorse—aye that's the thing—
Sweet! aw the sweet! astonishin!
If she'd d———d your eyes it' d ha' been the same—
Aw hard as steel and soft as crame;
Something betwix a hawk and a linnet—
Aw the music of her soul was in it.
Music! soul! you've heard tramhurns
740 And clarnets, and their twisses and turns,
And curlin and purlin, and pippin and poppin,
And booin and cooin, and stippin and stoppin—
Well they were all just fools, d'ye hear?
To that darlin vice, that—eh? What cheer?
Darling! yes *darling!* hillo! hillo!
All right! all right! well I didn say no!
All right of coorse! and what's up now?
Go it ye cripples! bow—bow—bow!
With *her*—eh—what? by the Lord above
750 I wasn! I wasn! now what is love?
In love with Christmas Rose! aye aye!
And the gel at the brew—and—navar say die!
And two of them—eh? now aisy! aisy!
Two of them—is it! my Michaelmas daisy!
Two of them—lookee, lads, what sense
Is there at you at all? The difference!
The difference! aw Betsy though!

---

727   in : into the house she goes.
728   ast: ask.
739   tramhurns: trombones.
745-67 *Omitted.*
752   brew: hill (ed.).

Betsy in heaven! you know! you know!
Betsy! Betsy! the one for me—
760 Betsy! Betsy! ma veg! ma chree!
Chut! that's Manx—they'll be axin to 'splain it—
Navar mind, lads! ye didn't mean it.
I was talkin about her vice, when you said
Something about Betsy—Betsy is dead—
Betsy is dead—I saw her die—
No I didn; but why then? why?
And—all at that time—and—come—come—come!
Shouldher arms and march to the drum!
Life is life, and the best foot fust!
770 'Scuse me, lads! I was thinkin just—
Thinkin—thinkin— Aw certainly,
Clear as a bell; but it's sharp it could be,
Sharp as a knife, and stingin, stingin—
But bless ye! the angels isn allis singin,
But a-hailin the divils; and "Enter not!"
They're shoutin, and givin as good as they got,
Lookin over the wall; for they leaves their hymns,
And fights like Turks—them cherubims—
I've read in a book°—but aisy! I say!
780 She was the one could hould me anyway—
And shake me too—could Christmas Rose—
And bless me the way she had with her clothes!
The slackin and tautin, and liffin and dippin,
And nippety-nappety trappin and trippin,
And a hitch to starboard and a hitch to port,
And a driggledy-draggledy all through the dirt;
And stuck to the mast or streamin free,
Or the wind gettin under and fiddle-de-dee!
How are they doin it, Billy—eh?
790 I don't know but they manage that way
That three or four foot of nothing—bless ye!
Is more to you till Europe or Asia.

But avast this stuff! anyway in she goes—
And me all right, and d—— the clothes!
And d—— the lot! Aw I did it grand!
Aw I gev it them nice, you'll understand—
And away, and shook them off, and tearin
Blue murder and all, and cussin and swearin

---

760   ma veg! ma chree! [*ch* as *k* or as in German]: my little one, my heart (ed.).
783   liffin: lifting.
792   till: than (ed.).

　　　　The skin off your face, and makin tracks
800　And down the road—but then I slacks,
　　　　And into the hedge and cries like blazes—
　　　　And up come people, and I knew their faces—
　　　　And souljerin on—as proud as you please,
　　　　And pretendin to look for blackberries—
　　　　And down to the shore, and up's with a creel
　　　　And into the boat with a kick of my heel
　　　　And off, and before you could preach or pray
　　　　I was crossin the tide and out to Mahay,
　　　　And agate o' the lobsters, and haulin in,
810　And destroyin them congers° like anythin—
　　　　Aye! aye! I could do that—chit nish!
　　　　There's no mistake but I knew how to fish—
　　　　And up with the grapplin, and home, and the tide
　　　　Dead again me, and springs beside,
　　　　And the back at me mostly bruk out of the henges,
　　　　And pullin—aw pullin—pullin tremenjous!
　　　　And landed and moored, and a skip and a hop
　　　　And a into bed, and a slep like a top.

　　　　Well there's an end of everything under the sun,
820　And I must tell ye the way it was done—
　　　　And was it my fault it's not for me—
　　　　Maybe it wasn nobody—
　　　　And if it wasn for what the Bible is sayin
　　　　About Him that hears us when we're prayin,
　　　　And navar a sparra drops for all°
　　　　But He's handy close to see it fall,
　　　　I'd think some black ould witch° was stuck
　　　　At the wheel of the world, and spinnin our luck,
　　　　And runnin the threads through her skinny fingers
830　Till our time was up, and then, by jingers,
　　　　It's whinkum-whankum, thrummity-thrum,
　　　　And she cuts you short with a snick o' her thumb.
　　　　But of coorse it isn, all the same,
　　　　It's Him—and blessed be His name!
　　　　They were tervil fond them three of the boat,
　　　　And they'd ha' had her whenever she could float;
　　　　But the Pazon was doin their schoolin at home
　　　　Hisself, you see, so they couldn come
　　　　Just as they pleased, but they had their taskses—

803　　souljerin: soldiering, sauntering.
808　　Mahay: a famous fishing ground.
811　　chit nish: come now.
825　　for all: however.

840 And grammar, and ciph'rin, and questions they askses—
Wonderful! aw I could tell ye a dale
About yandhar—but mind ye! when Pazon Gale
Was about in the parish, or when they were done
With the taskses—aw it's away they'd run
Like hounds for the shore; and her—yes her—
The fuss of the three, and in, and a spur
Rigged like a shot, and an oar I kep
A purpose for her, and off we swep,
Her with the rullock—aw bless your souls!
850 As proud—but ours was square in the thowls,
And pins, you know—and she'd pull, she'd pull!
Aw man-alive! it was beautiful!

One everin they come, and it's off to the Calf°
Behould ye! and long-lines° stowed there aft
Ready baited, and her that had never been there,
And—carry on! and navar care!
And a mist comin creepin up the Sound,
And wind to follow, you'll be bound—
But—*stuff-and-nonsense!* and a whiskin her hat
860 At the breeze, and "We'll do this and that!"
And George with the gun lookin out for a rabbit
On the cliffs° above; but James rather crabbit
On the middle thwart, and houldin the sheet
In his hand, and just a turn on the cleat;
And eyein the offin—aw, sink or swim!
A sailor every inch of him.
And "Is it back?" I says; "No! no!" says she,
"The sea! the sea! the open sea!"°
And a lot of rhymes; and George says "Blow it!
870 Give her it, Tom! put her gunwhale to it!"
Her gunwhale to it! aye! aye! my heartie!
Her gunwhale to it, says Buonaparte—
But it was *gunwhale-to-it*, and no mistake;
For the wind come stronger, and I didn spake,
And I knew well enough what ought we to do—
But—give in before her! not me! Would you?
No! d—— it! and her that keen to be sure—
Aw she'd have danced if she'd had the floor—
But she danced with her eyes—my gough! the light

---

846   spur: rowlock.
850   thowls: part of the oar which rests upon the gunwhale.
851   pins: pegs to keep the oar in place.
862   crabbit: crabbed (ed.).
863   sheet: rope for adjusting the sail; the end is secured to a "cleat" on the side of the boat (ed.).

880 Come into them! and the stretched and the tight—
Till they looked to be snappin fire in your face;
For the storm was in her—aw that's the place
That *was* the storm! aye, aye man! aye!
All urr o' the sea, and urr o' the sky,
Catching it with her mouth like suck,
Drawing the strenth of its heart till she shuck
And shivered again—and when the big cloud
Come up with the lightnin she gripped a shroud,
And she sprang to meet it like a bird to its nest,
890 Or a child to hang on its mammy's breast—
Or was it her sweetheart the cloud was lek,°
And her a-leapin on to his neck,
And sighin and sobbin and slakin her drouth
With the thunder-poison from his mouth?
Sobbin—aye! but not with fear!
Aw bless my heart! I cannot bear
Them women aboard in a storm—can you?
Instead of the divil's own hollabaloo
And faintin, for them to go and rejice—
900 It isn nice! it isn nice!
Nor right nor raison nor nothing—eh?
For them to be carryin on that way.
Women is women, and it's in the blood,
And they shud be freckened a bit they shud.

Well the dark it got, and the lightnin strong,
Lek it 'd slick up the sea with its red-hot tong,
And a little dead dirt of daylight left
In the west, and we began to dreft
On the rocks, for the boat couldn look at her coorse;
910 So it's down with the lug, and out with the oors—
Me with the one again them two,
And her in the stern with nothing to do
But enjoyin herself; and the head at her bare
And the lightnin lookin all mixed with her hair,
Like flowers of fire! my God! and a child!
But the wild she looked! O Christ! the wild!
And the glad and the mad—was her father and mother
Out in the clouds? chut! bother! bother!
There's strange things happens in storms though yit—
920 Well it makes me funny to think of it!

884	urr:	out
886	shuk:	shook.
904	freckened:	frightened.
913	the head at her:	her head.

So we pulled uncommon hard till we got
To the Thushla°—bless me! that's the spot—
That's where ye gets the strenth of the tide—
Aw the divil itself! but slack inside,
And shelter from the sea that's more;
So that's what we were making for.
"Three strokes! my hearts! three strokes!" I said,
"And d—— it all! we'll be round the head."
Three strokes was gev—aw the pluck of the lot!
930 Three strokes with a will—and in we shot—
Smooth water enough—but James had fell
Right aback from his taff, with his head in the well—
"Dead as a herrin, for sure!" thinks I,
And has him up immediately—
And feels the heart, and goin still—
But as slow as slow—aw terrible!
So I took him aft, and I put him restin
With his head on her lap, and it was just distressin
The way she sat, and not a notion
940 To hould him, or nuss him, nor navar a motion
To let him betwix her knees, or to spread
Herself upon him, or sthroog his head,
Or breathe on his cheek, or hould his hand,
The way with women, you'll understand—
But her knees that sharp all drew to a pint
Most comfortless! and every jint
That stiff! aw as sure as I'm a sinner
It was the divil of the storm that was in her!
Aye aye! and mind my words, d'ye hear?
950 I don't believe it was her that was theer—
Or if it was, I'll tell ye it,
Her soul was gone urr ov her for a bit—
Out and off! and up in the air,
With the clouds and the thunder—Lord knows where!
"Ger out!" says you, and "Stuff!" what *stuff!*
Aw it might happen, mind ye! easy enough—
Well—lave it alone! but I saw—I saw—
And I gave a cuss, but middlin low
That she wouldn hear; and I says "Miss Rose!"
960 I says, says I, "Lord only knows
If there's life in Masthar James, and maybe
You'll nuss him a bit," I says, "like a baby.
He hevn got no sense," says I,
"To know what are you doin—aw try now! try!"
I spoke middlin free; "and hise him," I says,

---

932   taff: thwart.

"Hise him, Miss Rose, agin your bress!
And warm him, and sing some ould tune to his ear!
Aw do, Miss Rose! aw do! that's a dear!"
I was trimblin when I said that word;
970 And afore it was out of my mouth—good Lord!
There come a flash that all the bay
And the boat and us was just like day—
Clap!—but betwix the darks behould yer!
George's face lookin over my shouldher
White as the dead! and eyein them two—
And I knew that minute what was there to do!
And I turned like a shot, and I saw her shaddhar
Wavin and shakin like a feddhar,
And up with the arms and down again
980 All of a heap, and the boy gathered in,
With his head in her clothes—I couldn tell how—
Aw the freckened I was that time! and now
When I remember—well lerrit! lerrit!
But what do you think now? was it the sperrit
Come back to her like a bird off the wing,
Or did she see George—eh? that's the thing!

Well we had a good two mile or more
To row agin we got to the shore—
And they were all that time? you're funny though!
990 Well there was something that hould't me, you know—
Something hould't me—I cannot tell what—
And the tired I was for the matter of that—
But I didn look at them once, I'll swear!
I couldn do it—I tell ye—there!
Navar mind! not a word from the one of us
Till the boat was up to her moorins just—
But then—*how was he?* I axed, *and his head?
Was it comin to?* "Aw he's better," she said;
"He knows where he is." "Thank God!" says I,
1000 And gets him ashore, and middlin dry
On a bit of the floorins; and me agate of him
And George, the two didn feel the weight of him—
And up to the house, and in to mother;
And the very first word she said was "Bother!"
Aw I heard her, but lettin on not—
And fixin her hair, and strooghin her brat,

---

965   Hise: lift.
983   lerrit: leave it.
988   agin: against, before.
989-94 *Omitted*

Fo'c's'le Yarns

And whippin a cheer amazin swivel,
And very nate and very civil—
Aw she could be that—and "Mother!" I said,
1010 "Masthar James must be put to bed
'Torectly," I says; "And get a sup
Of something hot, and I'll sit up"—
And this and that, and where and when;
For I was freckened there'd be a fight even then.
But there wasn though—no! I declare—
But "Aw the poor thing!" and "Dearee dear!"
And pityin, and lookin at Christmas Rose—
And—bless me! the way them women knows
What's up, in a general way—when you're seck—
1020 And also about young gels and the lek—
It's terrible in the world it is;
For if two craythurs hev took a kiss
Anywhere by day or night,
Every ould woman 'll know it straight.

So we got him to bed, and George run home
For th' tell the Pazon, and down he come,
And pale enough; and nothing to me
But "I see!" he says "I see—I see!"
And down to the parlour—not much of a light,
1030 You may aisy suppose; but aw! he turned white,
He did though, when he saw the lad,
For the faver was on him, and talkin like mad,
And navar knowin the father a mossel—
And down on his knees like the ould Apostle
With the chap in the Bible that nothin could handhar
But he must needs go and fall right out at the wandhar!°
But the sollum—aw the beautiful hearin!
Praying a little—but none of your tearin
And shoutin up to the rafters, like yandhar
1040 Premmitives, that calls like a gandhar
Before his gesslins—and what d'ye think
The Rose went and did? aw the bonny blink
Of her eye that time—they're tervil though—

1007   swivel: quickly.
1011   'Torectly: directly.
1021   in the world: intensive phrase.
1024   straight: immediately.
1026   th' tell: to tell (ed.).°
1027   and nothing to me: he said nothing to me.
1033   mossel: morsel.
1040   Premmitives: Primitive Methodists.°
1041   gesslins: goslings.

Them women—whether you like it or no—
She come behind, and she put her hand
On the ould man's head—My God! the grand
It was to see her, and how he turned
And looked in her face! aw it's me that yearned
In my very heart—and "Papa!" says she,
1050 "Papa!" aye just like that it would be;
But sweeter, bless ye! and like to cryin—
Aw she was a darlin—there's no denyin.
And didn the mother come? yes! she come—
And middlin snappish, and middlin glum
She looked; and her bonnet off, aw it was!
And titivated in our lookin-glass—
My gough! I was freckened, I don't know the fur—
But our little parlour, and a lady like her!
And upon my soul she made me jump
1060 With her hair like the handle of a pump
Stickin out, and no cap nor nothin, and as gray
As the divil—a sort of a wisp of hay—
And her never knowin I saw her theer
Combin away in the big arm-cheer.
But not till the mornin—not her, if you plaze!
What's your hurry? no lovin ways
With her—not a bit! and sittin as stiff
And rubbin her nose with her handkerchief;
And as grim; but mind ye! if you'd eyed her,
1070 You'd seen that woman had something inside her—
Aye! but navar mind! you'll hear!
"One at a time!" says Tommy Tear.

    Well the days went on though, and James could sit
In the bed, but—a cripple! aw navar fit
To earn his livin, nor nothin, but bent
All crooky—and crutches, and be content,
And hobble about! My gough! I grutched
A lad like him to look like wutched,
Or took at the fairies or that, and him
1080 A picthar to look at, every limb.
If he wasn that strong and that big like the brother,
I don't know where you'd ha' seen such another.
D—— it all! I loved the lad—
And to think of it now—it drives me mad.

1057   the fur: the for, the reason.
1077   grutched: grudged.
1079   took at: stricken by.

I don't know what was it at all,
Was it the bladder, or the lights, or the gall,
Or divil knows what—but somethin gev way
Inside—that's all the doctors could say—
A sort of a kind of mainspring,° I suppose—
1090 O Christmas Rose! Christmas Rose!

    Well just before he left our place,
And the doctors had settled about the case,
And cut, you know, I was sittin beside
The bed, us alone, and I cried and I cried;
And I said—"It was me! it was me! it was me!
Masther James!" I says; "of all the three
(Miss Rose don't count) it was me that done it—
It was me—yes it was—whosomever begun it—
I wish I was dead," I said, "I do!
1100 Dead and in the grave with you—
Or dead by myself, no matter what!"
"Now Tom," says he, he says, "what are you at?
The lot of us done it," he said, "I'll swear!
God d—— it!" he said, "what a fool you are!"
Aw the joy of my life when he said that though!
And just a little cuss, you know,
To keep me in heart! aw I thought I'd buss—
"Thank God!" says I; "he can cuss! he can cuss!"
And then he swore me that I wouldn tell
1110 What had he got—but I knew as well—
I can't say how—but chut! I knew it,
I did, afore ever he put the words to it.
That night aboard the boat when he woked
From the fit, and felt the way he was yoked
In Christmas' arms, and her breath on his face—
He didn know the time nor the place,
But only a sort of a dream I expec;
And he kissed her knees, and he kissed her neck;
And all the words the poor fellow hed
1120 Was—"Christmas! I love you—I love you!" he said.
Aw the poor lad! I loved him too—
Very good and gennal and true.
He said that—he did—and "Oh" he said,
"She lifted my head! she lifted my head!
And whispered something in my ear;

1085-90   *Omitted.*
1107   buss: burst.
1110   got: on his mind.
1122   gennal: kindly.

But I was that weak I couldn't hear,
Nor spake again; but her breath was warm
And sweet on my face; and the strain of her arm,
And all—and she loves me! she does!" say he—
1130 "And look at me! and look at me!"
He says—and he looks at himself like this—
"And will she ever—?" "Yes! yes! yes!"
I says: "Aw Masthar James, you knows
It's the rael thing is Christmas Rose:
And she'll be a good sisthar to you no doubt;
And fixin ye nice, and help ye about,
She's handy enough is Miss Rose, and 'll try—"
Aw then the red come into his eye,
And he swore the big oath by this and by that—
1140 And *what the divil was I dhrivin at?*
"Aw Masthar James!" I says, "Masthar James!
Cussin is cussin, and names is names—
If it's doin you good—aw go ahead!
But about Miss Christmas Rose," I said,
Aw Masthar James! be careful though!
Be careful for all! for how do you know
She loves ye?" I said: "Because you lay
In her arms, and she nussed ye into the bay?
Wouldn't any gel have done the lek?
1150 And you that was dyin! for gudness' sek,"
Says I, "be quite, and let me wash ye!
The poor gel only didn want to cross ye.
And besides I know—" but I jammed my helm
Hard a lee there; for I was goin to tell him
About George and the look in the boat—d'ye see?
Aw it was almost out at me—
It was though! and "What do you know?" he says;
And all the blood come into his face—
"What do you know?" and he swore the big oath,
1160 Uncommon big that I'd be loath
To say it again—aw 'deed I would—
But the boy was mad, and I done what I could—
And *it wasn nothin!* and bless me! the names!
And "Aw Masthar James! Masthar James! Masthar James!"
And "You'll be kilt altogether," I said, "you will;
You'll be kilt now, James, if you don't lie still."
Aw a hard fight for it at us—hard!
And *I was everything*; but I didn regard:
For the worse of it was the waker he got
1170 The angrier he was, and the cross and the hot:

1167   at us: between us.

And the flesh was wake, but the sperrit was strong,
And allis thinkin you were doing wrong.
And fits comin on him often, and ragin,
Like the man with the divil whose name was legion;°
And rollin and foamin till they had to tie him,
And then there wasn many 'd venture nigh him.
Aw dear! aw dear! and him I'd known
Such a hearty lad, and the strong and the grown!
Was it me? was it me? well the Lord he gave it,
1180 And the Lord took away—so there let's lave it!

But he'd be havin me with him whenever he could—
Not long at a time; for every flood
I was out at the lines: but the very fust
I was up to see him, it's go we must
The two of us alone to the Church,
And sittin there inside of the porch,
And the crutches at him, and strikin the pavin
Terbil vicious—he began a ravin
About the one thing, as you may suppose,
1190 Nothing but Rose! and Rose! and Rose!
And the very first time they were alone together,
He tould me, he looked and looked to see whether
Or not—"and nothing," he said, "in her face
But pity just, and gentleness."
And "What'll I do?" he says, and he grips
My arm, and frothin all at the lips,
But handsome—aw handsome! and proud and keen,
And full of the life that should have been.
"Aw! drop it!" I says, "aw Masther James,
1200 Drop it! drop it! it's only drames.
Isn she your sister?" I said, "since the day
God gave her to you from the sea?
Keep her what she is!" says I;
"And she'll be a blessin to you bye-and-bye."
"A blessin!" says he, "a blessin! a blessin!
Tom Baynes," he says, "you're a foolish pessin.
I'll spake," he says, "I will—and I'll know
Whether I'm to stay, or whether to go."
"Go where?" says I; and he gevs a stare,
1210 And pints to the graves, and answers "There!"
You're laughin, its lek? you're laughin? no?
But them so young—you'd let them grow
A bit fust, Billy? Strange! eh what?
Young craythurs carryin on like that—
Let them ate a bit more porridge fust
Says you: aw Billy! that's the wust

Of you, and it allis was, I'll swear—
You're coorse, man, coorse! aw yes ye are!
Aw it's coorse it is. And *Childher*, says you?
Young fools, you says; go on now do!
Fools, you said; and *they should be stript*,
I think you said, *at their mammies, and whipt*—
And *you'd warm them*—would ye? well listen to me!
I'm not a young fool, nor meanin to be;
And I say them *young fools*—wasn them your words?
Well—wait a minute, and I'll give the Lord's—
Lovin much is much forgiven;°
And—*of such fools is the kingdom of heaven.*°

Well he hed it out the very next night,
Just at the dark, but fire light.
For the Pazon and the wife was away
At another Pazon's, and George in the bay
Agate of the lines—and rainin for all,
And blowin hard, but we were bound to haul—
And him on the sofa, and her a clattrin
With the cups and saucers, and chittrin—chattrin—
Aw he tould me all! and bless me! he hed it
Just like a picthur—you'd hardly credit,
Now would ye! and him that mad, you know,
And distracted lek—aw he hed it though,
He hed it—and this and that and how
And where and when, and all the row,
And the backard and forrard and here and there,
And the light on the wall and the light on the cheer,
And the light on her all dancin lek,
And the tippin her head and the tippin her neck,
And the tippin behind and the tippin before:
And *Sarpints*, he said, *wasn nothin to her*,
Nor Royal Bengal Tigers—the way
She turned, a shakin the fire like spray
Out of all her clothes—aw the holy father!
I tell ye he beat me altogether—
The talk that was at him—he beat me clane,
I didn know half of it what did he mane.
The quality, ye see, is reared to that—
Noticin lek, and which and what—
Like some of them painter chaps that's mixin
A colour for everything, and fixin
The way it is; and him and her,

1222   *at*: by.
1233   for all: however.

1260 And the very place, and the near and the far—
Bless ye! the like of us wouldn be mindin
Was there light at all—let alone was it shinin
On her hips or her hocks, and *shaddhers fleein*—
Lord bless my soul! what things to be seein
When your life is on the cast! ho! ho!
The quality's very curious though.
Aye and what was this he said—
Burnt in—and something about his head—
Burnt in—*on his brain—on his brain!* aye *burnt,*
1270 *Burnt on his brain!* But it's lek it's turnt
His head was a bit; for, don't ye see?
How could it be? how could it be?
Aw turnt sure enough, and very bad!
Aw the poor lad! aw the poor lad!

    Well he was intarmint for to spake,
And out with it all, to mar or to make.
So he just said her name—as low as low—
But the way he said it! the way, you know!
Aw she come to her feet, and she looked at him straight—
1280 "My God!" he said, the hard and the white,
And the keen, took sudden, ye see, that way,
And watchin what was he goin to say,
And houldin herself like a hound on the spring,
And a tight'nin her heart for anything.
And *proud*, he said, she looked, and despisin
The leks of him—now isn it supprisin?
To think of that now! *proud*—let it go!
But *despisin!* her! no! no! no! no!
And she looked, and he looked, and then it came
1290 Out of his soul like the livin flame—
A storm, he said, a storm of fire,
A storm of rage and strong desire,
And love and hate and joy and sadness
All mixed together in a muck of madness.
And angels and divils, he said was scourin
The soul of him, and big d——s come pourin
Out of him; and talkin love
All the time, and "dear!" and "dove!"
And d——s again. Aye and he said
1300 Things that he shouldn—aw he ded! he ded!
He ded though, tervil things that never

1267-74 *Omitted.*
1275   intarmint: determined.
1299-1304 *Omitted.*

Shouldn be said to no woman whatever.
He couldn stop, he tould me, the sudden
The grip was on him, and the hard! he couldn—
But on and on—"till at last," says he,
"I said—never mind! she listened to me
Till then," he says, "and never a breath
But the studdy look and the sthrong as death—
But then she shivered all over, and put
1310   Her hands to her face, and I crept to her fut,"
He said, "like a toad—I crept and crept,
And I touched her frock—aw then she lept
Like a deer," he said, "when the dogs is slept—"
One leap—and she stood at the door and then—
"James!" she said, and she said it again—
And three times she said it—"James!" aw he fell
A cryin when he tould me that: "and the swell
Of her bress," he said, "and the eyes lookin down,
And the voice—it might have been a sound
1320   From Heaven," he said, "far off," he said,
"Like one that 'd be speakin from the dead,"
He said—"far off"—and "James!" says she,
"I am your sister," she says; "there's three,"
She says, "of us, and we love one another;"
She says, "O brother! brother! brother!"
She says, and—"yes! I will! oh yes!"
And she come, for he made his mouth for a kiss,
Beggin lek, and she gev him one,
And he fell as dead as any stone.
1330   That's all he remembered—but the sarvint was tellin
How she came to her, and her eyes all swellin
With the big of tears, and "quick! quick! quick!"
She says "Masther James is very sick,"
She says to the sarvint—that's all she said,
And never a bonnet upon her head
Nor nothing—and "Take good care of him, Jane!"
And out in the rain—aye out in the rain.
And "It's over," he said; "I know! I know!
It's time to go! it's time to go!"
1340   "But," I said, "Masthar James, she didn say
But what might be for all—" "*a year and a day*"!
Says he, "Oh yes! *and she'll think of it yit!*
Tom Baynes," he says, "you're a idiit!"

Well! George and me was comin in

1310-4   *Omitted.*
1313   slept: slipped, released (ed.).

That night, and a tervil time we'd bin,
With the wind off-shore, and blowin strong,
But him the hearty it didn seem long:
And shovin her nigh to the rocks, to cheat
The squalls; and says he all at once—" Did you see't?"
1350 He says; "See what?" says I, "A ghost?"
"Look out!" says he, "and let's come close!"
So it's close we pulled—and behould her lyin
On the bress of the rock—aw we thought she was dyin—
And her hands all clenched in the tangles there,
And the water sip-soppin up to her hair—
And her that limp you wouldn belave—
"George! George!" I says, "behave! behave!
Why George!" I says; aw he had her! he had her!
And the more I said the madder and madder
1360 He got; and he wrapped and wrapped her up
In his arms! Aw her mouth might have been a cup
Of the heaven's wine, the way he wrong
The kisses out of it—keen and strong.
"Lord bless me! Masther George!" says I,
"You'll kill her that way. Come! let's try!
Is there life in her at all? Be quite!"
I says; "and you know it isn right
To go on like that," I says, "with a craythur
When she doesn know—it isn nathur,"
1370 I says. Nor no more it isn—what!
Of coorse not—you knows better till that.
And *How was she there?* and *Bless my heart!*
And wondherin; and "Come! let's start!"
Says he; and in with her into the boat,
And covered her up with an oilskin coat
That was at us there. But mind ye! before
I could get him to studdy down to his oar,
He was at her again; and "She's spakin!" he said;
And list'nin, and houldin down his head
1380 To her bress—and sure enough she was—
"Take me home!" she said—aw an albathross,
Or a gannet wasn nothing to him then,
The way he pulled, like twenty men—
One, two, three, with a sweep and a swing!
And a four for the queen and a five for the king!
And into a gully that was lyin back
Under the church itself; and a track

1354   tangles: long seaweeds.
1356-71 *Omitted.*
1362   wrong: wrung (ed.).

Windin up through the goss; for I knew,
If we went to the shore, what a hullabaloo
1390 There'd be, and the talk—aw scandalous!
So up—and her goin a carryin at us;
Very wake, and treigh; but I saw
Masther George had to stow the jaw,
Let alone the kissin! aye!
He hed though, I tell ye! "It's you bein by,"
He whispers to me: but she straightened her head
That stiff on my shoulder—"Look out!" I said:
And "Look out!" it was; for, right or wrong,
He had to look out, he had, before long.

1400   The Pazon wasn at home when we got
To the house; so I stood out on the plat;
And George took her in—aw the gel could walk,
That time and then he come out for a talk
And a smook sittin under the sycamore
That stretched from the garden to the door;
A fine tree too, for the country, and tall;
For they're runnin rather stunty and small
Over there is trees—and the wind would come
And shiver it all, and make it hum
1410 Like a brave big top, and tappin the pane
Of the Pazon's study till he'd laugh again—
Aw he liked it well! but—I don't know
Trees is very curious though!
If there's ghoses takin anywhere
It's in trees it is! Aw they've got their share
Has churchyards and that—but mind you me!
I've seen funny things in a sycamore tree!
Aye aye! my lads! Aw lower down—
All right of coorse! all right, I'll be bound—
1420 You can grip them there, and feel the stuff
That's in them—aw all right enough!
But—up in the branches! my God! they're about;
But navar mind! look out! look out!
Well we talked and talked, and it was him begun;
And he gev a big sigh, and he says, "It's done!"

1388   goss: gorse.
1391   goin a carryin at us: being carried by us (ed.).
1392   wake: weak (ed.).
        treigh [pronounced like *tray*; *t* almost like *th*]: pale, miserable (*slack* in *1881* [ed.]).
1401   plat: small plot of ground (ed.).
1414   ghoses: ghosts.
        takin: haunting.

He says "it's done!" and he hung his head
And "I couldn help it, Tom Baynes!" he said.
And then he tould me the hard to bear
It was, and the trouble, and the care,
1430   And tryin and tryin to do his part,
And stampin the heavy upon his heart,
Puttin out the fire that kep burnin still—
Aw, he said, *it was terrible*.
Where does it come from? where? where? where?
Is it in the ground? is it in the air?
Is it sucked with your milk? is it mixed with your flesh?
Does it float on the top? is it caught in the mesh
Of a man's soul hanging deep and low
When the tides of life begins to flow?
1440   Where is it? what is it? The Lord above—
He only knows the strenth of love:
He only knows, and He only can
The root of love that's in a man.
Aw isn it true? And Him as quite,
Seein all in the clear sweet light
That's runnin through Him all day long,
And all the night—and the angels' song—
"Holy! holy! holy!" they're sayin—
And us poor craythurs prayin! prayin!
1450   And Him so quite—and "Gentle Jesus!"—°
And waitin—waitin—but by G—— he sees us!

What was I sayin? aw yes! *the fire*;
And what could he do? and *he wasn wire*,
Nor nails, he said: and how he'd kep
Out of her road; and the houldt and the grep
There was at him reglar; and allis out
After the lines, and knockin about
With the gun, and tryin to clear his head
And studdy hisself. "And James!" he said,
1460   "James!" he said—"God help us then!
Poor James!" he said—(Amen! Amen!).
"I thought," he said, "I thought I was stronger—
But O Tom Baynes! I can't stand it no longer!
Yes! Yes!" he says, "he loves her! he does!
And oh I think my heart will buss!
And I've tried and tried to give him fair-play—
Hevn I, Tom? now hevn I—eh?"
"You hev," I says, "but listen! listen!

1444   quite: quiet.
1456   reglar: he always maintained.

Masther George!" I says: "Now it is or it isn;
1470 But tell me for all what makes you suppose
That ither o' ye is for the Christmas Rose?"
"*What makes me?*" he says, and gives a cuss;
"And who is for her, if it isn us?
James or me?" he says. "Hullo!
I see!" he says, "I see! ho! ho!"
He says, and he jams his face chock up
Again mine, and he says—"Have you got a sup?
D—— it!" he says, "it's you ye manes!
You're for the Christmas Rose, Tom Baynes!
1480 You! by——," and he turned and he laughed—
Aw the bitter! and fore and aft—
At least up and down—and about with a wheel,
And churnin the gravel under his heel.
"You!" he said—"Well!" he said, "the cheek
Of some people! and what for don't ye speak?"
He says, quite quick, and stands as straight
As a boult before me: and "Will ye fight?"
He says, "or what will ye do? come! out!
Out with it! d—— ye! you're freckened, I doubt."
1490 "Masther George!" I said—quite studdy, you know—
"Masther George! it isn a minute ago
You were all in the dumps; and now it's fightin
You're after; and maybe you might or you mightn
Have the best of it: but there's one thing I thought
You couldn mistake, let alone the *ought*.
One thing, Masther George, you must ha' knowed;
Me for the Christmas Rose! my God!
Me for her! and you! yes you!
Knowin all about Betsy o' the Brew!
1500 Is there a thought?—You'll strike me, will ye?
(He was goin), or a wish I wouldn tell ye?
Hevn I tould you every word,
To the very keel of my heart—good Lord!
What can I do more? here I am!
Pitch into me! I don't care a d——!
Knock my head off! but navar a blow
From me to you! aw no! no! no!
Not this time, Masther George, if you plaze!
Not exactly! George!" I says.
1510 And I laughed—and be hanged! the two of us laughed—
Aw people in love is ticklesome craft:
For it's laughin and cryin and foolin and fightin
And cussin and kissin and lovin and bitin

1489 freckened: frightened (ed.).

All in the one—crabs and crame!
And the very birds is just the same—
Let alone monkeys and dirts like that—
Aw they've got their troubles I'll tell ye what!

    Well the laugh cleared the fog away nicely though
That was hidin us from one another, you know—
1520 You know what I mean—all hot and huffed—
And we talked chance talk, and puffed and puffed
At the pipe. And I remember the jump
He gev when he heard the jerk of the pump,
Thinkin the Pazon had come in
Unknownst at the back! And bless me! the din
There was at that pump; and apt to run dry,
And bad for the soak, and navar say die!
But work away!—aw a reglar brute!
And a rusty boult that roored like the hoot
1530 Of a owl or a dunkey; and suckin and sobbin,
And retchin and cretchin, and slibbin and slobbin—
It's lek you know how a hoss is goin
When the wind's bruck at him, and ah-in and oh-in
In his belly—they're ugly to hear in the night
Is them pumps, like a thing lek that wouldn be right
Someway! And the ould people used to be sayin—
But d—— it all! it was only Jane
The sarvint, gettin water of coorse—
But mind ye! she done it with a force!
1540 The arm she had—But it's idikkilis!
I'll never come to an end like this—
Pumps! my gough! Well we laughed, and a bat
Come wheelin about, and he gave me a pat
In the face with his d——d ould webby wings—
Aw the terrible I hate them things—
Away went the pipe, bruck out o' my cheek—
The strenth of the divil! and the boostly squeak!
Aw blast the father of him! I say—
I never liked them critters anyway.
1550 Aw then the laugh! But he come at me again,
And "Tom," he says, "I want you to 'splain.
You're in some sort of love with her, that's clear."
"Now what the divil!" says I, "look here!"

1514   crame: cream.
1526   at: with.
1527   soak: water poured into the pump when the *sucker* is dry.
1529   roored: roared.
1540   idikkilis: ridiculous.
1547   boostly: beastly.

Aw I got hot—"I'm not goin to stand
This talk," I says, "from the lord of the land.
I've tould ye and tould ye, and what's the good?
The more the tellin the less understood.
But mind my words, Masther George!" I says, "anyway—
The Christmas Rose isn for the one o' ye!
1560 No she isn—not a bit," I said:
She's far far far above your head.
Poor James!" I says; "poor James! well! well!
Of coorse—but you to come over the gel
With your dainty curls, and your bit of a stachya,
And the strong and the handsome; and "*Hev me! bless ye!*"
Thinks you; "most sartin, and only too glad!"
And *whistle and I'll come to ye, my lad!*°
Them's your thoughts; but where's your fax?
Where? aye where indeed! I may ax
1570 The where, bedad, and the when and the why."
Aw it's then he made a leap and a cry
Like a tiger, and at me; but I gev a duck,
And the fiss went over my shouldher, and struck
The tree like a hatchet—my gough! the smash
And his knuckles all jammy, and the blood splish-splash!
"You're not the man for me to be 'fraid of:
You're not made of the stuff that Christmas is made of!
No by —— " I said, "you're not."
Aw the leap again, and flew at my throat.
1580 But then I gripped him, and yeo! heave ho!
And a lift and a twist—and over you go;
And let him down the softest I could,
And it's only raison you allis should;
And give a man a chance—yis! yis,
And pick him up agin isn amis.
Well he was middlin giddy, ye see;
So I studdied him agin the tree—
And he says—"What's this for?" "For!" I said—
"For! ye come at me that vicious, ye ded!
1590 And me that was as quite as a lamb to ye!"
" I know you're strong," he says, "and be d—— to ye!"
And he hung the head middlin sulky though.
"Come, Masther George!" I said; "take a blow
Of the pipe," and I took and charged it for him,
And got it to draw; and—jann myghin orrym!
If he didn smoke it sweet enough!

1564   stachya: moustache.
1595   jann myghin orrym [pronounced *jen muh´ghun, gh* as *ch* in Scot. *loch*]: mercy on us.°

Hard to light though—ye know the stuff.
Well then I talked very sirrious,
Uncommon though; and I gev a cuss
1600 And I said—"It's hard for the leks o' me
To tell you how I love Betsy Lee,
And how I love the Christmas Rose:
But I love the two of them, God knows!
The two of them—so there ye hev it:
Aye aye! that's it! as right as a trevvit—
That's the words—and d—— it what's more,
I navar thought on it before—
The two of them—but the why and the whether—"
"How happy could I be with ether!"°
1610 Says he, half laughin—some dirty ould song
He had though for all—"Now ger along!
Masther George!" I says; "and listen, man!
I gor it now—the very plan!
Look here! you're lovin a nice young gel,
And she's lovin you—very well! very well!
That's right! that's good! that's—aw that's sweet!
And to meet and to part, and to part and to meet
Is all your thoughts—*and when will it be?*
Aw when? aw when? says you, says she.
1620 And it comes at last, and the bells is ringin,
And the Pazon waiting, and the ould shoes a flingin—
And home in the ev'rin, and settlin down—
And childher to foller, I'll be bound.
That's love; and thank my God it's in!
For without it we wouldn be worth a pin.
But, George," I said, "isn there no love
That's greater till that, that's risin above
The lek o' that—why can't there be
No love without wivin and all that spree?
1630 Couldn ye love, and navar make to her
No love nor nothing, nor navar spake to her?
Couldn ye look to her like a star
Up in the heavens quite reggilar,
Shinin down on all the same,
And maybe not even knowin your name?
Couldn ye love her up that high?
And kiss her with your soul through all the sky?
A sweetheart! aw Betsy ma veg! ma veen!

1598	sirrious:	seriously.
1609	ether:	either.
1622	ev'rin:	evening.
1624	it's in:	it exists.
1638	ma veg:	my little (one).

Christmas Rose

Aye aye! but a queen! a queen! a queen!
1640 That's another thing, and I don't care who knows,
My queen, my queen is the Christmas Rose!"
"Your queen indeed!" he says; "hear! hear!
Your queen! aw dear! aw dear! aw dear!
You're gettin quite rermantick," he said;
Who put that d—— nonsense into your head?
Why raelly," he says, "you're almost poetical!"
"Avast!" says I; "I'll hev no reddikil.
She's my queen, I beg to state!"
My queen! now wasn that first-rate?
1650 *Queen*—d'ye see? aw the fancies come quick
In my head them times, aye as thick—as thick
As the hairs outside; but now—hurroo!
The hairs is gone, and the fancies too.
Aw he laughed and he chaffed and he carried on,
But wasn I right? eh Billy? eh John?
Aye, and what is the love of God
The Pazons is shoutin about till they gets blawed
And black in the face?—you know their way—
"Love Him! love Him! you must!" says they.
1660 "*You must?*" how must? "Lord bless me!" thinks I,
"Tell me what is He lek, and I'll try."
"Aw He's this, He's that—you can aisy know:"
"He's nothing!" "He's something!" away they go!
"He's everything!" "He isn!!" "He is!!!"
Fight away your rivrinces!
Matthew, Mark, and Revelation—
Out with the dollop! I know my station—
Aw you're far too many for the leks o' me;
But I'm apt to love the things that I see,
1670 Anyway the beautifullest things
That God has made: and the birds they sings,
They does, and it's God that gives the notes,
Stretchin the bags of their little throats:
And the sun is bright, and the sky is blue;
And a man is strong, and a hoss is too,
And God's in all—But I'll tell ye the whan
You can see his face, if you avar can—
It's when He lights sweet holy fire
In the eye of a woman; and heises her higher
1680 Till all your thoughts, a woman true
But not for you la! not for you.

---

          ma veen: my darling.
   1647   reddikil: ridicule.
   1656-70 *Omitted.*

Who for? No matter! if you've got any sense,
Of coorse you'll know the difference:
You'll know when you're wanted and when you aint,
And navar make no surt of complaint,
But touch your hat—"My sarvice, Madam!"
And her not knowin you from Adam.
Bless me! d'ye think she's nothing to me
Because mayhap she doesn't know me?
1690 Har! har! I picks her out, and says I,
"You're my queen! keep up in the sky!"
I says; "keep up! shine on, my queen!
Who the divil am I? it's all serene!
It's all serene!" says I, with a bow—
Where's your huggin and ruxin now?
You've seen them picthers the Romans hess—
Merdonners they call them—women, I guess—
Women eh? with the blood in their veins,
And life and love, and the way they strains
1700 Their eyes to a height that's far above them?
Who can look on them, and not love them?
D—— all Popery, say I,
And idols and all that sort of guy!
And Irish divils anyway—
Protestant boys 'll carry the day!°
But whoavar made the likes o' them—
Their feet was in Jerusalem;
Whoavar thought that a woman could look
Like that—he knew the Holy Book;
1710 He knew the mind of God; he knew
What a woman could be, and he drew and he drew
Till he got the touch: and I'm a fool
That was almost walloped out o' the school,
I was that stupid, but d—— it! I've got
A soul in my inside, whether or not,
And I know the way the chap was feelin
When he made them picthers—he must ha' been kneelin
All the time, I think, and prayin
To God for to help him; and its lekly sayin
1720 He was paintin the Queen—they calls her the Queen
Of Heaven, but of coorse she couldn ha' been—
But that's the surt—a woman lifted
To heaven, with a bress like snow that's sifted,
And a eye that's fixed on God hisself—

1695   ruxin: glossed in *The Doctor* as "pulsing convulsively" (*CP*, p. 420—ed.).
1703   guy: toy, plaything (Moore).

Now where's your wivin and thrivin and pelf?
And sweethearts, and widdies well stocked with the rhino?
Ah! that's the thing likest God that I know.
Well up come the Pazon at last—no doubt
This time, and helpin the Misthress out,
1730 Very lovin; and a givin a screp
Of her skinny ould leg agin the step—
And "Oh Misther Gale!" and "How awkard ye are!"
And him a fussin and—"Well I declare!"
And "I beg your pardin!" Bless me! the perlite!
And Jinny dodgin about with a light;
And me with ould Smiler's nose in my hand,
The hoss that was at them, you'll understand,
And laughin like fun; and George goin nudgin
With his elber the way it was time to be trudgin—
1740 So I takes the hent, and away like a shot,
And down the gully and into the boat,
And pullin her round to the moorins all right,
And home, and mother sittin up straight
In her cheer, and a sulkin, and suckin hard
At her ould black pipe, and navar a word
But—"Here ye are! ye Lhiggey-my-traiee!
Go off to bed!" "I'm goin," says I.

Well poor James died—he did though—yis!
That was the fuss and the last kiss—
1750 He'd navar see her again—no! no!
Till the day he died—"Let me go! let me go!"
He'd say. It'd be some time about Harvis—
I was shearin that year for ould Juan Jarvis—
But I was up at the buryin; and, what's more,
That's the fuss white shirt that ever I wore.
Save us! the row the ould mawther made
About yandhar shirt, and the tervil 'fraid
It wouldn be ready—aw quite delighted!
And *me invited! me invited!*
1760 *She wouldn ha' cared if it wasn for that—*
And a black clout pinnin round my hat—
And the ould man's Sunday clothes took out
Of the chiss—and *mind what was I about!*
And none of my cryin and booin! she said;

1726	rhino: money (ed.).
1737	at them: they had.
1746	Lhiggey-my-traiee [pronounced approximately *lyi′guh muh thrai*; *th* almost like *t*, *ai* as in *air*]: unpunctual; Mx. *lhiggym y hraa*, "letting the time [pass]" (Moore).
1753	shearin: reaping (ed.)

I had other things to think of, I hed.
"Buck up" says she, "and look like a man!"
And how to walk and how to stand—
My gough! I was tired—"And don't let me see
A spec on that coat, ye fenodyree!°
1770 When ye come back"—she says; "but in case
You must cry, hould the handkercher to your face!
That's dacent enough—but drabbin still
On your clothes—it isn respectable"—
She said—"let alone the cloth goin a spilin."
God bless my soul! the woman was rilin.
I felt like a fool at the buryin,
For I couldn be sorry nor anythin
In them d——d clothes, but takin keer,
And mindin my eye like a prig at a feer.
1780 She'd gor a thing warped around my neck
Would ha' choked ould Harry himself I expec.
Well well! they're tervil—But even them clothes
Couldn hinder me lookin for the Christmas Rose.
And I saw her, I saw her sittin all alone
In a window—just like a block of stone—
Sittin, and lookin straight at the moul
That was heaped round the grave—upon my soul!
The way she sat—aw a queen on her throne!
But a block of stone—a block of stone!
1790 "Her heart was stone," says you—Well! well!
I suppose then Billy, you knew the gel?
You didn! no! I knew you didn!
Well then ould gandhar! stick to your midden!
Stick to what you're used of, Billy!
Christmas Rose, or Christmas Lily—
They're not much in your line, Illiam, eh?
Hard-hearted—well now *I've* heard them say
She *was* hard-hearted: but if they'd said
Strong-hearted, not *hard*, why then they'd hed
1800 Some raison—Look here now! is it the same—

1769 fenodyree [Mx. *phynodderee*, pronounced approximately as *funótheree—o* between the vowel in *odd* and *add*]: properly the "lubber fiend" of Milton; here *awkward fellow*; "a hairy satyr" (Moore).
1772 drabbin: wetting (see gloss for *Betsy Lee* 432—ed.).
1774 a spilin: getting spoiled.
1779 prig: pick-pocket.
1780 warped: wrapped, bound around (Cregeen).
1781 ould Harry: the devil.
1786 moul: mould.
1796 Illiam: William.

Hard and *strong?* and a craythur that came
Like foam from the sea—But it isn *strong*
Nor it isn *hard*: you're wrong! you're wrong!
It's far off it is, and different,
A kind of a surt of a splenthar sent
From another world—like moonstones juss—
They hevn got the same subjecs as us.
There's ones comes into the world like that,
Even among their own people—what?
1810   Hevn ye seen them? lonely things—
They hevn got crowns and they hevn got wings—
They're not angels azackly nor divils ether,
And us and them'll grow up together:
But their roots isn twisted someway with ours;
And the flowers that's at them is other flowers;
And they're waiting, I'm thinking, to be transplanted
To the place where the lek o' them is wanted:
And our love isn their love, and they cannot take it;
Nor our thirst their thirst, so we cannot slake it:
1820   There's no food in us for them to feed on,
There's nothing in us that they got need on—
So there they are, with kith and kin,
Sittin in the middle, and wondherin.
And *love* and *heart*—why how should it be?
There's no heart made in them yet, d'ye see?
Just wild-fire flashing here and there,
Or if it's at them anywhere,
It's like a bud that sucks the air
Through its baby lips, but open? no!
1830   Till the westlin winds begin to blow,
And drew at the sun with a strong sweet strain
It opens and nevar shuts again.
But, say what you like, and say what you will,
The Christmas Rose was a puzzle still.
It wasn no baby buds in her,
But a big woman's heart, that wouldn stir
To other hearts, but took its motion
From the winds and the clouds and the waves of the ocean.
It was bred in the storm;
1840   It was fed in the storm—

1805	splenthar:	splinter.
1807	subjecs:	substance.
1812	azackly:	exactly;
	ether:	either.
1815	at them:	which they have.
1821	got need on:	have need of.
1831	drew at:	drawn by.

She'd run to meet it, she'd see it comin,
She'd smell it, I b'live; she'd hear it thrummin
A hunderd miles off—out she'd be!
But secretly! aw secretly!
Crouchin and crouchin behind a wall—
I've seen her, but she didn know at all—
And lookin behind—Ah hah! my Queen!
Was she seen? she was thinkin, *was she seen? was she seen?*
And flittin like a bird, or a gel
1850 That's stealin away to the lad she loves well—
Ould eyes, she thinks, *aren't allis dim*—
"Hush! hush! that's him! that's him! that's him!"
And then to the rocks, and a loosin her hair
To the wind, and a rippin her bresses bare;
And her mouth all open, and a gaspin to't,
And the shivers of joy running down her throat—
What had she! what was at her, my men?
Was it her heart that was makin then?
But think of her father! think of her mother!
1860 That's it! so one thing with another,
And love for love, and tit for tat,
What 'd ye do with a gel like that?
There was another thing I seen that day—
A Pazon come from over the bay
For our Pazon lek, *to do the duty*—
That's their talk—well he was a beauty!
Well the purtiest little bit of a man
That ever I saw—and the little hand
And the little foot, and the little squeak
1870 Of his little vice; and the little cheek
So rosy and round; and the legs—my gough!
And the little hem! and the little cough!
Well he was a nice little divil though,
He was now; and his mouth like a little red O—
My senses! that little chap beat all—
A pippity-poppity—talk of a doll!
Why I'd just have liked to took and stowed him
In my trousis pocket, and had him and showed him
To the childher—only a penny a peep—
1880 Well he was the natest little sweep!
You might have put the little dandy
In your mouth, and sucked him for sugar-candy.
And he ups to the Pazon, and bless us! the sollum!
And the head goin like what-d'ye-call-em!

1857   at her: the matter with her.
1880   sweep: good-for-nothing (Moore).

And "A great affliction"—and—tiggle—taggle—
And *the Lord was great*—and—wiggle—waggle;
And the Pazon navar lookin at him,
But out to the round of the blue sea-rim
(It was clear that day); but what he saw—
1890 Navar mind! the little chap had the jaw.
Well, you see, I couldn cry, triced up
In the ould woman's rig, so I didn stop,
But out on the gaery—and what did I do
But off with the coat and the waistcoat too—
Aw laugh!—I did; and I hung the pair
On a lump of a thorn that was growin there;
And then I set to for a hearty bout,
And I had it out—I had it out.
But I was that disthressed and done, I tell ye,
1900 That harvis, I couldn go to the mheillea—°
Aw it's a fac! And Betsy theer!
Aw poor James! aw Betsy dear!

    Now, you see, after the buryin
George couldn help it but he must begin
To talk very comfortin lek and nice
To Christmas Rose, and once or twice
He put his arm round her, and called her name,
Just comfortin lek, and wantin the same—
Aw wanting it bad, for he loved his brother—
1910 And there they'd be, and the father and mother,
Tervil quite, just sighin and lookin—
The Pazon, I mane, and sometimes he'd be smookin,
But the pipe 'd allis be goin out,
And him navar knowin, and used to be stout,
And gettin thin, they were tellin me;
And the wife with the Bible on her knee,
Reading away, but very quick
And sharp with the temper, and givin a click
With her needles, and lookin up though still—
1920 George tould me it was dreadful uncomfible—
Quite—tervil quite—and the everins long,
And a sort of a choke at him, and right or wrong,
He couldn help it, but layin his head
On Christmas' shouldher, and "Dodgin," he said,
Aye! "dodgin," he said, poor fellow! for fear

1891	triced: fastened.
1893	gaery: piece of waste land.
1896	lump: good-sized.
1900	mheillea: harvest-home.
1921	everins: evenings.

The ould people would see; and dear! aw dear!
The way the Christmas 'd shake, and the shiftin
Onaisy lek, and the "Don't" and liftin
The big black eyes, and axin lek
1930 He wouldn do that; and curlin the neck—
And dhrivin him mad; and *why?* and *how?*
And "Mightn she now? aw mightn she now?"
And everything that miserble—
And all the house like a broken mill—
And wasn it her duty?—aye
Her duty, he said, *at least to try*
Could she love him, and not be that contrary?
Aw a fine brave lad, but simple very!
"And have ye spoke plain to her?" I said;
1940 "Yes! aw yes!" and 'deed he hed—
Plain enough—for the day before
He met her walkin upon the shore,
And he axed her *what was it*, and *what did she mane?*
That was middlin plain eh? middlin plain!
Well she was a darlin, for when them two
Was alone together—aw it's true! it's true!—
She met him as lovin, and she spoke
The way she ought—aw it's fit to choke
I am when I'm telling ye—yes—straight
1950 And plain to me as the gospel light—
To *me*—God knows how is it to me,
For George couldn twig it—ma chree—ma chree!
The strange—and him that eddicated!
Aw a power of schoolin! And he should ha' waited—
But still—what gud! aw the true and the keen!
My Queen! my queen! my queen! my queen!
I know it! I know it! but him—well! well!—
She said—"My darlin (didn he tell
Every word to me?)—my darlin," she said,—
1960 "My darlin brother!" (aw *the white and the red*
He was tellin me!)—"my darlin brother!"
(Aw he clasped her then!) "no other! no other,"
She said, "can ever be to me
What you are," she said (d'ye see? d'ye see?
Brother—eh?) "But oh!" she said,
And she cried very bad, and she stooped her head
Agin his bress, and he kissed her and kissed her—

1928   Onaisy: uneasy.
1948   it's fit to choke / I am: I'm nearly choking.
1952   twig: understand, comprehend (*OED*).
          ma chree: my heart.
1967   Agin: against.

(Aye aye! I know!) and "Darlin sister!"
And that—but then—"George! George!" she says;
1970 And the tears! the tears! and she lifts her face;
"George! George! no more! no more than this"—
And she gives him a long long lovin kiss;
And with that kiss—"George! George! here! here!
I give you all—oh dearest dear!
Oh brother mine—oh look and see!
It cannot be! it cannot be!
This—this! Forgive me, George, forgive!
I don't know how I come to live—
I should have died that time!" Ah Rose!
1980 And the strange! the strange! and the green grass grows—
"I'm so different—(she said it! she said it!)
And so unhappy—(aw let it! let it!)
Would God that I had navar been!"
She said—My Queen! my queen! my queen!
"It's strange," says George; "Well yes!" says I,
"Uncommon strange!" but I toul'd a lie;
For it wasn strange—the gel was right;
But a blind man navar 'll see the light.

And George, ye see, got desperate,
1990 And carin for nothin, and stayin out late;
And down at the public-house that was theer,
In the village, and heavy upon the beer,
Aw drinkin hard, I tell ye, hard!
For a lad like him, and didn regard
For nobody—but "Come! let's go
And have a pint!" and whether or no,
And in on the door—and the dirty ould trouss,
One Callow's wife, that was keepin the house,
Smilin and winkin, and plenty to say,
2000 And drawin and drawin, and scorin away—
Bad work! bad work! And cards, and tossin,
And glasses round, and winnin and lossin—
And me that was ouldher backin the lad,
And very bad! aw very bad!
But what could I do? what could you expec?
You see I was shockin fond of him lek—
And proud uncommon—aye that was it—
Proud—bless ye! proud! for there we'd sit,
Him, d'ye see? in the elber cheer,
2010 Hardly noticin was I theer;

1982   let it: let it be, leave it (ed.).
1997   trouss: slut.

And me on the settle; and him in his glory,
Singin a song, or tellin a story:
And all the chaps delighted, you know;
And "Isn he gud?" and "I tould ye so!"
And—"Listen! listen!"—and me nearly cryin
A thinkin of all; and tryin and tryin
Not to let on; and proud though stell—
And as much as to say—"Very well! very well!"
But lookin the way I'd say to the others—
2020 "Him and me is just like brothers!"
And, "Capital!" and "Go it! go it!"
Aw I shouldn ha' done it, and I know it.
What did ye say?—*if a chap's in the trim
To have a spree, that's a matter for him!*
And *why shouldn you have a spree with your fran?*
No! you shouldn with a gentleman—
No! no! my lads! it's a different case—
Honour bright! I know my place.
But still the proud! and *yandhar fellas!*
2030 *Who were they?* and middlin jealous.
For some o' them chaps 'd make too free,
And then I'd be hintin if it wasn for me
He'd see the lot at Jerusalem
Afore he'd make sport for the leks o' them.
And "Isn he fuss-rate, Tom?" and "Hip!
Hip! hooraa!" and me bitin the lip
As contimptible as contimptible,
And lookin to say "Of coorse! but still
What's that, bless ye! to the fun
2040 When him and me is together alone?"
Well drink is drink, and funny is funny,
And jink is jink, and money is money—
And a long score owin—that's the raison
He went partners with me for the mackarel saison.
Aw he was a partner—for I'll be dished
If a better fisherman ever fished—
Crafty uncommon, and never contented
With our ould dodges; but took and invented
New streamers, new poundrhels, new guts, new plyin,
2050 New everything, and tryin and tryin,
And changin often and calkerlatin,
And terrible tasty° about the baiting.
Aw if there was a fish in the sea

2017 to let on: betray what I thought.
2025 *fran*: friend.
2042 jink: money (Moore).
2049 poundrhels: weights.

He'd have it out though anyway—
Studyin lek. And that time o' the year
The nights is short, so we didn keer,
And maybe not in bed for a week,
But sittin in Callow's till the day would keek,
And out the very first skute of light,
2060 For that's the time the divils 'll bite—
Sittin—and maybe three or four
Of the other chaps upon the floor;
And all the fun and all the spree
Peaceful enough, and leavin to me
Mostly to watch—aw they knew who they hed—
Very wakeful and clear, they said!
And the clock goin tickin, and ould mawther Callow
A snartin and snortin in the parlour—
Disthressin bad—'deed many a night
2070 I've gone down, and pinched her to be quite.
And George 'd mostly be down with the head
On the table, and his arms outspread
For a piller lek; and the curly heer
Sthroogin among the rings of beer
And tobacco dust and the lek; and I'd take
And heise it up, and give it a shake,
And feel it a bit, for I loved him though,
And reddyin it, just with my fingers, you know;
And tuck it nice, and give it a ply
2080 Aback of his ears, and so—Oie vie!
But the first sign of day, or before it mayve,
We were down at the boat, and him rather heavy
And blundherin lek, and stumblin about;
But as soon as ever we'd get out
A mile or that, he'd say—"Here goes!"
And half-a-minute, and off with the clothes,
And over the side, and in like a shot,
And me lookin sharp, and markin the spot,
And measurin lek—and, I'll be swore,
2090 Maybe a cable's length or more—
And up with a jerk, and shakin the water
Out of his hair, and callin me ater—
And "Come in! Tom Baynes! come in! come in!"

2058   keek: peep.
2059   skute: squirt.
2074   sthrooghin: trailing.
2078   reddyin: combing.
2079   ply: twist (Wright).
2080   Oie Vie [*oie* like *ee*; *vie* rhymes with *ply*]: good-night.
2092   ater: after.

And the teeth that white, and the round o' the chin,
And his cheeks all red with the risin day,
Like another sun comin out o' the sea—
And the green water swirlin around the ring
Of his shouldhers, and fit for anything.
And—"Try it Tom! come! try, man, try!"
2100 "Go ahead! go ahead! go ahead!" says I;
I'm busy!" But, bless ye! heel or toe—
I never cared much for the water—no!
In the heat of the day it might do, ye see;
But they're very strange is the quality.
Well that's the style, and goin and goin—
And it's lek you'll ax was the Pazon knowin?
About Callow's?—well—I cannot say—
Lek enough—but he had a way
Houldin on, you know, and hopin still,
2110 And patient, patient terrible—
And livin in a sort of drame, I suppose,
And happy enough in the Christmas Rose—
And thinkin no evil, and trustin a dale—
Aw the best of fathers was Pazon Gale.
But he got to know it at last for all;
For who should go and give him a call
But ould Mawther herself—and *was he aweer?*
And this and that, and *the cards and the beer!*
And *well enough for him to spree*
2120 *That could easy afford it, but how about me!*
And *she'd better be takin a bag at once,*
And about the country, and *them that had sons*
Should look after their hours—and no disrespec!
And curtseyin and curtseyin, and trimblin lek.
And the Pazon, I'm told, got tervil red,
And "I'll spake to him, Mrs. Baynes!" he said:
But he didn say much—aw the man was aisy!
Lazy though, mawther said, or *crazy!*
Aw she wouldn spare! but bless her chatt'rin!
2130 Good people isn all the 'zac same pattrin;
For some is very strong and bould,
And some very tender, not willin to scould.
But whatever he said, poor George! he felt it,
Aw aisy froze and aisy meltit!
And I'll be bound to say he didn come
To the Bull for a week, and very glum
And silent lek; and the fellows lookin,
And navar a word, and smookin, smookin.

2130   'zac: exactly.

Christmas Rose

      But soon as bad as ever though,
2140 And gettin in at the window, you know—
      Aw I see the spot, and the very ould trammon—
      Faith! I'm not goin to deny it, I amn'
      Heisin him up there in the tree—
      I couldnt help but back him, don't ye see?
      And *The Rose? The Rose? it's lek she knew?*
      Well—I think she did; but what could she do?
      Was she to go and take him straight
      Because he was gettin drunk every night?
      And I'm not goin to say one thing or another;
2150 I know she loved him like a brother:
      And there's many a sister that's got to let be,
      And wait and see—and wait and see!
      But that wasn the way of coorse to come at her,
      Though maybe it wasn so very much matter;
      For the gel was moulded, ye see, and sent
      Into the world to be different.
      But still for all, if you want to catch
      Young love asleep, you must lift the latch
      Middlin aisy, I tell ye, for sure,
2160 And not go kickin at the door:
      And if you want to take a bird, my son,
      Alive for its beauty, no call for a gun;
      And snowdrops isn op'nin with puttin
      A candle to them, nor nither shuttin;
      And the brightest brass is the better for ilin,
      And navar no egg wasn hatched with bilin.
      Different—yes different!
      And navar meant! no, navar meant!
      But she couldn help noticin, whether or not,
2170 It's differenter the two of them got;
      And furder and furder from him he drev her,
      And lovin the Pazon more than ever.
      Aw a bird of the storm, if you like, but glad
      Of a bit of rest, and all that she had
      He done it, for, if the storm was in her,
      The calm was in him—so there they were.
      And she'd sit at his feet with her arms on his knees,
      And look up like a thing that was looking for peace,
      And axin lek—and all the big troubles

2141   trammon: elder tree.
2142   amn': am not.
2143   Heisin: lifting.
2147   straight: immediately.
2159   for sure: indeed.
2171   furder: further.

2180 A strainin in her eyes like bubbles
Of fire and wonder; and *who was she?*
And when and why? and the kind he'd be,
With his blessed ould face all full of love
And comfort for her to be drinkin of.
And she did drink too; and off she'd go
To sleep the way with the babbies, you know.
Aw he was a reglar ould nussin mother
Was the Pazon, and 'deed she hadn no other.
For the Misthress wasn no use, but hard
2190 And dry uncommon, and didn regard
For young craythurs, nor couldn fit
Her soul to theirs, aw not a bit!
It's lek you've seen a cross ould sheep
When the little things 'll creep and creep
Up to her tits, and she'll turn as swivil,
And bite and kick like the very divil—
Aw you might put a lamb to a hoss's tail,
But navar nothin to Mistress Gale.
And such suck for her heart as the Rose was drinkin
2200 It come from the Pazon's bresses, I'm thinkin.
Laugh on! laugh on! but you know what I mane—
Aw laugh then, laugh! and laugh again!
But there's many a man, I tell ye, Bob Shimmin,
That'll suckle a soul far better till women—
Aye! the soul of a gel too—think of that!
Now then what are you laughin at?
And *why didn she take and tell the Pazon
All about it!* is that what you're assin?
All about what now? come now, come!
2210 All about what? you're lookin rum—
And her not knowin herself what was at her—
It's aisy talkin, but no matter! no matter!

    And the two of them allis together though,
And larnin Spanish; and George stuck to,
And larnin with them, and larnin grand;
Aw quick at the schoolin, you'll understand.
I've got the book he was larnin from yit
In the chiss at me here—I'll show ye it
Some night—of course it's lingo to me,
2220 But George 'd be puttin it out quite free
In the English talk; and of all the stuff!
Aw terrible nonsense, sure enough!

2193-212 *Omitted.*
2218   the chiss at me: my chest.

Fightin and women, and I don't know what—
And the name they had to it was Don Quixotte—
A sort of a punch and judy, or the way
The Whiteboys° is actin a Christmas day—
Imprint craythurs! and Rosinante,
A skinny ould hoss that he had; and a banty
Fat little beggar called Sancho that got
2230 For a governor—aye! Don Quixotte!
And his shield and all the ould iron he wore—
Well the quality's—but I said that afore.
And the picthers raely is funny amazin—
Bless me! the barber and the bason!
And him agate o' the windmills—aye!
But I'll be showin ye bye and bye.
You see this book was wrote at a man
In London—he must ha' been a hand!
But that's the place where the divils is takin
2240 That can do the lek—and no mistake in—
And the number over the door,
And eighteen hundred thirty-four!

    Well the time went on, and George hed to go
To Oxford College, the way you know,
He'd larn for a Pazon—the for they're sent—
And the spree the night before he went—
At the Bull! and all the fellows theer—
And him with a speech and "Hear! hear! hear!"
And shoutin and tearin; and kissin ould Berry:
2250 But in the mornin thoughtful very
At the Coach: and "Tom! do you know where I'm goin?"
He says—and ould Cannel waein and woin—
"I'm goin to the divil!" and he turned his head;
Aw that's the very words he said!
And to the divil it was, for sure—
And spreein, and bills, and the Pazon poor—
Not rich at any rate, no no! not he!
Just a little bit of proppity
On the Northside, a place they called the Height,
2260 And mortgaged heavy to Tommy Tite.°
The Misthress, it's true, was gettin the name
Of a fortin somewhere; but how it came,

2226   Whiteboys: Mummers.
           a Christmas: on Christmas.
2237-42 *Omitted.*
2245   the for: reason why.
2249   Berry: Betty.
2252   waein: saying "way"; a call to a horse to stop (Moore).

Or where it was I cannot say;
But the women is allis big that way.
And when he come home—aw then the work!
And *what would become?* and that ould Turk
Of a Pazon's wife began to smell
A rat, and at him, and made him tell
About Christmas—and *he'd tried and tried,*
2270 *And he couldn help it, if he died:*
And heaven help him! and what was the use?
And he'd ither get her or he'd go to the deuce!
And at first she called him a fool; and she said
She raelly believed he was wrong in the head.
But she soon found that would navar do;
And then she came over to the Brew
To see ould Anthony's wife; and says she—
"Oh Missis Lee! oh Missis Lee!"
And *would she advise her?* and—"Oh Missis Gale!
2280 Sit down!" and—"You're lookin very pale!"
And *whatever?* And at it the two of them went,
And *a little sup of peppermint—*
"It's good for the narves"—and "Lawk-a-day!"
And "you gave me a start"! And "you don't mean to say!
Miss Christmas! mum—aw dear! aw dear!"
And out with it all—and "Did you ever hear!"
And *A tervil secret! and not to be tould*
On no account to a livin soul.
D'ye see how foolish the woman was?
2290 And it's often the way with people that's closs
And keepin back, and showin nothin—
They'll go to the very pesson they oughtn,
And demane theirselves to some ould churl
That's bound to blab it to all the world.
Aw dear! aw dear! they take a delight—
She tould it to Betsy that very night.
And what d'ye think the Pazon's wife
Had got to tell? God bless my life!
It wasn only George and Rose,
2300 But the Pazon! Well you'll hardly suppose—
But the Pazon, I tell ye! gettin too fond
Of Christmas, and *the carryin on—*
And—*navar sundered—* aw as jealous
As the divil himself—and who blew the bellows
But Anthony's wife? And "O Missis Gale!"
And "Yes! Missis Gale!" and "No! Missis Gale!"

2303   *sundered*: separate.

And *'deed and 'deed!* and *scoffers would mock;*
And *what a example to the flock!*
"And the family! the family
2310 You come of! Missis Gale," says she—
"Some of the very fuss that's goin!
And to think! and to think! but there's never knowin!"
That was a nice sort of talk, I'll swear,
For a wife, and a Pazon's wife to hear—
Aw takin it in as sweet as puddin—
And "Yes! my lady;" and *No! she wudn!*
And the fortin she'd brought him, and her a match
For the best in the counthry, and glad of the catch!
"Aye indeed! You'll 'scuse me, mam!
2320 But it's only spakin the truth I am!"—
And on and on. And would ye belafe
A woman that kep her soul in a safe,
And the keys hid away in the very guts
Of her d—— ould head, like worms in nuts,
Would give an ould craythur like Misthress Lee
The chance to take such a liberty?
But jealous! jealous! or mad? which is it?
Aw it's the divil's own claw in any one's gizzit!
And pride and dacency will go
2330 When that ould cock begins to crow.
And Misthress Lee—dy'e think for a minute
The ould humbug believed there was anythin in it?
Not her! that's just the talk ye see,
Ould Peggy was hearing and tellin to me
Long after; but the very next day—
To Betsy—it was another say—
Poor Missis Gale now! dear! aw dear!
What was at her! and—tervil queer!
And—the notions and the stuff she'd got!
2340 And *she ought to be ashamed, she ought!*
D'ye hear! of coorse! But true it ess—
Rael good women is very scess!

And the two of them made it up, I suppose,
To have it out with the Christmas Rose.
And old Anthony's wife was tellin how,
And what she said, and all the row.
And they got her in the parlour together,

2307	*'deed and 'deed*:	indeed and indeed.
2328	gizzit:	gizzard.
2338	*at her*:	the matter with her.
2341	ess:	is.

And George not at home, nor the Pazon ether:
And then she turned up the whole o' the middin;
2350 And Lee's wife backed her, but she said she didn,
But I know she did, but navar mind!
And first about George—*the good and the kind*
And the studdy he was used to be—
"Now wasn he? wasn he? Missis Lee!"
And "Yes;" and *what had come over him then!*
And allis down at that wretched den.
Manin the Bull—and *what was he doin*
At Oxford College? nothin but ruin!
And Christmas!" she says, "what are we to do?
2360 And—it's all—it's all—on account of you!"
And Christmas looked—but she sat quite still—
And looked; and her look was terrible—
Misthress Lee was saying—and with that look
The Misthress got quite 'cited and shook
And trembled all over, and went on quicker,
All flurried lek, like a woman in liquor—
And cryin and cryin! and *what hed she done?*
And—"Oh my son! my son! my son!"
But when she cried in that distress,
2370 The Christmas flew like a bird to her brest,
And clung and clung; and "Mother dear!
Oh let me! let me! let me be here!
Mother! mother! oh be my mother!"
And Missis Gale gev a kind of a shuddher—
"Oh I long for your love! oh if—oh if—"
But Missis Gale got very stiff—
"If I could always be like this!
Your child! your own! oh one *one* kiss!—"
And the mawther gev her a little pat,
2380 Betwix the shoulders, just like that!—
Coaxin though—"O mother! mother!"
Says Christmas, "George is a darling brother—
But more than that—" and she kind o' moan't—
"O mother! mother! oh don't! oh don't!"
And—"Some other time," she says, "I'll try,"
Says the Christmas Rose, "to tell you why.
But now!" she says, and she cuddled to her—
"I navar was like this before!
Love me mother!"—Aw the Misthress' face
2390 Was a thing to see—and "Listen!" she says—
"Will you have George? oh I'm goin mad!

2357 Manin: meaning (ed.).
2383 moan't: moaned.

O Christmas! have him! for the love of God!"
Then Christmas lifted her face, and sent
All the love and the wonderment
And the pain and the longin and the sighs
Straight into that ould woman's eyes.
And—"Be merciful!" she said, and bent
Her head again; but the woman meant
No mercy—no! "Stand off!" she cried,
2400   And all the rage and all the pride
And all the jealousy come tearin
In one blast through her soul, like the way you're hearin
A storm in the woods on a winter's day,
When the trees has no sap, and cranches away.
"Stand off! you viper!" she said; and *oh
If she'd only known this long ago,*
"I'd have smothered her, I'd have smothered her
In her cradle!" she said—Missis Lee didn stir,
But snivelin lek—"I would!" she said:
2410   "*Mother!* and *Mercy!*" and she spread
Her arms all wild—"Oh I know your art;
And you've robbed me of my husband's heart!"
And then she went on, and ravin and ravin,
That Misthress Lee thought it was time to be lavin.
But—"No! Missis Lee!" and "The wretch! and the schamer!"
And—"Look on her, Missis Lee! and shame her!"
And *what of Rose?* aye! what of Rose?
All the blood that was in her froze,
And she stood like an image made of stone,
2420   A dreadful thing to look upon,
Ould Lee's wife said; and nither fear,
Nor anger nor anything was theer;
But just the beautiful and the strong—
And she cowed that ould woman with the bitter tongue
Till she hadn another word to say,
But down in a chair and snivelled away,
And the two of them lek houldin in,
And sniffin and snuffin and slobberin—
And never a word all the time from Rose,
2430   But keepin her eye on them; and she goes,
And out on the door, and—"The fiend! the fiend!"
Says the Misthress then—my Queen! my Queen!
And was the Pazon's wife raelly jealous!
Yes! and a woman should allis tell us
If so be we're not lovin enough—
In our ways, I mane; for we're apt to be rough,

2415   schamer: schemer.

Fo'c's'le Yarns 104

      Bein men, you know, and not thinkin about it—
      But the women, you see, can't do without it.
      They like to be loved, and the love to be showed
2440 Middlin plain—aye that's the road!
      And there's odds of women and odds of men;
      And this Misthress Gale she wouldn pretend
      She cared, and dying all her life
      Because she wasn a happy wife—
      And the Pazon not knowin, the aisy he was,
      The fire that was undher all that frost.
      For she navar made no surt of complaint,
      And goin, and seemin well content:
      So that's the way she got mad, ye see;
2450 At least—well a sort of mad it 'd be—
      And plenty of love to hev for the asin—
      Aw the poor Pazon! aw the poor Pazon!
      I navar knew was he tould or what,
      But it's lek she'd be at him after that—
      I don't know, and I don't want to know—
      Poor ould man! But, whether or no,
      He'd enough to put up with, I'll be bail,
      Aw plenty! plenty! had Pazon Gale.

          And George to Oxford again, and wuss
2460 Till ever, and kickin a tervil duss,
      And making the money fly like blazes,
      As if the chap was as rich as Crayzus.
      But not for long—for one fine mornin,
      Without ever the smallest taste of warnin,
      What did he do but ax a lot
      Of chaps to his breakfast (a way they've got—
      The quality—chut! what a fool I am!);
      And there was the eggs, and there was the ham,
      Aw a tervil spread—but George, behould yer!
2470 Was off long ago, with a gun on his shouldher
      And a dog in a chain. The chap that was tellin
      Was at College with George; and his eyes was swellin
      With tears when he tould—and a nice sort of lad,
      And tould the Pazon all he had,
      Bein come a-purpose, you know, and tryin
      To tell it the best he could, and eyein
      The Rose—yes! yes! for George had tould

2441   odds: different kinds.
2448   goin: going about her ordinary pursuits.
2451   asin: asking.
2462   Crayzus: Croesus (ed.).

The sore he was, and the sick in his sowl
About her; and her eye met yandhar young man's,
2480 And then she hid her face in her hands:
And then the ould woman began with her talk,
And the Pazon gets up to go out for a walk;
And says he to the lad—"Will you come with me?"
And over the fields and out to the sea,
The young man said: but he didn tell
Much about that, and maybe as well.
But they walked till it was gettin night,
And the Pazon, he said, was very quite;
And at last he sat down on a big ould stone,
2490 And he says—"I'd like to be alone!"
But kind—and the young man bowed and went—
Aw a very civil surt of a gent—
Not so free; but stayin at the Bull,
And sittin there, and the kitchen full,
And lookin—you know the way they'll star,
And no pipe at him, but just a cigar—
And all of them knowin of coorse what for he
Was come, and very silent and sorry.
Aw the quality doesn't think, d'ye see,
2500 Such fellows has feelins—but let that be!
Well the next we heard of this poor chap—°
He was seen somewhere a drivin a trap
To a station, and navar a dog or a gun,
And carryin on though with jokes and fun;
And then a spreein away at a feer
Somewhere about in Lancashire—
And took up with a hurdy-gurdy gel—
And trampin the country—aw well well well!
And grindin the urgan; and her on the green
2510 A poundin away with the tambourine—
Aw mad though, and goin ahead like a fool;
And down at last to Liverpool;
And aboard a brig that was just a startin
For Australia—the Orpheus,° Captain Martin—
I knew the man—and up to the diggins,
And married there to a gel called Higgins,
I'm tould a dacent woman enough;
And him stickin to her, but fond of the stuff—
And all to that; and twins, bedad!
2520 The very fuss year! aw bless the lad!

2509   urgan: organ.
2515   diggins: gold fields (*OED*).
2519   all to that: so forth.

And losin the wife, and losin heart,
And losin all; and makin a start,
And beggin about among the farms,°
With them two childher in his arms.
That's the last I heard—aw every bit!
And I'm sore whenever I think of it.

    Wait then! wait! and I'll try to tell
About the gel—about the gel—
About her—yes! yes! I know! I know
2530 You'll not take rest—just so! just so!
Still—half-a-minute—and then—and then
(I'm feelin very strange, my men!)
Half-a-minute (very queer)—
Half-a-minute—(aw dear! aw dear!)
Half-a—d—— it then! here goes!
This is what happened to the Christmas Rose.
It was harvest-time, and terrible warm,
And me a-shearin on the Lheargy farm;
And rather late givin over though,
2540 And home and a good piece of road to go,
And takin the shortest cut I could,
And crossin a stream and a bit of a wood,
And out on the headlands over the bay,
And I saw a cloud very far away,
But comin, comin, bound to come,
And the deep low growl of its thunder-drum;
And steady, steady, sollum, slow,
As if it knew where it had to go;
Comin, comin, like it would be
2550 Comin a purpose for somebody—
(Was it *them* that had the power
Gave to them in that dreadful hour?)
And low, rather low; then higher, higher,
Till it kissed the cairn with a kiss of fire—
Once—like the twinklin of an eye—
Once—and the long back suck and the sigh
Of the silence—and terrible far away
Flash flashed to flash behind the sea;
And back and back till you couldn see fuddher,
2560 Like passin something to one another.
And—was it a sheep, or was it a flag

2530   not take rest: be satisfied.
2538   shearin: reaping (ed.).
           (Lheargy: sloping (Mx. *lhargee*).
2559   fuddher: further.

That white spot on the Belfry crag?
And curious though, and wondherin
And up through the goss, and up through the ling
As quick—it was her! it was her! Yes! Yes!
Dead though, dead, and gript in her fist
A bunch of blue bells that was growin there,
And sea-pinks twisted through her hair:
And never a spot and never a speck
2570 But just a black mark under the neck;
And her breast all open—my God! that breast!
The beautifullest and the loveliest!
But I covered it up—aw I did, and I ran
Down to the Pazon's like a crazy man,
And I shouted—well! well! that'll do! that'll do!
They took her—aye them two! them two!
They took her, it's lek, to be with them
In the Heavenly Jerusalem,
Or wherever it is. And you'll aisy belave
2580 Her grave is next to the darkey's grave—
And the Pazon is often sittin theer,
Partikler in the Spring of the year—
And to this day there's no man knows
Who or what was the Christmas Rose.

Castletown
Manx National Heritage

Captain Tom And Captain Hugh

YOU'RE wantin to hear about them two,
Captain Tom and Captain Hugh,
Very well! Very well!
But it isn much of a story to tell;
But—however—it's lek you know who you've got—
Middlin willin whether or not.

    Now these two Captains they were all allowin
Was the best that was sailin out of Castletown;°
And the two of them went to school together,
10 And navar no relations ether—
But up the Claddagh agate o' buck-kyones,
And ticklin troutses under the stones,
Or down at the Race, or out at the Mull,°
Or over plaguin Lukish's bull,
Or any divilment, ye see,
Where the one was, the other 'd be;
And stickin mortal close, and backin
One another up, whatever was actin—
Backin one another still,
20 And reared though very respectable,
Lek accordin to their station;
And goin a teachin navigation,
At Masthar Cowin that was general known
For the grandest masthar that was goin,
A one-armed man—aw, I'll be bound
You had to look slippy if you went to Cowin;
That's the man that could trim a scholar;

---

11   Claddagh [*dd* as *th* in *then*; *gh* as *ch* in Scot. *loch*]: marsh; low land along rivers (Moore).°
        agate: busy with (Moore).
        buck-kyones: small fish found in shallows (Moore).
18   actin: going on.
22   goin a teachin: being taught (ed.).
23   At: by.
26   slippy: sharp

Only wink, and the hook in your collar,
And wouldn listen to no excuse,
30 And workin the kiddhag like the deuce.

So these two lads got on though, aye!
Got on, I tell ye, and passin by
Ouldher men, and very much lek'd,
And studdier till you'd expect.
So from one thing to another they kem
To be skippers of smacks, the two of them—
Masthar Corteen's—you'll have heard of hem.
No? Well, raely! but that's the way,
And every dog must have his day.

40 So when they got married, they wouldn be beat,
But it was two sisthars they were schamin to get,
And got them, by the name of Sayle,
And a nice bit of money to their tail;
And right enough, and not felt on the farm—
Aw a little money 'll do no harm,
Not it, but only just to take keer
You'll hev it on the land, d'ye hear?
Aye that's your surt—aw very nice,
And the bigger the loaf the bigger the slice;
50 But still there's some 'll take the huff,
And grab 'ill navar have enough:
But what with the lean, and what with the fat,
Maybe a hundherd pound or that;
And a little inthress in the will,
Aye—aw very comfible.

Good wives they were, let alone the tin,
And chrizzenin for chrizzenin,
Lek clocks mostly, and allis prepar'd,
But runnin each other very hard.
60 And as handsome a breed as ever you'd see,
And very nice and orderly.

For the sisthars was livin next door to each other,
And civil to all, but cautious rather;
And wouldn hev their childher tearin
Out on the sthreet, and cussin, and swearin,

30	kiddhag [*dd* as *th* in *then*]:	left hand.
34	studdier till:	steadier than.
54	inthress:	interest.
56	tin:	money (ed.).

And raggin their clothes. And Ned Ballachrink,°
The uncle, that was mostly in dhrink,
Wasn navar suffered to come nigh them,
As if his very look 'd desthroy them.
70 And still they might have been his own
He was that fond of them; and you'll navar be knowin
What the lek is feelin; but ether woman—
No matter—let her see the uncle comin
And it was up the stair with the childher straight,
And longin shockin, but not a sight
To be seen of the one of them: and maybe he'd catch
A sound like little birds under the thatch,
Or the way they stirs themselves in bushes
Of a moonlight night—you'll hear these thrushes—
80 And the Ballachrink he'd look and he'd listen,
And them knowin parfec what was he missin,
But he darn say a word, or if he ded,
It was—*some chickens they'd got on the laff*, they said;
And no lie for all, just a way to spake—
Aw, exlen women, and no mistake.

Now, it wasn often the husbands 'd chance,
To be at home together, may be once
On the summer, ye know; and you'd see the whole crew o' them
Out in the garden that was doin for the two o' them.
90 They were looking fuss-rate was yandhar chaps,
And the women wearin their Sunday caps,
And all the little things as nate, ye know—
'Deed it was worth your while to go
Of an evenin there, and look over the wall,
And as nice and as happy though for all;
And every one with his little bason
Under the trammon, aw, putty amazin!

And even the poor Ballachrink 'd be gettin
Admission them times, and the way he'd be settin
100 And eyin the childher, and axin to taste,
Half tight, you know, but the love in his face—
The sowl—and well it's a pity too
Of the lek, and puzzlin what to do—
A good nathured craythur, and 'd allis be hevvin

---

83 laff: loft.
95 for all: however.
97 trammon: elder tree.
    putty amazin: amazingly pretty.

His pockets stuffed with knobs to be gevvin
To the youngsters; and watchin, you know, and 'd try
To pop them in their porridge on the sly.
But big at the talk, aw very big;
And disputin there about the rig
110 Of a vessel, and reefin, and lee shoors,
And this and that, and to work their coorse—
Aw, it's him that 'd larn them—and "Look!" he'd say,
"D'ye see the thing?"—and—"Here's the bay;"
And—*such a wind*, and how he'd contrive her—
"Up peak, my lads, down jib, and jive her!"°
Chut! of all the foolishness!
And Captain Tom with the chin on the bress,
And smookin studdy all the while,
And maybe just a little smile.

120   But that's the when you'd see, mind you!
The difference of Captain Hugh,
That 'd turn very sharp, and walk a bit,
And rux the shouldhers, and blow the spit,
Lek contemptible lek, and growl
Like a savage dog, and couldn hould
To hear such stuff—aw, that was the man—
Impatient mostly, you'll understand—
Hot, very hot, in general—
That was Captain Hugh for all.°

130   So the years went by, and the childher grew,
And the ouldest boy of Captain Hugh
Fell in love with the ouldest gel
Of Captain Tom—aw terrible!
"Love again?" now steady! steady!
Fell in love though did this laddie.
And the nither of them knew a bit
How they ever come to think of it—
Bein reared like a sisthar with a brother,
And used, you know, of one another,
140 And no newance nor nothin for them to go
And take notions like yandhar. But even so
The day will come, the mornin star,

105	knobs: sweetmeats made of toffee (Moore).
110	reefin: rolling or folding part of a sail (ed.).
115	jive: jibe.
123	rux: shrug.
125	hould: bear.
140	newance: novelty (Moore).
140-63	*Omitted.*

When the ould 'll be new, and the near 'll be far;
And the deep-sea-soundins 'll come to the surface,
And another face 'll look out of her face;
And a throuble 'll come between that'll change her,
And you'll look, and aw she'll be just like a sthranger—
And all will be sthrange, the sea, the shore,
The very boat, the very oar,
150 The very hooks, the very baits,
The very fields, the very gates—
New sun, new moon, new heavens, new earth,
New grief, new joy, new death, new birth—
Where's the gullies? where's the gills?
Where's the turn o' the road? where's the sit o' the hills?
Is that the head? is that the bay?
Is that ould Cronk-ny-Irey-Lhaa?
Bless ye! what are you thinkin of!
Changed! changed! The land is the land of love.

160   Are ye snorin, Billy? I thought I heard ye—
All right! all right! I was goin to blackguard ye—
But avast! I see, I see—guy heng!
A body snorin is a dirty thing.

   Well this Hughie though was a reg'lar bould chap—
They were callin him Hughie after the ould chap—
Hughie, not Hugh, for a differ lek—
Aw, a plucky lad and no mistake;
A splendid hand aboord of a boat—
Aw, he'd stick to anything that 'd float—
170 Would Hughie—aye—and none of your sauce
Nor brag; and the proud the father was
To see him when he was only a little mossel
With his two reefs tied, and his jib and fo'sail—
Stole of coorse; and the sea th'd be there!
And the owner shoutin on the pier—
And my lad with the taffystick in his fist,
And strainin his back agen the list—
Aw, into the rail! into the rail!
And as sollum as if he was carryin the mail—
180 And all the sheets trained aft to his hand—

---

154   gills: deep narrow glens (Moore).
157   Cronk-ny-Irey-Lhaa: Hill of the Dayrise (Kneen).°
162   guy heng: a petty oath (Wright).°
173   reefs tied: portions of sails rolled up and tied (ed.).
176   taffytstick: tiller, lit. stick of taffy.
177   list: leaning over of the boat.
180   sheets: ropes used to adjust the sails (ed.).

And to see him lie to was raelly grand,
Waitin his chance to come over the bar,
And the father 'd call, and the owner 'd swear;
And the little rascal 'd keek like a gull
Under his boom, and wait for a lull,
And humoured the boat, and pacified her,
Feelin everything like a spider,
Till he saw the nick, and afore you'd be knowin,
His helm was up, his jib was drawin,
190 And a lift and a leap and a jerk and a joult,
And he sent her in like a thunderboult.

    Then of coorse he'd have to make the best of it,
Jawin and lickin and all the rest of it,
And done him no harm, the little midge,
And the Captain sthooin him over the bridge—
But aisy to see, whatever he done,
It's proud enough he was of the son.

    He was rather silent lek was the Captain,
And not the sort of a man to be rapt in
200 A son or a gun—but he said one day
To the ould High-Bailiff° down on the quay
That Hughie 'd take a boat through the Sound
With any man in Castletown.
So the High-Bailiff gave a little laugh,
And, "What!" he says, "through the Sound of the Calf!
I doubt it, Captain!" he says, "I doubt it:"
And the people was tellin they had words about it.

    But that may be—but still, dear heart!
There's no doubt at all the lad was smart.
210 I've seen him myself coming under our quarter
And the skiff at him there nearly full of water;
And he'd lay alongside for a bit to bail her,
And then he'd cast off, and take and sail her,
And just a little latteen with a hook at it,
And he'd make the harbour when we couldn look at it.

184	keek:	peep.
188	nick:	of time.
195	sthooin:	driving
205	Sound of the Calf:	narrow channel between the Calf of Man and the main island (ed.).
211:	at:	with.
214	latteen:	also *lateen*, a triangular sail suspended by a long yard at an angle of about forty-five degrees (*OED*).
	at:	to.

Smart he was, but silent very,
Like the father, you know, and navar merry
Nor frisky lek, but thoughtful still—
For the skipper could talk when he had the will;
220 Aw, it's himself that had the bitter tongue,
Partikler when he was a little sprung,
And terbil standin on his right;
But as for the boy he was allis quite.
And if the father loved the lad,
He wasn showin it much bedad—
Short and sharp and hard to plaise—
Aw, he wasn a lovin man in his ways
At all—no! no! But the lad was lovin;
Even when he was a little thing he'd be shovin
230 Hisself betwixt the father's legs,
The way a little puppy begs;
And the Captain's hand on the little mop
Just absent-lek, and wouldn stop
Whatever he was doin, or maybe
Doin nothin at all; and the little baby
Rubbin and rubbin and feelin him,
And the Captain sittin very grim—
And navar a kiss for the little sowl,
Nor nothin, the craythur! so I'm tould.
240 But there's pessons like that though, isn there, John?
Starin out at the horïzon!
Some people's allis up the mast
Cockin their eye to a spyin-glass.
It's well to look a little nearer
And—bits of infants—what's more dearer?

But the son was lovin the father greatly—
Aw tuk up in him complately;
And grew to be the very prent
Of the skipper—he did—lek tuk and bent
250 To the shape of him—and the face and the walk,
And the turn and the look, and the nose like a hawk
And the chin like an egg, and the throat like a bell—
Grew lek, grew; and of coorse you will;
Not thinkin, you know, but lookin—aye!
Lookin, lookin, and takin joy—
There's childher that doesn, and childher that does—
A surt of comedher, I wouldn thrus';
But still a father you know—that way—

---

257   comedher [*dh* as *th* in *then*]: fascination.
      I wouldn thrus': I would not trust, I rather think.

And the fond and all, but it's hard to say—
260 There's men that's a charmin other men,
And hardly knowin the lek is in—
Hard men too, and gev to be close—
Some power that's at them, I suppose,
Like rubbed with somethin—what's its name?
Loadstun—aye; and women the same.
Hapes—that you wouldn be givin two screws for,
And gettin more love till they've got any use for,
And others aqual goin without,
And still a dale of it about.

270   Now this lad was a very gentle surt,
And hadn none of the fiery spir't
That was in the father—it's faithful he was,
Faithful, and houldin terbil fast
To them he liked, and perseverin
Uncommon—look at the ither steerin,
And you'd know the odds; for Hughie was all
For humourin, but the skipper would haul
On a wind no matter how it was blow'n
Just like a dog 'd be peelin a bone,
280 Greedy, you know, like a hungry dog,
Greedy, suckin his luff like grog.

    That's the way, and Hughie would look
On the sea like a man would read in a book,
Spellin big spells, and gettin them right,
But the Captain would stand like sniffin a fight
Far off—he would—like challengin,
Suspicious lek, like sayin—"Now then!
You're at it! are ye? Who'll strike first?
Come on ould stockin! do your worst!"
290 Like the sea and himself was swore in their teeth
To fight it out to the bitter death—
Half in anger, half in scorn,
Defyin it, as if he was born
A purpose to triumph and have the rule of it,
Or draw its cork, and make a fool of it.

    Chut! there's no luck with yandhar kind
But navar mind! navar mind!

261	is in:	that they exist.
276	odds:	difference.
281	suckin his luff:	sailing close to the wind (ed.).
295	draw its cork:	get the better of it.

Lookin so proud—but the lek 'll get lave!
Rather like lookin for a grave—
300 Seemin to me—but—very well!
And—maybe a notion—but time will tell.
And just the same ashore as afloat,
Allis restless, and facin to 't,
Like doubtin if he turned his back
The sea 'd be takin advantage lek.

Do you see the men?—well—does or doesn,
Annie they were callin the cousin—
A shockin nice gel, but slandhar though,
Slandhar, and very soople, you know;
310 And the hair she had, aw bless my sowl,
Cables and cables, and 'd take and rowl
And rowl them there, and stick a pin,
And the nice and the smooth astonishin.

She was a terbil modest gel was that,
And clane uncommon, and the little brat,
And the little strings, and altogether—
Not azackly handsome ether,
No, she wasn; but to see her smile—
By gogh I'd ha' walked a hundred mile—
320 I would—the sudden it came to be sure,
The sudden and the sweet and pure,
And spreadin out like some lovely rose,
And fadin away like the sunset goes,
When you'd think it wasn willin to die,
And it's fit to make a body cry.
So these two craythurs got in notions—
Like it 'd be a surt of commotions
Of throuble lek that was doin on them,
And hard enough to understand them,
330 Bein used of each other anyhow—
And why were they goin to be diffrin now?
Just like things that's caught in the trawl,
Wonderin what was there at them at all.

So of course they only got shier and shier,

298	the lek 'll get lave: such people will get leave—may do what they like . . . yet, etc.
315	brat: apron.
319	gogh: gough [*gh* as in Scot. *loch*], "a softened form of 'God'" (Moore).
326-36	*Omitted.*

Like two people shiverin over a fire—
Aw, as shy as any bird on the wing,
Till the mothers began to see the thing—
And lookin and signin, and hummin and hemmin,
And terbil plased—the way with women.
340 Aw, then the collogin that was done,
And her with the daugher, and her with the son;
And tuk a opportunity,
And had it out as nice as could be—
Hughie's mother that was spakin—
And—*whatever capers were they takin!*
And—"Why don't you laugh, and why don't you talk?
And why don't you hev a little walk?"
And—"Come, man! give your cousin a kiss!"
And—"Bless my heart! what foolishness!"
350 Aw, if Hughie didn make for the door
Like a shot, and Annie on the floor;
But hauled her up, and slacked the dress of her,
And coaxed, and wouldn take no rest of her,
And made her tell, and aised her shockin
The way her heart was goin a knockin—
Poor thing!—and a little taste of rum—
Aw, bless ye! it's terbil hard with some—
Aw, yis!—and people should be kind
To the lek, and get them to clear their mind.
360 (Now aisy that laughin, Bobby—what?
Well, you know, I'd *ax* you not.)

So she tould them though, and then they went
And looked for Hughie, and found him lent
Again the trammon; and "Why, man, why?"
And—"Nonsense! Hughie!" and "Try, man! try!"
And got him in, you'll understand,
And put them sittin hand in hand,
Aw, beautiful, and left them there,
And the dark, you know, he could hardly see her.

370 Then the two women took a sthroull
Along the shore, and the nither ould;
But still it's lek there 'd be a little sigh,
And I wouldn trust but a little cry,
Lek happy, you know, but middlin plain
Their time would navar come again.
And I was tould there was some that seen them too,

---

340   collogin: consulting.
345   *capers*: absurd ideas.

And they were sayin that Annie's mother threw
Her arms very lovin around the sister,
And hung to her a dale, and kissed her—
380　And so they went together linking,
And very peaceful lek, and thinking.
And tears is tears, no matter the from;
But he was a fuss-rate husband was Captain Tom.

　　　Fuss-rate he was—and gennaler
There couldn be, nor heartier.
Aw, happy was the people that bred him,
And happy was the woman that hed him.
But 'deed the happiest of the lot
Was the man himself the way he got
390　To make other people happy; his face
Was reglar bustin with happiness—
My sakes! the laugh! you navar heard!
It was allis snugglin in his beard
Somewhere, you know, bein curly very;
But when he gev way, a blast in a quarry
Was just a fool to it—Nebuchadnessar!°
Rattlin the very plates on the dresser.

　　　And the same man was terbil wise,
And givin people good advice—
400　About bezniss lek—there's some 'll remember—
But of coorse—my gough! the judge of tember,
And gardens and that—aw, every craft!
But he'd hev his laugh, he'd hev his laugh!

　　　But the fust these women had to do
Was to tell their story to Captain Hugh—
Mad—did ye say? God bless ye! *mad!*
No, not him—the mad or the glad,
Nor the yes or the no, nor the good or the bad,
Nor the nothin arrim; just a spit,
410　And a puff o' the pipe to see was he lit,
And his head on his chin° and his eye on the say;
So the women had to go away.
"Well!" says Annie's mother, "he's tould!"
"Yes!" says the sesther, but cryin, the sowl!

　　380　　linking: arm-in-arm.
　　382　　the from: the source.
　　384　　gennaler: kindlier.
　　409　　arrim: at him, on his part.

       And it's allis the same—aw, very nice,
And raisonable to rejoice
When two young things is comin together—
But there's sure to be a bit of bother
About it someway—aw, by George!
420 There's lumps in every body's porr'dge;
Like ould Jemmy the Red that druv to the packet,
One hos 'd go forrit, and the other backit—
"Dear me!" the people said;
"There's nothin puffeck," says Jemmy the Red.

       Now, Captain Tom was in Ireland over;
But the very minute they saw the Rover°
(The smack he was skipper of) makin the Mull,°
Aw, then the women took heart to the full—
'Deed if they were smellin Captin Tom in the offin
430 The whole of Castletown 'd be laughin
Mostly—the liked, you'll understand—
Aw, a terrible man, a terrible man!

       So somebody tould him, and he slapped the thigh
And come ashore in a blaze of joy—
In a blaze—and "Where is she? where is she, then?
The little rascal!" and—*how*, and *when?*
And—*bless his sowl!* and —*to think the deep!*
And, "Come here! come here! you little sweep!"
And—"Hughie! Hughie! Tyre and Sidon!"°
440 And—"Annie! Annie!" but Annie was hidin.
But caught at the mother somewhers in the yard,
"Ha! ha!" he says, "ha! ha! my bird!
What!" he says, "you don't know me, may be!"
And tuk her off her feet like a baby;
And clapsed her to his besom there,
And kissed her eyes, and kissed her hair,
And kissed and kissed her everywhere—
Shockin for kissin! noted for it—
Was Captain Tom. There's people horrit
450 That way with their slimin and slobberin,
But Captain Tom was differin.
But still—Well, in come Hughie, though,
And he dropt the gel, and he gev a crow
Out of him like a cock, very clear—
Like a cock that way—very pleasant to hear,

---

431   the liked: because he was so much liked.
438   sweep: good-for-nothing (Moore).
441   at: by.

Hearty—eh? and gript him straight,
And stood him off agin the light;
And—"The sakes!" and—"Deed on Hughie for all!
Capital! capital!"
460 And his face like the sun. And—"Hould up!" says he,
"Hould up for all! I want to see—
(And Hughie lookin rather semple)
The polished corners of the temple—
What's this ould David is sayin in the Psalm?
Bless my heart! the stupid I am!
The corners, it's sayin, *the polished corners*,
And—*splendid sheep*, it's sayin, and the *garners
Full of store.*°—I like you, my lad!
I like you! you'll do! you'll do!" he said.
470 And—"Where's your father?" he said to him then;
"Dear me! he isn half a man!"
And a passil of women outside gev a shout—
"You've gor it!" they said; and he turned about—
"Hulloah!" says he, and a surt of a roor;
"You're right!" says the women at the door.
"He's agin the match!" says the women, "he is!"
"Come now! I tell ye! be off out of this!"
Says Captain Tom's wife—*Well, dear heart!*
And—*it was only the truth they were tellin.* "Start!"
480 Says Captain Tom's wife; so the women cut,
And tossin the head, and—*A saucy slut!*
And, "Says is says, and thinks is thinks!"
And—*They were allis high, them Ballachrinks!*

And the talk was soon all over the town
That the one Captain knocked the other down,
And—*a desperate fight!* but of coorse they hedn,
And—*the evil eye that was on the weddin*
At Captain Hugh, and—*Careless! chat!
No use o' talkin—he was a black man*° *that!*
490 But—*Captain Tom!* and—"Did ye see him there?"
And—*that was the man! aw dear! aw dear!
Aw splendid!—the hearty and the kind!
Somethin like a father! aw, no fault to find,
But only them women!—a pair of slinks,
They hadn no patience with them Ballachrinks!*

---

458   Deed on: only to think of.
             for all: after all.
473   gor: got (ed.).
488   At: on the part of.

And it's lek there 'd be words; but—bless their stuff!
Captain Hugh was willin enough!
It wasn that. There's pessins that bright
The whole of their body is full of light;
500 Lek it's sayin in the Bible—"Take care!" it's sayin,
"If the light that is in thee turn dark again
(Lek some devil's runnet [God bless me!] thick'nin it),
Bless me!" it's sayin, "the dark you'll get!"°

But it wasn that. And still no doubt
There's people that turns theirselves inside out,
And others that turns theirselves outside in—
Was that the surt? you'll be wonderin.
No! I don't think it—or was he haunted
At some dirt of a sperrit? or was it wanted
510 Elsewhere he was? or a crick in his heart,
That he had to look another airt?
Or the devil himself, the ugly sweep!
Aw dear! aw dear! it's very deep!
They say the ould chap knows his own—
But I'll tell ye what, I'll lave it alone.

Well—this Masther Corteen I was tellin you of
Wouldn take no rest, but it's a schooner he must have—
Aw, smacks wouldn do for him at all—
Schooners! schooners! that's the call.
520 *Foolish*—you're sayin? Uplifted just—
Aw, uplifted scandalous!
For what is a schooner, if you come to that?
A slink of a thing with a side like a latt,
And bearins—eh? and stowage? my gough!
A bilge like a plane, and a hould like a trough—
That's your schooners—idikkilis!
Give me the little gel that'll kiss
Ould Bags in his teeth, and spin on her heel
Like a top, like your sweetheart dancin a reel
530 In the harvest moon—aw, a smack for ever!
Chut! you can twis' her tail like a heifer!
But—of coorse!—and them Douglas chaps 'd be talkin
And quiverin there—aw, big though, shockin—
Collister's ones, and Skillicorn,

---

502   runnet: rennet.
511   airt: way.
523   latt: lath.
528   Ould Bags: the wind.
533   quiverin: bragging.

And Moores, that was sailin a vessel for'n,
And the lek of that—aw, brigs and barks!
And galliotts, and Noah's arks!
Aw, you couldn touch the Douglas fellows—
No! and feelin middlin jealous—
540 And "I'll hev a schooner, up or down!"
And—*all for the honour of the town.*
And built at Boyds',° and no mistake,
And goin a launchin up the Lake,°
Or the Claddagh—is it? aye! and the scholars
Let urro the school,° and terbil colours;
And a canon there, and 'd hev a try,
And fired, and bust the bellman's eye—
Juan Jem—a squinty man he was,
And bust in bits—and—*not much of a loss,*
550 *At all*—I've heard the women say;
But useful is useful any day.
And a beautiful launch, you may depend,
And off the ways as smooth as a swan;
And Jacks, and Blue Peters, and stars-and-stripes,
And the name they gave her was the Clyps—
Or the Clops, or the Clups—what is it—eh?
Well, it's the Clyps they were callin her anyway.

    So then the talk was how would he man her,
And who'd be goin for a captain on her;
560 Aw, terbil talk—but of coorse they knew
It was either Captain Tom or Captain Hugh.
And a pazil of fellows down at the Crow
Was shoutin for Captain Hugh to go;
But the company over at the Crown,°
That was general countin the best in town,
Ould Mollachreest, and Corkish the baker,
Was all for Captain Tom to take her.
So you see the people was mortal divided,
And a bit of a row, and reglar enjoyed it;
570 And—*Wait then! wait!* and—*All serene!*
He wasn no fool, wasn ould Corteen—
No! And who was the head man d'ye think?
Who of coorse but the Ballachrink?
Down at the Crow there every night,
And glasses round, and as tight as tight;
And—*Healths apiece!* and—*What'll ye take?*

---

545   urro: out of.
554   Jacks . . . Blue Peters: Union Jacks . . . blue signal flags (ed.).
555   Clyps: *Cyclops.*

Bless me, the mischief them dunkies 'll make!
He gor a notion that time, you see,
A notion arrim how would it be
580 If he could just sundhar the captains a lill
That they wouldn be lek that agreeable
Lek they were used to be, on the one hand lek,
That the poor divil hadn the smallest speck
Of a chance, you see, to get his foot in
The either house; for he didn care a button
About the sesthars, but just he was cravin
For the childher—aye! aw, reglar ravin!
But how would it be now, how would it be!
"They'll have to give me more libbity!"
590 He says; and then he begun to think,
And he seen there wasn the smallest chink
Betwix Tom and the wife; and—"The smoother the wall
The harder to climb," says Ned for all—
Aw, Ned was sharp enough in his way—
He could tell was there shuggar in his tay—
Could Ned; he knew where to hommer a tack in,
So it's Captain Hugh that he was backin.
Backin uncommon; and tervil truck
Betwix them too, like an aigle tuk
600 To be friends with a pay-cock—that was about it—
And he puffed and he blowed, and he roored and he shoutit,
And he quivered the fiss; and "What!" he said,
"Captain Tom to walk over the head
Of Captain Hugh! What sense!" he was sayin;
And—*God bless his soul! and wasn it plain?*
Captain Tom! of coorse! of coorse!
But—Captain Hugh, they were on deffrin floors
Altogether—Was it blind they were?
Did they know who they had? Was there any compar?
610 And—"The two of them," he says, "is relations
Of mine;" he says, "but, my gough! my patience!"
And snaps the fingers, and taps the stick,
And gives a nod, and around as quick,
And faces up agin one of the men
Behind him there; and at it again—
And over the Craves, and all down New-street,
And up Kirk Arbory and Kirk Malew-street,
And the Green, and Cowles, and the Flukin' pool,°
Everywhere you'd hear this fool—

579	arrim:	at him, in his head.
598	truck:	communication, intimacy.
602	quivered:	shook (Moore).
616	Craves:	a street in Castletown.

620 But special at the Crow—Aw, there
He was all in his glory, and tuk the cheer,
And wondherful considern the gin—
You'd had thought it was the High-Bailiff himself that was in—
Proposed and seconded—and—*Them
That's in favour*—you know—aw, bless ye! it came
As natheral—amazin though
The way the lek can work the jaw—
And he stuck to Captain Hugh like a leech,
And grips the arm, and over the beach,
630 And past the quay, and down the pier,
Showin him off lek walkin there,
And the nose on the cock, like snuffin skallions,
Lek—*Clear the road!* lek these chaps with stallions.

But, howsomedever—Peter or Paul,
Captain Tom was the captain for all—
Aye, he was—of a Saturday night
The orders were out, and a reglar fight
At the Countin-house door—and—"Who then? who?
Is it Captain Tom? Is it Captain Hugh?"
640 And—"Hip hoorah!" and over the town,
And away to the Crow, and away to the Crown—
And the Ballachrink though, sittin as grand,
And the pipe in his mouth, and the glass in his hand—
Aw, a terrible big man at the Crow,
A sort of a gentleman, you know—
The way with these farmers—and his Sunday hat,
And a frill on his shirt, and all to that.
And—"Well!" he says, "There's no mistake
Who's goin for Captain; it's all correct,"
650 He says, "its settled," he says, "my hearties;"
And—*Of coorse!* and—*The influential parties
That was at Corteen, and not once nor twice;
But the man knew where to go for advice;
Aye! aye! and gor it; and what for wouldn he?
A brother-in-law! and what for shouldn he?
But wait! but still*—aw, dear! to think!
"I'll lave it to you then, Ballachrink."
In the parlour—aye! "But mind ye! my men,
You'll navar be mentionin this again!"
660 Aw, all in his glory—and the chaps goin nudgin
And winkin there, the way you'd be judgin
He'd see they were laughin; and did and didn;
Lek you'll see a cock upon a midden,

---

647   to that: so forth.

Scratchin—lek he was saying to the hens—
"Look out!" he says, "my gough! there's grains!
There's grains!" he says; and the dirt goin flyin;
And he'll scratch and scratch, and the hens 'll be eyein
One another, and smilin lek,
And may be bitendin to give a little peck,
670 For manners, you know, lek knowin his way,
But just the same lek mainin to say—
For all he thinks hisself that clever—
"The ould chap's gettin wuss till ever!"

Well, there he was, so in comes a lad,
And—"It's Captain Tom that's got her," he said—
Aw, the poor Ballachrink! "You sniffikin falla!"
(You could ha' heard him up at Ballasalla)°
"You blockit!" he says; "how dar ye!" he says;
"Ger urro that!" and quevers the fist—
680 Aw, the chap made tracks—And—"I muss I muss!"
Says the Ballachrink, "or else I'll buss."
And he laughed and he laughed—and "Keep her so!"
And—"Certainly! but knowin, you know!"
And the laugh—But it wasn long before
The whole mob-beg was outside of the door,
And no mistake, and "Hip Hooraa!
It's Captain Tom—where's ould Dadaa?"
Maenin the Ballachrink—the fond
He was of the childher; and—"*Where was he gone?*"
690 And—"Hurroose!" Aw, bless ye! no respeck
At these lumps of boys, aw, that's a fack!

But the Ballachrink begun to look queer,
And he gev a start, and he gev a stare;
And Corteen's head clerk come in through the row,
And no mistake about it now—
And the Ballachrink gev a leap and a cry,
Aw, dear! but he made the pint-joughs fly,
And his hair all on end, and his mouth all frothin—
"Hugh!" he said; but Hugh said nothin—
700 "I'll go myself," he says, "this minute;
I'll know what raison is there in it;
What right, what dacency, what sense!

---

669   bitenden: pretending.
676   sniffikin: insignificant.
679   Ger urro: get out of.
685   mob-beg: little mob; mob of boys.
697   pint-joughs [*gh* as in Scot. *loch*]: ale mugs.

Clear the road! I'll go at once!"
"Aw, stay where you are!" says the clerk; "when a bone
Is picked, it's batthar to lave it alone;"
He says, says the clerk—Aw, then the fury—
You navar—Herod, King of Jewry,
With all his tantrims, couldn touch him!
"*Ruch!* is he? the dirty ould fool! I'll *ruch* him!"
710 And out in the lobby, but he didn get no furdher—
"Here's ould Dadaa comin! Murdher! murdher!"
The people began; and he strooghed his clothes,
And studdied hisself agin the post,
And gev them a speech—aw, didn he though?
And this and that—and—*He'd hev them to know;*
And—*the rale ould blood; and—a black disgrace,*
And a shame and a scandal to the place;
And—"Justice!" he says; and—"We'll hev it bynby!"
And—Captain Tom! he wouldn deny—
720 *But him to be captain of a schooner!*
Did they think he ever worked a lunar
In his life, or heard of the lek? not him!
And Captain Hugh that knew the trim
Of every craft that ever floated
And could work his distance; and noted, noted!
Noted! he said, *for the navigation—*
"God bless me! let every man keep to his station!"
"Hooraa!" says the people, "that's the stick!
Gev it to them! gev it to them, Dick!"
730 And a hiss in his ear—"That'll do! that'll do!"
And turns—and there was Captain Hugh—
Like the thunder itself—and—"Draw these men
Some liquor!" he said to the woman; and then—
"Come!" he says, and just like a stone—
The poor Ballachrink! and liquor goin!
But it wasn no use—like a stone! like a flent!
"Stand back the lot!" and away they went.

And—"The childher! aw, the childher though!
Aw, Hugh, good soul!" and—*whither or no,*
740 And—*it wasn his fault—now was it? was it?*
"Aw, the childher! aw, the little closet!
Aw, Hugh!" and—"You promised! yes! you did!
Aw, let me see the craythurs in bed!"
And cryin—bless ye! Wasn Billy Fauldher

---

709   *Ruch*: rich.
712   strooghed: stroked, straightened.
721   lunar: an observation of moon and stars for navigation (ed.).

Sheltrin behind a yawl there?
And didn he hear? and fit to split—
But I'd be thinkin it was rather a bit
Sorrowful lek—but all depandin—
And he wouldn go on; and he kept him standin
750 Agin the boat—and—"Do la! do!"
"You're far too drunk to-night," says Hugh.
"No! no!" he says; "just look at me then!
The sober I am is astonishin!"
And coaxed and coaxed, and—*the careful he'd be!*
Till at last the Captain said he'd see.
"In bed! in bed! aw, honour bright!"
Says the Ballachrink; "All right! all right,"
Says Captain Hugh; "And you'll get them to say
Their little prayers though anyway—
760 Yes! yes! aw, Hughie! the little prayers!
Aw, whose is God listnin to, if it isn theirs?
Bless father and mother (the little birds!)
And uncle Edward! isn them the words?
Eh? Hughie, eh? aw, the lovely things!
Like angels, lek tuckin their little wings
Under their shirts, and the hands it's lekly
Goin clapsin there! aw, let's start directly!
Come Hughie!" "The dhrunk ye are to be sure!"
Says Hugh; and so they come to the door.
770 And they axed for a light, and it's up they'd go;
But the mistress didn half like it, ye know,
Deed she didn—and *What sort of a state*
Was that to be comin, and couldn they wait
Till the mornin—and the childher fast—
And it was reglar out of all order it was—
Yes! And she did objeck, she did,
And they'd better take and be off to bed
Theirselves. And—"As for that sot," says she;
"Aye, woman? Is it erluding to me
780 You are?" says the Ballachrink, "now is it?
Because, if a gentleman pays a visit
To his brother-in-law," he says, "he's expectin
Quite a differin way of actin—
Now look here!" he says, "I'll tell you what!
It's just the dirty temper you've got—
That's it! the dirty temper—aye!
Aw, ye needn begin to cry—
You're the talk o' the town," he says, "with your tongue!
Capers!" he says; "and you're not so young

---

750   la: interjection: Mx. *lah*, lad (Moore).

790 But you might have some sense," he says, "with it too!"
"Hould your jaw!" says Captain Hugh—
"The light!" he says; "I mane to hev it!
The light! the light!" and the woman gev it;
And the brat to her face, and followed them there,
And sobbin lek, and up the stair—
And freckened of fire, and stood outside
The door—the soul! and cried, and cried.

So these two divils in to the childher—
And a little boy, and a little gel there—
800 Aw, beautiful! as white as snow—
The very best of calico!
Bless ye! there wasn no houldin them chaps!
And the little frills around their caps
And all—aw, they'd hev it! aw, deed they would!
They'd hev it, and they'd hev it good!
And three bedrooms there, and all with ceilins!
Money! bless ye! like priddha peelins!
Aw, square was square, and round was round,
And Castletown was Castletown
810 Them times—aw, it's there the money was made—
Hapes! man; hapes! my gough! the trade!

So the Ballachrink made a run and a dart
And the little things wakened with a start—
And the big man there! and his face as red!
And the hair goin flyin about his head!
And slobberin, you know—but seein the father—
Aw, he was for atin them altogether,
Clane devourin—"Aw, dear! the soft!
The lovely!" he says—"Hands off! hands off!"
820 Says Captain Hugh—"Aw, just a touch!
Aw, one little foot! aw, it isn much!"
"No! no!" says Hugh; "Keep agin that wall!"
The women, ye see, was tellin all—
Knowin! God bless ye! Peggy Shimmin!
What *ar'n* they knowin? catch the women!

So the Ballachrink got quite, they were sayin,
Humble lek, and didn complain,
Nor nothin—but "The little prayer," he says,
"And the little hymn, and the little vess—
830 *Blessed Jesus! strong to save!*"°

---

794   brat: apron.
807   priddha: potato.

Aye! but he promised he'd behave.
So then these little things was riss,
And put on their knees agin the chiss
And "Our Father" they said though, very nice,
But rather trimblin with their little vice;
And then they rose the hymn—aw, dear!
Like little robin-redbreasts there—
Aw, the Ballachrink was done complate,
And he cried and cried most desperate,
840 Puttin them out, you'll understand;
And then these little mossels began,
And cried treminjus; and the mother couldn hould
Any longer, and she come in, poor soul!
And there was Ned, and the tears goin splatch,
Like the rain is drippin off the thatch:
But Hugh was turned away, and he stood,
And his face was fixed on the risin flood;
And a scran of a moon hung dead in the south,
And navar a word from the ither man's mouth,
850 But—"Jean myghin orrin, peccee hrie"—
The Ballachrink was groanin—aye!
Lek you'd be know'n, if you could understand him,
For the Lord to have mercy lek upon him—
Just so—And "It's not much *myghin* you'll get,"
Says the sesthar, and hushed the childher a bit—
"*Myghin* indeed!" But then she thought
He was her brother, and the ould spot,
And the times, you see, when they were young;
And she checked the anger on her tongue,
860 And she went and put her head on his shouldher,
And she saw the man the way he looked ouldher
And broken lek, and "Look up!" she said,
"Look up man, Edward! be comforted!
And come down stairs with me, man, come!
And warm, and then you'll be goin home!"
"Aw, no!" he says, "I like this place—
There's a dale of pace, a dale of pace
Here," he says; but she coaxed him though,
And coaxed, and got him persuaded to go,
870 And sat a bit, but didn spake;
And then the woman got him to take
A basin of milk to study him
And tuk and led him across the strame,

---

848   scran: scrap.
850   Jean myghin . . . hrie [pronounced *jen muh´ghun*; *gh* as *ch* in Scot. *loch*]: Have mercy upon us, miserable sinners.—*Litany*.°
854   myghin: mercy.

And into the town, and very quite,
And got the hoss, and home with him straight.

So you'll be thinkin? not a bit of it!
Bad blood! bad blood! and they couldn get quit of it.
For whataver you might do or say,
You know what was Hugh, so that's the way.
880 Bad blood! I tell you. And you'll aisy suppose
Whenever the Clypse was showin her nose,
By gough! the very first trip that was arrer
Captain Hugh was waitin for her
Aback o' Langlish; and the two of them,
The smack and the schooner in ballast trim;
Aw, he gev her a dustin—and raison he wud,
Just a dead beat at them all the road—
Aw, she could hev gev the schooner 'crase,
Mortal sleppy in her stays
890 Was yandhar smack—the Mona's Pride°
They were callin her, and built at Boyd
The same as the Clyps, but a dale more spring,
With the worked, you know, and everything
Like shuttles runnin; but new or ould
A smack with a schooner! bless my sowl!
So it was allis racin after that,
Racin, racin, for he wouldn be beat:
Blow high, blow low; come fire, come thunder,
Everything she could shiver under—
900 Sky-rakers, moon-scrapers—
And talk about them in the papers.
And he'd be hidin there with his topsail low'rt
In Dreshwick somewhere, or under the Fort;°
And Captain Tom 'd be lyin to,
To see would he go ahead, you know;
But the fo'sil 'd be over like a shot,
And he'd wait; and it's wuss and wuss he got,
Stickin to Captain Tom like a leech,
And they navar come to no manner of spcech
910 About it at all—Captain Tom 'd hav' lekt,
But Hugh—well, you see, you could hardly expect.

882	arrer:	at her, she had.
884	Langlish:	Langness (the peninsula forming the eastern shore of Castletown Bay—ed.).
888	'crase:	increase, start.
893	with the worked:	on account of having been worked so much.
903	Dreshwick:	Dreswick Point on Langness (ed.).
906	fo'sil:	foresail (ed.)

Then the Ballachrink got a notion, you see,
It was his duty to look after the family
When Hugh was away—aw, terbil big!
And he'd come and he'd sit outside in the gig,
And call to the sesthar; and—for her *to look smart*—
And—this and that—and—"Bless my heart!"
And—"Look here!" and—*did she understand?*
And—*mind she wasn extravagan!*
920 And—"Hould this hoss!" and *he'd hev a look;*
And—*was she puttin everythin in a book?*
And in with him there; and piffin and puffin,
And op'nin the cupboard, and sniffin and snuffin;
And—"Very well!" he'd say, "but you see
Of coorse your husband is lookin to me!"
And up the stair, and eyein about him.
It's a wonder to me she didn clout him;
But no! she didn, but held the hoss—
A patient craythur if ever there was.

930 One day he come, and spades and picks,
And the manservant with him, and—*They were goin to fix
The garden*, he said; and—what did they do
But tuk and divided the garden in two
With a lump of a hedge? So the women said—
"Whatever!" "I'll tell ye *whatever*," says Ned:
"The *whatever*—it's a sundherin;"
He said, "A separationin!
Come now! that's the whatever!" says he;
Says the women—"Where's your 'torrity?"
940 "'Torrity!" says Ned, "aw, dear!
Is it 'torrity?" he says, "look here!
Whose writin is that—eh? Chapter and vess!
I think you'd better go in," he says.
And sure enough he had the letter
From Captain Hugh; so says he "You'd better
Go in," says the Ballachrink, "and mind
Your business," he says; and the women cryin,
But went; and the hedge was finished grand—
Separationin! bless the man!

950 So that's what Captain Hugh wanted,
And a fuss-rate job, and quicksets planted
By the time he come home—and the Ballachrink
To show him all; and—"See that sink!"

---

934   lump of: good-sized.
939   'torrity: authority.

He says, "and the barrel there agen it!
See the splendid brass tap that's in it
This side!" he says, "to share the water!
Aw, dear!" he says, "look at yandhar daughter
Of Captain Tom's," he says, "she's smilin!
Imprince!" he says; but Hugh was silen'.
960 But the Ballachrink was cock of the walk,
And swellin the breast, and workin the talk—
And wheelin the pipe, and pintin to this,
And pintin to that—and—"It isn amiss!"
And—"Take that handle! turn that tap!
Sherwood's best! I wouldn gev a rap
For your rubbidge," he says; "just feel that movemen'!"
He says, "chut! a terrible improvemen'
Altogether, you know! aw, dear!"
And in to get a drop of beer.

970   And sure enough it was Annie they seen,
That was standin there with Bella Corteen,
A grand-daughter of the owner's—aye!
Aw, a reglar lady! but noways high—
Aw, very gennal, aw, reglar frens!
She's married to a pazon since—
Yes—and indeed it's smilin she was
Was Annie; and she hed a cause;
For she loved her uncle—the sort of a man
That women 'd love, and not understand
980 What for were they lovin—the deep, I suppose,
And the dark, and the strong—but, goodness knows!
An uncle anyway—and the poor little woman!
Smilin—eh? and Hughie comin!
And 'deed he was entrin on the door
That very minute, and happy thallure;
And out in the garden, and gev a run,
And over the hedge like the shot of a gun,
Hardly mindin the lek was in—
But the Ballachrink was noticin,
990 Watchin there, cocked up in the windher;
And he turns, and "Hulloah!" and "Did ye see yandher?"
He says to Hugh—"You'll jump it, will ye!
Jumpin! jumpin is it, my gillya?
But for all the jumpin, if I was you,
I'd teach him——" "Drop it! drop it!" says Hugh;
And he turned, and he looked at a picture though

---

985   thallure: Mx. *dy liooar*, enough, galore (Moore).
993   gillya: lad.

Of the wife afore they were married, you know.
And he looked very long, and then he went
And kissed her there; and then he lent
1000   The head of him agen the chimbley;
And then the wife come, very thrimbly,
Very lovin and gentle lek;
And she put her arm around his neck;
And you could see by the way his shouldhers was hove
The terrible the strong man strove—
And navar a word! navar a word!
But the woman was prayin to the Lord
In her heart, poor soul! fit enough to brek—
Aw, bless them! bless them! bless the lek!
1010   And the Ballachrink could only stare,
And gor up, and tuk and left them there.

    And the hedge—aw, well it was left to stand;
But what d'ye think these sweethearts planned?
Hughie that schamed it—They tuk and sowed
A passil of plants that as soon as they growed
'd creep over the hedge, and mix the flowers—
And Hughie was settin convolvolars,
And Annie was setting these—what's their name?
Painted ladies! aye, the same—
1020   Like butterflies mostly—lovely things,
With their little curly catchy strings!
"So you see," says Hughie, "whatever there 'll be,
These flowers 'll be standin for you and me;
"And they 'll be twisted together," he says,
"And breathin in one another's face.
And when I'm far away, little gel!
There they 'll be whisprin and snugglin still.
And at night there 'll be none of your goin to bed
For them like for us; but coortin" he said,
1030   "Coortin there till the mornin light—
Aw, the hard it is to say good-night!
Aw, Annie——" But bless me! what am I at?
Well—of coorse their talk 'd be somethin like that—
Just fancyin lek—aw, I wouldn say knowin;
But I'll be bail there was kisses goin.

    So when these flowers begun to grow,
They said you navar seen the show!
Astonishin the strenth! like clover!

1011   gor: got (ed.).
1019   painted ladies: sweet peas.

	And the hedge goin cov'rin over and over!
1040	And little Annie 'd come and listen,
	And settin two of them a-kissin—
	And a notion at her she heard them ringin,
	Like a surt of a cling-a-ling-a-lingin,
	Like a weddin, you know—and she'd take and kiss them
	Herself, the little bough! and she'd bless them;
	And she'd coo upon them like a little dove,
	And all in a wonderment of love—
	Longin you know—the little honey!
	Aw, dear, the sweet they are and the funny
1050	With their little ways—aw, they're very nice,
	Aw, yes they are. But she heard a vice,
	And who was there but poor ould Ned—
	And—"This place is goin to ruin," he said;
	"It's altogether goin to ruin—
	What's these painted-ladies doin?
	I see!" he says—"from the other side!
	I'll larn ye," he says, "I'll tame your pride!
	I'll make you know your place, ye trash!"
	And out with the knife, and he gev a slash—
1060	And—"Uncle! uncle!"—poor little Annie!
	"Aw, don't then! don't then!" "*Don't!* your grannie!"
	Says the Ballachrink—"I've a very great mind"—
	"Aw, uncle, be kind! aw, uncle, be kind!
	Lave them, uncle! lave them; will ye?"—
	"Very like a trespass, I can tell ye"—
	Says the Ballachrink—"by gough it is!"
	But, however, he'd consider the case;
	But didn do nothin—just puffin and blowin—
	And so the flowers was left alone.
1070	It was maybe a twelvemonth after that
	Captain Hugh come in with a flat—
	That he took in tow—I forget her name—
	And everybody praisin him.
	But the people said he was terbil queer,
	Heavier and silenter
	Till ever, they said; and takin no joy
	Of anythin; and the light in his eye
	Like a turf, like smouldhrin in a pit;
	And there's plenty said he wasn fit
1080	To be in charge of a vessel at all;
	But howsomedever they hedn no call,

1045   bough [*gh* as in Scot. *loch*]: poor (little thing).
1071   flat: "a broad, flat-bottomed boat," such as a scow (*OED*).

And it wasn no business of theirs—but still
Somebody ought to be 'sponsible.

    But before he went to sea again
He sent for Annie one evenin:
And the freckened she was, not knowin the for,
But the aunt and the mother persuaded her;
And—*Maybe*, they said, *he was goin to be kinder*,
And in on the door, and shut it behind her.
1090 So there they were alone together
I dessay half-an-hour or betther
In the little parlour; and I've heard them tell
They couldn hear a syllable—
The women? The women! who else would it be?
Listnin? Listnin! certainly!

    But when Annie come out at yandhar door,
The change, they said, you'd ha' hardly knew her—
Wondherful, they said, the step
Of the gel, the springy it was, and the lep
1100 The tight, and the nails dug into the hands,
And the fingers at her just like strands
Clinched, and the head thrown back like a hoss's,
Lek you'll see these picthurs of people on crosses,
With their body all stretched like steel, like wire,
With their noses all spreadin lek with fire,
Lek lifted up, lek crucified—
The love, the misery, the pride—
My gough!—They're knowin what you're not knowin,
They're seein him upon the throne;
1110 They're sure of somethin—yes! that's it!
Bless ye! they don't care a bit!
What's the world to them? you see them—do ye?
Glory, glory! Hallelujah!
But goodness me! well, hard to say,
But it's the thruth I tell ye, from that day
The gel was changed, whatever there 'd been,
And she'd sit like seein things unseen;
And Hughie with his arm around her neck—
But very heavy and absent lek—
1120 And—"I raely think father is wrong in the head!"
"Don't say that again!" she said.
I don't know is it catchin it is
Or what—impossible to guess—

1084-1127 *Omitted*.
1086   the for: the reason (ed.).

But people that's mad has got a power—
Eh? Aw, they hev! and this little flower—
Well, well, for all—aye, even so—
Aw, a little gel, a child, you know.

    So the very next tide he was settin sail
For Liverpool; and Billy Quayle,
1130 That was used to work for him, took to his bed;
He didn like his looks, he said—
Just 'scusin; and, behould ye, though,
The Ballachrink took a notion to go—
Knowin about a vessel? not a cent!
But took a notion, and by gough he went.
And the son, young Hughie, was servin mate,
Just the three: and, of coorse, the concate
Of the Ballachrink—and criticisin
Terbil, you know, and the big advisin,
1140 And all to that—but you know the man,
Cacklin there like an ould hen
All the way—and a beautiful scamper
Before the wind; and the best o' temper
Comin up the river; and the way he was drast,
And the style altogether—there was people ast
"Who's your passenger?" 'deed they done—
And the 'spectable—astonishin!
That's what they were sayin comin up the river—
Aw, a credit to any vessel whatever!
1150 Just lek a Pazon—aw, the coat as black,
And his hands in the tails behind his back
As tight—and the sate of his trousis showin
The tasty, every step he was goin—
For the thieves you know, bein warned that way—
Aw, bless ye, whatever ye may say,
The biggest man on the Prince's pier
And Maddharell's° and everywhere—
Aw, the Ballachrink was the man that cud—
Aw, bless ye! it was in the blood!

1160   I was over there myself that time,
Just a running job with a cargo of lime
For Jefferson's; and the Clyps was moored
Alongside of us; so I jumps aboard,
And axed them were they wantin a man,
And glad enough of an extra hand,
So ships like a shot, and urro the basin

1166   urro: out of (ed.).

That tide—and the schooner, the trim for racin
She was in! but navar a notion arr us
That Captain Hugh was waitin for us
1170 Just outside the Bell bwee;
But, however, there he was, you see;
And every stitch, and more prepar'd,
And riggin out a stunsil yard
Like a fishin-rod goin slingin across;
But bless me the deep in the water she was!
"She'll navar carry that canvas," says I:
Didn I see her high and dry
In the harbour only a week afore,
And noticin the strained and the wore
1180 She was in the bottom—and natheral—
Nothin done to the boat at all
For years—*and whatever was he at!*
Draggin, draggin her like that!

So he got the wind of us, you know;
"Let's gev him a hate!" says Billy Crow,
That was at the helm—"let's gev him pepper!"
"Aisy! aisy!" says the skipper;
"Aisy," says Captain Tom, "my lad!
Just keep an eye on him," he said.
1190 Then says Billy—"He started sooner"—
"Silence! silence aboard this schooner!"
Says Captain Tom; and a look at the clouds,
And twisses his arm in the weather shrouds;
And keeps his glass on the Mona's Pride—
"Silence!" terbil dignified!
Aw, he could be that, for all
The hearty he was in general.

So on we went, but keepin a view of them,
And maybe a mile betwix the two of them.
1200 *How was the wind?* A leadin wind,
And very little of it to begin—
Hardly a list to it, bless your sowl—
But about mid-channel a long dead rowl
Come up from the South; and far away

1168   arr us: at us, in our minds.
1170   bwee: buoy.
1173   stunsil: stunsail, "a light sail, sometimes set on the exterior of a hull . . . when the wind is fair" (Kimbrough).
1185   hate: heat, race.
1193   weather shrouds: ropes supporting the masts on the windward or "weather" side of a ship (Kimbrough).

A white mist creepin over the say,
Creepin, creepin, the dirty thief,
Creepin—"All hands stand by to reef!"
Says Captain Tom; and reef we did—
"Get out your storm-jib! quick!" he said—
1210 All right! and then by gough it come
With a rip and a roar, and a hiss and a hum—
Bizzz—and the schooner lept her lenth,
And if there 'd been another brenth
Of canvass out, it isn here
I'd ha' been to tell ye, navar fear!
Rip-rip-rip—you know the scranch of it,
And into the hatches, every inch of it!
But come to her bearins beautiful,
And shakes herself, and away like a gull.

1220   And what was the Mona's Pride about?
Anythin off her? not a clout!
Every stitch—and the green-seas flyin
Over her cross-trees, and navar a sign
To shorten sail; but—*on you go!*
Slash her through it! keep her so!
And us that was sailin as light as light,
And humourin, and only right;
And Captain Hugh with his broadside to 't,
Reglar buryin the boat.
1230 "Well, that's no sailin!" says Dicky Homm,
That was mate o' the Clypse; but Captain Tom
Kep his eye upon her strick,
For the free she was sailed she was bearin quick
Upon us, you know, as if she meant
To overhaul us, and make a slant
Across our bows; and every man
On the schooner with a coil in his hand,
For any minute they were knowin
The smack might founderh like a stone.

1240   And Hughie was tellin us afterwards
How the father took a pack of cards,
From a locker, and cut them with his thumb,
And—"Now," he says, "for kingdom come!"
"Father! father!" says the son,
"Take somethin off her, or we'll be done!

1209   storm jib: small triangular sail set on the jib-boom in stormy weather (ed.).
1213   brenth: breadth.

>   For God's sake, father!"—and he made a spring
>   To the weather halyards—"Touch a thing,"
>   Says Captain Hugh, "and I'll strike you dead!
>   You coward! say your prayers," he said.
> 1250 "Look here! look here!" says the Ballachrink;
>   "If you'll go on like that, she's bound to sink!
>   You're mad!" he said, and outs with his knife—
>   "Villyan! villyan! for your life,"
>   Says the Captain—"Villyan!" and struck him full,
>   And down on the combins like a bull—
>   And a lurch and a rowl, and a shake and a shiver,
>   And the Ballachrink was gone for ever.
>   "Father! father! you've murdered him!"
>   And he looked, but the Captain's eye was dim,
> 1260 Like wakin from sleep, and he gev a yawn,
>   And—"Hulloah!" he says, "hulloah! that's one!"
>   Then Hughie drew a long long breath,
>   And gripped him there for life or death—
>   The despard grip; and the tiller dropt,
>   And the smack flew up, and the fo'sail flopt,
>   And tuck aback immadient,
>   And all sheets fast, and down she went.
>
>   "Stand by!" says Captain Tom, "stand by!
>   Listen if you'll hear a cry!
> 1270 Look out!" he says; and it wasn long
>   Afore we saw Hughie swimmin strong,
>   And heaves him a line, and hauls him in
>   Like a shot, and—"Where's your father, then?"
>   Says the Captain, but Hughie couldn spake;
>   And the whole of us strainin our eyes on the wake.
>   But Billy Crow that seen him fuss,
>   Driftin right under our stern he was,
>   Driftin lyin on his back—
>   "About! about on the other tack!"
> 1280 Says Captain Tom, and heaves a rope—
>   But he didn look at it—"More scope! more scope!"
>   Says the chaps, "Hould on! my gough! you'll lose him!
>   Noose him! Captain, noose him! noose him!"
>   And the noose went flyin over his head—
>   "Studdy! studdy!" the Captain said.
>   But he turned on his face, and he slipped his neck—
>   "For God's sake, Hugh! for Esther's sake!"

1247 weather halyards: ropes for hoisting or lowering sail on the windward side of a vessel (ed.).
1255 combins: covering of the hatch.

"Father, father!" says Hughie, "try!"
Then the two clenched fists went up to the sky—
1290 "Navar!" he says; and a big sea tore
Right over him with a race and a roar
Like a thousand guns, and just a minute
We saw the black head wrigglin in it—
And round and round—aw, it's thrue! it's thrue!
And that was the last of Captain Hugh.

Aw, it's an ugly job to be comin
Home with news like that to a woman—
And the way she'll look, and the way she'll sob—
Aw, bless my heart! it's an ugly job—
1300 And the childher wondrin, and no help in for it,
And questions axin—aw, it's horrit!
But the wuss of all the trouble they had
Was with this Annie, that navar shed
A tear, but standin like requirin
The blood, you know, lek made of iron.
And they said she struck Hughie in the face,
And wouldn have him in the place,
And wouldn belave him, wouldn belave him!
"Why didn ye save him? why didn ye save him?"
1310 That was all her cry, like savage-lek,
Savage,—lek the uncle put a speck
Of some mad stuff in her sowl, that was brewin
And spreadin there, or somethin doin,
To bother her that way. And she'd wake with a start—
And—"What's these tangles round my heart?"
She'd say, "the sticky they are, and the stingin!
Listen to yandhar bell that's ringin!"
She'd say, "and the shilly siftin, siftin;
And the sand like paste, and liftin, liftin!"
1320 And—"Give me a chance?" and "Where's the boat?"
And—"What's these crabs around my throat?"
And—"Oh! is this the road to hell?"
Disthressin the mother terrible.

And nobody could understand the state of her,
And ould women and pazons and all agate of her—
And they were puttin little babies in her arms,
And tryin prayers, and tryin charms,
And trying harbs; and a meetin over her

1302-61 *Omitted.*
1318 shilly: shingle (ed.).

At the locals, but they couldn recover her—
1330 Couldn! couldn! And at last they sent
For Docthor Bell, that was well acquent
With the family. And—"Lave her! lave her!"
Says Dr. Bell: and he didn give her
A mossel—"Just humour her! Time 'll do 't"—
Aw, by gough it was himself that knew 't—
"Time!" he says—aw, wondherful though!
What is it that he didn know?
Dr. Bell—aw, dear! aw, dear!
And lek enough the best of a year
1340 Afore she come to—bless me! surprisin
Wasn it? the strenth of the pison
That was in her there, howavar, it was—
But working urror her at last.
And then she soon begun to get stronger;
But she wasn a little gel no longer,
But a brave big woman, sweet and kind,
And aisy and sensible in her mind;
And the little gel, and her sorrow, too,
Went down for ever with Captain Hugh.
1350 Well, she was a lovely blossom—
Let him rock her on his bosom—
Let him hev her for his own—
Till God 'll call him before the throne!

    A fine strong woman—and lovin the lad?
Lovin! who'd she be lovin instead?
Lovin—aye! but none of this bother
These sweethearts has got with one another—
Allis ready for a fight—
Aw, very quite! very quite!
1360 Because, ye see, these sweethearts will—
But comfible, aw, comfible!
And married him, and what 'd prevent her?
Married him that very winter—
Aye—and a nice little lump of jink—
Wasn she heiress to the Ballachrink?
Aw, a beautiful proppity,
And no mistake, and so you see—
But of coorse—and love it was! aw, yis!
But still whatever was hers was his—
1370 Aw, married—and the very weddin day

1329   at the locals: on the part of the locals—the Methodist lay preachers who stay in one locality (ed.).
1343   urror: out of (ed.).

Yandhar hedge was took away—
And the place where it stood they put a row
Of lilies, corcusars, you know,
Polyanthers—and every thing
That's comin up early in the spring—
Makin a garden very bright—
And so I think I'll say good night.

'Lugger' or Dandy Smack, 1840

Port St. Mary
Manx National Heritage

Tommy Big-Eyes

DEAR COUNTRYMEN, whate'er is left to us
    Of ancient heritage—
Of manners, speech, of humours, polity,
The limited horizon of our stage—
Old love, hope, fear,
All this I fain would fix upon the page;
That so the coming age,
    Lost in the empire's mass,
Yet haply longing for their fathers, here
    May see, as in a glass,
What they held dear—
May say, "Twas thus and thus
    They lived;" and, as the time-flood onward rolls,
Secure an anchor for their Keltic souls.

I NEVER knew a man in my life
That had such a darling little wife
As a chap they were callin Tommy Gellin:
So how he got her is worth the tellin.

    Now, Tommy was as shy as a bird:
"Yes" or "No" was the only word
You'd get from Tommy. So every monkey
Thought poor Tommy was a donkey.
But—bless your sowl!—lave Tommy alone!
He'd got a stunnin head of his own;
And his copies just like copper-plate,
And he'd set to work and cover a slate
Before the rest had done a sum:
But you'd really have thought the fellow was dumb—
He was that silent and bashful, you know;
Not a fool—not him—but lookin so.

Ugly he was, most desperate:
For all the world like a suckin skate.
But the eyes! the eyes! Why—blow the fella!
20 He could spread them out like a rumberella—
You'd have wondered where on earth he got them
Deep dubs of blue light with the black at the bottom—
Basins of light. But it was very seldom
You could see them like that, for he always held them
Straight on his book or whatever he had,
As if he was ashamed, poor lad!
And really they were a most awful size;
And so we were callin him "Tommy Big-eyes."

The way that chap was knocked about
30 Was just a scandal. You hit him a clout
Whenever you saw him—that was the style:
Hit him once, and you'd get him to smile:
Hit him twice, and he'd drop the head;
Hommer away till you'd think he was dead.
And he'd stand like a drum, as if his skin
Was a sheep's, and made for hommerin.
Then, his hair was so thick it was nice to grab it,
And pull it back like skinnin a rabbit,
Till he'd have to look up, as you may suppose;
40 And then you could welt him under the nose.
I do believe the cruellest fien's
In the world is a parcel of boys in their teens,
One of them stirrin up the other.
But still, for all, the divil's mother
Should have looked a little more to the way
The chap was rigged; for it isn't fair play
To dress a lad that's goin to school
As if he was born to be a fool.
Fancy a frill around his neck!
50 What in the world could the woman expec'?

18	skate: ray fish (ed).
22	dubs: pools.
44	for all: after all.

Skate

And his trousers buttonin outside
Of his jacket, like these fellows that ride
At the races. Surely, it might occur——
Well, she'd a deal to answer for.

And that's the for this Tommy had
Such girlish ways—oh, very bad!
Just give him a needle and a bit
Of calico, and there he'd sit
In a corner, as happy as a prince,
60 And the gels goin on with their imperince,
And—"Are you wantin a sweetheart, Tommy?"
Poor thing! as innocent as a lammie!
They said, if you'd give him a doll he'd frock it,
But he owned to a pincushion in his pocket.
"*Where did he come from?*" did ye say?
Somewhere over Lough Molla' way;°
And a road runnin in on the opposite side,
A long sort of road that went to Kirk Bride,
And joinin together, and leadin down,
70 And over the bridge, and into the town;
And about a mile, I think it will be,
On the Kirk Bride road there's a path you'll see
Betwix the brews that the sheep have wore,
And a cart-track leadin to the shore;
And a pleasant little place they're callin—
What's this it is now?—aye, "The Vollin"°—
And a little house, and a garden to't,
And a little croft, and a mackerel boat,
And some trees they've planted, but they haven't thriven,
80 And that's where Nelly Quine was livin.

So you see these two would be meetin there

---

55   the for: the reason (ed.).
66   Lough: lake, pronounced as Scot. *loch* (ed.)
73   brews: hills.

Ramsey Mackerel Boat

Every mornin, rain or fair.
For, mind ye, if this Tommy was late—
And he tried to be—little Nelly would wait.
Wait she would, and pretend a nest,
In the briars, you know; or had to rest;
Or a pin or somethin she was losin;
Or sittin down to put her shoes on.
Then Tommy would come, and he'd give a peep
90 Round the corner, and then he'd creep
Close in to the hedge, and wouldn allow
He saw her a bit, and on like a plough.
And there they'd go—you'd have split to seen them—
One on each side, and the road between them—
And little Nelly lookin, lookin;
And this poor bashful divil hookin
The best he could. And every turn
In the road, no matter the bend, he'd burn
With the shame; and he'd crib himself into a O,
100 Like feelin her bearin on him, you know.
And sometimes Nelly 'd give a race,
And get before him, and look in his face,
And he'd stop as dead—and she'd give a little snigger
Of a laugh in her nose, like the click of a trigger,
And lookin under to see could she prize
His big head up with a lift of her eyes—
Botherin this chap. But when they'd be near
The school, she wasn willin they'd see her
Comin with Tommy; and she'd tuck up her clothes,
110 And she'd shake her hair, and away she goes;
And the little feet twinkling—ha! ha! my men!
He'd look rather sharp, would Tommy, then.

And Dick, and Nick, and all the rest of them—
Miss Nelly could plague him with the best of them—
Indeed she could; and boo and hiss,
And put out her mouth like wantin a kiss,
And dance around him, and ask him to carry her—
"Do, Tommy!" and—*when was he goin to marry her?*
"When, Tommy! when la'?" just bewild'rin—
120 That's when she was with the other children.
"*Fiends*" I called them, did I? Well,
I shouldn then. It's hard to tell;
And it's likely God has got a plan
To put a spirit in a man

---

119   la': interjection; Mx. *lah*, lad (Moore).

Tommy Big-Eyes 149

      That's more than you can stow away
      In the heart of a child. But he'll see the day
      When he'll not have a bit too much for the work
      He's got to do. And the little Turk
      Is good for nothin but shoutin and fightin
130 And divilment; and God delightin
      To make him strong and bold and free,
      And think the man he's goin to be—
      More beef than butter, more lean than lard;
      Hard, if you like; but the world is hard.
      You'll see a river how it dances
      From rock to rock, wherever it chances—
      In and out, and here and there:
      A regular young divil-may-care!
      But, caught in the sluice, it's another case,
140 And it steadies down, and it flushes the race
      Very deep and strong, but still
      It's not too much to work the mill.
      The same with hosses—kick and bite
      And winch away—all right, all right!
      Wait a bit, and give him his ground,
      And he'll win his rider a thousand pound.
      Aw dear! aw dear! I've had my day,
      And it's a merry month is the month of May—
      Little Peggies, little Annies,
150 Little Nellies, little Fannies—
      And you with Kitty, and me with Sal,
      And coortin like the deuce and all;
      And playin weddin's, and pretendin to go
      To the Vicar for a licence, you know—
      And a book, and sayin the very words—
      Bless ye! as innocent as the birds!

        So what did a lot of us do but join
      And persuade this Tommy that Nelly Quine
      Was desperate in love with him there—
160 And "Spake to her, Tommy! spake to her!
      Spake to her, for all!" we said:
      "Yes, dyin in love!" And he hung the head
      Like a clout, poor chap! But we stuck to him still—
      And "If you'll not spake, there's others that will,"
      Says one of the imps. And how she'd be blushin

---

    144   winch: wince.
    161   for all: however.
    163   clout: dish cloth.

When they'd tell her the bad that Tommy was wushin
To be her sweetheart, but afraid to make free.
And "Aw, my gough! the plased she'll be!"
Says the imp. Then Tommy looked up, but slow
170 And the big blue eyes began to blow
Like—"Bladders" was it I was sayin?
"Rumberellas?" Try again.
"Bubbles," was it? What d'ye call—
"Blow'n," I said. Just aisy all!
"Blow'n," of coorse; and the bigger the lies
The wider Tommy was spreadin the eyes.
"She said you were handsome; she said you were smart;
"She said she was almost breakin her heart";
"She called you a duck"; "She called you a dove";
180 "She called you her darlin darlin love";
And the tasty dressed, she said she never;
And the splendid trousis he had however;
And the way they were stitched, and the beautiful gimp.
"She didn!" says I. "She did!" says the imp:
And "Buck up, Tommy, and bring her a present."
These imps is terrible onpleasant.

    So one day Tommy took the road
The very earliest he could;
And into the school as quite as a worm,
190 And claps his basket under the furm—
His dinner, you'd think—and waited there
Till school began; but just in the prayer
A fellow gave a shove—worse luck!
At Tommy's basket; and "Tuck-tuck-tuck!"
And the master stopped, and we all of us stopped;
And "Tuck-tuck-tuck!" and out she popped—
A beautiful little hen—and she flew
This way and that way—and "*Shish!*" and "*Shoo!*"
And over the desks; and we all gave chase,
200 And she flapped her wings in the master's face—
And the dignified he turned to look!
And "*Shoo!*" he says; and "Tuck-tuck-tuck"—
And away to the window; and scratched and tore;
And the feathers flyin. "Open that door!"
Says the master; and, glad to be shot of us,
So out goes the hen, and out goes the lot of us—
Helter-skelter, boys and gels—
Sticks and stones, or anything else:

---

190   furm: form; bench (ed.).

"Catch her!" "Watch her!"
210 "Stop her!" "Drop her!"
"Here she is!" "There she is!"
"Tommy's I'll swear she is!"
"Tommy's! Tommy's! Hop chu naa!
Three cheers for Tommy!—Hip-hip-hooraa!"
And a stone come flyin, and a flip and a flutter—
And down went the poor little hen in the gutter,
And her leg was broken; and "Take her up!"
And "The poor little thing!" and "Stop, then; stop!
Here's Tommy himself!" And Tommy came,
220 And he stood like dumb. "It's a dirty shame!"
Says one of the gels, and begun a-cryin.
Says an imp, "He brought her for Nelly Quine!"
And, "Nelly! for Nelly!" and took and caught her!
And, "Nelly's his sweetheart! It's for Nelly he brought her!"
So when Tommy heard that, he stooped down low,
Like to take the hen, and the tears to flow
Most pitiful, and shivered all over—
And, "Look at him, Nelly! look at your lover!"
But Nelly sprung like a flash of light,
230 And her eye was set, and her face was white;
And she put her hand upon his head,
And, "Was it for me then, Tommy?" she said—
"Was it for me?" And he snuffs and he snivels;
And, "Yes," says Tommy. "Hooraa!" says the divils.

Then Nelly faced round like a tiger-cat—
"You brutes!" she said, "gerr out of that!
Gerr out, you cowards!" and her face all burned
With the fury of her; and she turned,
And she took this hen that Tommy confessed,
240 And she coaxed it, and put it in her breast,
And kissed and kissed it over again.
"My own little hen! my own little hen!"
Says Nelly; and then she got Tommy to rise,
And took her brat to wipe his eyes.
But away goes Tommy over the street
Like the very wind, and Nelly gave sheet
As far as the bridge; but it wasn no use,
For Tommy could run like the very deuce—

---

213   Hop chu naa: burden of a Manx song.°
236   gerr: get.
244   brat: apron.
246   gave sheet: ran (sheet: a rope or chain used to extend a sail to increase the speed—ed.).

        And the hen in her arms and all, you see—
250 So she stood and laughed; and didn't we?
        Laughed and laughed—the little midge!—
        And leaned against the wall of the bridge,
        And laughed again; but I'll be sworn
        There was many a day after that you darn
        Say much before Nelly about Tommy—no!
        She wouldn't have it! Touch and go,
        Was Nelly. Three words, and by jabers you'd gerrit!
        Aw the gel, ye see, had a splendid sperrit!
        Just the least little *chuck!* was enough, and then
260 You couldn't coax her back again.
        "And why did she laugh herself"—did ye say?—
        "The time poor Tommy was runnin away?"
        Well, everythin of coorse in raison!
        And the fool he looked, you know, was amazin.
        But, even then, when she heard us behind her,
        Singin out "Tally-high-ho-the-grinder!"—
        (The *grinder!* if you know what that is!)
        She turned and looked like thunder at us—
        And, upon my word, there's a lot of thunder
270 'll go in a little noddle like yonder.
        So she rolled the little hen in her brat,
        And its little heart all pit-a-pat—
        And as dignified as dignified—
        And starts, and away with her, home to Kirk Bride.
        And didn come to school that day, nor the next—
        Oh, Miss Nelly was desperate vexed!

        But Tommy come the very next day—
        And if he didn catch it—eh!
        By gum! *He'd make an impression*,
280 The master said; and he gave him a threshin
        In the good old style, with your thwickumy-thwackumy!
        Slishin-slashin! bick-o'-me-back-o'-me!
        And, "Fowls!" he said. "What next?" he said—
        "Ducks and geese!"—and, "Hould up your head!"—
        Pigs and geese, as like as not!
        Bulls of Bashan! ° *You couldn tell what!*
        The whole of the farm! "But, look ye here!"
        He said—and he caught him a clip on the ear—
        "You insolent vagabone!" he says,
290 "Who's goin to see the end of this?"

---

    257   gerrit: get it.
    266   Tally-high-ho-the-grinder: chorus of an old song.°

Was it fowls!! Well, well! had it really come
To fowls!! Why, it abslit struck him dumb,
He said. *Of coorse*, he said, *marbles he knew,*
And even, now and then, an apple or two;
And liked his scholars to be cheerful;
But—fowls!!! he said—*it was simply fearful!*
No, he couldn, he couldn pretend,
He really couldn, to say where would it end.
Abominable, he said, *the habits*
300 *Of childher now-a-days!—the rabbits*
And rubbish! he said; and "Fowls!" he said—"Fowls!!"
And he lifts his voice, and reglar howls.
And the lot of us poor little blokes
Takin care to laugh at all his jokes.°
Oh! he said, *it wasn no use!*
And down came the cane like the very deuce.
By Jove! he laid into him like greens,
Till poor Tommy was all in smithereens—
Poor little divil! the way he was tanned!
310 But stood it grand! stood it grand!

    So when Nelly come back, the whole of the row
Was over, you know; but anyhow,
The master didn't say a word
To her at all; but of coorse she heard—
"Tuk and pounded him into jammy!"
We said. And the way she looked at Tommy!
But Tommy didn look to her.
Tommy kept his eyes on the floor.
But I never saw anythin beautifuller
320 Than Nelly's little face, and the colour
Comin and goin in her cheek;
And her eyes, that, if they didn't speak—
Well that was all. And weren't they pretty!
Yes; but now they were wells of pity—
Wells of pity, full to the brim;
And longin to coax and comfort him.
Aw, she couldn take them off him, I swear!
But whether this Tommy was aware
I cannot tell; for he wouldn look,
330 But the head of him down on the slate or the book
Like nailed; but still a way with his back,
Or his body altogether lek,
And a sort of a snugglin with his head
That showed he was a little bit comforted.

So that evening she wouldn let Tommy go home
By himself at all; but collared to 'm,
And wouldn leave him; but, step for step,
The quick or the slow, till they came to the Clip,°
Where the roads divide. Then Nelly spoke—
340 And Tommy fit enough to choke—
And, "I'll give you a kiss," she says, "Tommy, for that"—
And she wiped her little mouth with her brat.
"Here now, Tommy!" and made a lip to 'm;
But Tommy ran; but Nelly gript him;
And Tommy turned this way, and Tommy turned that way;
And poor little Nelly couldn tell what way—
And first cockin one ear, and then the other,
Till at last says Nelly, "My gough! the bother
There's with you, too!" And, "Turn for all!
350 Turn, ye donkey!" But he stood like a wall;
And whatever she did, and whatever she said,
She was forced to kiss him on the back of his head.
And then if Tommy didn cut!
But Nelly stamped the little foot—
And, "Well, I never!"—and, "Fiddlededee!"—
And, "After all, he's a fool!" says she.

"*She was right,*" you're sayin? Poor Tommy, though!
"*Right enough?*" Well, I don't know——
If a chap won't take a kiss when it's gev him,
360 *You suppose the only way is to lave him?*
Yes, I suppose so. Aw, Nelly was furious!
But still, for all, it's very curious,
The little foot was slack enough
Before she got home, and all the huff
Washed away in bitter tears—
And as white as a sheet: and so it appears
The mother noticed. And, *What was the matter?*
And, "Dear me!" and clitter-clatter.
And, "It's just these boys! and you'd better confess!"
370 "Aw, no!" says Nelly; "Aw, no!" she says.

But if Nelly was sorrowful, then trust me
It was Tommy that was happy. "She kissed me!
She did! she did! she did!" And over
The hedge, and into a field of clover,
That was very fine; and he threw himself down
In the thick of it; and never a soun
But the corn-crakes crowin very clear—
You know they're about that time of the year—

Tommy Big-Eyes

Just to be happy, you know, and think—
380 The little chap! And the last sweet blink
Of the day, and the big cloud sailin across.
And *oh!* he thought, *the happy he was!*
Bless ye! he's tould me many a time.
Why, this Tommy could put it in rhyme!
He was a bit of a poet, was Tommy—aye!
Aw, never say die! never say die!
A poet, I tell ye, reggilar!
And—— *The Star!* that was splendid about the star!
Of coorse, he didn make it then:
390 It 'd ha' puzzled him to do that, my men!
No, the long years after this
(But even at school he wasn amiss
With his little songs). I wouldn trust
But I've got it here—I think I must—
Wrote at Tommy. Aisy all!
That's not it. Rather small
Is Tommy's writin. Wait a bit!
"Star of Hope"—that's it! that's it!
Will you read it, Jemmy? Give him a light!
400 Jemmy's a scholar. All right! all right!
    Jemmy reads:—
        Star of hope, star of love,
        Did you see it from heaven above?
        Love was sleeping, hope was fled—
        Did you see what Nelly did?
        I know it was only the back of my head—
        But did you, did you, did you, did you,
        Did you see what Nelly did?
        You're my witness, star of joy!
410   Was it a girl that kissed a boy?
        Was it a boy that kissed a girl?
        Oh, happy worl'!
            I don't know!
            Let it go!
    I thought I'd have died, and nobody missed me,
    But Nelly has kissed me! Nelly has kissed me!
        Come down! come down!
        Put on your brightest crown!
        Slip in with me among the clover.
420   Now tell me all about it—I'm her lover!
        Did you see it? Are you sure?

---

390   It 'd ha': It would have.
395   at: by

Is she lovely? Is she pure?
Smell these buds! Is that her breath?
Will I love her unto death?
Ah, little star! I see you smiling there
Upon heaven's lowest stair!
   I know, I know
   It's time to go;
But I'm only waitin till you have blessed me,
430 For Nelly has kissed me! Nelly has kissed me!°
First-rate, Jemmy! that'll do!
Capital readin! Aw, it's aisy for you.

   Well, however, this Tommy fell asleep,
With the light of the stars on his face, poor sweep,°
And when he awoke the night was half over,
And the star was really down in the clover.
So Tommy felt rather shiverin,
And home like the mischief, and creepin in—
Poor craythur! and never a bite or a sup for him,
440 But only the father sittin up for him—
And took a stick, and gave it him hot;
And *for-shamed* him, and sent him to bed like a shot.

   But, of coorse, this was rather too much for the lad;
So Tommy was taken very bad.
It was weeks, I believe, afore he was out,
And even then only creepin about—
And, I really can't azackly explain,
But he never come to school again—
At least to ours—I don't know did they get
450 To hear the way the lad was beat.
But, however, he was sent to another school—
Somewhere down by the Ballagoole;°
And that'd be close to his father's house,
That owned a croft and a couple of cows,
And a pig or two—aw, a dacent ould blade.
The man was a blacksmith to his trade,
And worked at it, too: at least, if he didn,
There was the smithy aback of his midden.
He was a hard man, though—very hard—
460 And a man that didn much regard
For the people that was over him:
Pa'sons, churchwardens, sumners, and them.°

---

434   sweep: a good-for-nothing (Moore).
462   sumners: officers of the Ecclesiastical Court.

There's no doubt he was rather fond of a fight;
But any way he'd have his right—
The commons, the quarterlands, the cess,
Intacks, easements, and all the rest.
That's the man that could rattle them off—
And only ownin this bit of a crof'.
I believe the joy of his life was to go
470 To a vestry meetin, and have a jaw
With the Archdeacon, that was capital
For keepin the temper; and the louder he'd bawl,
"The bark," he'd say, "is worse than the bite of him;"
And bore with the chap, but hated the sight of him.
That was Gellin—quarrelsome rather;
And, anyway, he was Tommy's father.

But "Nelly!"—certingly! Nelly!
Always after the gels, I see!
Well, I really don't think she cared a toss
480 About poor Tommy, how he was.
I can't say, of coorse—they're very queer—
But still for all it didn appear
She took up with any of these other chaps—
So that's the way, you know—so p'rhaps—
But dear me! a fellow that couldn take a kiss
Just in a way of friendliness—
Well, of coorse, a chap that 'd act that funky—
She must have thought him rather a donkey—
Must, you know—a soft sort of craythur—
490 Aw, there's no mistake—it's only nathur—
And none of us didn say nothin to her,
And she didn stay over a quarter more,
Being wanted at home for a baby they had,
And fish was scarce, and times was bad,
And the mother was sick, and Quine was cussin,
And isn it strange how they'll take to the nussin—
These gels, you know? So we hadn a chance
To see much of Nelly; but only once
Me and another chap had a boat
500 On the Vollin shore, just waitin to float,
And we took a notion we'd go up for fun,

---

465   quarterlands: divisions of land ranging from 120 to 140 acres (ed.).
cess: assessment (ed.).
466   intacks: intakes, pieces of land "taken in from a moorland, common, etc." (*OED*).
495-516 *Omitted.*

And see how Nelly was gettin on.
So up we went; and, 'deed for sure,
There was Nelly at the door,
Sittin on the step, and rockin
The baby in her arms, that was cryin shockin.
So I leaned on the hedge there, just like this,
And "My compliments, Miss Quine," I says;
"You'll 'scuse our callin without any warnin;
510 And how is Tommy's hen this mornin?"
Oh she made a grab, and a stone at her foot
As big as a turmit—didn we cut?
But shoutin all the way down the glen—
"Tommy's hen! Tommy's hen!"
And finished off with three good cheers,
And I don't think I saw her again for years.

    Well, after a while this Tommy was sent
To work on a farm that was called Renshent—°
Jurby way, runnin out on the shore,
520 Somewhere aback of the Ballamoore;
And a sandy sort of a place; but still
The farm was runnin up to a hill
Slopin south: and, just when you come
On the top, the brews went down like a plumb
To the shilley behind; no rocks at all,
Just clayey stuff, but as steep as a wall,
And the jackdaws workin their holes in it clever,
The divils, bein soft, you'll observe: but, however,
You know the sort of place I mean—
530 Snug, I can tell ye—Archie Cain
They were callin the farmer—but come with the wife;
But what's the odds! dear bless my life!
Fairish plough-land—couldn be beat,
I've heard for turmits—a little wet
In the bottom, no doubt, a sort of a gaery,
But splendid for geese; not much of a dairy—
Well, you wouldn expeck—just enough that would do
For themselves—a nice little meadow or two—
But it paid them well—that gaery piece—

---

512   turmit: turnip (ed.).
524   brews: Mx. *broogh*, "brink . . . precipice" (Cregeen).
525   shilley: shingle.
535   gaery: waste.

540　Bellies like bollans! tremenjis geese!

　　　　Oh, I knew Renshent—and a beautiful garden—
　　Bless me! wasn Cain a warden?
　　And a round of trees, if it's trees you'd call them,
　　For, the way the salt of the wind 'll scald them
　　Over there, they're rather like bushes—
　　But still, for all, these lumps of thrushes
　　Of a summer's evenin, an' the way they'd be shoutin
　　After the sun, as if they were doubtin
　　Would he ever come back to them again—
550　And, "Be sure! be sure!" you'd think they were sayin—
　　Rum things is birds though—yes, indeed—
　　Astonishin the places they'll breed—
　　Very curious that way—
　　Fanciful I call them—eh?
　　Fanciful—Dear me! the dub
　　That was there for the ducks, and a sort of scrub
　　Of jenny-nettles and that, where the hens
　　Was layin on the sly, in the lee of the fence
　　That ran by the gable; and a splendid old trammon
560　For the fairies. But, bless my soul! what gammon!
　　As if it was any odds to you—
　　But, ye see, I like them places, I do.
　　However, this Cain had a very nice spot of it—
　　About a hundred acres 'd be the lot of it.

　　　　So Tommy was put to Renshent all right,
　　And ould Gellin had a despard fight
　　About the wages, and all the rest of it;
　　And I don't know which of the two had the best of it.
　　But of coorse *he'd hev a understandin,*
570　And a row, if it was only to keep his hand in.
　　But Cain was his match; so, with a deal of bother,
　　They settled it betwix them some way or another.

540　　bollans: a round-shaped sea-fish.
546　　lumps of: fine big.
559　　trammon: elder tree, planted at the gable of a Manx house as a
　　　　protection against fairies.

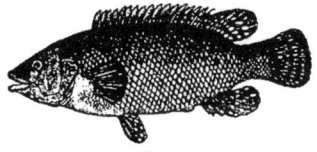

Ballan Wrasse

        And Tommy made a fuss-rate servant—
"Diligent in business, fervent
In spirit"—it's sayin in the Bible—eh?°
There's no doubt that Tommy earned his pay—
Aye did he—earned it to the full:
For, ye see, the chap was as strong as a bull,
And handier till men that was twice his size,
580   And uncommon watchful, and willin, and wise.

        Well, now, this Tommy, after a bit,
Got to be a terbil favourite
With the misthress there, that was one of the sweetest
Women you ever, about the completest
Every way a woman *should* be—
I don't think a better woman *could* be—
For patience, for gentleness, and that—
She was one of the Shimmins of Ballarat—°
They were all of them nice—aw a capital strain!
590   But the nicest of all was Missis Cain.
And she took to Tommy very much.
For, you know, there wasn the smallest touch
Of divilment in Tommy—no!
But all the other road, and so
The woman was feelin quite at her aise with him,
She said *he had such studdy ways with him.*
For there's some of these country lads is rough,
And cheeky, and impudent enough;
And carryin on with the gels, and slinkin
600   Off to the public-house, and drinkin,
And stayin out without any leave,
And not the smallest notion how to behave.
And, at dinner, they'll sit till they're nearly bustin,
And belchin perfectly disgustin
And hardly fit for pigs to eat with,
Let alone a Christian to have his meat with—
Never taught no manners, I doubt—
They've often got to put them out
Afore they're done; and they'll lie like logs
610   In the haggard somewhere—regular hogs!
I've seen a chap myself, without any jokin,
Took to the door, and all but chokin;
And of coorse these fools of gels must laugh,

---

579   till: than (ed.).
603-16 *Omitted.*
610   haggard: stackyard (ed.).

Whatever they'd do, and him stumblin off
And slouchin away with his head on his breast,
And the misthress lookin quite distressed.

    But Missis Cain was a woman that 'd be
Always for order and decency.
She wasn strict, so much to speak,
620 But pitiful, and lovin, and meek:
And when that woman was in a place
You'd think there couldn be nothin but peace—
It seemed to breathe from her very skin—
The pure and white astonishin!
She wasn a stirrin woman at all,
Nor given to scouldin, and hadn no call;
For the woman had only just to sit
In any room, and you'd see it lit
With a soft sweet light, that was just the holy
630 She looked, and the pure; and all sin and folly
And dirt, and evil talk, was driven
From her; and her smile was like an angel in heaven.
Do you believe, if a picture of Christ was hung
Somewhere, that a fellow could do what was wrong
Before it at all? I don't think he would.
But we're tould these Romans——but what's the good?
God knows the heart; and I don't like to be sayin
Too much, you know; but Missis Cain—
Dear me! it's no use! wasn she a Shimmin
640 Of Ballarat?—most splendid women!

    And Tommy had nice ways with him, too;
Indeed, for his station, there 'd be very few
That would have such sense and manners, both;
The very way he was suppin his broth,
Missis Cain remarked (and she was right, bedad!)
Was showin the proper feelins he had.
No puffin and blowin, no stuffin and chewin,
And scroogin and nudgin, and the elbers goin
Like a shoemaker; but Tommy would dip
650 His spoon very delicate-like, and the lip
As tight as a puss; and no slushin and sloppin—
And, besides, the fellow knew when to be stoppin.
Where he learned it, I don't know;
Not from his father—I never saw

653-79   *Omitted.*

A man like that agate of his grub—
My eye! I've seen him at a club—°
Beef and mutton, fowls and pork,
Pies and puddins—he was up to his work
Was Gellin, you'd think he'd never be finished,
660 And "Will you have your plate replenished,
Mr Gellin?" says the Archdeacon, looking sly—
"Just wait a minute!" he says "and I'll try!"
But what the Archdeacon had in view
Was to stop his eternal hollabaloo
As long as he could, and "Try the bacon!"
(Aw, bless my soul! that ould Archdeacon!)
"Try it, Mr Gellin; I think you'll find
It's very excellent;" and "Well, I don't mind,"
Says Gellin, and, dropping a button, and scowlin,
670 "There's not priddas enough;" and his eyes a-rowlin
Like cartwheels there—and, "Ring the bell!"
Aw, the Archdeacon was capital!
Understood the chap, you know.
Understood him—aye, just so,
Understood him, every art,
Understood—but, bless my heart!
This'll never do for a man that's tellin
A story—I fancy I'm rather like Gellin,
That didn know when to stop. All right.

680   Now, Missis Cain she took a delight
In Tommy—reg'lar delight it was,
The decent woman! ye see, because
She was thinkin the nice example he'd be
To all the rest of the family.

And it wasn't only eating either,
But just his conduct altogether—
Modest—and when the work was done
Of an evenin, and every one
Was getting sleepy, Tommy would take
690 His book, and keep them all awake—
Beautiful readin—and a lovely voice,
And the gels would say it was very nice,
And listen, grand; but the boys would be laughin,

---

655   agate of: busy with (ed.).
669   button: lump (ed.)°
670   priddas: potatoes (ed.).
675   art: "airt," point of the compass (Moore).

Tommy Big-Eyes

And tryin to carry on with their chaffin:
But the gels would shame them, and then they'd be quiet;
And then some of *them* would take and try it;
And then the gels would laugh till they were shakin—
The idikkilis mistakes they were makin—
And then they'd give in; and all the while
700 The misthress 'd be havin a little smile—
And Tommy as happy, and explainin there—
A good-natured craythur, never fear!
And simple; and then he'd take the book,
And a gel would look, and a boy would look,
And back into a corner, and start
A little bit of courtin—dear heart!
What harm?—And you'd hear a kiss go *pop!*
And the misthress would be lookin up,
But no-ways cross, just a sort of surprise;
710 But Tommy 'd never lift his eyes.
What was he readin? All sorts of things—
Lives of pessons—Queens and Kings—
Travels—history, you know—
Pilgrim's Progress—Robin Crusa—

    And Tommy had a fiddle too,
And I don't know what was there he couldn do
With yandhar fiddle, the way it 'd mock
Everything—it 'd crow like a cock,
It 'd hoot like a donkey, it 'd moo like a cow;
720 It 'd cry like a baby, it 'd grunt like a sow,
Or a thrush, or a pigeon, or a lark, or a linnet—
You'd really thought they were livin in it.
But the tunes he was playin—that was the thing
Like squeezin honey from the string;
Like milkin a fiddle—no jerks, no squeaks—
And the tears upon the misthress' cheeks.
And sometimes he'd play a dance—and what harm!
But she wouldn have it upon the farm,
The misthress wouldn—dancin, I mean—
730 It didn matter so much for the play'n:
But she'd often stop him, and ask would he change
To a nice slow tune, and Tommy would range
Up and down the strings, and slidder
Into the key; and then he'd feather
The bow very fine, and a sort of a hum,
Like a bee round a flower, and out it 'd come—
"Ould Robin Gray," or the "Lover's Ghost"—°
That's the two she liked the most:

                And the gels, that only a minute afore
740   Were ready to jump and clear the floor,
                Sat still on the form, but onaisy though,
                And terbil disappointed, you know.
                And sometimes they'd be coaxin Tommy to take
                The fiddle out in the orchard, and shake
                His funny-bone over a jig or a reel—
                Something to tickle a body's heel,
                Says one of the gels—and "I'll give you a kiss!
                Faith, I will then, Tommy!" she says:
                And Tommy that blushed to the roots of his hair;
750   But still, he said, *no matter where,*
                If the misthress wasn't willing,
                He wouldn—and "Tommy, we'll give you a shillin!"
                And coaxin away: but he didn regard them.
                And anyway, you know, she'd have heard them.

                    Well, ye see, in a country place
                The gels is apt to be rough in their ways:
                But Missis Cain was particular,
                These wild huzzies wouldn do for her.
                There's farms, no doubt, where they're very bad;
760   But she'd have them dacent, whatever she had—
                Dacent it is—*dacent*, I tell ye—
                Dacent—but still of course, at a Mheillea,
                Or a tay-party, on an Eril Vary,
                Or the like of that, young folks 'll get merry.
                And, dear me! when it's after dark,
                It's seemin right to have a lark
                In rayson—depanding the way it's meant;
                So I wouldn trust but these gels at Renshent,
                For all they couldn have a dance,
770   Took their fun when they had the chance.—
                I've helped them myself? I thought you'd guess it.
                'Deed, maybe it's just as well to confess it.
                Capital gels! just so, just so;
                But rather hard on Tommy, though.
                And that was encouragin these other chaps,
                That 'd take this Tommy on their laps,
                Or some stuff like that, being undersized,
                And pretendin to nuss him; but rather surprised

---

755-88   *Omitted.*
762   Mheillea: harvest home (ed.).
763   Eril Vary: Eve of Mary, Christmas Eve (Brown's note to *Christmas Rose* 65—ed.).

When Tommy buckled to one day,
780 And me, as it happened, to show fair-play,
And gripped the biggest of the lot,
And put him on his back like a shot—
And the women lookin; but the clean he was thrown
And the quick, he thought he'd leave Tommy alone;
And when he got up, the whole of them slanted;
So Tommy got peace, and that's all that he wanted,
And they'd more respeck for him from that day—
Poor Tommy! that wouldn have hurt a flea!

But Cain himself? the master, you mean—
790 Oh, a very nice man was Cain.
Very, very—couldn be beat.
But you'll hear something more about him yet.
Cain was a "Local," you'll understand—
Yes! aw, the very head of the plan.
They said to preach he was only fair,
But you couldn touch him for a prayer—
Soundin out like a trumpet-blast;
And shockin powerful with a class.
I don't know much about their rigs,
800 These Methodists that has their gigs,
And travels about; but Cain preferred
To stay at home, and preach the Word
To his neighbours there. So he got to be
A sort of Apostle among them, you see,
A prince and a ruler among his people,
A tower of the truth, a reg'lar steeple
Was Cain; and had his mortgages,
And money out at interest,
With all the *members*—isn that the name?—
810 And even the chapel itself the same.
But still he counted all but loss—°
"A humble servant of the cross,"
He said—and *the people liked him*, he said,
And who was he to deny the bread
Of life to hungry sinners? No!
He said *he didn want to go*
And leave the little flock that loved him—
And d——m him! if they'd took and shoved him

---

793   "Local": a Methodist lay preacher serving in only one locality (ed.).
799   rigs: arrangements, games (ed.).
811-32 *Omitted.*

Over the brews—I've seen the Archdeacon—
820 But steady! steady! put the break on!
Hould her in!—oh, a child of grace!
Got it shinin in his face!
He said *he really couldn tell
Why he was so acceptable—
No! the unworthy*, he said, *the unworthy!
He knew it, he knew it! of the earth, earthy—
But run upon the Potter's wheel,*°
Sealed with the everlasting seal—°
That was it—"By grace ye are saved"—°
830 *Look at Peter, look at David!
The call*, he said, *the heavenly call!
Look at Abraham, look at Paul!*
I've heard him there—a tremenjis voice—
"Rejoice!" he'd say, "my friends, rejoice!"
And up the high you couldn think,
And up, and up—but afore you could wink,
Down like a gannet, like he wanted to pin
The divil in soundin's! and then he'd begin,
And he'd wrestle and groan, and he'd thump and he'd thwack—
840 A black-haired man, and his eyes was black.
So he says one day to Tommy at last—
"You seem to have gifts with that fiddle," he says,
And he flattens his hand like a dab of mortar
On the little chap's shoulder, and a kind of a sorter
Lookin right over him, a way he had,
Because a big preacher from Douglas said,
After chapel one night, he *navar beheld
Such a look*, he said, *all doubt dispelled,*
He said. He said—"You know what I'm maenin,
850 Like lookin to the heavenly Canaan,"
He said, and "they that seek shall find,"
And "showin a lovely frame of mind"—
So, "Gifts," says Cain, "and gifts, my friend,
Is from the Lord, that knows where to send
His gifts," he says; "and so you see,
They must be used accordantly,"
And a little pat, and the lift of the eye,
Like talking to somebody twelve foot high.
I was there myself, and listenin to'm;
860 For almost every time I come home

---

820   break: brake (ed.).
838:    soundin's: shallow water.
846-53 *Omitted.*

I'd be out, bein allis in a friendly way with them,
And takin joy, and havin my tay with them—
Well, of course, there was gels there too—
But look here! confound it! what's that to you?
"Now," he says, "This fiddle here,
Is very pleasant to the carnal ear,
To the ear of sense, that's aisy plaised,
But them that's got their affections raised,
How is it with them?" and his voice quite holler,
870 And took a hitch in Tommy's collar,
That was restless rather, and studdied him
Like a little sack—"How is it with them?"
And "Oh, the unconverted will!"
He says, and his eye on Canaan still,
And a twist with his knuckle, and "the aisy yoke,"°
He says, and Tommy fit to choke,
Till at last the misthress said, rather fearful,
She thought the fiddle was very cheerful
And nice, and makin people happy.
880 Oh, he turned upon her as snappy as snappy—
"I'll ask your opinion when I'll want to,"
He says. I don't know where Canaan was gone to
That time at all. "It's unbecomin,"
He says, "It's clane again Paul for a woman
To talk in the Church."° "But at home," she said,
"In the house, I don't see," aw, his face got as red
As the fire, aw, you navar seen the complexion.
"Silence!" he said. "Subjection! subjection!
Subjection!" he said, "this minute! this minute!"
890 And he gave her a look—not much Canaan in it,
I fancy, but rather the other style:
So the woman dropt it. Then he gave a smile,
Very holy and peaceful lek,
"And now," he says, "I've a propogicion to make,"
And Tommy stoops and Tommy shifts,
"Thomas Gelling," he says, "your gifts
Is only a snare to you, after all,
A snare," he says; "but hear the call—
Take," he says, "and dedicate
900 These gifts to His service; there's a handy seat
Under the pulpit," he says, "in the middle
Of the aisle," he says. "What! play the fiddle

---

862   takin joy: *to take joy*, said of persons meeting after a long separation, or unexpectedly.
884   again: against.

In the Chapel!" says Missis Cain; but he gave
A sweep with the hand, and "By your lave,"
He says, very dignified, "I was comin
To that," he said, "but, of course, a woman!
But navar mind (a tongue on a wire!)
This fiddle may go on the back of the fire,
Or the midden, or any other place;
910 You'll be cultivatin the viol bass,
Of course, the proper instrument,"
He says, "and begin immadient.
We'll get it from Ramsey," he says, "you'll see;
And it'll be the chapel's property,
And paid in instalments out of the fund—
It isn very expensive they run,
These viol basses; and you'll have permission
To use it, but only on condition
You'll lead the singing. So there you have it:
920 And now your talent 'll be His who gave it,
And you'll be sitting in the front pew,
And God 'll be glorified in you."
And he sniffed, and Tommy said nothin whatever.
"I've no doubt," says Cain, "you'll do your endeavour;
But we're all of us wake," he says, "and you know
Where we're privileged to go,
Thomas," he says, and——on and on,
Till I thought he never would be done.
So at last I left him there in the thick of it,
930 For, upon my soul, I was fairly sick of it—
A thund'rin rascal, anyhow;
But, however, you'll hear, you'll hear just now.

    So, you see, this bass viol
Was sent for from Ramsey at first on trial,
Apprerbation, or whatever they call it,
And Tommy there to overhaul it,
And see was it right, and couldn take to it
At first at all, *not able to spake to it*,
He said, *like the fiddle*; aw, longin shockin
940 For the fiddle, for all, that was used to go cockin
On his shouldher so handy, you know, or sittin
Upon his breast like a little kitten,
Nustlin there agen his cheek,
And coaxin the lovely little squeak
Out of its innards, somewhere or another,

---

940   for all: however.

Just like a baby with the mother—
And the misthress loved to hear him like that,
*It went to her soul, she couldn tell what
She was feelin, no, she couldn, she said,*
950 But, *comforted*, aye, *comforted*—
And she had her troubles with yandhar man,
Poor thing! and it wasn with him they began—
No—and this Tommy delighted to plaze her.
But when he got this roarin baser,
He was put out most pitiful;
For, however he'd screw, and however he'd pull,
And see-sawin
And Margery-Dawin,
He'd get nothin with all his scrapes and his scrubs
960 But a surt of yowlin molligrubs.

So Tommy was bothered, and you see the raison,
For he thought it couldn do nothin but bas'in,
And hadn no notion the awkard brute
Could play as soft as any flute.
And deeper and deeper still he was goin,
And sawin the bass to the very bone,
And no music at all; till at last the fact is
The misthress axed him to have his practice
Somewhere else. So away to the barn
970 Goes Tommy with his big consarn,
Determined, I tell ye, to have it out with it;
For he hadn the smallest bit of a doubt with it
But the tune was in it somewhere, you know.
So there he was; and he tried the slow,
And he tried the quick; till at last, by jing!
He come upon the tenor string,
That he'd come upon many a time afore:
But this time, Tommy said, you'd have swore
It was altogether different,
980 Astonishin the way it went,
Whatever the touch, or whatever the turn,
Like butter comin on the churn,
When you're nearly beat—*like butter*, he was sayin,
Like butter, or something like bleedin a vein,
The oozy it come, and the cloggy lek;
And then it'll draw to a pint, and brek
In a reglar sthrame—Aw he worked it grand!
Like a livin thing, he said, *under his hand;*

---

960   molligrubs: a stomach-ache or a fit of ill temper (Wright).

Like rivers of water in a thirsty land.°
990 So Tommy ran up the string like a paper
'll run up to a kite; aw he made her caper,
Rejisin, you know, the high he got
After yondhar basser's, aw workin it hot,
And rispin and raspin, and thrimmin and thrummin
Till the very thrashin boord was hummin.

So all the people was wondherin
Outside; for Tommy had locked himself in.
Says the boys—"Hulloah! it's like enough, may be,
The viol bass has got a baby!"
1000 But the gels said—*hush!* and stood like cravin,
For the sweet it was—they said it was *heaven!*
Heaven! they said; and *to hould their noise:*
Gels is musicaller till boys—
Just so—takin a interest—
Much more easier empressed.

So the next night Tommy began in the kitchen
And the misthress couldn help droppin her stitchin,
And starin at Tommy, the look he had,
Just like a body goin mad—
1010 With his head thrown back, and his eyes like moons,
And his hair all ruxed, and tunes and tunes.
And the lads very quiet, sittin back-o'-behind,
And the women that 'cited they couldn mind
Their wheels, lek afraid if a sound 'd be missin,
And smoothin the brat a' purpose to listen;
And the tenor string as clear as a bell,
And Cain from home, and just as well.

Then Tommy was at the misthress to get her
To think that the viol-bass was better
1020 Till the fiddle itself, *bein full of power,*
Says Tommy, *and the fiddle apt to be sour,*
And thin in the top; but the viol, he said,
Was studdy, and sure, and keepin its head
On the small edge of nothing; no baby, not him!
But a fine big lusty cherubim,
That takes the half of Jacob's ladder
At a leap, he says, or—"may be, rather,
Like a beautiful man, that loves you," he says,
"And turns your sorrows to happiness."

1011   ruxed: disordered.

1030 'Deed the misthress looked to see what he meant;
But—innocent, bless ye! innocent—
Hadn a notion, not him, the sowl!
Aw, as innocent as a biddhag bowl!

But, after that, the life they led with him
I'm tould was shockin—must have it in bed with him,
This viol, and reachin to his nose,
And the stick of it tanglin in the clothes,
And strugglin, and gettin out on the floor,
And at it still—aw, well to be sure!
1040 At it, I tell ye, from night to mornin;
And the chaps that was sleepin with him gave them warnin;
And Tommy had to go over the stable;
But, if he'd been put on the top of the tower of Babel,
Tommy wouldn have been offended,
Just the thing for him, got on most splendid—
But terrible partikkilar;
No! he said, *he wouldn dar,*
He couldn; they really must excuse him
No! nothin in the world 'd induce him,
1050 *He said, to go in the chapel yet:*
And Cain couldn understand him a bit,
And very impatient; and no wonder e'ther—
They were runnin away with him altogether,
Them gifts, he said, and to build on the rock;
And often enough a stumbling-block—
Aye, and remindin him of Paul,
That didn think much of them at all,
But rather bothered him,° yes indeed!
Aw, there's no mistake, a troublesome breed;
1060 "And, for all the carryin on there's about them,
The Church could do very well without them."

But Tommy was firm: he said he was wantin
To see the Vicar—"What gallivantin!"
Says Cain—"The Vicar! the Vicar! eh?"
"Yes," says Tommy, "he asked me to play
A piece with him, to see how it 'd go,
And him to work the piano, you know"—
"Well," says Cain, "of course it's carnal;"
And—*how about the life eternal?*
1070 And—*a very unsatisfactory sperrit;*

1033   biddhag [*dd* like *th* in *then*]: cream ready for churning.
1060   carryin on: fuss.

Vicars indeed! but, however, lerrit!
Lerrit! he said. So Tommy went
To see the Vicar, that was well acquent
With Tommy, a wonderful aisy man
Was Pazon Croft—he was an Englishman,
But despard shy, for wherever he came,
He was just like walkin in a drame—
Very white in the face. I've heard it stated
That Pazon Croft was eddikated
1080 In one of them big Churches they've got
Over in England—*Cathedrals*—what?
Cathedrals—aye: and, the lovely he sung,
He was put to the urgans very young—
Not much like this music that's driven in
Hapes of people, but what he was livin in.
For, the finest music that ever was done
He'd hardly be knowin when it begun,
Or when it left off—just so, just so—
Havin it all inside him, you know.
1090 And if the trees, or the stacks in the yard,
Had struck up, he'd been perfectly prepared.
Bless me! if yandhar man had met
A quire of angels that was just let
On Snaefell to practise their hosanners,
He'd ha' axed to look over a book with the tannors—
That's all. So, the first he heard
This Tommy and the fiddle, never a word,
Never a wink, as a body might say;
But, still for all, the next day
1100 There he was, and the next, and the next,
Till Cain was gettin rather vexed—
And, *Couldn they bake on their own griddles?*
And, *Well to be lookin higher than fiddles.*

So this was the Vicar. So Tommy come;
And, *If he wouldn be throublesome*—
And this and that; and, "Come in! come in!"
And down to the piano, and at it like sin;
And jingin and jangin, and bahin and bowin,
Till at last they heard the bellows blowin
1110 For breakfast, you know. So then they left off—
He was a single man was Pazon Croft.

1071 lerrit: let it (be).
1093 let: lit (ed.).
1094 Snaefell: highest mountain in the island.

So Tommy come home, and a book at him there
As big as the parish register—
Somewhere about the weight of a sack
Of potatoes, and every bit of it Back—
Back! yes, Back—you don't know what I mean?
Of coorse, of coorse! Well, you see I'll explain—
Tommy that was tellin me,
And showin the way, and how would it be.
1120 Well, it's a difficult sort of music, look'ee!
Slantindicular, that is, crooky,
Up and down, in and out—
Bless me! what am I talkin about!
Complercated—heads and tails—
Scientific, that is, scales—
I don't know whether you've ever heard—
Fidgets, fuges! that's the word—
Fuges, fuges, that's what I meant—
Excellent though, excellent!
1130 Fidgets—good! but avast these nudges!
I'm goin to tell you what a fuge is—
Fuge—dear heart!
What a start!
Well, obsarve! away goes a scrap,
Just a piece of a tune, like a little chap
That runs from his mammy; but mind the row
There'll be about that chap just now!
Off he goes! but whether or not,
The mother is after him like a shot—
1140 Run, you rascal, the fast you're able!
But she nearly nabs him at the gable;
But missin him after all: and then
He'll give her the imperince of sin:
And he'll duck and he'll dive, and he'll dodge and he'll dip,
And he'll make a run, and he'll give her the slip,
And back again, and turnin and mockin,
And imitatin her most shockin,
Every way she's movin, you know:
That's just the way this tune 'll go;
1150 Imitatin, changin, hidin,
Doublin upon itself, dividin:
And other tunes comin wantin to dance with it,
But haven't the very smallest chance with it—
It's that slippy and swivel—up, up, up!

1115   Back: Bach.

Down, down, down! the little pup—
Friskin, whiskin; and then as solemn,
Like marchin in a double column,
Like a funeral: or, rather,
If you'll think of this imp, it's like the father
1160 Comin out to give it him, and his heavy feet
Soundin like thunder on the street.
And he's caught at last, and they all sing out
Like the very mischief, and dance and shout,
And caper away there most surprisin,
And ends in a terrible rejisin.
That's Backs, that's fuges—aw that's fine—
But navar mind! navar mind!
Of coorse! of coorse! But, however, the day
Come at last for Tommy to play
1170 In the chapel: and they said it was raelly splendid,
But, as soon as the second hymn was ended,
Tommy went on, and it wasn no use,
On he went like the very deuce.
Fuges! aye! just so—for a part
Of the tune they'd been singin was just like a start
For one of these fudgets. So it got in his head.
And he couldn stop—and his face as red,
And his eyes like tar-barrels—only blue,
And—tuttee, tuttee, tuttee, tooh!
1180 I lave it to your imagernation
The feelins of that congregation—
Feelins, is it? Well, I'm blest!
Tremenjers! couldn be expressed!
And first a look at one another,
And then, you know, a kind of a smother
Of a groan; and then—*hush! hush! hush! hush!*
And then a roar, and then a rush:
And Cain on his feet, and—"Hould him! I say;
Hould him! hould him! anyway;
1190 Dear me! take the viol from him!
Lick him! kick him! smash him! d—— him!"
Did he? in the chapel too! I'll engage
He did: and wasn he black with rage,
And his dickey all spotted with blood—the hard
He was bitin his tongue? but took off his guard—
Aye! aye? and talk to reprove him,
I can tell ye, and even to remove him—
Talk! but—*the excellent man!* and—*the pity!*

1192-1207   Omitted; d—changed to maul.

                And left it all at last to a committee
1200   Of Cain's own friends, with just one goose
                Of a chap they were callin Billy Baroose,
                That was knowed to be his enemy—
                To make it to look like fair, ye see.
                Aw, they made it all right for him after a bit—
                "The zeal of thine house,"° they said, *that was it*—
                "The zeal of thine house," and wasn it plain;
                And well if all was like brother Cain!

                But Tommy? Tommy! aw, Tommy was ragged,
                And Tommy was shook, and Tommy was dragged,
1210   And cast into outer darkness; there
                Shall be weepin and gnashin of teeth;° and I'll swear
                If the preacher didn't get up, and thumbed
                The Bible there; and hemmed and hummed,
                And them very words, or very lek them—
                And—*this is the way the Lord 'd correck them*
                He said—*this unfortnit young pessin,*
                No doubt, he said, *it was very disthressin;*
                But here he was! a figger-head—
                Figger, I mean—what's this he said?
1220   *A lively figger*, he said, *of them*
                That's called—but—chosen? No! He came,
                Like many others, bid to the weddin;
                But hed he the garment?° *No, he hedn!*

                So Tommy, you see, was in disgrace,
                And very nearly losin his place.
                But Cain thought better of it, for all he grumbled;
                And he said he thought *the lad was humbled*—
                Converted—eh? Well—evident not;
                But still such a servant couldn be got
1230   Every day, so he stayed; but he wasn
                Suffered to rub a bit of rosin
                On that viol again. And indeed it was bruk
                That night in the row, and had to be tuk
                Down to Ramsey for repairs,
                And if it ever came back who knows and who cares?
                Anyway Tommy got over it clever,
                And worked the fiddle the same as ever.

                But he'd never go to chapel again,
                No, not even for Missis Cain.
1240   Sunday morning, the very first thing,
                When his porridge was supped, he'd be off on the wing

Fo'c's'le Yarns 176

    For the Curraghs down—and away for hours—
    Butterflies, insecks, beetles, flowers—
    G'ology, botany, and such,
    And a book to tell him which was which;
    And a bit of a glass that wasn as long
    As your thumb. But, goodness me! the strong!——
    Microscope. Hulloah! look out!
    Aye, man! aye! and what do *you* know about
1250 Microscopes? You're took on the sudden.
    Well, you know, I wish you wouldn.
    But—however. So he liked the Curraghs well,
    Did Tommy; and they've got a beautiful smell,
    Upon my word, them Curraghs; yes!
    Even in the spring they're not amiss,
    When the soft little sally buds is busted,
    And all the sthrames about is dusted
    With the yellow meal: but—in summer! I'm blowed!
    Just before the grass is mowed—
1260 Kirk Andreas way, St. Jude's, Lezayre—°
    Just lie down, no matter where,
    And you'll think you're in heaven: and the steam and the heat
    Fit to smother you, the sweet—
    Splendid too, when a chap is home
    From a voyage; very wholesome to'm,
    Clearin the blood—astonishin
    The way it exthracks the salt from the skin—
    Soft as cream, sweet as honey.
    And I'll tell you another thing that's funny
1270 Comin off the sea—the close you've got
    The horizon, like the lid of a pot—
    Just enough to make a pair of breeches,
    And then the sallies and the ditches.

    So this is where Tommy allis was hauntin—
    Every mortal thing he was wantin
    He could find in them meadows—wonderful land
    For harbs! and him that could understand
    The sorts, you know, and the virtue they had,
    And were they good or were they bad—
1280 And them that was p'ison—aw, first rate;
    Bless ye! the p'isons was just like mate

    1242   Curraghs [*gh* as *ch* in Scot. *loch*]: marshy meadows.
    1250   took: caught, as when seized by a sudden illness (Wright).
    1256   sally: willow.
    1268-73 *Omitted.*

To Tommy, that liked to feel the strong
They were, and rowlin them on his tongue
As comfibil as any kid
Would suck his mammy, or me my quid.
Well, he was curious, I tell ye—
"Look here!" he'd say, "I could take and kill ye
With a drop of this stuff!" For he'd boil it, and strain it,
And still it and steam it, and draw it and drain it,
1290 Till he'd nothin left but the very last squeeze
Of the Divil's own clout—aw, as nice as you please—
What's this he called it—"concockit?" "decockit,"
Aye, stowed away in his waistcoot pocket.
Many a time I've tould the chap
To take care for fear he'd get into a scrape
With this dirt, that nobody navar can't trust—
Abominable dangerous!

    So, flowers springin,
Linnets singin,
1300 Church bells ding-a-ling-a-lingin—
There was Tommy in his glory.
So, one day, I tell ye, afore he
Knew where he was—now, what d'ye think?
Nelly! Nelly! And the start and the blink
Of her bonny blue eye—like some *haythen goddess*,
Tommy was tellin; and curtseys as modest:
But dear me! the mischief and the sauce
There'll be under all that! and the quick little toss
Of the head; and then—"I suppose," says she,
1310 "You don't know me, Tommy?" "Know you!" says he,
And his face all burnin like the very fire—
"Know you!" and daren't look any higher
Than her knees. "It's lek I've grew," she said—
"Grew?" says Tommy, and as red as red—
"Grew?" "Would ye think," she said, "I'm the same
Little gel that used to answer her name
At Creer's—the same you were such a friend to—
The little gel you brought the hen to?"
"Think?" says Tommy, "think!" and it all
1320 Come over him like the burst of a squall
When the mornin lifts—"Dear me!" she says,
"Look up!" and he did, and he saw the breast,
And he saw the woman, the full and the round—
And—*who was he?* and he made a bound,°

1289   still: distill.

And cleared the hedge, and away like a deer—
Did Nelly laugh? Well, I didn see her—
But—I'd rather think not, but—take the hint!
She was goin to church,° so of coorse she went.
But mind ye! that was the road the gel
1330 Had to go. So, very well!
Where was Tommy now would ye be thinkin
The very next Sunday? and sneakin and slinkin
Behind the very same hedge? Dear me!
What else? and hid that a crow couldn see
Where he was hidin; and as still as a block,
Still,—but felt the whiff of her frock,
And shivered, and waited till she'd pass,
And kissed the print of her foot in the grass,
And kissed, and kissed: so, of coorse, you know,
1340 He loved her again—poor Tommy though!
Again he loved her! it hadn died
In his heart—this love; just stupified
Like a fire that's slacked, like a spark in the tinder;
Like you'll wake with the light, and jump to the winder—
Jump to the winder—she's comin! she's comin!
Aw, by gough! this love is a rum 'un!

  But at last poor Tommy, with all his blushes,
Got pluck, and 'd twiss hisself out o' the bushes
Like a little hedgehog before her there—
1350 A hedgehog makin up to a hare,
Rowlin—his legs were rather crookit—
And maybe flowers for her to look at,
Or tarroodeals, or ladybirds—
That's coleopthar's—terrible words!
Aye, but Tommy took heart of grace;
And, the second Sunday, he looked in her face;
And the third, she didn come alone,
And Tommy gave a sort of a groan,
And cut; and the fourth, they had a talk;
1360 And the fifth, I believe they had a walk—
Two fields or so—and left in the lurch with her
At those other gels, but wouldn go to church with her—
Catch him! so she tould him how it was,
And she was come for a sarvint to the Ballaglass,
The principal house in the parish—aye—
Captain Moore°—aw, terrible high—

1353 tarroodeals: devil's bulls (a kind of beetle).
1362 at: by.

Splendid family them Moores—
Deemsthars, Clerk-of-the-Roulses, brewers—
All sorts of swells, you know, that's goin,
1370 Was belongin to the Moores—no knowin
The ould, that family; blood, man, blood!
Aw, the rael thing—from the time of the flood—
Officials, Staff-of-Government,°
And all to that. So this here gent
Was countin among the first of the land,
Not rich, exactly, you'll understand:
But breedin, bless ye! There's plenty 'll cock
Their chin, but still you know the stock;
And wool is wool, and silk is silk,
1380 And you can't get your nose out of your mother's milk.

    So this is where Nelly Quine was livin
For a housemaid with them. I don't know were they givin
High wages or not; but it was a sort of a place
That was very grand, for Manx at *laste*—
The people was lookin up to it uncommon—
And the misthress, you know, an Englishwoman—
And a hape of sarvints, and a sort of a style
With them altogether: and the best part of a mile
Of plantin and that;° and a gardener (Scotch)
1390 And a butler with a gold watch—
And bulls, and stallions, and a little laddy
With buttons runnin all over his body
Style, you know—his name was Kelly.
So all that summer Tommy and Nelly
Was meetin in the meadows there;
But still, for all, he didn dare
To ax her would she love him a bit,
Only they'd linger a little, and sit
Till the bell 'd be out. And once she stayed
1400 So long, you know, that she felt afraid
To go in at all; and cried and cried;
Aye, and wouldn be pacified,
And wouldn spake to him. And Tommy said
He was very sorry—but she turned and fled
Like a pigeon (you know she could run rather fast),
And away with her to the Ballaglass.

    But when the winter weather come,

1368   Deemsthars: judges.
              Clerk-of-the-Roulses: Clerk of the Rolls, a Manx official.

Mrs Moore was keepin the sarvints at home,
And a surt of a praychin, just to shuit
1410 Their hours, and I'm tould it's well she could do't—
For the Captain and the son, ye see,
Were at church as strick as the pazon 'd be.
So what was Tommy to do? Every man of ye?
What would *you* have done? Now, one of ye!
Spake now!—Billy!—All right! You'd *ha' gone
After dark, and had some fun
At the Ballaglass?* Well, there's a quid
For your guess! That's just what Tommy did.
But the *fun?* my gough! aw no, no, no!
1420 Poor Tommy! Bless ye! if he could only go
To the house at all, it was just as much
As ever he could—aw bless ye! to touch
A thing she'd touched, a can, a besom—
It was wonderful the trifle 'd please him—
Pleasin isn' the word! He'd get it
Away with him somewhere, and coax it, and pet it,
And listen (he tould me, and I wouldn doubt it)
If there was any sound of her about it,
And put it back. *Did he ever see her?*
1430 Never to spake to her—*aw dear!*
Says you—why, bless ye! you don't know the fellow—
He'd ha' been turnin blue and green and yellow,
And red, and primin, and black and white,
If anybody 'd seen him, and brought a light!
Fancy Tommy in the sarvints' hall
At the Ballaglass, and ould Missis Ball
That was housekeeper, and all the rest—
And Tommy lookin east by west!

No, no! but still there'd be gels about,
1440 Bless ye! often slippin out
On the sly, and sooryin with their chaps,
And the darker the night the better perhaps—
Dear me! what's the use to scould them?
Where's the boults or the bars that'll hould them?
The lot of them mostly; for, don't ye see?
They like to coort in company—
Two or three pairs in the haggard—eh?

1423   besom: broom (ed.).
1433   primin: the color of priming paint, pink in Britain (ed.).
1441   sooryin: courting (Moore).
1442-83 *Omitted.*
1447   haggard: stackyard (ed.).

And the nither can hear what the other 'll say,
Nor any sound that could atthrack,
But a little sigh comin round the stack—
And bless me! that might be the air—
Some sort of a draught you can't tell where.
No! says you? Well, seemin to me then—
I think these stacks is allis breathin.
Aw, laugh, if you like—yes, yes, yes, yes!
But ye don't know the country, that's what it is.
Now, look here?—once for all I tell ye—
I've been to a weddin, I've been to a mheillea;
I've been coortin lek in general,
And I'll lay my life there isn no call
For the scand'lous talk some people has got—
And it's just dependin, whether or not,
On the place and the people, and the dacent care,
And the masther and misthress, and the kind they are,
And the considerate, and like to see
Their sarvints all of a family,
And happy and respectable—
Well now, are you laughin still?
Indeed!—well look here! one word is as good
As two, but I'd like to be understood,
And I'll tell ye what—a chap is a fool
That thinks the country is like Liverpool.
A country lad, in the Isle of Man,
Sucks something wholesome out of the very land,
That fills his head with sense, d'ye see,
And fills his heart with liberty—
The pick of men—there's good and there's bad—
But just you take a dacent lad,
And give him a chance to be dacent—aye!
Give him a chance, and—I'm tellin no lie—
That chap'll be dacent—bake or brew,
And he'll like his gel to be dacent, too.

Well, of course, the gels 'd watch
For the signs of the boys, and lift the latch
The way no finger on earth will guide it
But a gel's, when her lad is waiting outside it.
So that was Tommy's trouble, the sowl!
The poor little divil! out in the cowld,
And no gel in his arms, nor him in hers,
That's better than mittens and comforters,

1448   the nither: neither pair (ed.).

Soup and blankets—and cowld is bad,
But what was driving this Tommy mad
Was thinking if Nelly was one of the crew,
And, if she was, then *who, then? who?*
Who was the chap? And he'd be creepin and creepin
All around, and peepin and peepin,
And seeing her shaddher on the blind,
And very nearly out of his mind;
And hearin a click, and 'd have to jump,
1500 And hidin himself behind the pump;
And gettin in the way of others that was lookin
After their own sweethearts, and hookin
Over into the garden, and stumblin
Agen some others, and all of them grumblin—
And often chased, but never caught;
Till at last they got freckened, for of course they thought
It was ghosts; and—*the night was very injurious*,
Mrs Ball was sayin: but the boys was furious,
And had a reg'lar hunt, but no use,
1510 For Tommy would dodge them, and off with his shoes,
And away like the wind. So the chaps was fo'ced
As you might say, to give up the ghost.
But a terbil disappointment, it's lek,
For the Captain's gels was the very pick
Of the sarvints about—aw, splendid lasses—
Shuperior, you know, was the Ballaglasses.
So the chaps was coming from far and wide,
Sulby way, Ballaugh,° Kirk Bride—
Chaps, you know, that had any consate
1520 Of themselves, and likin to be nate
And dacent—dacent—none of your scum—
Why, light-keepers was used to come—
Light-Keepers! yes, and eireys too—
Eireys—'deed I could tell ye the who—
But still, for all, it's hardly worth—
Just the tip-top coortin on the North.

And was Nelly one of them? No; *and why?*
Well, I'll tell ye the raison bye and bye.
But, of course, you can fancy the disthress
1530 Of this poor little Tommy. I remember a verse
Of a little song he made—let's see—
How's this it is?—"I think of thee"?

1523   eireys: heirs to farms.
1526   North: northern division of the Island.

No, that's not it—"So it's home——"—just so—
I've got it now—when he was leaving, you know—
    "So it's home to Renshent
      My weary way I wind;
     For I must be content
       With her shadow on the blind."
On the blind, ye see. *Renshent*, that's Cain's—
1540   All right! all right! I know what you manes,
Yes, yes! of course, that's the tune you're hummin to.
The misthress and Tommy—that's just what I'm comin to.

    Well, I tould ye the way he was punishin
These beetles and things—it was raelly astonishin
The stores—till these gels began to mock,
And *was he goin to have them in pickle like stock?*
And *did he want a barrel? or where would he put them?*
And *would he like them to help him to gut them?*
So he was quite offended, if ye plaise,
1550   And took and made a sort of a case—
And every inseck with a little hook through
And a pane in the lid for a body to look through—
For you mustn open—all hatches battened
On Tommy's decks; and the flowers he flattened
(And still there wasn room for half)
In a big ould Bible he found on the laft.
And often of an evenin
The misthress would ax him to bring them in,
And Tommy would sit, and Tommy would 'splain—
1560   And who so happy as Missis Cain?
Aw 'deed she was happy for all—
"Yes," the misthress would say, "he's small
Is Tommy," she says, "but his heart—his heart
Is big enough." And *he gave her a start
Many a time*, she said, *to see
The perfect happy he could be
With nothin, and the full of it too—*
Yes—and she liked his eyes to be blue,
She said, *it was making them so clear—*
1570   *Such room*, she said, *he had in them there—*
Such an arch, such a spread, like the round of the sky—
No cloud; no shadow of a lie.
Some eyes, ye see, is nothin but fog,
And some is just like weak grog;
And some is like leeches, and some is like slugs,

   1556   laft: loft

And some is like bullets, and some is like bugs—
Muddy, some is, and some is sharp,
And some like a cod, and some like a carp—
Differin sorts. But Tommy's was loops
1580 Of light in light, just hoops in hoops
Of soft blue fire, and feathered about
With a kind of grey fluff, and openin out,
And out, and out—the eye of this chap—
Hoops, you know—like ye'll see a map
That's showin all the planets and things,
And the sun in the middle, and rings and rings—
No doubt you've seen the lek in a book.
So the misthress would sit, and look and look,
And give a little nod, I'm tould,
1590 And bless this Tommy in her sowl.

Well, troubles came upon him for all—
Troubles! troubles! where's the wall
That'll keep them out? As the Scripture saith—
Dig the foundation as deep as death:°
Plumb it, and plaster it, every chop of it;
Build it to heaven and put glass on top of it—
No go, my lads! you'll pay your fine—
And a chap that's in love should spake his mind:—
Spake he should—there's never known'—
1600 Does he think the gel is a stock or a stone
That it'll stay where it is till he choses to pick it?
He should speak, he should speak! You can't get a ticket
For Love, at all: it's rather a free thing,
Is to Love,° I tell ye—call it a he thing,
Call it a she thing—wilful—eh?
And there's other boats besides yours in the bay—
That's the thing. But this Tommy? What?
Shy? my gough! But, whether or not,
He was over one night at Captain Moore's,
1610 And watchin the windows, and watchin the doors,
And as silent as a little trout,
And a dale o' coortin all about,
And chased at these divils, and couldn see her,
And into the garden, and hid himself there,
Behind the summer-house—Holy Moses!
The smotherin it was with roses,

1599   known': knowing (ed.).
1599-606 *Omitted.*
1613   at: by.

Yandhar place; but only Spring
The time I'm tellin: but thatched with ling.
So there was Tommy aback of a bush,
1620 When—aisy! aisy! hush, hush, hush!
Two people comin on the walk,
And the nearer they come he could hear them talk—
Aw—Tommy, Tommy, Tommy mine!
The young Captain, and Nelly Quine!
Aw 'deed it was! aw 'deed for sure!
Nelly, and young Captain Moore—
The son—and into this arbour place,
And sat, and his arm around her waist,
And—the ould ould music, sweet and low—
1630 Music! music! aye just so—
Whoever was the first to set it—
Music, music, wherever you'll get it.

And Nelly's tears was just like rain;
And Tommy could hear what the Captain was sayin—
"Do love me, Nelly! do then! do!
Aw Nelly, the same as I love you!
Nelly! Nelly! I am in earnest—"
If that wasn a burnin fiery furnace
For Tommy—my gracious! he said the bite
1640 He took of his tongue to try and keep quiet,
And his head goin round and round and round,
Till he thought he'd fall; but he held his ground
And they looked so lovely! he said—good Lord!
That's where, he said, *it come very hard*
On the leks of him—and he didn know
Whether to stay, or whether to go,
Or what to do—but, rain or fair,
Of coorse he wasn't wanted there—
But—Nelly cryin—and—*Would he take her part?*
1650 *But how?* and the cables of his heart
Goin crackin. And then he thought, was it right
For him to be sneakin there in the night
Like a spy upon her? for he wasn apt
To be thinkin evil, wasn this chap—
No, he wasn, and he didn now;
But he waited till, he couldn tell how,
Nelly's head gave two little slips,
And—aw poor Tommy! lips to lips,
Breast to breast! aw Tommy, my son,
1660 You're beat! you're beat! the game is won!
Was and wasn—and meant is meant—

But he picked up the bits of his heart, and went,
Bits! aye, bits! and a swish and a swirl
Of all his life, like the wheel of the world
Had gone over him with its lumbering load,
And left him dyin on the road—
Tommy! Tommy! But, afore he got home,
He begun to think what good could come
Of work like that—and—*oh! and oh!*
1670 *Would the Captain marry her? And—No:*
No, no, no! he was goin to deceive her,
Make a fool of her, and leave her.
"She's lost!" he said, "She's lost! she's lost!"
And he staggered, and his head was frost
And fire in a minute, and he turned to go back,
And—"I'll save her! I'll save her!" and he looked to the black
Black sky, and he shouted—"Nelly!" he said,
"Nelly! Nelly!" and fell like dead.
Aw dear! the little sowl!
1680 And some chaps that was knockin about on the sthrowl
Found him there, and picked him up,
And of coorse they thought he'd had a sup,
And home with him, and laughin and jeerin,
And up to the door, and Cain appearin
With a light, and terbil aggravated,
And—"Here's your Tommy, tossicated!"
And cuts. "Indeed!" says Cain, "indeed!
The pump, I suppose," and wouldn heed
For Tommy, whatever he could say—
1690 "Drunk," says Cain, and drags him away—
"Drunk," says Cain, "indeed!" he says,
And Tommy that wake he couldn resist—
And under the very pump; but then
The misthress came, and—"Cain! aw Cain!
Cain!" she said, "aw listen, listen!
He isn drunk, he isn, he isn!
It's trouble," she says; and—"Lave him to me!"
So Cain dropped him, and—"Come" says she,
"Come in now, Tommy!" Then Tommy to ax
1700 *Could he spake to her alone?* "The fac's
Is dead agen ye," says Cain; "but still—
Trouble—eh? well—pozzible—
Pozzible"—and shakin the head,
And takes the candle, and off to bed.

1680   knockin about on the sthrowl: strolling, loafing.

So then it was that Tommy tould
All the secrets of his soul—
And Nelly—and how it began at Creer's
When they were little things, and all the years
He'd loved her since; so she gave a smile,
1710 Did the misthress, you know, and—"Dear me! child,"
She says—"that's not such a terbil case";
And she took his hand, and she looked in his face.
"But now," says Tommy, and *where he had been
That very night! and what he had seen!
And the way the Captain was spakin to her,—*
"Captain! what Captain?" "Young Captain Moore."
"Captain! Captain!" Aw, she dropped his hand,
And the two of her own clasped in the one,
And pressed to her heart, like man when he's shot,
1720 And her face like paper, and just a blot
Of blood on her cheek, and drawin her breath
All tight and shivery through her teeth,
Tommy said—*like shot,* he said—
And, if it hadn been for Cain that was overhead,
There's no doubt, he said, she'd have sent a cry
Right up through the roof, right up through the sky—
Poor thing! to God himself in Heaven,
But Cain was betwixt—and past eleven.

Now, what had Tommy done? You'll get lave!
1730 He'd stumbled into an old grave—
Had Tommy, sent his foot through the lid
Of a coffin—that's what Tommy did—
Of a coffin, where her heart's true core
Was nailed down, stamped down for evermore.
That's what the misthress thought, it's lekly,
But I'll tell you all about it directly.

Well, whatever it was, it was see-saw,
For a while at the misthress. Would she hould her jaw
Altogether, or just to spake out
1740 To Tommy at once, like a doubt in a doubt—
For to spake at all wasn aisy to her—
And to spake to Tommy—that was more.
For ould sorrows comes over you sometimes
Like ould tunes, like ould rimes,
That's runnin in your head, and makin ye
A sort of happy, and sometimes they're takin ye

1729   You'll get lave [leave]: All right!°

   Like the frost takes the whalers in the fall of the year
   And gunpowder cannot blast you clear.
   And still, for all, she had to say something,
1750 For of course this Tommy would think it a rum thing
   For her to be carryin on like yandhar:
   And besides—she loved him—Alexandher!
   I'll throuble you to look sirrious!
   Loved him—that's the way it was—
   Bless ye! and isn it Natur tells us
   To pour our souls into somebody else's?
   And that's what she'd longed for, but hard to find;
   So navar couldn make up her mind,
   Part wondherin if Tommy would shuit,
1760 But stopped at the pint, and didn do't.
   But now the confidence—what bother!
   Love then! Love!—as old as his mother—
   Love—and the feelinger and the truer
   There couldn be; and that's what drew her—
   And—holy, holy—indeed! you object to it?
   Holy, I say! I'll tell ye, I'll stick to it—
   Holy—so that's the raison she dar;
   So she tould her saycret, so there you are!
   Only just think now! Pazons and preachers,
1770 Pastors and masters, class-leaders and teachers,
   Shuperintendans and conferences,
   Archdeacons and bishops, and all their expenses
   Paid. Think of that! the whole machine
   That was workin around her, or else should have been—
   Priests and Levites, that was used to go
   Every day to Jericho,
   And back very likely—and navar eyein
   The craythur that lay by the roadside dyin—°
   And this little chap, that just kep in his place,
1780 Like a dog might keep, and look up in her face,
   But looks like axin her to tell—
   Aye, that's it! aw well, well, well!

    Now, listen! this is the way it was—
   This Captain Moore, of Ballaglass,
   The father, you know, when Misthress Cain
   And him was young, lek the people is sayin
   Young and foolish—eh? but still
   Fell in love with her terbil—

1762-7 *Omitted.*
1767   dar: dare.

And her with him? Well, never say die!
1790 I think he's a chap with one eye,
A chap with one eye, that is,
Or else with a slit, the way a cat is—
Her with him! for goodness sake!
It was—*her with him*, and no mistake—
Her with him; and that's the way—
The man 'll go, but the woman 'll stay.

And was he desavin her? Honour bright!
True and honest as the light
Was Captain Moore. But what was the good?
1800 Think of the fam'ly! think of the blood!
First-class—my gough! the very first
In the Island you know: and that's the worst—
What for won't people be content
With their equals? And—*The heiress of Renshent?*
I knew she was, and a Ballarat—
But, bless my soul and body! what's that,
When you're spakin of Moores? It couldn be,
And they might ha' knowed it. *But wasn he free?*
Nonsense! nonsense! it isn no use!
1810 *He ought to have married her?* Go to the deuce!
Most certainly not! the Ballaglasses
And the Ballarats! you stupid asses!
What stuff are you talkin? Is wine the same
As jough? Is water as thick as crame?
What are you comin to? Silk and leather!
Confusion and folly altogether!
No, no, my lads! The Captain was maenin
All right enough—there's no complainin
About him at all. But of coorse the fuss
1820 His people was makin was scandalous!
Dreadful! And it's only raison too
His love wouldn be that through-and-through
And deep and strong like the misthresses,
So that's, you see, the way it is.
And they had him away to England there,
And he'd ha' married her like a shot, navar fear!
And half the parish at the weddin,
But he wasn allowed, and so he didn.
And years afore he was back—behould ye!

1790-7   *Omitted*.
1808-19 *Omitted*.
1814   jough [rhymes with Scot. *loch*]: ale (ed.).

1830   He married the English lady I tould ye,
      So that's, you see, the way it was done,
      And settled down, and had this son,
      Their only child, and spoilt him rather,
      And went for a Captain like his father.

        So Misthress Cain—that's Shimmin, you know,
      That was then—was taken uncommon low,
      And wouldn ate and wouldn spake,
      And gettin very thin and wake.
      And it wasn no matter what they were tryin—
1840   Aw 'deed I believe she was out of her mind,
      For a while, at least. And Parson Craine,
      A rum ould chap that was vicar then,
      Was axed would he come and pay her a visit.
      So they tould him the way. "A dumb divil, is it,
      She's got?" and they looked! "Aw, well, I guess
      You'd better lave her alone!" he says—
      Like maenin, *It's well to be rid of their talk,*
      The *women*, you know. Aw, a hearty old cock
      Was Craine, I've heard, a rael ould Turk.
1850   So then the Methodists went to work
      And the lot of them hummin about her like midges;
      And got her to be a sort of religious;
      Lek stupid lek, and very meek,
      And had her converted in a week—
      In a week she got pace; and rather blamin her
      The slow she was, like a sort of shamin her,
      Pace! Aw, 'deed, I'd aisy belave
      She *had* pace; but was it the pace of the grave?
      Well, well, there's many worse places.
1860   *Pace!* it's a word I'm fond of, pace is.
      Pace, pace from all her woes!
      Pace, pace! God only knows—
      Perfect pace—the people was sayn;
      Perfect pace——and then—comes Cain!

        Yes, he come—he come from the South,
      And butter wouldn melt in his mouth—
      Yandhar man! And the holy, you never!
      And gettin the name, you know, of the clever!

    1834   went for: was called (ed.).
    1855   pace: peace.
    1865   South: southern division of the Island.

    At the Methodists—bless ye! brought him over
1870 A purpose to see would he do for a lover—
    Renshent's heiress! my gough! they knew
    Which side their bread was butterin too.
    So nither way no *love* was meant
    She got *religion* (!), and he got Renshent.
    She hadn a notion, I expeck
    To have him for a husband lek
    Lek husbands is, you know, but just
    A guardian lek, that was put in trust
    With her sowl, like a guide the Lord had given
1880 To lead her studdy on to Heaven—
    A Christian brother and a Christian sisther,
    And if this Cain had ha' tuk and kissed her,
    He'd ha' spoilt it all. But—cautious! cautious!
    Bless ye! that's the stuff that washes!
    And her to tell him the whole of her story,
    And hand-in-hand with him on to glory—
    That's what she thought—*her foot couldn slip
    In such holy communion and fellowship.*
    The big Tom-cat! the smooth and the sleek
1890 And the soft, and the whisker on his cheek
    Just like blackin on a boot,
    And his nice white hands, and——ough! the brute!
    And—"Oh," he says, "the unselfish love!"
    Renshent, you know, he was thinkin of!

    Aye, Cain—so the uncle come to die—
    Him she was gettin the propitty by—
    And rather an awkward way he was givin it—
    And so they got married, and come to live in it.
    And so you'd think they'd be goin jog-jog—
1900 Aw bless ye! they turned a new leaf in the log
    That day, they did; a leaf that was scored
    With blood and misery, every word—
    Death sealed it up at last, and tuk it
    To owners, that has never bruk it,
    And navar will till God 'll sit
    Upon his judgment throne—-that's it.

    But still you'll hear everything almost,
    No matter how they may keep it close—
    The neighbour women? Of course! what else?

1869 at: among.
1907-16 *Omitted.*

       Fo'c's'le Yarns

1910 And the boys with sweethearts, and also the gels—
   They'll talk! they'll talk! aw never fear!
   And then what she tould this Tommy theer
   That time, you know, and all the rest of it—
   I believe I've got the proper twist of it—
   I believe so. But—however, you'll see—
   This is the way they were tellin me.

    Well, this Cain was not content—
   He'd got the woman, he'd got Renshent;
   But there was one thing he hadn got,
1920 The woman's love—he hadn got that—
   The bargain! the bargain! she didn pretend—
   A pious friend! a pious friend
   Here below, and Heaven above—
   And she shivered at the name of love.
   She was beautiful—I know she was;
   She was young—too young to be nail'd on a cross;
   Aye—and so of coorse he'd fall
   In love with her beauty—aisy all!
   Couldn help it! Well, that's a fact—
1930 *And wantin her to love him back*—
   Any more? any more? Cain's love! my gough!
   Cain's! A pig 'll love its trough,
   I dessay he will—do you think I'm hard?
   Cain's love! do you think I don't regard
   For the feelings of a man? I do!
   There's not a feelinger man in the crew—
   And you know it—But let it be *love* then—there!
   There's odds of love, and I don't care—
   I know what I mane, and I know what I say—
1940 But how about the bargain—eh?
   Obey him? serve him? so she was doin;
   But—*love* him? That's another tune.
   She couldn, it wasn in her power:
   Her love was as dead as a dead flower—
   Stick it in the ground! will it grow?
   Mould it! water it! just so—
   Will it blossom like the rod for Aaron?°
   Will it bloom and blow like a rose of Sharon?°
   Its stalk is bruk, its leaves is shed—°
1950 Dead! she tould him it was dead.

  1925-40 *Omitted.*

Now, some men's nothin but muck and mire,
And some is aequal full of fire:
But Cain was both, like these bogs they're tellin,
That's allis burnin there and swellin—
Rushes above, and turf, and that,
But underneath they're just a vat
Of pitch and brimstone, and all the rest,
A big black fire of greediness—
That was Cain. And the pride of the man
1960 To think he couldn get her love like land—
Rent it, or buy it, so much an acre—
That, if she wouldn love him, he couldn make her.
Make! make! make? No, you won't, my boy!
Let's have that joy! for it is a joy!
You can't! you can't! Oh isn it glorious?
Love victorious! love victorious!
Victorious—eh! ah dear! the strength of it!
And the height and the depth and the breadth and the length of it.°
Make it—will ye? Make a woman's heart!
1970 Scoop it, and scrape it in every part!
Send blood through its chinks, let it beat, let it burn,
God bless your soul! make a tub, make a churn!
Your granny's picthur!—But—he *loved her*—eh?
He loved her,—he loved her;—well, in a way,
I'll allow he did. But what thanks to him then?
Could he help it? You navar seen her, my men—
My goodness! could he help it? There!
He was welcome to love her. But was it fair,
When she couldn love him, and when he knew,
1980 Was it fair for him—I'll lave it to you—
First to sulk, and then to complain,
Then ragin fury, then sulks again,
Till he settled down in the dead sea
Of bitter hatred and cruelty?
Where was the saint that she thought would direct her
On the road to Heaven, that she thought would protect her
Against herself, against the love
That was still in the deep of her heart, and strove
With the love of God? Where was he to lift her
1990 Above everything on earth that could drift her
From the anchor of her sowl°
Sure and steadfast, like we're tould
In Hebrews—do ye remember the hymn—

1951-9 *Omitted.*
1973-7 *Omitted.*

Jesus lover—Say't for them, Sim!°
Can he? my gough! is it *can he*, ye said?
Now, then, Simon, go ahead!
        Jesus, lover of my soul,
          Let me to thy bosom fly,
        While the threatening billows roll,
2000   While the tempest still is nigh.
One verse, that's enough, that's all we're wantin,
Just to show the way it's slantin.
He could say every word. Well, you'll easy see,
He wasn the man he was seemin to be
When the misthress married him:—it was just like wakin
Out of a dream; like a cloud 'd be breakin,
Like scales goin peelin off her eyes,
When she saw what he was. There's some of them dies
Directly almost, and some drags on—
2010 But she knew the man! she knew the man!
So there you are—a sweetheart? a lover?
Hadn he taken advantage of her
When the poor thing didn know what she was at?
When she was stupid lek, with religion and that—
Stupid—low in her mind, not knowin
What she was doin nor where she was goin,
Or what she was eatin, or how she was dressin—
Not fit to marry any pessin.

    Well, he hated her. Reglar spite and malice;
2020 But still, for all, the man was jalous
In his very blood, in his very bone;
So he couldn lave the woman alone.
That's the worst she had to endure.
And *Captain Moore, Captain Moore!*
And *Captains, was it? Captains! aye.*
Indeed, she was lookin middlin high!
Captains! Captains! very strange!
Could she fancy a Colonel for a change!
Mockin, you know, upcastin lek—
2030 And about *the duty* and about *the respeck*,
And then he'd fire the Screpthar at her,
Texes on texes, chitter-chatter—
Daniel there, and Zechariah—
Ezekiel and Nehemiah—
Proverbs and Leviticus—

  2002   it's slantin: it goes.
  2011-87 *Omitted.*

What was the rule, he said, *from the fuss?*
Wasn the woman to cleave, it was sayin,
To the man, and the two to be one, Mrs Cain?
One flesh,° he said; and then he'd fall
2040 On his knees, and pray like Peter and Paul,
And ax her to pray—to pray, by Jove!
To pray for love! to pray for love!
Love for him! A nice request!
Love for *him—that her heart might be his—*
God's and his, he said, *he'd share it,*
He was willin of that—oh, yes, he could bear it.
He could bear it, he said; and he'd hould her
Like a vice, till her arm, right up to the shoulder,
Was just like ink—with his savageness.
2050 And he'd stand her off, and he'd look in her face
Like some hungry brute, like watchin the signs
Of a *chance* of love, lek in two minds
Would he choke her, or would he not?
Choke her? kill her upon the spot?
And her like the dead: but navar took
Her eye off his, and the pitiful look!
And—*how would it end?* and—*who was to save her?*
Till he'd fling her agen the wall, and lave her.
By gough! he's been seen; aye, aye, he has!
2060 A pane of glass is a pane of glass—
But hadn no notion, not him—but still—
Very well! very well!

But religion! aw the divil was keen—
He was more religious till ever he'd been;
Strict uncommon, and strict he kept—
I wonder if that man ever slept—
One eye open I should think—
Navar touched a drop of drink;
And just the same when I got to know him
2070 Long years after. "A happy home,"
He'd say, "is the thing"—*unworthy, no doubt,*
Unworthy—but what was he talkin about?
            Grace was free,
            And who were we?
            And—fiddledee!
And the cup to his mouth, and sippin and sippin,
And lookin at the wife as sweet as drippin—
"Yes!" and he'd sigh—"a blessed privilege!"
But why he didn call it divilege,
2080 When he was about it, it's hard to say—

I suppose there's privilege
That *is* divilege—
But—that's the way!
My gough! to see him smoothin his chin,
And scraped like a priddha to begin,
Just like paintin (maybe he was)—
Paintin out the Divil's cross.

    So that's the story she had to tell,
Like a craythur cryin out of hell
2090 To any body passin, to see
Would they pity her in her misery.
Yes, she tould him—he didn try to stop her—
But very nice, you know, and proper—
Like shuitable for him to hear—
Aw, that was the woman! navar fear!
And—"Tommy, Tommy," says Missis Cain,
"The curse is come upon them again—
The curse! the curse!" And—*she'd send a letter*
The very next day to Nelly, to get her
2100 *To come—and most particular.*
And Tommy of course, you know, not to be there.

    And so she did: so Nelly come,
And this Cain, for all, was away from home.
So ups with Nelly, and took and tould her
All about it. She didn scould her—
No, no! not her—but just the way
It was; and the people had got it to say—
"What people?" says Nelly, and the stiff she stud!
"What people? if you'll be so gud?"
2110 "A friend of yours," says Mrs Cain,
"A lovin friend"—"That's the *people* you mane,"
Says Nelly, as sharp! So she didn deny,
Didn the misthress, but fit to cry;
For she thought this Nelly was rather hard,
For a young thing like that, and wasn prepared.
And bless ye! maybe *a bit of a brazen*,
Thinks the misthress: but everything in its saison—
I navar wasn for imprince—no!
I don't like it. But, even so—
2120 My gough! there's things—why, bless your noddy!
Musn a body stand up to a body,
When there's one body botherin at him,
And another body at the bottom—
And you don't know, but still you've a guess!

My gough! I'll tell ye what it is—
That's hard, if you like! your life, your love,
Your heart of hearts—and they'll take and shove
Their fist in there! aw I know it well!
But still it's differin for a gel?
2130 And *the misthress,* you says, *that kind*—well, yiss—
And fisses!—my goodness! the misthress's fiss!
All right! all right! just the pride and the pluck,
And the *touch-me-not!* look out, my buck!
Will she? won't she? what's the use?
Aye, and see ye at the deuce!
As quite as a lamb, and as bould as a ferret—
Some women's got a terbil sperrit.

"He loves you dearly." "Who loves me?" says Nelly,
"Who loves me?" and up with the head like a filly,
2140 Like sniffin the wind—they're splendid craythurs
Is them, lek accordin to their nathurs,
Splendid—like sniffin—"Who loves me? who?"
So the misthress tould her. "Aw, that'll do!"
Says Nelly—and a little laugh—and she says,
"I think I'll go now, ma'am, if you plase;
If you plase ma'am, I'll be goin, I think"—
And the misthress felt her heart go sink—
But held on, for her sowl was cravin to her,
This Nelly, the very first minute she saw her,
2150 For she saw that she was the raal stuff,
That's it! and no matter for the huff—
Huffed! but wasn it like prent,
The beautiful and the innocent?
The sweet and the true? But—whether or not—
Chut! the misthress loved her like a shot—
And *how to save her?* She seen the sowl
Was trimblin all over, for she couldn hould,
No matter the huffed—aw hard to hide!
Love is a stronger thing than pride.

2160   So the misthress tould her all the same
She done to Tommy, only the name
She didn tell—but *a gentleman*
That was far above her, and how it began,
And how it ended—*no doubt, for the best*—
No doubt—but oh! the bitterness!
And "Nelly, I wouldn be tellin you this,

2152   prent: print.

If I didn' love you—give me a kiss!"
And *Nelly darlin!* and—*Nelly sweet!*
Then Nelly ran to the misthress' feet,
2170 And laid her head in her lap, and flung
Her arms around her, and clung, and clung,
And sobbed and sobbed a good while—
Aw, bless ye! what was she but a child?
Then the misthress took her bonnet off,
And slackened her a bit abaft,
And caught her round and round the neck,
And spread herself upon her lek—
Aw, Nelly herself has towld me—and she lay,
And the gathered, and sheltered, and hid away,
2180 And nussed, and coaxed, and folded in,
She said it was just astonishin
The complete the world seemed all to go
From her lek—that she didn' know
Nothin at all, but just the door
Was shut on all sorrows for evermore.

But when Nelly got a bit peacefuller,
Then the misthress sthrooghed her hair,
And reddied it, and made it nice—
Dear me! the tender and the wise—
2190 Eh? my gough! till she brought it round
To spake about Tommy, and the way he was down
Altogether, lek low in his mind—
And *the good, and the faithful, and the kind*—
And—*any woman, no matter who,*
Might be proud to marry him; and—"it's you!
It's you he's lovin more than his life!
Oh Nelly, couldn ye be his wife?
Aw, try, Nelly! aw, I think ye could—
Aw, Nelly! there's no mistake he's good."
2200 But Nelly shivered in every limb—
And—"Oh! don't talk to me about him!"
She says, "for if he's as good as gool,
He's a fool," she says, "and a stupid fool."
My word! she was up again like fire.
But the misthress thought she wouldn' try her
That way any more, but just
To pet her, and coax her, the way you must
With the lek, you know, if it's peace you're for—
Or else—my gough! look out for war!

2188   reddied: arranged.

2210   Aye—but she got her as quiet as quiet,
And then she went, but that very night
The misthress made up her mind to spake
To Captain Moore himself, to take
Some order someway with the son—
Hard it was, but it had to be done.
And she saw the captain; but what occurred,
To tell ye the truth, I navar heard—
Only the misthress came home very weakly,
And off with her to bed directly;
2220 And whiter till white; and it was raelly too much—
Ould love is a dangerous thing to touch.

    But listen to me! Just a week after that
I was down at Renshent; and the whole of the lot
Sittin up all night there in the kitchen,
Afraid of the storm, that was nearly hitchin
The roof off the house—Nor-West by Nor—
Dead in, you know, upon the shore—
Great guns—and impossible for me
To get home, so stayed for company.

2230   And Cain was there, with his face in a frown
Like thunder; but the misthress was lyin down,
They said, in the parlour; very sick—
So these boys was up to every trick,
Pretendin they had to hould the gels
For the freckened they were—dear me! what else!
And snugglin up, and whisperin—
And very lovin and comfortin—
Bless ye! coortin away like dust—
Takin advantage scandalous.
2240 And Cain someway didn seem to be heedin,
And he had a book, but he wasn readin—
He seen them well enough, I'll be bail—
But he looked to be thinkin there a dale.
But Tommy wasn with them at all;
And so I says to Harry Phaul—
One of these chaps—"Where's Tommy to-night?"
And the wink went round upon me straight,
And nudgin and lookin, till one of them said—
"Haven you heard——?" "Silence! ye jade!"
2250 Says Cain, and looks at the gel like murder—

    2245   Phaul: son of Paul.

"This talk," he says, "must go no furder—
It isn accordin to your station,
And it isn to the use of edification."
So the gel gev a frump, like *dear me?*
"Look here!" he says, "you're talkin too free—
Yes—and very undesi'ble—
And I'll read you four chapters in the Bible
In a minute," he says, "like a shot," he says—
"Four chapters, every vess—"
2260 *Four chapters, if a finger stirred o' them!*
Four chapters, every word o' them!
"Silence! I say." And he stamps the foot—
"A chatt'rin, aggravatin slut!

But this young Baynes," he says, "may ax
What has happened—I'll state the fax!
I'll state them," he says, "ye jack-daw!
And every one of ye hould your jaw!
This is the fax. Our Thomas Gellin,
For raisins best known to himself, has fell in
2270 Love with a person they're callin Quine—
Ellen; if I rightly mind.
Now, this gel was a sarvant in Captain Moore's,
That should have turned her out of doors
Long ago—but, however,——this Nancy—
Nelly, I mane, takes the captain's fancy—
The young captain's. They'd words—all right—
Him and the father—that's Wednesday night.
Thursday—that's yesterday—Nicky Freel
Brings the captain's yacht from Peel,°
2280 And anchors her inside the bay;
And there she was lyin the whole of the day.
At six o'clock this evenin
This young pesson isn in—
Nither's the captain—can't be found—
And then, wherever she was bound,
This yacht they're callin the Waterwitch°
Is off to sea with every stitch—
And a woman aboord.—Well, it's nat'ral rather,
And, puttin two and two together,
2290 It isn cuttin it very fine
To think this woman is Ellen Quine—
No—so the people have got it they're off
To Scotland of course,° and I'm tould their craft
Is small, and very bad prepar'd—
And certainly it's blowing hard—

And Gelling—that was allis short—
Don't take his affliction the way that he ought;
But's gone clane mad, and out on the shore,
And says he'll navar come back no more—
2300 See the carnal mind, see!
Where's his faith? perplexin to me!"
And when he was speaking there come a strain
That rocked the house—"It's blowin," says Cain:
"Blowin!" says I; "she'll navar live!
That thing 'll go down like an ould sieve,
If she tries her course—I know the boat;
But she'll navar show the canvass to 't
Her only chance is to run—d'ye hear!"
I was gettin rather 'cited theere—
2310 "And where'll she run to? I give you warnin
That vessel 'll be ashore afore mornin."

    I tell ye the words were hardly gone from me
When the door burst open, and in comes Tommy—
My gough! the drippin! and white as a ghost,
And his eyes all ablaze, and his voice all hoast—
And—"Run!" he says, "the lot of ye, run!
She's on the Rue! she's done! she's done!"
"The Rue!" I says, "just so! that's it!"
(The Rue is a point to the westward a bit)—°
2320 *The Rue*—"Come along!" says I, "let's slope!"
"Get a ladder!" I says, "and plenty of rope!
Light the lanthorn! bear a hand!"
Says Cain,—"You're quite a perfessional man!"
I raelly thought he was going to bother
About some humbuggin thing or another
Even then—but he wasn so bad as that—
'Deed he was as active as a cat,
Was Cain—and skillful, and houldin out—
Under orders? no doubt! no doubt!
2330 Of course! guy heng! and who was he,
To work a wreck, compared with me?
Well, I should think so! only raison!
And everybody in his saison.

    The day was bruk when we got to the Rue,
And there was the Waterwitch full in view.

  2315   hoast: hoarse.
  2328   houldin out: enduring.
  2330   guy heng!: bless me!°

Fo'c's'le Yarns 202

        She wasn on, but very near it,
        Just makin her last tack to clear it:
        They'd tried to anchor, but the cable went snap;
        They'd tried her with her jib and a scrap
2340 Of a mizzen, but it wouldn do—
        Closer, closer to the Rue!
        And, when we came upon the beach,
        They were settin the mainsail reefed to the leech—
        And the only chance there was for the ship—
        When there came a squall, and the mast gev a rip
        And out of her, and there she was!
        Roullin on like a dead hoss—
        Helpless, you know, "Stand by now, men!
        She'll strike, and strike, and strike again,
2350 Afore she'll settle"—I says; and she gave
        A heel to starboard; and then a wave,
        Like an elephant, took her on his back,
        And in with a run, and crack—crack—crack!
        And then a scrunch, the way I said,
        And the Waterwitch had made her bed—
        Fast—stuck fast in a sort of a jint
        Betwixt two rocks, that lay off the pint
        About a thirty fathom or so,
        And covered them; and the tide 'd flow
2360 Maybe an hour after that—
        My gough! like a mouse with a cat!
        And the short seas herryin her,
        And the long seas buryin her,
        And the tearin and sawin on the rocks—
        You could see she was breakin up like a box.
        So says I—"The work has got to be done!"
        And sthrips—says Cain, "Go on, my son!"
        "No!" says Tommy, "I'll go!" says he;
        "I'll go!" he says, "it's me! it's me!"
2370 "Look here!" says I, "just wait a second!
        Look here now, Tommy! how long do ye reckon
        You'll live in that sea? The very first flop
        'll rowl ye over like a top.
        If you want to be drowned, that's another story.
        But are you detarmined to go to glory
        All at once—eh, Tommy?" says I.
        "If I die," he says, "I'd like to die!"

2343   settin the mainsail reefed to the leech: adjusting and securing the mainsail that was partially rolled up and tied to its edge (ed.).
2362   herryin: harrowing, tearing.

"Indeed!" I says, "aw dear! aw dear!
Whisper, Tommy!" and I stooped to his ear—
2380 "Whisper—patience just a bit!
Maybe you're goin to have her yet!"
Aw! by gough, he was just like a lamb—
Coaxin! that's the way I am!

So I says to the chaps—"Is any one wantin
This job?" I says, "for it's time to be slantin."
Not a word—"Are ye sure now?—Right as a riddle!"
And I ties the rope around my middle,
And ready coiled, and how—God knows!
But I shut my eyes, and in I goes!
2390 *And wasn I divin under the says?*
Divin! divin, if ye plase?
Teach your granny to suck eggs!
But it's terbil nasty about your legs
A rope like that—and payin it out
Far too free—bein willin, no doubt,
But no 'sperience, you know—hard work!
And no mistake! There was a regular turk
Caught me half-way—my gough! what a brute!
I'll swear I thought I'd navar get through't.
2400 And these divils ashore—it's worse they got—
I'd a mind to go back, and kick the lot—
But—however—what with tuggin and luggin,
And givin and takin, for all their humbuggin,
Just when I thought I had enough,
Somebody gript me by the scruff,
And afore a man could turn on his heel
I had my arms round Nicky Freel.
No time for talk!—"The stump o' the mast!
Bear a hand, Nick! make fast! make fast!"
2410 And gives him the rope—when there came a rowl,
And a bump! and I don't know in my sowl—
But he dropt it—*Nicky?* Out of his hand!
Dropt it! and these chaps on the land
Haulin for all they felt the loose—
Haulin away like the very deuce—
Like they'd got a whale—he dropt the rope—
Nicky Freel! like soap! like soap!
And him a sailor!—all very fine!

2385   slantin: going.
2414   for all: although.
          the loose: how loose it was.

"Nicky!" I says, "where's Nelly Quine?"
2420 And I looked, and there they had her lashed
To the cabin companion—my gough! the washed
The craythur looked, the washed and the wore—
Half drowned, you know—"I'll take ye ashore,"
I says, and the Captain standin by—
"I'll take the young woman ashore," says I.
He looked at me very hard, and then
He loosed the lanyarn, and—"Listen, friend!"
Says the Captain. "Suppose I don't live," he says,
"To reach that shore, remember this!
2430 Whatever happens, dyin or livin,
Nelly's as pure as an angel in Heaven."
And so he gave her to me, and so
I says—"It's time for us to go;"
And made her fast across my hips—
"Now, then!" I says, and in I slips—
Easy, you know, very easy, and humours
All I could, and makes these boomers
Ride me as nice as possible,
And treadin the trough, you know; but still
2440 She hung upon my back like death—
Not a word! no, no! not a sound! not a breath!
I thought she was dead—not the smallest tick
In all her body—so I struck out quick
And hard; but a sea come tearin along,
And caught me up, and wrenched me that strong,
And bothered me, that the next that came
Knocked me over like a bame—
Senseless—like a log of timber—
And so, of course, that's all I remember
2450 Till I felt the smell of a body smookin,
And a lot of people round me lookin,
And three of us side by side there lyin—
The Captain, and me, and Nelly Quine—
Her in the middle—but they'd turned her head
Away from the Captain, because he was dead—
Dead, poor chap! But Nelly, the sowl!
Was sleepin just like a two-year-old.
"Hullo!" says I; "hullo!" says Nickey—
Him that was smookin, and likewise Mickey—
2460 Clague, I mean. So then they stated
How the young Captain waited and waited

2421   cabin companion: a covered stair or ladder (ed.).
2427   lanyarn: lanyard—a small rope (ed.).

Till he seen the lot of them landed there,
And then he jumped, and swam very fair,
Strong, they said, but cautiously—
When, all of the sudden! the boom, d'ye see!
That was soulgerin about in the trough,
Gave a heave, and a drop! and hit him, my gough!
Hit him just aback of the skull,
And knocked him over like a bull—
2470 Killed him, it's lek, upon the spot:
For when the body come in, they got
No signs of life, nor nothin in it—
Killed him, I expec, that minute.

So Cain must have a bit of prayer over us—
The way the Lord was extending His care over us,
He said; and so it's prayer we had:
And then we took and sent a lad
For a cart for Nelly, and another to go
So quick as he could, and let them know
2480 At the Ballaglass. So we got the cart,
And Nelly a heisin, and made a start.
But the Captain's body was left in a cove,
And chaps to watch it. So on we drove,
And the poor gel there hangin all of a dangle,
Sthrooghin just the same as a tangle—
The limp, you know; and her clothes all twisted
And ruxed about her; and the way she listed
This way, that way, as if her neck
Hadn no bone in it. But I didn leck
2490 The way that chap was lookin at her—
Cain? Aye, Cain—but no matter! no matter!
Cain, sure enough—so we done our endeavour,
And up to the house with her howsomedever—
And *where to put her?* and—bear a hand there!
And—"The hayloft 'll do for the lek o' yandhar—
Says Cain—"The hayloft!" and I gev a star—
"Is it wantin to feed the rots ye are?
Haylofts!" I says. So he grunted though;
But what was he goin to say I don't know;
2500 For the misthress come, so soft and swift,
Like ghoses comes, ye know—just a whiff

2466   soulgerin: soldiering, knocking about.
2481   a heisin: being raised.
2485   sthrooghin: trailing.
2496   star: stare.
2497   rots: rats.

Of somethin white—like an owl's wing—
And she ran at Nelly like a greedy thing;
And Nelly lifted up her head,
And fell in the misthress' arms like dead.

So Cain was lookin rather foolish then,
And of coorse, you know, no use of men—
So we stood to one side; and, I'll tell ye what!
The divil a one but off with his hat,
2510 Lek round a coffin: and the gels there cryin,
And huddlin and cuddlin, and Nelly lyin
On the whole of their laps, and goin a carryin
In on the parlour, exac like a buryin—
And—*to keep away!* and the door shut;
So Cain stood glasses, and so I cut.

But *Tommy?* Tommy, did ye say?
Aw, he was over the hills and far away°
Long afore that. And, dear me now!
You'd ha' thought ould Cain had ha' kicked up a row
2520 About Tommy breakin articles
Like yandhar—*Noticin,* is it? Bills
Of ladin, contracks, charter-parties,
And all the rest of it—go it, my hearties!
Breach of promise? Breach of something—
And ould Gelling, too! But that's a rum thing—
Just when you'd ha' thought the man 'd been furious,
To take it that aisy—wasn it curious?
Not a bit of it! bless your soul!
But you'll be tould! you'll be tould!

2530   So Tommy was gone; but Nelly got better,
And then the lot of them was at her
To stay for a servant with them there,
And so she did: and the best of a year
No news of Tommy; but the people was sayin
They were hearin a sort of music playin
In the air sometimes—like a sort of disthress—
Like a fiddle cryin bout the place—
Like a *cry,* they said, and a surt of a moan to it—
(I've axed Tommy himself, but he wouldn own to it).
2540 So the people said it wasn right
At all: but Cain tuk a gun one night,
And fired it out at the front door,
And then they navar heard it no more.

Aye, aye! but afore the next Mheillea
There was wonderful news of Tommy, I tell ye—
Just so! just so! aw, hould your luff!
Wonderful, wonderful, sure enough!
Well now, this is the way it was—
Nelly's father, ye see, was lost
2550 Off the Shellags° one night, with Illiam Crowe,
One-eyed Illiam? exactly so.
And the widda come down most terrible,
And all the mouths she had to fill—
I don't know the number—and it's hard for such,
And Nelly helpin, but it wasn much—
What could she do? aw a reglar battle,
And *executions*, and I don't know what all.
And the bed goin sellin from under them,
And all to that, till at last it came
2560 She had to give in. And Nelly took heart
To ax this Cain to take their part,
Just, you know, to spake to the Coroner°
For the mother, poor soul! that he wouldn be purrin her
To the road altogether, and no expense,
And did. But Tommy's tould me since
That Nelly was sayin she'll navar forget
The way he looked when she axed him that—
Lek the divil gev him a dig in the ribs,
Or the back, or somewhere—and takes and cribs
2570 His eyes like pennywinkles just—
She didn know the better or wuss
Nor the nothin them times—but I'll be bail—
Bless ye! looks 'll mane a dale,
A dale will looks: but helped them though;
And then the widda thought she'd go
To Douglas, to live with a sisthar theer;
And so the Coroner got them clear,
Or clear of them. And so Mrs Quine
Off to the sisthar——but—very fine!
2580 Sisthars! will they? Not a bit o' them!
Showed her the door, and all the kit o' them.
And too proud to go back—you know, the disgrace—
And Douglas is hardly a Christian place:
Bless ye! Douglas, as a rule,

2546   hould your luff: pay attention (ed.).°
2550   Illiam: William.
2559   all to that: so forth.
2563   purrin: putting.
2570   pennywinkles: periwinkles.

Is just as bad as Liverpool.

So she wandered about on the bare street,
And not a stockin to her feet;
And worer and ragg'der, and thinner and starveder,
Till one of these bobbies tuk and obsarved her—
2590 That's their word—and brought her up
Afore the High-Bailiff°—not a bit or a sup
At the woman for days—and the childher all round her
Cryin; and that's where Tommy found her—
In the Coort? In the Coort. "Is there one of ye knows her?"
Says the High-Bailiff: "I was used *to*, Sir,"
Says a little chap in the crowd; and, blow me!
If the little chap they had wasn Tommy—
Tommy, for sure! And—"I'll take care o' them,"
Says Tommy there—"I think there's a pair o' them,"
2600 Says the High-Bailiff, and he laughed, and he turned
The leaf of his book, and the bobbies girned—
Of coorse! of coorse! But still they were plazed,
Aw yes, they were, and the woman amazed;
But stuck to Tommy, and out on the door—
And—"Mind you'll not come here no more!"
Says the High-Bailiff. But when she got out,
And tuk a look at the chap, no doubt,
And seen the surt, she lost all heart—
Poor soul! and actual made a start
2610 To cut and lave him. But Tommy caught her,
And Tommy entreated and Tommy besought her,
And these little midges set up a boo!
And the woman didn know what to do—
"Tommy, ye dunkey! it isn no gud!
Ye cudn!" she says; "I cud! I cud!"
Says Tommy: "try me! try me!" he says;
"I've got a terbil shuitable place,"
Says Tommy—"Come, Mrs Quine, aw come!"
And so she went, but very glum—
2620 Lek shamed, you know, at the undersize
And that, lek thinkin he wasn wise.

So Tommy done the best he was able,
And tuk a lodgin in Guttery Gable,°
Or somewhere—just one room they had;
But he worked like a haythen naygur, he did.

2601   girned: grinned.
2608   the surt: what sort he was.

And the woman wasn a bad soul ether,
Only a little cretchy rather—
Cretchy, or something of the kind,
And uphouldin the days she lived with Quine.
2630 *She shudn!* No, of coorse she shudn;
But—*that's the times she got the puddin,
Heavin it down the sink*, she said—
*Plenty of botther to her bread
Them times*, she said: you know their way!
Women *muss* hev somethin to say—
Muss—and——yes, it was rather hard
On Tommy. But, bless ye! he didn regard.
Tommy had a hope in his bussum,
Had Tommy—and 'd take the childher, and nuss 'em,
2640 Or wash them, or anything at all:
Till at last the sisthar gev a call
One evenin: and she saw the nate
And comfibil, and—gettin late,
And—*could she sit till mornin theer?*
And cuddled her up in an arm cheer,
And had her breakfast, and liked the tay,
And never left them anyway—
Pride, eh? Turn your back, and Pride
'll ate all you'll give him, and more beside.

2650 And all in a little bit of a room
About the length of a lugger's boom—
And dacent lek, ye know, in their habits,
But all in a little room like rabbits.
Bless your sowl! there wasn no harm in,
But the people said Tommy was turned a Mormon—
Two wives, they said, *and it ought to be looked to*,
And—*Pazon Dobson should be spoke to.*

So Dobson come in with a speech to make to them,
But he laughed that hearty he cudn spake to them.
2660 For, the time he come, they were goin to bed,
And the women had rigged a hammock, he said,
And rove it up to the roof with a tackle;
And the minute they heard him, my gough! the cackle!
And "Tommy, you fool!" and "Tommy, you dirt!"

2627 cretchy: querulous.
2650-83 *Omitted 1881; restored 1889.*
2651 lugger's boom: the spar extending from the bow of a small vessel rigged with lug sails (ed.).

And Tommy standin in his shirt—
"Here's Pazon Dobson! for all the sakes!
Tommy!!!" and in a brace of shakes
Heaves, and whips him up to a bame,
Like a flitch of bacon, and makes fast the same,
2670 And laves him danglin under the laths,
And turns about, and smooths their brats,
And—"Good evenin, Sir!" and curtseyin—
My gough! the Pazon laughed like sin.
And "Tommy, how are ye gettin on up-stairs?"
He says, and "Did ye say your prayers,
Tommy?" that's all, bein gev to jokin,
And out, and down the sthreet, and chokin.
But still a dale more dacenter
To have the falla slung up there—
2680 Just a block, and a strong hook,
And a promise at Tommy he wouldn look,
And then they could sthrip, and out with the light,
And in to the childher with them straight.

So that's the news that come to Renshent,
And Nelly hed ha' tuk and went
Over the mountains like a shot
That very minute, but the misthress said not,
And coaxed and coaxed, and—"Nelly! Nelly!
You relly are too hard now, relly!
2690 Isn it all for you he's doin it?
And it'll be your fault if he's ever ruin it—"
And—*to do unto others*—"arn we bidden?"
And—"Don't, Nelly, don't!" So Nelly didn.

But still there was other things both'rin the gel—
Cain? Aye, Cain—most terrible!
Aw there's no mistake the man was bad,
At laste, ye know, if he wasn mad—
A touch of both—I wouldn thruss—
But Nelly didn see it at fuss—
2700 No she didn—if you'd only ha' ast her,
She'd ha' said he was such a *nice* master—
Nice she'd ha' said, *nice*, d'ye mind!
Pious very, but terbil kind—
Kind she'd ha' said—*such gentleness!*
Such——that's the way the women is—
It's no use o' talkin! they will! they will!

2698   I wouldn thruss: trust (I rather think).

That's the way with the women still—
Kind and pious! folly and blindness!
That's the piety and the kindness!
2710 Vanity and consate—that's it:
Well—howsomdever—just wait a bit!

But the misthress saw it—like a weather-glass
Is these wakely women; not a speck 'll pass
But they'll have it there—aw, I don't know the wake
Or the what—it's lek the delicake
And the hung that fine—but let that be—
They'll see what nobody else 'll see.
And—*What for would she care?* What for would she care!
Well, that's a clever chap, I'll swear—
2720 Clever he is now, yes he is—
Very deep—what is it he says?
She didn love Cain from the day of the weddin?
No, I'm happy to say she didn—
Nor never after—that's more!
(I thought I'd settled that afore);
Never after she didn love him:
So you want to make out that that's what druv him
Wrong altogether? Now, is it that?
Is it? Or what are you drivin at?
2730 Eh? I'll stick to it like glue,
Cain was a divil, so that'll do—
A despard divil. But still, guy heng!
If you'll give me a chance, I'll tell you a thing.
I'm as willin as any man can be
For th' be raisonable, don't ye see?
Raisonable—that's the surt;
But contindickin, and all such dirt
Is boosely! boosely! and I'd have you to know!
And I'll throuble you to hold your jaw!

2740   Yes, of coorse, the way I'm statin,
If chaps is only accomodatin,
And raisonable, raisonable—
That's the thing—I'll engage I'll be able
To clear the clew: but, bless my guzzit!
Raisonable is the thing that does it—

2718-69 *Omitted.*
2735   th' be: to be (ed.).°
2738   boosely: beastly (ed.).
2744   clear the clew: untangle a ball of twine or thread (ed.).

Raisonable—aye—*and ar'n ye?*
All right! but just I want to warn ye.

Now, here's the way—*No love*, you said,
For Cain! no love—is it barley-bread,
2750 This love? Is it leeks—is it—-what is it now?
Yes, yes! my gough! I'll allow, I'll allow—
Love for Cain—No, none that *I* know of—
Oh, of coorse! the woman he got the rhino of—
Of coorse—but the heart, as God's in heaven,
It was never given! it was never given!
You were talkin of love—Well, Nelly there,
Wasn there no love for her
At the misthress, I mane? Why, warn ye tould
She loved her like her own sowl?
2760 And for her to be singed with the fire of the breath
Of that man's—love—it was worse than death.
Aye, and look here now! what d'ye think?
Was the misthress a woman that you'd fancy would wink
At work like that? Could she have it at all?
Come now! was it pozzible?
Could she have it about her? Could she have it near her?
Anywhere? Any way? Aw, never fear her!
You didn't know Mrs Cain—my chree! my chree!
That was full of nothin but dacency.

2770   Aye, but there's more—there's more though still,
And so I'll confess it, aw, deed I will.
Do you know—my gough! it's an ould song—
What it is to be right, and yet to be wrong?
Not her fault—no, no! but—look!
Swore upon the Holy Book—
Swore—d'ye see? Aw, it's no use denyin—
Swore—and still, if the woman was dyin,
What could she do? she hadn gorr it—
Love! what love? the only thing for it
2780 Was death, not love: death, death's the cry!
Sell love? sham love? no, die, die, die!

But more than swore, more than swore—
Ten thousand times more! ten thousand times more!

2753   rhino: money (ed.).
2758   at the misthress: on the part of the mistress (ed.).
2768   chree [*ch* as *k* or as in German]: heart (ed.).
2778   gorr: got.

Here was a man that was goin to ruin
Most terrible—and whose doin?
Whose? Aw, don't be hard! aw, don't!
Yes—*she* thought so, but *me!* I won't!
Navar! Navar! God help me then!
Navar! Navar! Christ's sake, Amen!
2790 She thought so—yes, just what you'd expeck—
But, oh! be pitiful to the leck!
That's the thought that done the jeel,
Goin like a threddle to a wheel,
Thrib-throbbin night and day,
The sore that sucked her life away.
She hadn loved him! and who could tell
What might have been? aw well, well, well!
I know, I know—if she could have done it,
If she could, if she could? but who begun it?
2800 Who made it unpozzible from the fuss?
No, no, my lads! I'll not cuss—
But this if—if—if! what's the gud of *if?*
What'll it carry? what'll it lift?
If she cud—just the smallest taste—
Just so—*if, if!* in case, in case!
And all the rest of it, I suppose he'd ha' got
To be a reglar angel—what?
This Cain—an angel, cocked in a bush
Like at Moses theer°—ah I only wush
2810 These *ifs* were not so sharp and crook'd,
And catchin, and houldin, and gettin hook'd
In the very flesh, and no aisin to 't
Till Death 'll haul you into his boat,
And wrench the hooks, and set you free
From all the throuble and misery.

      Too late! too late! I'm glad it was—
The slack'd fire broke out at last,
Lek the Divil had lit a fiery sun
That scorched her face to look upon.
2820 What! Cain? Yes, bless ye! plain as plain—
He didn make no secret didn Cain—
It seemed as if all care was past,
It seemed as if he was happy at last,
Happy, happy, or goin to be it.

2792   jeel: damage.
2793   threddle: treadle.
2796-834 *Omitted 1881; restored 1889.*

And still this Nelly didn see it.
Wonderful! wonderful, I've heard
About *the state of her sowl!* good Lord!
Yes—aw yes—and 'd give her instruction
Himself, you know—"The introduction,"
2830 He was used to say, "of this young pessin
To the truth is deeply interessin—"
A lamb of the flock, he said; aw dear!
And wolves, he said, *prowlin everywheer;*
Wolves, he said; *but the fold was near.*
The scroundhrel-villyan! and allis tuk her
To chapel himself, and up and stuck her
In the front pew—and high and low
Could see, but Nelly didn, no!
Such a fatherly man, she thought, *so good,*
2840 *And holy, you know;* and there she stood
In the chapel, like a primrose in the spring,
And as sweet and as foolish as anything—
And the starin—but she didn know what it meant—
Terrible, terrible innocent—
Terrible in the world for sure,
The sweet, the innocent, and the pure—
And very beautiful! she *was* that—
And then this tremenjis ould Tom cat
Purrin there in the pulpit, and prayin,
2850 And praechin, and hardly knowin what he was sayin
For lookin at Nelly: and Nelly 'd look
Up at him from off her book—
And nothin in the craythur's mind
But pride and wondher—poor Nelly Quine!

But others seen it—what? *the gels?*
Seen it of coorse—my gough! who else!
Likewise the boys—of an evenin theer
At home you know—and the Book, and the cheer—
And—"Aw!" he'd say, "the power of grace!"
2860 And put a finger in the place,
And his other hand on Nelly's head—
"The power of grace! of grace!" he said;
And pattin theer, and the big smooth smile,
And—"The Lord is daelin with this child."
"Oh!" he says, "it's grace that's in,"

2843-54 *Omitted.*
2855-906 *Omitted 1881; restored with minor changes 1889.*
2858   cheer: chair.

And the hand goin sliddherin under her chin.
And then he'd be readin all the chapters
That's talkin of love—"Oh!" he'd say, "the rapthurs!
The puffick joy! And lizzen to this!
2870 *Greet one another with a holy kiss!*°
See!" he'd say, "my childrin, see
The joy of Christian liberty!
If it hadn been for *the unrighteous leaven,*°
See what kisses we'd be hevvin!"
"Dear me!" he'd say, "if you were all God's sons
And daughters, we might begin at once;"
And dhrops the book, and sticks his thumb in
His oxther, and gives a surt of a hummin,
And lookin the way you could aisy tell he
2880 'd like uncommon to begin with Nelly.

Did they wink? did they nudge? enjoyin the spree?
Certainly, most certainly!
And sometimes he'd be lookin very black at them;
And sometimes, d'ye know! he'd be laughin back at them—
Actyall! yes! he wud, he wud!
Dhrunk? No—the pison in his blood;
Or—— I don't know; but in general,
He wasn takin no notice at all;
But just like a body in a dhrame,
2890 As sweet as sugar, and as soft as crame,
I believe in my sowl—honour bright!—
The man was thinkin he was all right.
Sometimes? Yes; and weeks at a time—
Lek nothin in the world could annoy 'm;
Just azackly as if he was livin
In another world, *saved and forgiven,*
With other loss and other gain,
With another Nelly and another Cain.
Decavin himself? No, no! d'ye see!
2900 Navar not decavin nobody
Such times—like settled long ago,
And no use to be spakin nor nothin, ye know;
But just to be happy, and have no bother
This way that way, one thing or another—
Happy, happy; allis the same—
But just to go on, and dhrame and dhrame.
Like yandhar Chineses, did ye say?

2878   oxther: oxter, armpit (ed.).
2907-14   *Omitted.*

Chineses, Chineses! Aye? What way?
Oh, I understand you—Whanko Fum.
2910 Just so—agate of this opium?
Well—no—no—no—that wasn it.
No! not with Cain; not a bit, not a bit!
Far more, I tell ye; far more! Because
He was raelly happy. Yes, he was;
Raelly happy. For this Nelly at Cain's
Made the man's blood go sweet in his veins—
Lifted the falla up from the mire
Of his spite, and his hate, and his hell-fire;
Grew like a lily or a pink
2920 'll grow by the side of some dirty sink,
Or a midden—— *Hard?* No, I'm not hard!
A midden in a farmyard!
A midden, by gough! I'll stick to that,
A midden or a tanyard vat—
My senses! a midden's twice too gud for him.
A beauty for pinks and lilies to bud for him!
There now, there now! Labour in vain!
You've got him, you've got him! So take your Cain!
It's no use, my men; keep quiet! keep quiet!
2930 How could it be right? how could it be right?
Heaven above, or earth beneath;
Right is right in the Devil's teeth.
Lovin Nelly! What did ye say?
That was sugar for any man's tay?
Certainly! and no thanks to be gud,
If you were lovin her; I think you shud!
And her lovin you—aw, at that price,
Ould Nick himself 'd 'a' tuk to be nice—
Yes, there's no doubt; but I can't discover
2940 How he had any right to love her—
Any right, or any sense.
My gough! he knew he hadn a chance
To get Nelly to love him. What was there in him
But muck and mash and hissin venom?
Could he love? He could hate—he hated his wife!
Put a dhrop of love into that man's life;
Run a river of love—what's the gud of it all?
It'd only turn to the bitter gall.
He had soaked himself in spite—d'ye see?
2950 He had steeped himself in cruelty.
He was pison to the very brim—

2915-3403   *Omitted 1881; restored with minor changes 1889.*

All the love on earth couldn sweeten him.
Plant a apple tree in a bog—will it root?
In a hungry bog—will it bring forth fruit?
Plant love in Cain—don't you know what would happen?
It wouldn be love; it wouldn have the sap in,
Nor nathur, nor nothin: it would breed grubs;
It would rot; it would stink. It 'll do in dubs,
Will dirty water; but, so soon as it flows,
2960 Stand to one side, or hould your nose!

 Aw, he had to keep quiet—his only look out;
And as long as he could, there isn no doubt
The man had a surt of happiness,
A surt of peace, a surt of rest—
A surt—but still he knew if he'd spake
One word that Nelly couldn mistake,
One word! his dhrame would go like a puff—
That's what my lad knew well enough.

 So he had to humour his dhrame that way,
2970 To spin it out, to coax it to stay—
Lek all that was ever like to be—
And it made him as peaceful there, and free—
Bless your sowl! he was gettin quite kind
To the misthress even, lek he'd made up his mind
Lek all to be happy like in a story,
Lek Nelly 'd got them up to glory,
Nor where, nor when, nor how, nor who—
And the misthress to be in it too.
But who and how, and where and when,
2980 Must have an answer, must, my men.

 And so there was times when the divil awoke,
And seen he was just the fool of a joke,
And sickened at these slops of love,
Or whataver trash he was dreamin of.
And then the seven divils came°
And filled his sowl with rage and flame:
And his shouldhers shuck, and his face fell,
And his heart was like a coal of hell.
And he'd take for the shore or anywhere—
2990 Lek chokin, ye know, lek catchin the air—
I've talked to people that heard him there.
It was hard to understand him rather,
They said, bein mostly stormy weather
Such times he was after these games; and mixin

Religion and that; but still they were fixin
Putty middlin; and the despard way
He'd shout to the land, and shout to the sea,
And—"God in Heaven!" he'd say, "O God!
I know thy rod! I know thy rod!
3000 She can't be mine! she can't be mine!
O Nelly Quine! O Nelly Quine!
But why? O why? Isn there a place
In all the world, a little space,
Nowhere? nowhere? a space, a spot—
Oh, is there not? Oh, is there not?
God of mercy, in all these lands,
Where I can flee from thy commands?
Somewhere! somewhere! there must! there must!
O God, I am but feeble dust,
3010 A worm, a fool, a stupid liar—
O give me but my heart's desire!
God in Heaven! what's the gud o' me?
I cannot do the thing thou wud o' me—
I was navar convarted. I only shammed—
I'm lost already! O God I'm damned—
I navar loved Thee, nor Thy word—
Lave me to myself, O Lord!
I'm weak, O Lord, I can't stand firm!
What's all this bother about a worm?
3020 Drop me! Lave me! What matter to you?
Give me Nelly, and that 'll do."

That was a praecher—rummish docthrine
For a man that knew the way, and walked therein
With sweet assurance—I've heard him talk—
Rather a curious road to walk!

But Nelly navar knew a scrap—
Ye see, the parties that heard the chap
Was terbil deep Methodisses,
That's apt to hide a thing like this is,
3030 Hush it up, lek thinkin *it best*,
They're sayin, *for the Chapel intheress*—
Aw, crafty uncommon! a Christian brother—
Dear me, but they 'll stick to one another!

But how was it the misthress didn spake

2995   fixin: describing it.
2996   putty: pretty.

To Nelly? Now, for God's sake!
To Nelly? The misthress? You havn a grain o' sense—
Wasn it just in Nelly's innocence
That the misthress had her only pleasure,
Her only joy, her hidden treasure—
3040 In Nelly's peace, in healin the smart
Of the sore that was still in Nelly's heart?
In seein her bud again and blossom,
That would ha tuk her to her bosom
Every minute, and rocked her and rocked her
Like a baby there—and Cain for the doctor!
My gough! let's see—
Doctor Cain, M.D.
And so long as the gel was cheerful
And happier gettin, the misthress was fearful
3050 To move a finger—and she didn know
About his tantrims. She only saw
The smilin the man was got, and the silly,
And evident all by raison of Nelly.

    And sometimes she started like a thing that was stung,
When she looked at the man, and seen the young
And sthrong he was seemin: and then she thought,
My gough! I don't know what!
Death, and darkness, and despair—
But other times, sittin there,
3060 Just the three of them, and no winkin nor nudgin
At these boys and gels, it was hard to be judgin
And Cain that tuk up, and contented, and cuddlin—
If it was only a piece of old man's muddlin
After all; and, if so,
Then he was very happy, ye know—
And was *she* makin him happy? poor woman!
Cud she? and mightn the man be comin
To an anchor lek in still water,
And Nelly to be to him like a daughter!
3070 Besides the religion—aw, deed, I'll bet
The misthress was thinkin a dale of that.
For, ye see, for all the good-hearted,
And the sweet, this Nelly wasn convarted—
No—and still it was rather expected,
After all her trouble, she'd be *directed*
And that—you know—and only proper—
And even talk of Cain to adop' her.
So who was knowin when it 'd come—
The great change—very slow with some—

3080 Yes, I suppose so—and to try to forget
      The Captain theer—aw, they wouldn be beat—
      Poor lad! Was he in the same thrim?
      I wondher what change there come to him.
      "We shall not all sleep," it says,
      "But we shall all be changed," same vess—°
      All, now? What is he maenin by *all?*
      A terbil hand was yandhar Paul.

      But I tell ye, it got so bad in the Chapel
      That these unfornit locals had to *grapple*
3090 *With this question*—that's what they called it—
      And the Shuperintendan overhauled it
      One everin with them, havin come
      Special o' puppose from Douglas, by gum!
      Aye! but of coorse, you know, they'd contrive it
      To be a meetin lek in private—
      Private, aw, private—yes, but still
      The lek will out, of course it will.

      So the meetin was in the everin,
      So the next day they summoned Cain
3100 To *appear* before them—*for divers grave*
      And weighty causes—aw, you'll get lave!
      Like lawyers just—ould Bobby Kirkbride—
      And as dignified as dignified.
      But the chap that had to sarve this writ
      Didn like the job a bit—
      No, he didn, aw, deed, no, man!
      So he started off the very momen'
      It was in Cain's hand, and he over the hill,
      And heard him shoutin terrible—
3110 "Young man! come here!" but he didn mind him,
      But ran lek he'd got the Divil behind him.

      But Cain to the chapel—and that's the place
      They had the row, and every taste.
      And who was tellin me? Tellin? tellin?
      Why, bless your souls! ould Harry Gellin,
      Tommy's father; aye, but it was, though,
      Just one day there shoein a hoss though—
      Aw, whatavar there's goin, the blacks and the whites of it,

---

3082   thrim: trim (ed.).
3101   you'll get lave: say what you like.
3113   taste: bit of it.

It's in a smithy you'll get the rights of it—
3120 And him a local: but tuk the huff
About something, and left them long enough
After he was tellin me the fun.
So Bobby Kirkbride it was that begun,
Bobby—and "Brother Cain," he says,
"We're in a very great disthress,
Brother—very," he says—"The Church,"
He says, "is troubled. 'Twere gud to search
Your heart, brother, and ascertain
How is it with thee, brother Cain.
3130 It's for our brother's own sake,
And indeed the case is delicake,
Yes, it's delicake uncommon—
I may say it's about a young woman,
Livin under your own roof,
I understand, but kep aloof
From the rest of the sarvants. We've heard this;
And then, in this sacred edifice,
We're tould of conduck, as one might say,
Conduck, conduck, in a general way.
3140 Furthermore, it's said in the neighbourhood,
That this faymale pessin is well-favoured,
Also, we're informed her state
Is hopeful, or *was*, at any rate—
Hopeful—and makin her to be
A pleasin subject—spiritually—
Spiritually—in another respeck,
We've heard of captains and the lek—
We've heard, no doubt, and a trouble that came
On a fam'ly I'm not goin to name—
3150 A trouble, yes. So, if he's inclint
To clear his mind upon this pint,
We think, in a spirit of Christian unity,
Our brother should have a opportunity."

And then he axed the Shuperintendan
To *open the Scripthar for their understandin,*
If so be they might see the light,
And lead the doubtin Church aright.
So then the Shuperintendan prayed,
But *very cautious*, Gellin said—
3160 Cautious, cautious, like an ould drake,
And cautiouser still when he come to spake,
Eyein Cain; ye know, that was theer,
Sittin in the Communion cheer—

Bless ye! as happy as a bird,
Nid-noddin at every other word:
And when the prayer was over, he set
The Amen as bould as a clarionet;
And slicked his lips like slickin a label,
And cocked himself on the communion table.

3170 So then the Shuperintendan 'spounded,
And the way it was, and where they found it—
Corinthians—and Paul *enlargin*
How a man is to do with his vargin—
If he think he's behavin uncomely toward her,
St. Paul is sayin, he's bound to take order
To get her married some way; but still,
If the party's got power over his will,
And *hath so devised in his heart*, says Paul,
He needn marry her at all—°
3180 "That's Paul," he says; "we've his own word,
It's only hisself, and not the Lord—
But I spare you, says Paul,"—and this and thus,
And whips them back to Leviticus,
And works the texes—*But still, of coorse,*
The law of Moses hadn no force—
And then there was David, when he got ould,
And sufferin greatly from the could,
Tuk yandhar Abishag,° that nussed him,
And seemed to be a ancient custom,
3190 *But differin from the case in hand,*
And not the same for every man—
But no doubt, for the sake of the congregation,
Their brother would gev an explanation.

Says Cain—"It's beautiful, it is!
A splendid exposition," he says—
"Splendid, splendid! Dear me! the way
That scripthar was opened, just like day,"
He said, "like day. But how? But how?"
Was it larnin? "No, I trow:"
3200 *Was it readin, was it study?*
Was it pokin in the muddy
Waters of the carnal mind,
Pokin, pokin, till you're nearly blind—
Was it? And he looked round,
And he smiled like butter a shillin the pound—
"No!" he says, "it's just the habirtual
Comparin spir'tual things with spir'tual"—

And—"Hem!" he said, and ups with the eyes,
And smacks his lips like somethin nice.

3210   Nice! by gough! aw, nice enough!
It was Nelly he was thinkin of.
Aye, aye! it had got a name,
It was there, *he was spoke to*, it wasn a dhrame—
Spoke to! spoke to! Yes, and, beside,
I believe the chap had a surt of a pride
The way he was lifted altogether
Above Shuperintendans, or Locals e'ther,
Lek on wings of the mornin,° and these craythurs to run
With their farlin candle to see the sun
3220 Just when it was goin to rise—that's it!
To rise, to rise—that's the thing that lit
His face till it shined like polish just—
Heaven or Hell, love or lust—
Take your chise! but, as Gellin 'd say,
It must have come from somewhere—eh?
"The exposiiton," he says, "is grand;
But now let's come to the point in hand,
To the point," says Cain; "I'm not deny'n
A word that was said about Ellen Quine.
3230 I think you'll allow it's only natur,
The way she came to us, we'd trate her
Special lek, bein in a sense,
Entrusted to us by Providence—
Trusted," he says, "I think you'll agree,
Trusted to Mrs Cain and me.
She come to us a poor lost sinner,
But we seen the seeds of grace that was in her,
And—the beauty, yes, the carnal beauty—
No doubt, no doubt; but what was our duty?
3240 That's the thing. Our duty was plain
Before us—me and Mrs Cain.
Seeds—now ought we to leave them there,
To be picked and pecked by the birds of the air?°
To be choked with the thorns, to be burnt with the heat—
Is that our duty? I beg to state
It's not. No matter the time or the place,
Seeds of grace is seeds of grace.
To raise the fallen, to seek the lost,
That's our duty, whatever the cost.
3250 *But the gel is good-lookin?* that's admitted—

3219   farlin: farthing (ed.).

Is she any the less fitted
For a vessel of grace? Good looks is fax—
What *is* there in good-looks, I ax.
Must she be ugly? Is there anything carnal
In good-looks? Is the life etarnal
For ugly women, and ugly men
Only? No, no! my brethren.
That's carryin Election out of all raison:
The works of Nature, in their saison,
3260 Might teach ye that. The very flowers
Of the field, God's work, you know, not ours—
Has the blossoms of Spring a lovely breath,
Or are they a savour of death unto death?
They're beautiful—aye! There ye gorrit!
Beautiful, and ye like them for it.
And then in the Bible everywhere
The beautiful the women are!
Not one neither, but every one of them,
Aye, bless ye! every mother's son of them.
3270 They're all beautiful! Look at the way
They're in the picthars—as you might say—
Puffeck beauty, not a stain nor a spot,
Not an ugly one in all the lot.
Yes, and holy women, too.
Of coorse! of coorse! we've nothin to do
With Jezebel and Herodias,°
And hapes of the like, as bould as brass:
But Queen Bersheba that wouldn be done°
But she'd hear the wisdom of Solomon;
3280 And the Shunamite,° that we're taught to consider
A type of the Church; and—altogether—
What do ye say to the likes of them?
And 'the daughter of Jerusalem.'—°
See the Prophets, see the Psalms;
See that Hagar of Abraham's,°
And Ruth, and Rahab,° that hid the spies,
And Leah°—only the blinky eyes—
And dozens more, if they were wanted—
See the way they're represented!
3290 Beautiful? Of coorse they were—
Beautiful—and I'll tell ye the for.
It's a gift is beauty, a gift it is,
And used for improper pupposes

3264   ye gorrit: you have got it.
3291   the for: the reason.

  At the Divil—no doubt a snare to catch
Unwary souls: but God's his match.
This gift is *his* gift after all,
Not the Divil's, in spite of his gall;
And God is usin it to bend
Our hearts, that so we may befriend
3300 Poor things that has been led astray,
That so His banished may find a way
To return to Him; the effeck of whuch,
My beloved brethren, is such
That this beauty, this snare of the ould Dragon's,
Is the banner of love: 'stay me with flagons
In the banqueting house; yea, comfort me
With apples from the apple tree—
I am sick of love,' the bride is say'n;°
And so with me and Mrs Cain.
3310 We love this young pesson; the Lord has guv her
Unto us that we might love her,
That we might lead her unto Him;
And if she was like a cherubim
For beauty, or just the *vice versies*,
We umbly thank him for his mercies."

  And he stopped. To hear ould Gellin arrit
Was good! he had every word, like a parrot—
Stopped a minute, did Cain; and the fashion
Of his face was changed, Gellin said; no passion;
3320 No love nor hatred to be seen;
But just the cunning of a fiend—
Cunning. And then he says—"The occasion
Was seemin to want an explanation:
And now ye have it," he says. "But still,
If you're only convinced against your will,
If this meetin isn satisfied,
Then," he says, "I wouldn divide
A Christian body," he says; "no, no!
I can go," he says, "and I'm willin to go.
3330 But," he says, "I'll always be jealous
Over you with love: no malice
Has place in my heart, but only a yearnin
In the bowels of the Gospel for them that's returnin
Evil for good. But—no more of that.
One thing," he says, "I musn forget—

3294 at: by.
3316 arrit: at it.

It's a matter of business," he says, "I fear,
But better perhaps to have everythin clear.
I'd be very sorry, certainly,
To give any trouble to the Committee,
3340 Or the congregation in general,
Very sorry: but—still for all—
There's certain moneys; and it's handy, rather,
For the man and the money to go together—
So no doubt you'll be makin arrangements for payin
The mortgages on the Chapel," says Cain,
"With all the interest that's owin,
For I think there'll be foreclosin goin.
But I'd better give you a day or two
To think about it—that'll do,"
3350 Says Cain, "Good evenin!" and takes
His hat, and a smooth of the elber, and makes
For the door. "Stop!" says Gellin, "Stop!"
He says, and he gave a skip and a hop,
And got hoult of the door. "Stop!" like commandin;
"Aisy!" says the Shuperintendan;
"*Aisy*, Mr Gellin!" he says;
"*Aisy?* What sort of talk is this?"
Says Gellin. "Aisy! I'd have you to know,"
And set to work, and gave them the jaw,
3360 Most terribil—the way he was tellin;
Aw, by gogh! he could do it, could Gellin—
Could and would—*They'd heard a lecthur,*
He said, *about women that's drew in a pecthur.*
Concubines, and ould men's misses;
Was this the talk for Methodisses?
Were they Protestans? See, then, see!
Wasn this flat popery?
What else in the world? "Pecthurs!" he says,
"Pecthurs, graven images!
3370 "It's as clear as daylight," says Gellin; *but then—*
The mortgages! And at it again.
Mortgages, he said, *indeed,*
He'd like to see the trust deed;
He called for it to be produced—
Yes, and he'd hev it. They couldn be loosed
From the obligation under the Trust—
Was it gud in law? Was it right? Was it just?
Mortgages! There couldn be—
And how about the mortgagee?
3380 *He could tell Mr Cain, if he'd lent that money,*

The position he was in was more till funny;
It was danger's it was, a reg'lar fix.
And he'd better be makin quick sticks
To get out of it, or he'd see what the Coort
Of Chancery would say. And he roort
And he shouted: *and he'd hev it tried,*
He said, *if it beggared him, if he died;*
He'd take it to every Coort in creation—
It was just *"a corrup' consideration."*

3390   And Cain looked thunder, and well he might;
But the Shuperintendan got a light
From all this talk; so he stroked down Gellin
The best he could, that was puffin and swellin
Most awful—and then he turned to Cain,
And—"I think we'll let the matter remain
As it is," he says, "I believe I express
The general feelin—as it is, as it is;"
And looks round at the others, that gave a sort
Of a grunt or a groan, or a sniff or a snort,
3400   Maenin yes—and "Let us pray;"
And down on their knees, and pegged away:
But Gellin only said—*Chit!* and *Chut!*
And tuk and slammed the door, and cut.

So the very next Sunday ould Cain was as clever,
Fiddlin there with Nelly as ever,
And wrappin the shawl—and it wasn rainy—
But just lek the gel was made of chayney.
And Nelly as rosy as an apple,
With the blushes, and linkin down the chapel,
3410   As happy, bless ye! and content—
Innocent! just innocent!
For the capers this Cain was carryin on
She didn hardly understand;
Only she thought it was mayve a manner
With pious pessins—oh Susannar!°
But of coorse there was people 'd have their say,
And the praecher looked another way;
And Crellin there, and very glum;
But the hour had come, the hour had come!
3420   Come, I tell ye! make or break—
For on the road he begun to spake

3381   *till*: than (ed.).
3409   linkin: going arm in arm (ed.).

About the young captain, and worked it round,
Till she *must* understand; and she gave a bound,
And off like a deer, and the night was black,
And this divil couldn follow the track,
And lost her there; but Nelly went
Across everythin, everythin, straight for Renshent.
My gough! what would the poor craythur be?
Just mad with fear and misery!

3430   *The misthress! the misthress!* That was her thought:
She wasn freckened to be caught—
Poor thing! not that—but *there! oh there!*
To be with her! to be with her!
Safe, safe with her! And just the strength,
And in on the parlour, and fell full length
At the misthresses feet. And—*what was there at her?*
And—"Nelly, Nelly! What's the matter?"
And never a word, and never a moan—
Poor Nelly lay as dead as a stone.
3440 But coaxed her, and petted her, and raised her—
And—"Nelly! Nelly!" and 'mazeder and 'mazeder.
"What is it, Nelly?" (you understand—
A pious man! a holy man!
Where was *he?* My gough! What odds?
The heart of an innocent gel is God's—
Let scoundrels skulk, let divils chafe!
Nelly was safe! Nelly was safe!
Safe with the misthress). But when she woke,
And when she looked, and when she spoke,
3450 And when she tould—the misthress heard,
But she didn say a single word,
But turned like a sheet. It had come at last,
And the bitterness of death was passed.

    "Misthress!" says Nelly, "Misthress! mother!
My own! my own! for I haven no other,
Or if I have—O kindest friend!
O sweet! O good! O . . . *mother* then!
Mother, my heart is like to break!"
But the misthress, you know, she couldn spake—
3460 "Oh Misthress, is your heart turned hard to me?
O Misthress, won't you spake a word to me?
Just a word! a word! Oh spake
Any word—for Jesus' sake!
Am I a naughty gel, Mrs Cain?
Am I? am I? I didn mane—

Misthress! Misthress! I didn know—
Am I! am I! Must I go?"

But the misthress sat in her chair quite stiff—
So Nelly got in a sort of a tiff,
3470 Lek, you know the way with such,
Half-cock, hair-trigger, and off with a touch—
That was the wuss o' Nelly, aw yes!
'Deed it was, and 'deed it is.
But—dear me! clean your own winder—
Flint is flint, and tinder is tinder—
And knew no more till the man-in-the-moon
All the mischief she was doin—
That was Nelly. And "Misthress," she said,
And she stood on her feet, and she back with the head,
3480 And her bonnet fell off and draggled there—
"You *won't* hear, you *won't* hear!
I'm not worth, I suppose; I see't! I see't!
I'm only the dirt beneath his feet!
I'm no matter. I haven a friend,
And you think I'm a liar, and——there's an end!
I believe ye knew! I believe ye knew!
Yes, I do! yes, I do!
I believe ye made it up between ye,
And I'm sorry the day that ever I seen ye."
3490 *Quick work*—you'll say; aw, quick is the road;
But oh, if Nelly had only knowed
What the misthress was feeling then!
But—however—what's the use, my men?

So Nelly gev an awful cry,
Like the yowl of a dog, but no reply
From the misthress, no reply at all.
So she took her bonnet and her shawl,
And away, and locked herself in her room,
And left the misthress to her doom.

3500 And the sarvints was freckened, and didn go near,
But they heard the misthress on the stair
Lek staggering, lek—and then—no more,
Not even a foot upon the floor—
And sat up for Cain: but he didn come in
Till daylight, and *blew about with the wind*,
They were sayin, *rather*, and up to bed—

3490   road: way.

And there was the misthress lyin dead!
She was lyin dead. *Pison?* yes!
A mug of it upon the chiss—
3510 Pison, though—poor thing! she was gone
To the happy place, where it's all one—
Prepared? my gough! what *iss* prepared?
The d—— ould murderer stood and stared!
He shouted? Yes, enough for three!
Shouted—but not immadiently.
No, no; but aisy! wait, then, wait!
Don't get 'cited, at any rate!

Well, now, you may think the work
There was in that house; and Christy Quirk,
3520 The Coroner, comin and the inquest arrim,
And everybody on the farrim
Callin there; and couldn agree
For *temporal insanity;*
But just it was pison, pison—what's
The name of that poison they're given to rots?
But by whose hand administered—
Minis, minis—that's the word—
I think so. Well, they couldn say;
So to bury the body anyway,
3530 And service over it all right—
And so they did, but late at night.

And poor Nelly, they said, was just like a ghose,
Creepin about, and packed her clothes
To be off; but the women coaxed her for all
To stay with them over the funeral.
But Cain knew well that she'd settled to lave
When the misthress went out: so before the grave
Was filled—aw bless ye! hardly a spatter
On the coffin-lid, he was home and at her—
3540 Aye he was, and had some tay
In the kitchen, and tould the rest to stay
Outside till he'd want them in to prayer;
But *he'd something very particuler*
To say to Ellen Quine, he said—
Aw, by gough! and so he had.

3509 chiss: chest.
3520 arrim: at him, held by him.
3521 farrim: farm.
3522 callin: being called.

  And—*would she forgive him?* That was the game,
Would she forgive him? He felt the shame
Of his conduck the other night—aw dear!
The shame, he said, *but still it was clear*
3550 *He was left to himself,* he said, *that time—*
And would she forgive him? and would she try him?
What was man? he said—*the best,*
He said, *the very holiest*
Of men was wake—and what says Paul?
"Let him that standeth take heed lest he fall."°
No doubt, no doubt, he said, *it was sudden:*
But what was he to do? he couldn
Allow her to go, and his heart to break;
And if he didn spake now, when was he to spake?
3560 *It was his one chance,* he said, *and he took it;*
And the dear departed would overlook it.

  And Nelly tried to stop the man—
But, my gough! she said, the tongue of him ran
Like a wheel, she said. *And would she be this?*
And would she be that? and all the list
Of the things he'd do, and the things he'd give her—
And—"I will! I will!" and on like a river—
And promisin *the kind (!) he'd be—*
And—"Oh, I'll make you happy!" says he,
3570 And—"Will ye, will ye be my wife?"
And he stopped to get wind. "I'll send this knife,"
Says Nelly, "through your black heart,
If you'll spake another word." The start
He gev! and the cup fallin out of his hand!
"Through your black heart, you bad man!"
Says Nelly, and she tuk a step
Towards him, and the divil kep
His eye on her still; but he backed and backed,
And out on the door; and—aw it's a fact,
3580 Nobody said another word
About *prayers* that night that ever I heard—
No: and the next mornin the gel was sayin
Good-bye to them there, when in comes Cain.
"Clear out of this!" says Cain to the gels:
"I must spake to this pessin, and nobody else
Is wanted here." So of course they went.
"Now, Nelly," he says, "you're leavin Renshent;

But you'll return," he says, "for Lammas,
And marry me. Promise now! promise! promise!"
3590 But Nelly made a dart at the dresser,
And had a knife in a minute, bless her!—
The gel was quick. But Cain gev a sign,
And two policemen, that was eyein
The whole, unknownced, gript Nelly, by George,
Like a shot,—and "I gev this pessin in charge
For the murder of Mrs. Cain," he says;
And he stands like a rock, and his hand in his breast.
Poor Nelly! poor Nelly! and haulin and pushin,
And a car there to take her to Castle Rushen.
3600 But just when they started he tried once more,
And stooped, and whispered somethin to her.
But the people didn hear what he said,
And Nelly only shook her head—
And, "All right!" and nothing more to say with them,
And up goes the driver, and off and away with them.
The divil! I think I see his hoofs!
But he'd got his proofs, he'd got his proofs.
His proofs—aw yes: for who was it bought
This pison but Nelly, that little thought
3610 What was goin to happen: and then the fight
She had with the misthress that very night—
The servants would swear to as soon as wink,
And looking middlin ugly, I think.

Now, when Tommy heard this news,
He was clane crazy. "Don't be a goose!
Don't be a goose!" says Mrs Quine;
"Of course the case 'll be goin a try'n;
And Nelly was allis a bit of a fury,
Aw, 'deed she was: but no doubt the jury
3620 'll consider the young the craythur's yet—
And it's only transportation she'll get."
"*Transportation!*" says Tommy, "and *me!*"
"Well, well," says Mrs Quine, "we'll see."
"See!" says Tommy, "I'll go to Duddon
This very minute." "Well, I wouldn,"
Says the mother. "I wouldn be so selly.
She was allis very short-tempered, was Nelly.

3588   Lammas: church festival held on August 1.
3599   car: a small horse-drawn vehicle such as the phaeton in 3681 (ed.).
           Castle Rushen: the jail of the Island (in Castletown—ed.).
3617   goin a try'n: will be tried.

And Duddon the very first lawyer goin.
Duddon! Bless ye! it's only throwin
3630 Your money away—it is, indeed!
And goodness knows, there's not much need.
Look at the childhar!" and so she went on.
And, "Stop now, Tommy!" but Tommy was gone.
Ye see the chap was doin fair:
He'd got in with some masons and builders there—
And contraks and that, and good at the measurin,
And plannin, and cipherin, and takin a pleasure in
All surts of inventions, and layin the gas—
Aw, bless ye! makin money fast.

3640   But Duddon that was the chap for the law—
Terbil, but terbler for the jaw—
Aw, a mortal hand! He's laid on the shelf
Since then. But he'd bully ould Harry himself
Them times. By gough—fire and slaughter!
Put Duddon on them, and they'd cry for quarter.

   So it's Duddon Tommy wanted to see,
And tould him all; and, "Lave it to me!"
Says Duddon, and bitin his pen, and lookin
As deep as deep: so Tommy was hookin.
3650 Poor Tommy, though—the shaky and shivery
He was. And "The General Jail Delivery"—°
That was the time. And them words seemed cut
In every stone the craythur put
In a wall. They seemed to be wrote in the air,
On the sands, in the harbour—everywhere.

   And Tommy got lave for the mother and aunt
To see this Nelly. And so they went,
And Tommy with them, in a car,
And into the Castle; but didn dar
3660 To go in the place where Nelly was,
But pretended to be lookin after the hoss.
And Mrs Quine was weepin a dale,
And the sisthar, of course she wouldn fail—
Aw, dacent women! But when they were done,
And just sittin together, the mother begun
To ask a hape of questions, you know;
And this and that, and terbil though—
Till at last she said, "And, Nelly, then,
What did ye give her the pison in?"
3670 Aw, Nelly jumped to her feet, and she turned

Away from them, and the cheeks of her burned
With fire and shame; and she wouldn spake,
And didn—and so they had to make
Tracks of coorse; and—"She's very queer!"
Says the mother to the jailer theer.

But just it was goin about a week
To the trial, Duddon sent to speak
With Tommy. And—*everythin was in train;*
But he'd like to have a talk with this Cain.
3680 *And would Tommy go with him at once? and statin*
The for. And the two of them off in the phaeton.
So when they got there, it was—"How do ye do, sir?"
"You know me," says Duddon. "Who wouldn know you, sir?"
Says Cain, very smilin. But when he seen
Tommy there, his face got as keen
As the Divil; and—"Thomas Gelling, is it?"
He says, and "What's the cause of this visit,
May I ax?"—quite stiff, ye know. But Duddon
Wasn the chap to wait for the puddin,
3690 But in it at once: and—"A pessin is lyin
In the Castle, by the name of Quine—
A servant of yours—in custody,
Upon your information, it seems to be,
For murderin your wife by pison.
Now, Mr Cain, it's very surprisin
You don't perceive how much better
It would have been for ye all to have dropped this matter.
If your respected pardner had died
By her own hand, by suicide,"
3700 *There you were: but there was people enough*
That didn know when they were well off.
And the jury hadn seen their way
To "temporal sanity," and he dare say
He could guess the raison. "But I don't care a toss,
It was suicide, and *you know* it was!
That's my conviction, and you can't remove it;
You know it, my friend, and you can prove it—
Yes, you can. And look here, Mr Cain—"
And he eyed him sharp—"Look here, I'll be plain.
3710 There's no doubt at all the law 'll considher
The two of you to be in it together,
Her the insthrument, and *you*—
Well, Mr Cain! But here's my view—

3681   the for: reason.

Mr Cain, Mr Cain, the law 'll go furdher,
And bring you in yourself for the murdher—
Yourself alone!" (Ould Cain gave a jerk)—
"So just you set your wits to work,
And give me that proof—you know what I mane—
Or I'll have you arrested, Mr Cain.
3720 By this time to-morrow—the proof! d'ye hear?
So now you know the way to steer.
Good day, Mr Cain—" and turns on his heel.

That everin Cain was off to Peel,
And a Tommy Artlar in the bay,
And her anchor tripped, and goin to sea
Directly. And Cain just settled his passage,
And sent a passil and a message
By a chap on the pier—by gough, it's a fact!
And away to Ireland aboord of this smack,
3730 And got the steamer at Queenstown, bedad!
And off to America—Catch my lad!
Apt to come back? By gough, he isn—
If he'd show his nose, he'd be clapt in prison
Like a shot—not him! else what did he run for,
Eh? and so that divil is done for!

But what was this paper? The paper! wup!
This was the paper. When Cain went up
And found the misthress lyin dead,
He found this paper on the bed,
3740 And tuk it, and read it, and kep it by 'm—
The dirty villain! all the time.
This paper was written by his wife,
And statin *the tired she was of her life—
And the wishful to die*—that's the way it was tould—
And the Lord to have mercy upon her sowl!
And somethin about her weddin-ring——
Disthracted-lek; poor thing! poor thing!

So the trial was held, and the jury sat,
And—"Appear to coort!" and all to that—
3750 And Duddon got up, and the speech he made
Was grand—aw by gough he knew his trade—
And the foreman at them was Corlett the Draper—

3724   Tommy Artlar: Arklow fishing-boat.
3727   passil: parcel.
3736   wup: woa.

And Duddon handed up the paper,
And the Deemster read it, and "Do ye agree?"
And "Not guilty! not guilty!" what else could it be?
"Three cheers! three cheers!" aw I'll engage—
And the Deemster black in the face with rage!
And Tommy outside of the Castle wall
With a car; but he hadn the mother at all
3760 That time: and Nelly very pale—
The way with women comin urrov a jail—
And the people all lookin lek expectin
She'd go to Tommy, lek a surt o' directin,
And in with her straight, and stooped the head,
And—"You've beat me, Tommy! you've beat me!" she said.
But, half-way to Douglas, this Nelly got bouldher,
And the head was slipt on Tommy's shouldher,
And the whisperin in Tommy's ears,
And his arm round her waist, and tears—tears—
3770 Tears—I'll lave it to any man livin,
Sweeter to Tommy than the rain from heaven.

And so of coorse they got married at once?
Bless ye! where would be the sense?
But it's married they got; and this little wutch
Worked with Tommy, and Tommy got ruch.
And the farm on the North—Renshent, ye know,
Was comin to the heir-at-law,
That lived in England, and willin to let it,
And Tommy terbil wantin to get it,
3780 And got it—the very primmisis,
And there he is now—aw faith he is!

It was only last year I had a spell there,
And Tommy and Nelly and me and the childher
Went out for a walk on the Mooragh there,
Just to enjoy the lovely air:
And we tuk for the beach, and we come to the Rue,
And Tommy looked, and I looked too—
And we thought, you know; but it wasn grief—
And the water floppin upon the reef—
3790 And the little things busy with their play—
And Nelly as happy as the day.

3761   urrov: out of (ed.).
3784   Mooragh: waste land on the shore.

Explanatory Notes: Betsy Lee

3   *Lawyer's Clerk*: In Victorian narratives, lawyers' clerks range in character from the despicable Uriah Heep in *David Copperfield* to the well-intentioned but fallible Philip Christian in Hall Caine's best-selling novel, *The Manxman* (1894), a work with borrowings from the *Yarns*. In both cases the clerk goes on to become a lawyer. His showy watch chain (10) is an early sign of the class distinction between him and the derisive narrator; later his way of addressing Tom—"There's a sixpence . . . for your pains— / A sixpence, my man!" (344-5)—suggests an effort to sound as English as possible. In readings by Dollin Kelly, Taylor speaks in a parody of Oxbridge English, and his name indicates English origins, although later references to his father imply that he was born on the Island.

Rival suitors from different social classes appear in a number of nineteenth-century works in which a prudent, sometimes scheming landsman contrasts with a bolder, more impulsive suitor (or husband) who goes to sea to make money and reportedly dies, as Patrick G. Scott has shown in a survey of sources and analogues in *Tennyson's Enoch Arden: A Victorian Best-Seller*, Tennyson Society Monographs, no. 2 (Lincoln: The Tennyson Society, 1970). Scott notes the parallels in plot between *Enoch Arden* (1864) and such forerunners as "The Parting Hour" (1812), a poem by George Crabbe (whom Brown admired); "Homeward Bound" (1858), a poem by Adelaide Procter; and the novel *Sylvia's Lovers* (1863) by Elizabeth Gaskell. Earlier analogues include *The Odyssey*, Thomas Southerne's tragedy, *The Fatal Marriage* (1684), and Lady Ann Lindsay's popular ballad, "Auld Robin Gray" (1772), cited by Brown in *Tommy Big-Eyes* (737). In the basic plot of these works, the husband (or the favored lover) goes on a journey and apparently dies, leaving the field clear for a rival suitor. The fame of *Enoch Arden* in the 1860s might have influenced Brown to adapt this plot in *Betsy Lee* at the end of the decade, but many works could have influenced him.

12   *divil*: A term of contempt here, *divil* expresses admiration and affection elsewhere (see 411). In the dialect *devil* was "reserved for serious occasions" (Moore); *divil* is used literally, however, in 447.

51   *the marks and the signs*: A mark is a "fishing-ground distinguished by various land-marks. . . . The bearings for the marks are given with great reluctance, as the fishermen consider them as somewhat in the nature of a trade secret" (Moore).

57   *yawl*: "Baulk" (longline) yawls were small fishing boats with a single mast and oars: see *Manx Sea Fishing, 1600-1990's: Resource Book* (Douglas:

Manx Heritage Foundation, 1991), p. 18. The lines, traditionally made of horsehair, might be as much as a mile long. Hooks would be baited at intervals along the lines.

161   *glory*: To compare the beloved to a figure with a halo in a painting may sound conventional, but for Low Church or Methodist Manxmen at the time a "glory" was a particularly foreign image. Despite his Low Church background, Tom has a fondness for Catholic iconography, as shown later when he compares Little Simmy to the cherubic figures in paintings in Roman Catholic churches (see 390ff.). In *Christmas Rose* he insists upon his Protestantism while praising the paintings of the Blessed Virgin; in *Tommy Big-Eyes* he reports the Methodist indignation of a blacksmith who has just heard a man talk of pictures of beautiful women in the Bible. In the last of his yarns, *Job the White*, Tom compares the central figure to Christ at the Transfiguration and gets scolded by a Protestant listener after saying that a "glory" surrounded the young man. This undercurrent of conflict (and humor) may reflect Brown's own mixed feelings after his exposure to the Oxford Movement when he left his Low Church Island for the University in 1849, although late in life in a review of Henry Liddon's biography of Edward Bouverie Pusey he wrote that at Oxford "we belonged to the school of Muscular Christianity," as if he had had no Puseyite leanings. See *National Observer* 10 (7 October 1893): 541. (The review was unsigned.) For evidence that he was indeed drawn toward the Puseyite side at Oxford, see Tobias, pp. 59-61.

193   *courtin times*: Called "sooreyin" in the dialect, courting was carried on at the woman's home, with the couple spending long winter evenings in a room with her parents. Brown treats the custom at length in *The Manx Witch*, where the suitor is accompanied by a friend, the "dooiney molla" or man of praising, whose function was to praise the suitor and perhaps to distract the parents with conversation. Some Manx ballads voice the suitor's complaints about the rigors of courtship: see "*Arrane Sooree*" (Courting Song), in *Manx Ballads and Music*, ed. and trans. by A. W. Moore, preface by T. E. Brown (Douglas: G. & R. Johnson, 1896), pp. 81-2.

379   *little Sim*: As a cabin boy, Sim might be as young as ten or eleven, and he seems no older than that in Tom's description. If he is that young, then the story is being told around seven or eight years after the final narrated event, since Simmy, who could barely talk then, was about three at that time. He would have been two when Tom returned two years after his first voyage (1171). Probably at least another year passes before Tom finds Simmy in Liverpool.

443   *Tommy Tite*: A miser, as the name indicates, Tite holds the mortgage on Pazon Gale's property in *Christmas Rose*. He is mentioned also in *The Doctor (CP, p. 388)*.

627   *Spreadin sods and flowers at the mouth of his mine*: Mining primarily for lead was an important occupation around Foxdale and the Laxey Valley on the Island, but Tom never puts it on a level with the traditional tasks of fishing ("God's own work" —659) and farming. In *The Manx Witch* (1889), Tom finally tells a story about lead miners; but in spite of making friends with two of them, he indicates that miners and sailors do not mix, the miners being "more of a clan" (*CP*, p. 526).

664	*All your own among the hay*: That cattle barns had a role to play in rustic Manx courtships is indicated by the first stanza of a traditional Manx song, "*Arrane y Blieh*" ("The Grinding Song"):
	    O the oats are great for humans and cattle
	    It keeps them warm and gives them mettle
	    And in the straw for the bedding is the best place to cuddle.
	The last line—*As ayns coonlagh corkey mie dy lhie*—is more literally translated as "And in the oat straw [it is] good to lie." See *Folksongs of Britain and Ireland*, ed. Peter Kennedy (New York: Shirmer Books, 1975), p. 183. Mona Douglas's very free adaptation of "*Arrane Sooree*" ("Courting Song") forms a still more explicit parallel with the passage from *Betsy Lee* when the suitor in the song tells of eventual happiness:
	    But soon her scruples vanished,
	      Resolving in a smile,
	    Then together in the cow-house
	      We lingered for a while,
	    And our hearts to-gether beat
	      To a mellow tune and sweet,
	    While the sweet breathed cows
	      In two dark rows
	    Lay grunting at our feet.
	Twelve Manx Folk Songs (London: Stainer & Bell, n. d. [c. 1925]), p. 18. Unless Mona Douglas knew of another version which ended with the lovers in a cow-house, she might have been thinking of the passage from *Betsy Lee*, provided that she knew the uncensored 1873 text. In A. W. Moore's closer translation, there is no cow-house.

673	*Gentle Jesus*: a once popular children's hymn by Brown's favorite hymn writer, Charles Wesley (1707-1788): see Brown's letter to S. T. Irwin (3 December 1893): "One Charles Wesley, sir, and no other" (*Letters*, 1: 237). Tom quotes the first stanza of "Gentle Jesus, meek and mild" after 1285. Brown might have had in mind the setting called "Innocents" from *The Parish Choir*, 1850.
676	*Sing Glory be*: probably the "*Gloria*," beginning "Glory be to the Father, and to the Son, and to the Holy Ghost."
721	*Like Sammil when he was riz from the dead*: At King Saul's request, the Witch of Endor calls up the ghost of the prophet Samuel (1 Sam. 28:7).
831	*Stack*: a large black rock shaped like a haystack just off Scarlett Point on the west side of Castletown Bay. Another rock called the Stack lies just off the Calf of Man on the west side; another is on the west coast of the Island near Peel.
832	*Rantipike schooner*: "three-masted topsail schooner. . . . generally engaged in the transportation of pig iron from Glasgow to Liverpool" (*OED* quoting R. de Kerchove, *International Maritime Dictionary*, 1948).
837	*Pazon Gale*: An important figure in the *Yarns*, he has a major role in *Christmas Rose*, which deals with the loss of his children. He appears also in *The Doctor*, *The Schoolmasters*, and *The Manx Witch*. He narrates in standard English *Bella Gorry: The Pazon's Story* (written in 1880, published in 1889). The character apparently reflects the traits of clergymen known to Brown in his youth. In addition to his own father, there was William Drury (1808-1887), who succeeded Robert Brown as vicar of Kirk Braddan and like Pazon Gale had two sons. William Corrin (1799-1859) was identified as the prototype of Pazon Gale in A. W. Moore's *Manx*

Worthies (1901) and by Brown himself in "Manx Characters: The Castletown Aristocracy" [report of a lecture], *Ramsey Courier*, 21 January 1893. Corrin served as curate for Brown's father at St. Matthew's Church, Douglas, before becoming vicar of Kirk Rushen in the southern part of the Island. For a discussion of these figures, see Tobias, pp. 35-7.

869 *rings on their fingers*: Cf. the nursery rhyme,
> Ride a cock-horse to Banbury Cross,
> To see a fine lady upon a white horse;
> Rings on her fingers and bells on her toes,
> She shall have music wherever she goes.

891 *roaring ranthers*: "Ranters" was a term for the Primitive Methodists, who had split off from the Wesleyan Methodists. The anonymous *Illustrated Guide and Visitor's Companion Through the Isle of Man* (Douglas: J. Quiggin, 1837) reports that "In 1819 the people called Primitive Methodists, or Ranters, established themselves, and have erected many chapels in different parts" (p. 32). This branch of Methodism apparently is the target of Brown's satire in *Tommy Big-Eyes*, where the villain is a preacher; and Ranters hold a camp meeting during the cholera epidemic in *The Doctor*. Doctor Bell calls them "rascals" and orders them home (*CP*, p. 372).

899 *where I was livin*: apparently Castletown Bay. Between this bay and Derbyhaven the land "runs out" to Langness Point and Dreswick Point on the southern end of Langness. That Tom's fictional village, the "Lhen," is near Castletown in this poem seems evident from a passage in the 1872 text where he says he took the road to Castletown when coming home from Ramsey by way of the southern mountains: see Textual Notes for 1659-62. Brown makes it impossible to pin the place down, however, and distances from Castletown to the Calf of Man are too far to match certain references in *Christmas Rose*. The location in that poem seems to be further to the west, as it probably is in *The Doctor*, where Tom says a yacht anchored "inside of the Carrick" (*CP*, p. 436). The Carrick is a rock in the broad Bay ny Carrickey (Bay of the Rock) between Scarlett Point on the east and Port St. Mary on the west. A boat from the yacht is sent to Tom's village somewhere along this bay, which is just west of Castletown Bay. The mythical village apparently shifts places. In *Tommy Big-Eyes* the narrator never explains how he could be going to school in the north of the Island; in *The Schoolmasters* the Lhen has moved from the southern coast to the northwest near Jurby—apparently not far from the actual Lhen, a broad trench that drains the Curraghs (marshlands) into the sea. With these shifting references, readers are left free to form their own image of the place.

977 *Boanarges*: Boanerges, the name given by Christ to the two sons of Zebedee: "he surnamed them Boanerges, which is, the sons of thunder" (Mk. 3:17—unless otherwise noted, Biblical quotations are from the King James Version). The Pazon smokes like a son of thunder, but he does not preach like one, as Tom has already pointed out (883-91).

981-2 *Aldebarn . . . Orion*: Aldebaran (the "follower") is the brightest star in the constellation Taurus; Orion is the constellation near Canis Major, named for the giant hunter in Greek mythology.

985 *what was man*: Cf. Psalm 8:3-4.
> When I consider thy heavens, the work of thy fingers, the moon and the stars, which thou hast ordained;

> What is man, that thou art mindful of him? and the son of man, that thou visitist him?

1086   *seven-times heated furnace*: See the story of the three children of Israel and the fiery furnace: "Then was Nebuchadnezzar full of fury . . . and [he] commanded that they should heat the furnace one seven times more that it was wont to be heated" (Dan. 3:19). Brown used this image later in "Roman Women" (*CP*, p. 65).

1136   *Absalun*: Absalom, who rebelled against his father, King David, and was slain in battle. Tom's next line echoes David's lament:
> "O my son Absalom, my son, my son Absalom!
> Would God I had died for thee, O Absalom, my son, my son!"
> (2 Sam. 18:33)

1146-9   *And I cried like Peter*: Cf. Matt. 26:75: "And Peter remembered the word which Jesus had said, Before the cock crow, thou shalt deny me thrice. And he went out, and wept bitterly."

1159   *China bound*: The same phrase names the destination of Enoch's ill-fated ship in *Enoch Arden* (122).

1159   *the Waterloo*: Around the time of the story, two large vessels are listed under this name in *Lloyd's Register of British and Foreign Shipping*. A ship of 796 tons, built in 1848, sailed to Australia and by 1865 to India, with London as the home port. Another *Waterloo* of 1245 tons, built in 1865, sailed from Liverpool to India. The captain is listed as T. Kelly, not "Davis" as in the poem.

1163-4   *the Liverpool clipper . . . the Marco Polo*: A *Marco Polo* of 1400 tons, built in 1851, sailed from Liverpool to Australia by 1862. In the 1850s it sailed to Mobile, Alabama.

1205   *ghoses*: To be mistaken for a ghost is a common experience for characters who return after being thought dead. It happens in the ballad "Auld Robin Gray," in T. W. Robertson's play *Caste* (1867), and in the novel *The Manxman* (1894). In *Sylvia's Lovers*, the title of the chapter in which the sailor reappears is "The Apparition." The threat to the peace and welfare of the living posed by such returns is apparent in old ballads about ghostly lovers. Brown names "The Lover's Ghost" along with "Auld Robin Gray" in *Tommy Big-Eyes* (737). In a ballad such as "Sweet William's Ghost" the return of the dead brings death to the surviving lover. Christopher Ricks notes Tennyson's long preoccupation with the idea expressed in the sailors' line from "The Lotos-Eaters": "we should return like ghosts to trouble joy" (119): see *The Poems of Tennyson*, 2 (London: Longman Group UK Ltd, 1987): 1129.

1231   *Lloyd's*: As ship insurers, Lloyds of London kept records of lost ships.

1234-5   *Night and day the ould people was at her— / And would she marry Taylor?*: Cf. "Auld Robin Gray," after the report of her lover's death, when the girl is being pressed to marry her elderly suitor:
> My father argued sair—my mither didna speak,
> But she look'd in my face till my heart was like to break;
> They gied him my hand, but my heart was in the sea. . . .

The Book of Scottish Songs, collected by Alex Whitelaw (Glasgow: Blackie & Son, 1844), p. 205.

1253   *Doctor Bell*: The protagonist of Brown's longest yarn, *The Doctor*, Bell is an Englishman who comes to the Island after losing his first love, the daughter of an aristocrat. Following his heroic service in the cholera epidemic of 1832, he makes a bad marriage. After learning, too late, that the lady is now free to marry him, he becomes an alcoholic. His son becomes a pimp and his oldest daughter a prostitute.

1344 *hip and thigh*: After the Philistines killed Samson's wife, "he smote them hip and thigh with a great slaughter" (Judg. 15:8).

1383 *Wasn he paid to look after ghos'es?*: Pazon Gale's behavior here contrasts with his later role in *The Manx Witch* as the voice of rationalism, opposed to the popular belief in witches and other expressions of preternatural power. The strength of Manx folk beliefs in other-worldly beings has been shown by several scholars, including Margaret Killip and W. W. Gill (Gill complained that Brown slighted these beliefs).

1431 *Her love is a star that'll keep you right*: Cf. Shakespeare's Sonnet 116: "It is the star to every wand'ring bark. . . ."

1437 *Flying Foam*: *Lloyd's Register* lists several ships of this name. One of 604 tons, built in 1851, sailed from London to China; two others sailed to India in the 1850s and 60s, but their home port was not Liverpool.

1443 *Spreein away in Liverpool*: Liverpool figures in the *Yarns* as the epitome of all that is corrupt and corrupting in English urban life—although in *Tommy Big-Eyes* (1880), Tom does allow that "Douglas, as a rule, / Is just as bad as Liverpool" (2584-5). Most English tourists arrived in Douglas from that city. In portraying it as a center of corruption, Tom has certain facts on his side: Victorian Liverpool had some of the worst slums in Europe, and the waterfront where Tom goes on sprees had "formidable problems of crime, vice and drunkenness": John K. Walton, *Lancashire: A Social History, 1558-1939* (Manchester: Manchester University Press, 1987), p. 254. What Tom tends to ignore is that he is part of the problem, especially in *The Doctor*, where he calls England a "savage" place, unworthy of "the name / Of a Christian country," just after describing his arrest for kicking in a window in Liverpool (*CP*, pp. 358-60).

1445 *Sailor's Homes*: The Sailors' Home at Canning Place in Liverpool was established in 1844 to provide seamen with room, board, and medical care "at a reasonable charge" and "to encourage them to husband their wages, to promote their moral, intellectual, and professional improvement, and to afford them the opportunity of receiving religious instruction." Along with a savings bank and a library, the Sailor's Home kept a "register of character" to be used in "securing to the well-conducted seaman a rate of wages proportionate to his merits": *Gore's Directory of Liverpool and Its Environs, 1860* (Liverpool: Maudsley and Son, 1860), p. 73. Tom has obvious reasons for avoiding such an institution. The poet's brother Hugh, the popular Baptist preacher in Liverpool, supported it as chairman of the Liverpool Seaman's Friend Society: see *Hugh Stowell Brown: His Autobiography, His Commonplace Book, and Extracts from His Sermons and Addresses*, ed. W. S. Caine (London: George Routledge and Sons, 1887), p. xix.

1480 *Wappin'*: Wapping, a street on the waterfront running along the quay behind the King's Dock to the Queen's Dock.

1487 *Jack in his glory, and Jack's delight*: a Jack-tar (sailor) drunk with a prostitute.

1562 *Irish curs*: Irish immigrants came in thousands to Liverpool during the Great Famine and often had menial jobs. Tom's attitude was representative of the Manx, who had a saying, "*Cur da, she Yernagh eh* [Hit him, he's Irish]": Sophia Morrison and C. Roeder, *Manx Proverbs and Sayings* (Douglas: S. K. Broadbent, 1905), p. 6. The hostility was mutual: Lord

Teignmouth reported in 1836 that Manx sailors in the Royal Navy passed themselves off as Irishmen partly "from apprehension of the animosity evinced by the Irish towards them": *Sketches of the Coasts and Islands of Scotland and of the Isle of Man* (2: 208). Brown himself did not share Tom's anti-Irish attitude, and in a sermon he warned Manx fishermen against trying to proselytize Irish Catholics or arguing with them over the question of Home Rule: see "Fishermen's Valedictory Service: Sermon at Peel by the Rev. T. E. Brown," *Isle of Man Examiner*, 3 October 1893, Manx Museum Library. See also the note to *Christmas Rose* 1705.

1589   *Whitehaven*: To reach this small port on the coast of Cumberland, Tom would have to go around 100 miles north from Liverpool.

1597   *To "ordher myself to all my betters*: part of the response to the question, "What is thy duty towards thy Neighbour?" in the Catechism in *The Book of Common Prayer*: "To submit myself to all my governours, teachers, spiritual pastors and masters: To order myself lowly and reverently to all my betters. . . ."

1611   *Over the hills and far away*: The refrain of a song from George Farquhar's play, *The Recruiting Officer* (I, iii); it appears later in *The Beggar's Opera*, I, xii, from which Brown cites a song in *Christmas Rose* (1609). As Dollin Kelly has pointed out, Tom Baynes probably would be thinking of the nursery rhyme, "Tom, Tom, the Piper's Son."

1622-4   *Ramsey . . . Ballacraine*: Tom lands at Ramsey on the northeast coast, goes west through Ballaugh and south to Kirk Michael on the west coast, then south past St. John's near Ballacraine and on towards Castle-town along the "mountain road" up from Foxdale by South Barrule.

1643   *In heaven makin signs to me*: In identifying a star with Jenny and later with Betsy, Tom may be reflecting the old Manx belief that "every human being has a visible star in the sky which corresponds to, or is in sympathy with, him or her. More than once I have heard from a companion looking up at the night sky the speculation, 'I wonder which is *my* star?' " W. W. Gill, *A Second Manx Scrapbook* (London: Arrowsmith, 1932), p. 105.

1651-2   *Suffer / The little children . . .* : Mk. 10:14.

1653   *Glory be*: See note for 676.

1655   *Let dogs delight*: from "Quarrelling," a children's hymn by Isaac Watts (1674-1748). Tom remembers these two stanzas:

    Let dogs delight to bark and bite,
      For God hath made them so;
    Let bears and lions growl and fight,
      For 'tis their nature too.

    But, children, you should never let
      Such angry passions rise;
    Your little hands were never made
      To tear each other's eyes.

Ironically, Tom at this point still wants to kill his rival. The next quotation has not been found in nineteenth-century collections of English children's hymns.

1659   *the Lhen*: Tom's fictional home village: see note for 899. In the 1872 edition "Castletown" was used instead of the Lhen, which first appears here. It is used early in *Christmas Rose* (126) and frequently in *The Doctor*, as well as in *The Schoolmasters*.

1667,88 *Claddagh*: The Manx word meaning "low land by rivers" (Moore) or river bank (Cregeen) could refer here to a low meadow between the bay and the parish church of Kirk Malew north of Castletown.

Baulk Yawls

Explanatory Notes: Christmas Rose

54   *hunder-thirty-nine*: Wrecks were common on the Isle of Man; Teignmouth, in his *Sketches of the Coasts and Islands of Scotland and the Isle of Man* (1836), urges the building of a safe harbour for shipping in the Irish channel, and speaks of "the numerous and disastrous shipwrecks which have already taken place, and still occur every year, attended with the lamentable destruction of human life and property" (2: 406). The poet's brother describes a major storm that struck the Island on a Sunday morning at the beginning of January 1839: see *Hugh Stowell Brown: His Autobiography, His Commonplace Book, and Extracts from His Sermons and Addresses*, ed. W. S. Caine (London: George Routledge and Sons, 1887), p. 25. Manx newspapers do not report any exceptionally big storm hitting the Island around Christmas 1839. But a spectacular shipwreck occurred at Christmas in 1852 when the brig *Lily* was blown by "fierce winds" into the Sound between the Calf and the main island and wrecked on the islet of Kitterland. Some of the crew escaped, but on the morning after Christmas the forty tons of gunpowder carried by the *Lily* went off in an explosion that shook windows eighteen miles away in Douglas and killed twenty-nine men who were there to guard and watch the ship. See Terry Cringle, R. E. Forster, and G. N. Kniveton, *Here is the News: An Illustrated Manx History* (Douglas: The Manx Experience, 1992), p. 96. Tom's reference to the heroine as the "Christmas Lily" (1795) might reflect Brown's memory of the disaster.

61   *Jem—Jemmy—Jem*: called Jemmy Jem in *The Schoolmasters*, where he is the father of Tom's friends Mark and Maggie (*CP*, p. 494).

65   *Carvels. . .the Ail Varey*: The Christmas Eve service was an important one. "It was the custom for the people to go in crowds to the Parish Churches on this evening to attend a service, the main feature of which was the singing of Carols, called in Manx *Carvals*, many of which were of portentous length . . . . After the prayers were read, and a hymn was sung, the parson usually went home, leaving the Clerk in charge. Then each one who had a carol to sing would do so in turn, so that the proceedings were continued to a very late hour" (A. W. Moore, *Folk-Lore of the Isle of Man* , pp. 127-8, cited in Paton). Paton explains that "These old religious poems [in Manx] are of great interest. They were written by men of all classes, including several clergymen, a sumner, two vicars-general, a privateersman, several farmers, etc. They are usually long . . . often from a hundred lines to double that length . . . . The subjects are various. The Nativity is *not* the most common topic . . . . They were sung in various ways. One way was for the singer to start at the west end of the church and take one step towards the Table at the

end of each verse. I have been told also that sometimes two men would get up, one on each side of the church, to sing a carval. Probably it would be one of the carvals which have 'Question and Answer' in alternate verses" (pp. 89-90).

68 *carryin on outside of the door*: Paton cites Kennish's mention of "jocular remarks from 'wags around the door' while a dull carval was being sung, and this is complained of also in one of the carvals" (p. 89).

70 *the ould man*: Tom's father. We hear of his mother's reaction to his father's death in *Betsy Lee* but it is not possible to date this exactly. His death occurs sometime after the wreck which brought Christmas Rose to Man and before Tom's courtship of Betsy Lee.

77 *the houses stript*: Teignmouth describes the construction of houses thus: "The cottages are in general of a very inferior description; often built of earth, or sod, thatched with straw, fastened down by ropes of the same material. A funnel of sail-cloth, covered with a coating of lime, serves as a substitute for a chimney." An exception is the village of Cregneish, near Spanish Head. Here were "cottages built of stone . . . neatly thatched and whitewashed, and equally clean within, as most of them were provided with chimnies which carried off the smoke" (2:219).

98 *Conisthar head* : "Conister" is the name of a reef in Douglas Harbor, now covered partly by the pier and marked by the Tower of Refuge. Meaning "head of the reef," the word might apply to another reef besides this one, but Kneen lists no other instance of this place name on the Island. Douglas is too far to the northeast to be in credible range of the Calf at the southwest point of the Island where later events occur, and "the Scranes" where the ship breaks up are off Langness Point near Castletown. Derived from the Manx plural of rock, *skeryn*, "Scranes" could apply to other rocks than these, such as the "Skerranes" near Port Erin, but the treacherous currents around Langness make it the likely spot for a "ten-knot tide." Near Derbyhaven in *Betsy Lee*, Tom's home in *The Doctor* is apparently further west, closer to Port St. Mary. A yacht anchors "inside the Carrick" (*CP*, p. 436), the "Carrick" being a large rock in the Bay ny Carricky, the bay west of Castletown Bay. A boat is sent from the yacht to Tom's village. The location of "the Lhen" is left ambiguous, and apparently it shifts about: see the note for *Betsy Lee* 899.

118 *the Whitby light*: The harbor of Whitby, in Yorkshire, is situated between steep cliffs. Tom refers to the practice of lighting fires at night on the tops of the cliffs to confuse navigators so that ships would run aground. He angrily rejects Billy's suggestion that the wreck from which Christmas Rose came was caused in this way. Notwithstanding Tom's righteous indignation, there is evidence that "wrecking" did occur on Man. Margaret Killip speaks of such activities taking place at Maughold Head, not far from Ballure (p. 154).

124 *Praise God from whom*: the first half of the line of the doxology, "Praise God from whom all blessings flow."

125 *You'll get lave*: A "literal translation of the Manx 'Yiow kied,' " the expression "has many shades of meaning" (Moore); these might range from "You may say what you like" to "Say what you like, but I'll never agree with you."

126 *Lhen*: Tom's fictional home village. See the note for *Betsy Lee* (899).

129 *custom-house sharks, and the coastguard force*: The animosity towards these bodies was not only on account of their overseeing of the salvage

from wrecks but because of their role in stamping out smuggling. Teignmouth quotes a "respectable native" as saying that "[t]he local trade [smuggling], so long carried on here to the detriment of the crown, being now totally suppressed by the care and attention of his Majesty's civil government in the Isle, aided by the vigilance and activity of the revenue officers and cutters, they [the Manx people] have turned their hands with uncommon spirit and diligence to cultivate the more innocent and laudable, though less lucrative, art of agriculture, and the linen manufacture" (2: 206). It is unlikely that smuggling was "totally suppressed," and even if it had been severely curtailed the animosity against these enforcement agencies would die only slowly. See also Killip, ch. 11.

130 *Lloyds and Droits*: Lloyds is the foremost insuring agency for shipping. *Droits* refers to "Droits of Admiralty," which are "certain rights or perquisites, as the proceeds arising from the seizure of enemies' ships, wrecks, etc." (*OED*). Both Lloyds and officers of the Admiralty would try to prevent the taking away of salvage. Tom Baynes' comment that "we've made a lef" (133) simply means that they took what salvage they could when no one was looking. This was easy to do:
> Previously to the passing of the Act of 1846 the only substantial protection against plunder which owners of a wrecked ship could get was to apply to the admiralty judge for a commission enabling them or their agents to take possession of what came ashore . . . . [B]efore the commissioners arrived at the scene of the wreck a valuable cargo would have disappeared and been dispersed through the country. Plunder of wrecks was common, and the crowds that collected for the purpose set the law at defiance (*Encyclopaedia Britannica* [1921] 23: 802).

138 *took to the graves*: hid salvage in the graves.
149 *the point*: Langness Point is next to the Scranes (151), the rocks lying just off shore.
159 *no life-boats, nor apperaturs*: Teignmouth mentions one life-boat in the area—at Douglas, introduced by Sir William Hillary:
> This spirited individual has himself repeatedly incurred the utmost risk in rescuing the crews of wrecked vessels. He never allows the men employed in his service to wear cork jackets, or to be lashed to the boat, deeming such precautions calculated to diminish their intrepidity: nor does he himself, though unable to swim, make use of them. Sir William has received several medals from the Royal Humane Society, in recognition of his distinguished services in the cause of humanity. (2: 192-3)

It might be in the context of these deeds of derring-do that Tom Baynes is rather defensive when asked if the people aboard the *Hidalgo* could have been rescued. (No vessel with this name is listed in *Lloyd's Register of British and Foreign Shipping* for 1838 and 1839.)

183 *a little child*: Shortly before Brown published *Christmas Rose*, the old motif of finding an unidentified child reappeared in *The Maid of Sker* (1872), R. D. Blackmore's first novel after *Lorna Doone* (1869). Serialized in *Blackwood's Magazine* from August 1871 through July 1872, the novel depicts a little girl coming to shore in a drifting boat in the calm before a storm (ch. 4); the storm breaks up a slave ship and no one survives (ch. 9). For another depiction of a black man saving a child, see the ballad "Butler of Bewsey" in which "a faithful negro" protects the "infant heir" of Sir John

Butler and, in a nineteenth-century version by John Fitchett, falls while fighting off the attackers: *Ballads and Songs of Lancashire*, ed. John Harland (London: Routledge, 1875), pp. 1, 16. See also George MacDonald's novel *Sir Gibbie* (1879), where a black sailor is murdered after befriending and protecting a little boy (ch. 8).

213   *crown of life*: Rev. 2:10.

249   *the very vess*: the verse on the headstone; see note to 213.

280   *the Christmas Rose*: Christmas roses (Helleborus niger) bloom from December to February, their large white petals partly concealed under glossy foilage. Although in legend the Christmas rose first bloomed to provide a little girl with a gift for the infant Christ, this poisonous plant when considered as hellebore has ambiguous associations. Since ancient times hellebore (veratrum) has been known for both its medicinal and its noxious properties. T. F. Thistelton Dyer in *The Folk-lore of Plants* (New York: Appleton, 1889) wrote that hellebore, "in addition to guarding the homestead from ill . . . was regarded as a wonderful antidote against madness" (p. 315) and a means of purging melancholy. According to Charles Skinner, "it also purged human habitations of such evil spirits as had gained entrance" (*Myths and Legends of Flowers, Trees, Fruits and Plants* [Philadelphia: Lippincott, 1939], pp. 135-6). On a lighter note, Tristram Shandy's father recommends that Uncle Toby cool his sexual ardour, a particular type of "love madness," by application, to the offending part, of "syrrup of hellebore" (vol. 8, ch. 34). But Spenser placed this plant amongst those "direfully deadly black, both leaf and bloom / Fit to adorn the dead and deck the dreary tomb" (Book II, Canto vii). And Dyer noted that "our forefathers, in strewing their floors with this plant, were introducing a real evil into their houses . . . the perfume having been considered highly pernicious to health" (p. 315). In the poem, Mrs. Gale will see Christmas Rose as a viper, poisoning the household.

316   *Sarah in Genesus*: Abraham's wife mistreats his concubine Hagar once this woman conceives: see Gen. 16:6.

390   *Doodoss*: W. Walter Gill in *Manx Dialect: Words and Phrases* (London: Arrowsmith, 1934) says that in Brown's writing this is not much stronger than "my word" or "by Jove." Gill derives the word from Irish Gaelic *dubh-dhoight*, "terrible," but literally "burnt black" (p. 46).

393   *Like a brother or that?*: The question apparently means "like a brother or something like that?"—if the final phrase indicates approximation as it does later when Tom speaks of sailing "a mile or that" from shore (2085).

472   *canokes*: "a punishment or penalty in the game of marbles. The knuckles are held down and the marbles are rolled against them" (Moore).

473   *Duckstone*: "a boy's game in which the 'duck' is a small stone placed on top of a larger one. The players in turn throw . . . stones at the 'duck' and endeavour to knock it off" (Moore).

Hommer-the-let: "a game in which one boy hits another with a ball; then he who first picks up the ball hits the nearest boy with it, and so on as fast as possible" (Moore).

585   *Bible says about Moses*: See Ex. 34:29 ff.

610   *backin and fillin*: going "backward and forward" (*OED*) like a ship avoiding an obstacle. To "back" a sail is to set it so the wind blows directly against the front of it.

624	*image set on a fine hair spring*: Brooches which consisted of an enamel butterfly or bird affixed to the pin by a hair spring were popular in the nineteenth century.
627	*jig-a-maree!*: literally, "will he come with her," if *a* represents Mx. *eh* (he). The *OED* glosses the phrase as "a sportive or cunning trick, a maneuver."
667	*stud*: probably a misprint for *shud* in 1873 (rhyming with *cud*). *Should* is used here in 1881, apparently meaning "should go up [to the church]."
687	*aw cheeagh voddie!*: a puzzling phrase, apparently garbled. *Cheeagh* means the female breast or pap (Cregeen); *voddi* (normally spelled *voddee*) means dogs. The initial consonants are aspirated from *keeagh* and *moddee* because the words are in the vocative case. In Manx word order, *voddi* should identify whose breast or pap is being invoked, so a literal translation might be something like "dogs' tit." If Brown meant to use the singular, *voddey*, it would not have rhymed with *body* in the next line, since the final *ey* would be pronounced like "uh." Manx speakers on the Island did not agree on the meaning in 1995. The Victorian Manxman who annotated the 1873 text presented by Brown to Robert J. Moore pencilled in "hearty dogs?" in the copy in the Manx Museum. Perhaps for grammatical reasons and possibly to avoid giving offence, Brown evaded the task of glossing the phrase by deleting it from the 1881 edition.
711-12	*a mixture / At them and at me*: a mixture of play actor and jack-a-dandy and of myself—that is how I placated her.
779	*read in a book*: apparently *Paradise Lost* (VI), although Tom hardly seems that literate. He does speak of Milton, however, in *The Manx Witch* (*CP*, p. 584).
810	*destroyin them congers*: "The dried conger, which the English fisherman will seldom eat, and the Scotch hold in abhorrence, from the resemblance of the eel to the snake, is in Man a favourite article of food" (Teignmouth 2:220).
825	*But never a sparra drops for all*: See Matt. 10:29.
827	*black ould witch*: Margaret Killip speaks of "days long past [when] there were witches in the Island who sold wind to seamen bound up in the knots of a length of thread. The sailors were permitted to loosen two of them, but if the third knot was undone it would unleash a hurricane and they would be shipwrecked" (p. 126). Tom pictures the witch as a composite of the three Fates in classical mythology.
853	*Calf*: the Calf of Man, a small island on the southernmost tip of Man. The "Sound" (856) is the narrow stretch of water which separates it from the main island.
854	*long-lines stowed*: Tom's fishing-boat is a "baulk yawl" (Mx. *baulk*, a long line), used for fishing with lines having hooks baited at intervals. Made of horsehair, the lines for cod fishing might be as much as a mile long. Tom's boat has one mast with a lug sail; if it is as big as the regular Manx yawls around 1850 it would have three or four benches (thwarts) for the rowers. See *Manx Sea Fishing*, p. 18 and Card 7, cited in the note to *Betsy Lee* 57.
862	*cliffs*: if they are sailing west toward the Sound, and in sight of it, the cliffs would be those around Spanish Head.
868	*"The sea! the sea! the open sea!"*: first line of a lyric by Bryan Waller Procter (Barry Cornwall, pseud.), "The Sea," first published in *Friendship's Offering* for 1831 and set to music by Sigismund Naukomm: The sea! the sea! the open sea! The blue, the fresh, the ever free!

Fo'c's'le Yarns 250

The third and fourth stanzas prefigure Rose's love of storms and her sense of having no human mother:
> I love, oh! *how* I love to ride
> On the fierce foaming bursting tide,
> When every mad wave drowns the moon,
> Or whistles aloft his tempest tune,
> And tells how goeth the world below,
> And why the Sou'west blasts do blow.

> I never was on the dull tame shore
> But I lov'd the great sea more and more,
> And backwards flew to her billowy breast,
> Like a bird that seeketh her mother's nest,
> And a mother she *was* and *is* to me;
> For I was born on the open sea!

"The sea! the sea!" echoes the famous cry of the weary Greek soldiers upon finally gaining sight of the Euxine Sea in Xenophon's *Anabasis*, 4.7.100.

891 *Or was it her sweetheart the cloud was lek*: Tom is imagining a dangerous spirit ("With the thunder-poison from his mouth") who resembles the "Stromkarl" described by an earlier Manx poet, Elizabeth Cookson. The speaker in her rhapsodic poem of this title stands on a cliff by the sea, consumed by "a yearning fierce for things unseen":
> I felt as I were drawn away
> By kisses falling swift as spray
> Upon my lips so red and warm,
> Upon my shuddering yielding form.
> Delicious horror! I was press'd
> With eager arms to some cold breast. . . .

In her "wilful crazy mood" she feels herself flying with him, then fleeing "to darkness where the demons are," before being rescued by an angel. See *Poems from Manxland, with Legends and Translations from the Manx and German* (London: Eliot Stock, 1868), pp. 5-7. Tom thinks that Rose's soul leaves her body and goes up "With the clouds and thunder" once "the divil of the storm" possesses her (954, 948). The woman's orgiastic sense of becoming the "bride" of this mysterious power is echoed later in *Christmas Rose* when Tom tells how the girl would steal to the shore to meet the storm, her lover (see 1852-6).

922 *Thushla*: a dangerous rock between the Calf and Kitterland, a very small island just off the main island.

1026 *th' tell* : *the* can mean *to* (Moore); Mx. *dy* = *to* before verbs, and sounds like *the*.

1036 *fall right out at the wandhar*: Cf. Acts 20:9: "And there sat in a window a certain young man named Eutychus . . . and as Paul was long preaching, he sunk down with sleep, and fell down from the third loft, and was taken up for dead."

1040 *Premmitives*: "[I]n 1776, the Methodists, who directed their attention particularly to the Celtic portion of our people, in Cornwall and Wales, finding in their disposition to religion and to religious excitement, unregulated by education . . . the utmost encouragement, obtained a footing in the Isle of Man . . . . The Methodists have now erected chapels in almost every parish" (Teignmouth 2:254). At first the chapel services were arranged so as not to clash with those of the church, but Teignmouth adds in

Explanatory Notes: Christmas Rose 251

a footnote: "In the towns, the Methodists now open their chapels during Divine service, a practice which many of them consider a great evil" (2:259). The "Primitive" Methodists, sometimes called "Ranters," began establishing chapels on the Island in 1819 (see note to *Betsy Lee* 891).

1089 *a kind of mainspring*: In a letter to A. M. Worthington dated 5 April 1892, Brown writes, "I believe it is all up with me. I may go for a few years more yet, but the mainspring has been rudely shaken, and I shall be a simulacrum, an approximation to the manes and lemures of fable" (*Letters* 1:153).

1174 *whose name was legion*: Mark 5:9; Luke 8:30.

1227 *much forgiven*: Cf. the account of the woman who washed and anointed Jesus' feet: "Her sins which are many, are forgiven; for she loved much" (Luke 7:47).

1228 *kingdom of heaven*: Cf. Matt. 19:14: "Suffer little children . . . to come unto me: for of such is the kingdom of heaven."

1450 "Gentle Jesus": "Gentle Jesus, meek and mild"—first line of a children's hymn by Charles Wesley; see note for *Betsy Lee* 673.

1567 *whistle and I'll come to ye, my lad!*: from the chorus of a song adapted by Robert Burns, published in George Thomson's edition of *Scottish Airs* in 1799. The last two lines of the chorus are

Tho' father an' mither an' a' should gae mad,
O, whistle an' I'll come t'ye, my lad!

1595 *jann myghin orrym*: properly *Jean myghin orrin* (Moore). *Orrym* = "on me," not "on us" as in Brown's gloss.

1609 *"How happy could I be with ether"*: sung by the highwayman Macheath when Lucy and Polly both lay claim to him in Act II, scene xiii of *The Beggar's Opera* (1728) by John Gay:

How happy could I be with either,
Were t'other dear Charmer away!

1705 *Protestant boys 'll carry the day*: "Though the Manks and the Irish have descended from the same stock, venerate the same patron saint, and speak nearly the same language, they entertain a deep-rooted antipathy to each other. The feud between them . . . is indicated by frequent broils, especially in the streets of Peel. It arises chiefly from religious differences, aggravated by the affinity of the two people, which invariably, when it does not produce closer union, occasions bitter animosity. The Irish despise the Manksmen, as having degenerated from the faith of their fathers: the latter, seeing the total neglect of religious practices by the Irish, so contrasted to their own scrupulous adherence to them, regard them as infidels, or to use the term applied to them by a Manks fisherman while conversing with me, as 'not men,' or as he explained it, as wicked and of no religion" (Teignmouth 2:276). The antipathy was further exacerbated by considerable numbers of Irish mendicants coming to the Island (2:266). Teignmouth also mentions that Manxmen who entered the navy concealed their nationality and passed for Irish "from apprehension of the animosity evinced by the Irish towards them" (2: 208). See note to *Betsy Lee* (1562).

1769 *fenodyree*: Cregeen gives the following: "*Phynnodderee* a satyr; Isa. xxxiv. 14 . . . . derived from *Fynney* (hair or fur), and *Oashyr* or *Oashyree* (of stockings or hose); the name seems to imply that its hair or fur is its covering." Paton says this denotes "a kind of Manx brownie" (p. 48). In Kathleen Killip's telling of the story of "The Phynoderee of Glen Chass" he is the one who makes sure the wife and son of the fisherman are safe whilst the man is at sea. The phynoderee is described as having a "head like a man and a coat all shaggy like the cattle"; he is "as shy as a wren and as quiet as a shadow" and lives, almost invisibly, in the trammon tree. He delights to help people but is offended if given presents in return: *St. Bridget's Night: Stories from the Isle of Man* (London: Hamish Hamilton, 1975), pp. 115-23).

1900 *mheillea*: "This term is used for the finishing of reaping corn, when the last handful is cut; this is bound up with ribbons, and what wild flowers come readily to hand, and borne by the Queen of the Mheillea, some female favourite of the harvest-field, to the highest part of the land where the reapers express their joy in loud huzzas. On these occasions it is usual for the farmer to provide a supper at which the reapers, young and old, assemble with the family and friends of the 'Big man,' all being on that occasion on an equality; the evening is often concluded with a song or merry dance" (Paton p. 11).

2052 *tasty*: probably from *tastagh* "knowing, sagacious, intelligent, discerning" (Cregeen).

2226 *Whiteboys*: Paton says,"At Christmas-tide the White-boys went the round of the houses, performing the old play of 'St. George and the Dragon.' " He cites an account of the proceedings by William Harrison:
> the *dramatis personae*—St. George, Prince Valentine, King of Egypt, Sambo and the Doctor—as their designation imports, are attired in white dresses, showing their shirt sleeves, fantastically decorated with ribbons, fancy-coloured paper, beads, and tinsel. They wear high caps or turbans of white paste-board similarly decked out, with a sprig of evergreen or "Christmas" stuck in them, and each carrying a drawn sword in his hand. The Doctor is in *full black*, with face and cap of the same, armed with a stick, and a bladder tied to the end, with which he belabours those who press too close upon the performers. He generally carries a small box for contributions, and is a kind of Merry Andrew to the play. . . . The performance is often wound up by a song. (p. 96)

2260 *Tommy Tite*: a miserly neighbor of the Lees: see note to *Betsy Lee* (443).

2501 *this poor chap*: not George's friend but George himself. Later editions have a paragraph break here to make the reference less confusing.

2514 *Orpheus*: A ship with this name but a different captain is listed in *Lloyd's Register* in the 1850s. It was launched in 1841, with Liverpool as the home port through 1852.

2523 *among the farms*: For the needy to go from farm to farm asking for alms was a common practice in the Isle of Man. Tom Baynes seems to be superimposing a local custom on Australian life.

Explanatory Notes: Captain Tom and Captain Hugh

8   *Castletown*: the site of Castle Rushen on the south coast and the seat of government for the Island until 1869, when Douglas became the capital. Hampered by a shallow harbor, the town had a population of a little over 2000 in Brown's lifetime, falling behind Ramsey and Peel, while Douglas increased to over 19,000 by 1891. But Castletown "remained an area of residence for the upper classes and a seat of learning"—King William's College, which Brown attended, being nearby: Vaughan Robinson, "Social Demography," *The Isle of Man: Celebrating a Sense of Place*, ed. Vaughan Robinson and Danny McCarroll (Liverpool: Liverpool University Press, 1990), p. 142. In *Armadale* (1866) Wilkie Collins gives this description of the town which for Tom Baynes once epitomized wealth and elegance (see 805ff.):

>Beginning with the waterside, there was an inner harbour to see, with a drawbridge to let vessels through; an outer harbour, ending in a dwarf lighthouse; a view of a flat coast to the right, and a view of a flat coast to the left... The few shops open were parted at frequent intervals by other shops closed and deserted in despair.
>(Bk I, ch. 3)

Describing the scene at low tide on August 30, 1855, George Borrow reported a long "waste of mud and seaweed; to the north-west, far in the distance, were brown mountains, down whose sides the mists of evening began to roll; then there was to my west the muddy river crawling... to the bay...." See "An Expedition to the Isle of Man in the Year 1855," *The Works of George Borrow* 16 (London: Constable & Co. Ltd., 1924): 483.

11   *Claddagh*: The stream forming the Claddagh is the Silver Burn, which runs through Castletown into the harbor. The marshy area at low tide just up from the main harbor is called "the Claddagh."

13   *down at the Race, or out at the Mull*: Mull (or Meayll) Hill, the high, bare headland rising up on the southwest point of the Island, across the Sound from the Calf. Teignmouth refers to "the Race of the Calf" as "a narrow sound, through which the tide runs from east to west with great rapidity" (2: 190). This channel is about six miles to the west of Castletown. The swift tides around Langness Point at Castletown Bay might also be called a "race," and a millrace off the Silver Burn ran near the town.

66	*Ballachrink*: farm of the hill (Kneen), a common place-name. Kneen lists two in the parish of Kirk Malew, which contains Castletown. The uncle's surname is Sayle, but as owner of this farm he is "the Ballachrink."
115	*"Up peak, my lads, down jib, and jive her!"*: The command would be to raise the peak of the fore-and-aft sail, lower the jib sail, and cause the vessel to change course (jibe) by shifting the fore-and-aft sail.
129	*That was Captain Hugh*: By giving his own name to the congenial Captain Tom and his older brother's name to the stern Captain Hugh, Brown could be reflecting his sense of the profound differences in temperament between himself and the well-known Baptist preacher in Liverpool. He alludes to ill feeling between them in a letter of 1850, but by the 1870s the differences apparently had been resolved. See Tobias, p. 41.
157	*Cronk-ny-Irey-Lhaa*: a high hill on the southwest coast about five miles northwest of Castletown. Also named *Cronk ny Arrey Laa*, "hill of the day-watch" (Kneen).
162	*guy heng*: *guy* is a "disguised form of the word 'God' " (Wright). Brown's gloss is "go hang" (*CP*, p. 236).
201	*High Bailiff*: an officer charged with maintaining order. He ruled on disputes concerning debts of under forty shillings, and directed repairs and the upkeep of the town (see Teignmouth 2:237). Castletown, Douglas, Peel, and Ramsey each had a high bailiff.
396	*Nebuchadnessar*: Nebuchadnezzar was the king of Babylon who conquered Judah in the reign of Jehoiakim, and took captives back to Babylon. See Dan. 1-4.
411	*his head on his chin*: possibly a misprint of *head* for *hand*, but thus in all editions.
426	*Rover*: This was a common name for vessels in *Lloyd's Register of British and Foreign Shipping* in the middle of the nineteenth century. Under "Local and General News," *Mona's Herald* for Wednesday, 6 December 1848, reported that "on Tues. night last week Mr. Thomas Kneale, master of the *Rover* of this port" [Douglas], was "washed overboard and drowned, almost an hour after the above vessel had left Wick, on her voyage to Belfast. Mr. Kneale was a quiet and inoffensive man. . . in the prime of life and has left a widow and four children to lament his untimely death. . . ." The captain of a different ship drowns in the poem.
427	*making the Mull*: coming around the high headland on the southwest tip of the Island as the smack sails home from the west.
439	Tyre and Sidon: cities on the Syrian coast. Cf. Matt. 11:21-22.
466-8	*the polished corners. . . Full of store*: See Psalm 144: 12-13 in *The Book of Common Prayer*:

> That our sons may grow up as young plants: and that our daughters may be as the polished corners of the temple.
> That our garners may be full and plenteous with all manner of store: that our sheep may bring forth thousands, and ten thousands in our streets.

489	*black man*: "dark," with negative connotations, and perhaps also "unknown," as in *black stranger*, "an unknown person" (Moore).
500-3	*"Take care". . . the dark you'll get"*: Cf. Matt. 6:23: "But if thine eye be evil, thy whole body shall be full of darkness. If therefore the light that is in thee be darkness, how great is that darkness!"

Explanatory Notes: Captain Tom and Captain Hugh 255

542   *built at Boyd's*: Tom's account of the launching of the *Cyclops* resembles the one in *Mona's Herald* under "Local and General News" on Wednesday, 20 December 1848:

> On Tuesday week a handsome schooner, registered 51 tons, was launched into Castletown harbour, at the tide time. She went off beautifully into her distinctive element, amid the cheers of hundreds of spectators. Her name is the *Cyclops*. She was built for Mr. Thomas Boyd, blacksmith, by Mr. John Moore, to whom she does credit. . . .

Although Tom never gets the name right and the owner of the schooner is not Corteen, his report is based on fact, and like the journalist he speaks of "a beautiful launch" (552). The captain of the *Cyclops* listed in *Lloyd's Register* is P. Sayle. Brown was in his last year at King William's College at the time. Since the original text had no gloss identifying the *Clyps* as the *Cyclops*, Tom's trouble with the name would have been an in-joke for Manx readers in 1878 who knew of this schooner.

543   *the Lake*: a pool behind the harbor where a low dam crosses the Silver Burn. Between the Lake and the main harbor is the marshy Claddagh, with mud banks lying exposed at low tide.

545   *the school*: apparently Brown's old school, King William's College (opened in 1833), outside Castletown.

564   *the Crown*: "The Crown Arms" and "The Rose and Crown" were both public houses on the Quay at mid-century, but none called "The Crow " was in Castletown.

618   *the Flukin' pool*: "Flukes" on the Isle of Man are plaice; the pool is in the bay near the town.

677   *Ballasalla*: a village about two miles northeast of Castletown.

830   *Blessed Jesus! strong to save!*: unidentified, but possibly a misquotation of what became the "Navy Hymn":

> Eternal Father, strong to save,
> Whose arm hath bound the restless wave,
> Who bidd'st the mighty ocean deep
> Its own appointed limits keep;
> O hear us when we cry to Thee
> For those in peril on the sea.

The words were written by William Whiting (1825-78) for *Hymns Ancient and Modern* (1861).

850   *peccee hrie*: Moore corrects the quotation by changing *hrie* to *hreih* (miserable).

890   *Mona's Pride*: The name does not appear in *Lloyd's Register* from 1849 until 1866, when a 100 ton schooner from Peel was built to sail to the Mediterranean. The vessel in the poem is only a smack, used for coastal shipping.

903   *Fort*: the round Derby Fort is on St. Michael's Island, just off the north end of Langness, guarding the harbor of Derbyhaven; another fort, in ruins, stands at the south end of the peninsula.

1156-7 *Prince's pier . . . Maddharell's*: the pier by Prince's Dock in Liverpool Harbor; "Maddharell's" represents Tom's pronunciation [ma*th*arel's] of *Maddrell's* or *Madrell's*. In directories for 1851/2, William Gibbons Madrell was the proprietor of an ale house at 10 James Street off Strand Street next to the docks. Given the Ballachrink's fondness for drink, the ale house would be a likely destination. A second possibility would be the porterage service of William Matheral on Brunswick Street nearby, if the Ballachrink went there with the captain to arrange for carrying material to the vessel. (The editors are indebted to Miss E. Organ, Liverpool Record Office, for this information.)

'Lugger' or Dandy Smack, 1840

Explanatory Notes: Tommy Big-Eyes

66   *Lough Molla'*: (or Mallow) "lake of the plain," according to Kneen, who notes that although the lake is gone "the name is still preserved in Lough Mallo road and bridge" (p. 536). The place is in the northeastern part of the Island, south of the hamlet of Kirk Andreas; the bridge is inland over a mile west from what is now North Ramsey.

76   *The Vollin*: probably "The Vowlan," shown on the large scale Ordnance Survey Map of 1870 as a place on the shore not quite a mile north of Ramsey Harbor. In mid-Victorian times it lay well outside the town, along the "Kirk Bride road" that runs north from Ramsey. Tom's references indicate that Nelly's home lies "about a mile" north of the "town," and Ramsey is the only town in that part of the Island. Approached from the north, the bridge over the River Sulby would have led "into the town" (70) at the time of the action. The school in the poem might be in Ramsey. Nelly chases Tommy from the school to the bridge when he starts home (247). When Tom says that Nelly then went "home to Kirk Bride" (274), he must mean that she crossed the river into her home parish, not that she went all the way north to the little hamlet of Kirk Bride. "The Vowlan" is on the shore and the hamlet isn't. Later in *The Schoolmasters* when listing schools in the north of the Island, the narrator says that Tommy and Nelly went to school "In the Town, where none of us went of a rule" (*CP*, p. 494), and again the only possibility is Ramsey, unless he meant Peel on the west coast. (Tom seems to forget that he went to school with them also.) For identifying "the Vollin" the editors are indebted to Mr. Les Quilliam of Peel.

213   *hop chu naa*: usually *Hop-tu-naa*, the refrain of a verse that Manx children said while making their rounds at Hollantide (All Hallow's Eve), carrying lanterns and collecting pennies for a "taffy spree." Brown recited it in a lecture reported in "Castletown Fifty Years Ago," *Isle of Man Examiner*, 23 November 1895 (Scrapbook J10/16x Manx Museum Library). Moore gives the version used at Peel, with the refrain of "Hop-the-nei" [*ei* as in *weight*], derived from Mx. *hop! ta'n oie*, lit. "Hip! it is the night." He reports that the verses were recited antiphonally, with one speaker saying the refrain and another responding, in this version:

            Hop-the-nei!   Put in the pot;
            " " "   Put in the pan.
            " " "   I scawl't (scalded) me throat;
            " " "   I feel it yit.
            " " "   I went to the well;
            " " "   I dhrunk me fill.

			On me way back
"	"	"	I met a foul-cat;
"	"	"	The cat began to grin,
"	"	"	I begun to run,
"	"	"	Where did you run to?
"	"	"	I ron to Scotlan'.
"	"	"	What were they doin theer?
"	"	"	Bakin bonnags and roastin sconnags.
"	"	"	Jinnie the Winnie went over the lake,
"	"	"	The griddle in her han' ready to bake.
"	"	"	I asked her for a bit;
"	"	"	She gave me a bit as big as me big toe.
"	"	"	I dipped it in milk;
"	"	"	I wrapped it in silk.

Hop-the-nei!
If you're goin to give us anything, give us it soon,
Befoor we run away be the light o' the moon.

Several versions are printed by Paton, pp. 78-82.

266 *Tally-high-ho-the-grinder*: According to A. L. Lloyd, the song originated in the 1860s when the Sheffield grinders of cutlery protested a government report: see *Folk Song in England* (London: Lawrence and Wisehart, 1967), pp. 373-5. But Roy Palmer identifies an earlier source for the refrain as "Tally i o, the grinder"—"a comic song about marital incompatibility": see *Poverty Knock: A Picture of Industrial Life in the Nineteenth Century Through Songs, Ballads and Contemporary Accounts* (Cambridge: Cambridge University Press, 1974), pp. 30-33. Mr. Palmer has very kindly supplied a text of the earlier song, which the school children might have sung at least in part in the 1840s:

Tally I O, the Grinder

If ever I marry a wife,
   I'll marry a widow for fun;
I'll set a cockade in her hat,
   And then she'll follow the drum.
Tally I O, tally I O, the grinder!
Tally I O, I O, tally I O, never mind her.

I have a ship on the sea,
   And I have a pilot to mind her;
I have a wife at home,
   And she's a terrible grinder.

    Tally I O, &c.

If you want to see my wife,
   I'll tell you where to find her,
She is at the back of the door,
   Playing with Harry the grinder,

    Tally I O, &c.

>   There was a wee bit wife,
>   And she had a wee bit daughter,
>   Who had two bonny black eyes,
>   And she was a terrible starter,
>   Tally I O, &c.
>
>   I left my wife at home,
>   And there I thought to find her;
>   But long e'er I came back,
>   She was off with Harry the grinder.
>   Tally I O, &c.
>
>   My mother went down to the mill,
>   My father went down to find her,
>   He put her in the mill hopper,
>   And then began to grind her.
>   Tally I O, &c.
>
>   There's never a lass on the sea,
>   Nor is there a lass on the sea,
>   There's never a lass on the land
>   Shall be a heart-breaker of me.
>   Tally I O, &c.

A Garland of New Songs ([Newcastle]: Angus, Printer, n. d.), pp. 5-6. Reproduced here in modern type, the text apparently was published in the late eighteenth century, according to Palmer, who reports that the printer was probably Thomas Angus (d. 1788), although printers named Angus worked in Newcastle up to 1825. Palmer notes also that a tune entitled "Grinders," which "would fit the words of the song" appears "in John Clare's manuscript books of fiddle tunes" (letter to editor, 16 February 1995).

The "marital incompatibility" depicted later in *Tommy Big-Eyes* takes a less violent form, but the husband's feeling toward his wife is murderous in both the yarn and the song.

286   *Bulls of Bashan*: Ps. 22:12: "many bulls have compassed me; strong bulls of Bashan have beset me round."

303-4   *us poor little blokes / Takin care to laugh at all his jokes*: Cf. *David Copperfield*, ch. 7: "Mr. Creakle cuts a joke before he beats him, and we laugh at it—miserable little dogs, we laugh. . . ."

338-9   *the Clip, / Where the roads divide*: Brown recalls the "Clyp" near his home parish of Kirk Braddan (*Letters* 2:214), and the place-name *Clypse* occurs in the neighboring parish of Onchan, but the editors have not located a place with this name near Ramsey. W. W. Gill relates *clypse* to a Manx word for a smaller rock by a large one in the sea: *A Manx Scrapbook* (Bristol: J. W. Arrowsmith, 1929), p. 222.

430   *Nelly has kissed me*: Cf. Leigh Hunt's "Rondeau" (1838), which begins and ends with "Jenny kissed me."

452   *the Ballagoole*: This place-name is not listed in Kneen. Mr. Les Quilliam suggests that it might be a corruption of *Balladoole*, the name of a farm near Ramsey.

518   *Renshent*: "blessed division" of land (*sheaynt*, "blessed with peace"—Cregeen). Kneen lists a farm of this name in Kirk Malew by Stoney Mountain near Foxdale. The name does not appear in the parish of Jurby on

the northwest coast, where the Cains' farm is located. The place that best matches the description in the poem is Sartfield, less than a mile to the north of the Jurby parish church of St. Patrick's. Beyond the farm buildings, the land rises and breaks off in steep sandy cliffs by the shore; cliffs run southward toward Jurby Head but do not carry on to the north. The marshy land below the buildings forms "a sort of a gaery," still "splendid for geese" in 1995. Sartfield lies "aback of the Ballamoore" (520), the "great farm" which is the only major estate near Jurby. It is about a mile and a half east of Jurby Head. Called "the Ballaglass" in the poem, it is the fictional home of the Moores.

574-5   "*diligent. . . spirit*": Rom. 12:11: "Not slothful in business; fervent in spirit; serving the Lord."

588   *Ballarat*: A farm with this name is found near Grenaby, in the south of the Island to the north of Castletown.

656   *club*: a "friendly society" providing benefits for sickness or burial. The club would hold an annual dinner, as in William Barnes' "Whitsuntide an' Club Walken.' "

669   *dropping a button*: "Button" could mean lump or morsel by analogy with the Manx word *cramman*—"a lump, bulb, or button" (Cregeen).

737   "*Ould Robin Gray*" . . . "*Lover's Ghost*": Written by Lady Ann Lindsay (1750-1825) to the tune of "The Bridegroom greits when the sun goes down," "Auld Robin Gray" (1772) was later sung to a tune composed by the Rev. William Leeves, although the first verse retained the "old air": see Alex Whitelaw's collection, *The Book of Scottish Songs* (Glasgow: Blackie & Son, 1844), p. 204. In the ballad, a young woman tells of her unhappy marriage to an older man after her impoverished young lover has gone to sea and she hears of his death in a shipwreck. He returns in the flesh, however, after she has become old Robin's wife, and the original version of the ballad ends with these stanzas:

> I hadna been his wife, a week but only four,
> When mournfu' as I sat on the stane at the door,
> I saw my Jamie's ghaist—I couldna think it he,
> Till he said, "I'm come hame, my love, to marry thee!"
>
> O sair, sair did we greet, and mickle did we say:
> Ae kiss we took—nae mair—I had him gang away.
> I wish that I were dead, but I'm no like to dee;
> And why do I live to say, Wae is me!
>
> I gang like a ghaist, and I carena to spin;
> I darena think o' Jaimie, for that wud be a sin.
> But I will do my best a gude wife aye to be,
> For Auld Robin Gray, he is kind to me.

Lindsay added a continuation much later to provide a happy ending; the whole text appears in *The Book of British Ballads*, ed. S. C. Hall (London: Henry G. Bohn, 1853), pp. 417-20. See also the Explanatory Notes for *Betsy Lee* (3, 1205).

A version of "The Lover's Ghost" appears in *Everyman's Book of British Ballads*, ed. Roy Palmer (London: J. M. Dent and Sons, 1980), p. 49. The ghost in this version is a woman; usually it is a man. In "Sweet William's Ghost," for example, and "The Suffolk Miracle" (No. 272 in F. J. Child's *English and Scottish Popular Ballads*) a girl dies after the return of her lover's ghost. As in the ballads, Mrs. Cain learns that "Ould love is a dangerous thing to touch" (2221), and Nelly must put behind her the memory of a drowned lover.

811   *he counted all but loss*: Phil. 3:8: "I count all things but loss. . . ."

827   *Potter's Wheel*: Cf. Jer. 18:3-4: "Then I went down to the potter's house, and, behold, he wrought a work on the wheels. And the vessel that he made of clay was marred in the hand of the potter—so he made it again another vessel, as seemed good to the potter to make it."

828   *everlasting seal*: Cf. Rev. 7:2-3: "And I saw another angel ascending from the east, having the seal of the living God: and he cried with a loud voice to the four angels, to whom it was given to hurt the earth and heaven the sea, Saying, Hurt not the earth, neither the sea, nor the trees, till we have sealed the servants of our God in their foreheads."

829   *"By grace you are saved"*: Eph. 2:5.

875   *the aisy yoke*: Cf. Matt. 11:30: "For my yoke is easy, and my burden is light."

885   *talk in the Church*: Cf. 1 Cor. 14:34-5: "Let your women keep silence in the churches. . . . And if they will learn anything, let them ask their husbands at home . . . ."

989   *rivers of water in a thirsty land*: Cf. Isa. 32:2: "And a man shall be as an hiding place from the wind, and a covert from the tempest—as rivers of water in a dry place; as the shadow of a great rock in a weary land"—and also Isa. 35:7: "And the parched ground shall become a pool, and the thirsty land springs of water. . . ."

1058   *But rather bothered him*: See 1 Cor. 14, where Paul warns against speaking in unknown tongues without an interpreter. About spiritual gifts, however, he does not reach Cain's conclusion that "[t]he Church could do very well without them."

1205   *zeal of thine house*: John 2:17, quoting Ps. 69:9: "The zeal of thine house hath eaten me up."

1211   *weepin and gnashin of teeth*: Cf. Matt. 8:12, 22:13.

1221-3:   *weddin. . . garment*: Matt. 22:11-12: "And when the king came in to see the guests, he saw there a man which had not on a wedding garment: And he saith unto him, 'Friend, how camest thou in hither not having a wedding garment?' And he was speechless."

1260   *Kirk Andreas. . . Lezayre*: places in the north central part of the Island. The parish of Kirk Christ Lezayrs lies just south of the parish of Kirk Andreas and has marshlands (curraghs) along its northern border.

1324   *he made a bound*: The shy man is a rustic type notably represented by Hardy's Joseph Poorgrass in *Far From the Madding Crowd* (1874). Because Tommy falls in love and marries, however, he has more kinship with the character in William Barnes' poem, "The Shy Man" (1859), than with Poorgrass.

1328   *church*: St. Patrick's, the Jurby parish church, standing stark and white on the bare headland west of Ballamoar ("Ballaglass").

1366   *Captain Moore*: Although the title might be military, as the principal landholder he would be the likely "Captain of the Parish"—the official who calls parish meetings and goes to the Tynwald (the Manx governing body) when the laws are read: see E. H. Stenning, *Isle of Man* (London: Robert Hale, 1950), p. 81.

1373   *Staff-of-Goverment*: the Appellate Division of the Manx High Court (see Stenning, p. 377).

1389	*Of plantin and that*: The description of the Moore estate could have been inspired by Ballamoar ("Ballamoar Castle" today). With an imposing tree-lined drive, a park, a lodge, and a summer house in Brown's time, it was the greatest estate in the area.
1518	*Sulby way, Ballaugh*: Sulby lies inland between Ramsey on the east coast and Ballaugh on the west. (Ballaugh rhymes with "off" in *Betsy Lee* (1622-3).
1594	*Dig. . . death*: Despite Tom's claim, this line is not in the Bible. He might be thinking of the Song of Solomon 8:6 ("For love is strong as death").
1604	*is to Love*: perhaps a confusion of *to* with *the* (which can mean *to* in Anglo-Manx), although no need for the article is apparent. Capitalized and personified, *Love* does not look like part of an infinitive.
1729	*You'll get lave*: Brown's gloss ("All right!") gives only one of the meanings he found in the phrase. At the start of an argument it might signify permission for an opponent to have his say, while later it might mean, "'You may talk until Doomsday. . . but all the same I don't agree with you, and don't intend to" ("Manx Idioms: Interesting Lecture by T. E. Brown at Castletown," *Isle of Man Examiner*, 5 January 1897 (Scrapbook J10/16x, Manx Museum Library).
1947	*blossom like the rod for Aaron*: See Num. 17:8.
1948	*rose of Sharon*: See Song of Sol. 2:1

1949	*Its stalk is bruk, its leaves is shed*: The imagery suggests versions of "The Unquiet Grave" (Child No. 78):
	    O think upon the garden, love,
	      Where you and I did walk;
	    The fairest flower that blossomed there
	      Is withered on the stalk.
	    The stalk will bear no leaves, sweet-heart,
	      The flower will neer return. . . .
	See *The English and Scottish Popular Ballads*, ed. F. J. Child, 4 (Boston: Houghton, Mifflin, and Company, 1894): 475.

1968	*height. . . length*: Cf. Eph. 3:18.
1991	*anchor of her sowl*: Cf. Heb. 6:19.
1994	*Sim*: Tom's adopted son, "little Simmy" in *Betsy Lee*. The author of "Jesus, Lover of My Soul" (1740) is Charles Wesley (1707-88).
2039	*One flesh*: See Gen. 2:24.
2279	*Peel*: a port on the west coast some eleven miles southwest of Jurby Head.
2286	*the Waterwitch*: Several vessels bore this name: the *Manx Sun* for 29 May 1852 reported that a schooner, the *Water-Witch*, had been "swept onto the Chickens Rock and eventually sunk" off the Calf of Man.
2293	*To Scotland of course*: Under Scottish law, a couple could be married without any delay.
2319	*The Rue*: Gob Ruy, "red naze or point" (Kneen, p. 594), lying about a five miles northeast of Jurby Head. It could not be "westward a bit" from Renshent if this fictional farm is supposed to run "out on the shore" (519) near Jurby. The Rue is westward by about four miles from the Point of Ayre, the northernmost tip of the Island.
2330	*guy heng*: According to Wright, *guy* in northcountry dialects is a "disguised form of the word 'God,' used in petty oaths." Brown's gloss elsewhere is "go hang" (*CP*. p. 236).
2517	*Over the hills and far away*: the refrain of several songs: see note to *Betsy Lee* (1161).

2546	*hould your luff*: according to Professor Elizabeth Schultz, this might mean to get on course or mind your business. On a ship the command would mean to sail close to the wind while keeping the sail from luffing (fluttering). Cf. Hall Caine's novel, *The Deemster* (1887), where a Manx fisherman says, "If I was the old Bishop's son I'd hould my luff too. . . . But we've got ourselves in for it . . . and we're the common sort . . . and there's no sailin' close to the wind for the likes of us" (ch. 23 of the one-volume edition).
2550	*Shellags*: Shellag Point is on the northeast coast, about a mile southeast of Kirk Bride and near the imagined location of Nelly's home, just north of Ramsey.
2562	*Coroner*: an important official, especially before 1832, when some coroners had police and magisterial powers (Stenning, p. 82). Teignmouth equates the coronor's duties with those of a sheriff in England (2:238).
2591	*High-Bailiff*: a local official serving as superintendent of police whose duties included "abating nuisances" (Teignmouth, 2:237); Douglas, Castletown, Peel, and Ramsey each had a high-bailiff.
2623	*Guttery Gable*: a street in Douglas "from Arch Lane. . . leading into Howard Street" (Kneen, p. 223).
2735	*th' be*: *The* can serve as *to* in Anglo-Manx (Moore); it sounds like Manx *dy*, which means *to* before a verb (Cregeen).
2809	*at Moses theer*: See Ex. 3:1-6, where the Lord speaks to Moses from a burning bush.
2870	*holy kiss*: 1 Cor. 16:20: "Greet ye one another with a holy kiss."
2873	*unrighteous leaven*: Cf. 1 Cor 5:8: "the leaven of malice and wickedness."
2985	*seven divils*: See Matt. 12:43-45: "When the unclean spirit is gone out of a man, he walketh through dry places, seeking rest, and findeth none. Then he saith, I will return into my house from whence I came out; and when he is come, he findeth it empty, swept, and garnished. Then goeth he, and taketh with himself seven other spirits more wicked than himself, and they enter in and dwell there: and the last state of that man is worse than the first."
3084-5	*sleep. . . changed*: 1 Cor. 15:51.
3172-9	*Paul. . . marry her"*: Cf. 1 Cor. 7:36-7.
3186-8	*David. . . Abishag*: See 1 Kings 1:1-4: A "fair damsel," Abishag the Shunamite, is brought to lie in bed with the aged King David to keep him warm.
3218	*wings of the mornin*: Ps. 139: 9-10: "If I take the wings of the morning, and dwell in the uttermost parts of the sea; Even there shall thy hand lead me, and thy right hand shall hold me."
3242-3	*Seeds. . . birds of the air*: See Matt. 13:3-7, the parable of the sower.
3276	*Jezebel. . . Herodias*: See 1 Kings 16:31ff. and Matt. 14:3-12. Jezebel, the wife of King Ahab, persecuted the prophets; Herodias caused the beheading of John the Baptist.
3278	*Queen Bersheba*: Beer Sheba is a place in southern Palestine (see Gen. 21:31-3), but Cain thinks of the Queen of Sheba in 1 Kings 10.
3280	*Shunamite*: Abishag (3188) or the woman whose son Elisha restores to life in 2 Kings 4, but Cain confuses her with the beautiful young Shulamite in the Song of Solomon (6:13)—a figure sometimes interpreted as a "type of the Church" (3281).
3283	*daughter of Jerusalem*: The phrase with "daughters" recurs in the Song of Solomon.
3285	*Hagar*: See Gen. 16. Hagar was Abram's concubine.

Fo'c's'le Yarns 264

3286   *Ruth. . . Rahab*: See Ruth and Josh. 2:1-21. Left a widow, Ruth was famed for her devotion to her mother-in-law Naomi, and later she married Boaz; Rahab was the harlot in Jericho who sheltered the spies sent by Johsua.
3287   *Leah*: see Gen. 29:16ff. She was (in the King James version) "tender eyed."
3305-8   *banner. . . sick of love*: Cf. Song of Sol. 2:4-5.
3415   *oh Susannar*: "Oh Susanna," popular Negro Minstrel song by Stephen Foster. In the context of Cain's attempt first to seduce and then to frame a young woman, the name might also call to mind the story of Susanna in the Apocrypha.
3555   *"lest he fall"*: 1 Cor. 10:12.
3651   *The General Jail Delivery*: The Criminal Court that makes the final ruling after the accused has been found guilty at the Deemster's Court (see Teignmouth, 2:232-6).

Manx Fishing Smack c. 1820

Textual Notes:
Copy Texts, Treatment of Variants, and Editions Cited

Except in the case of *Betsy Lee*, this edition is based upon the first printings of Brown's texts. *Betsy Lee* was first printed privately at Cockermouth by I. Evening in 1871 or 1872, the later date being more likely. For the Macmillan edition of 1873, Brown changed the name of the lawyer's clerk, omitted four lines that Macmillan said sounded like someone else's, and dropped the couplet where "w——e" rhymes with "door." He also deleted six lines near the end that suggest a definite location for Tom's mythical native village (after 1658). These omissions were more than offset by additions that give a detailed account of how Tom Baynes and his newly adopted infant son got back from Liverpool to his home on the Island (1588-91, 1612-25). Because only two deletions look like self-censorship and the additions develop a previously sketchy segment of the poem, the 1873 version has been chosen as the copy-text.

Christmas Rose was also printed privately at Cockermouth; both *Captain Tom and Captain Hugh* and *Tommy Big-Eyes* were printed at Douglas in booklet form; they also appeared serially in the *Isle of Man Times*, as *Betsy Lee* had done before them. Brown's manuscripts for all these poems have vanished, except for one page of *Tommy Big-Eyes* in the Manx Museum Library. Brown relied upon the original printings when adding a gloss and preparing copy for the Macmillan edition of 1881. Apparently referring mainly to the problem of writing the gloss on already printed pages, he defended this procedure in a letter to Macmillan: "I am preparing printed copies, not a new MS., as, on the whole, the advantages of print overbalance the objection to crammed space and unsightly erasure. But, if your people find my *scoring* a nuisance, and would rather [have] a MS., I will do my best: only I hope they will manage with the printed copies" (17 November 1880). The reference to erasures and crammed space might indicate that he was doing more to the text than adding a gloss.

Since his marked copies have vanished along with his manuscripts, the nature of any substantial changes he might have made before receiving a letter of admonition from Macmillan's partner in early December 1880 remains unknown. In three cases he might have been expanding the poems, if his counting of their total lines can be trusted. On November 27, he wrote Macmillan that *Christmas Rose* had 2627 lines, which was around fifty more than it had in 1873. He wrote that *Captain Tom and Captain Hugh* had 1554 lines—177 more than the booklet version in 1878. At 3927 lines, *Tommy Big-Eyes* was now 136 lines longer than the 1880 text. *Betsy Lee*, on the other hand, was by his count of 1635 lines almost a hundred lines shorter than the

Macmillan edition of 1873. Brown makes no mention of these discrepancies. Unless he miscounted, they seem impossible to explain. Perhaps he added some lines to the printed copies and then omitted them once he was told to shorten *Tommy Big-Eyes*. If he had already cut passages from *Betsy Lee*, the deletions would have made it easier for him to comply with the publisher's recommendation; and they might explain why Brown requested only minor restorations of this text in 1889, while insisting that eleven omitted pages be restored to *Tommy Big-Eyes*. These are guesses; any chance for an authoritative explanation of the discrepancies has vanished along with the revised copies he sent to Macmillan.

Changes in the Copy-Texts for this Edition

Obvious misprints have been corrected when possible by comparisons with other editions, as shown in the Textual Notes. Where an exclamation point or question mark was not in italics following an italicized phrase, italics have been added, as in later editions. Not noted are the variants in the use of apostrophes for such words as *goin*, *runnin*, *isn*, and *didn*. This edition leaves out the apostrophes, following the uncluttered style of the 1873 text of *Betsy Lee* and the 1881 and 1889 editions of *Fo'c's'le Yarns*. After Brown's death, the 1900 edition regularly inserted these marks in place of a missing final *g* or *ot*. As one of the editors, Henley apparently preferred this fussier form, having used it for the last yarn, *Job the White*, when it appeared in his *New Review* in December 1895. The published texts may reflect printers' styles instead of Brown's own. The Cockermouth edition of *Betsy Lee* (1872) has no apostrophes in these places as a general rule, and neither does the Macmillan edition of 1873. The Cockermouth text of *Christmas Rose* generally follows the same rule, although apostrophes often mark the missing letters in *wasn* and *doesn*. The Douglas editions of *Captain Tom and Captain Hugh* and *Tommy Big-Eyes* tend to make apostrophes the norm, but there are many inconsistencies. Macmillan regularized the form by omitting these marks until the 1900 edition; subsequent editions, including the two-volume edition by the University Press of Liverpool in 1952, reproduce the busy markings of the 1900 texts. Whether Brown really cared about such matters is unknown. The single page of surviving manuscript from *Tommy Big-Eyes* has no apostrophe for the missing final *g* in two places but it may have it in two others where his marking is unclear. At any rate, the uncluttered form apparently satisfied him in 1872, 1873, 1881, and 1889, and it is restored here.

Unlisted Variants

The following sorts of variants have not been noted:
1. the use of a comma after such expressions as *oh*, *aw*, *aye*, *eh*, and *well*: commas were generally added here in *1900* along with the apostrophes after contractions or such words as *runnin*; both marks in these places are unlisted as variants;
2. the insertion of a colon before a dash in *1900* and the presence or absence of a hyphen between *a* and a participle;
3. spelling changes of such words as *gud*, *blud*, *cud*, *tuk*, and *surt* to *good*, *blood*, *could*, and *sort*;
   ether or *ither* or *nether* to *either* or *neither*;
   avar and *navar* to *ever* and *never*;
   ded, *hed*, *hev*, and *gev* to *did*, *had*, *have*, *give*, *gave*, or *given*;
   mayve and *tervil* or *terbil* to *maybe* and *terrible* or *terr'ble*; *cheer* to *chair*;
   theer to *there*, *masthar*, *sisthar*, *sesthar*, or *sesther* to *masther* and *sisther*;
   fuss or *fust* to *first*; and *oh* to *o*.

Additional unlisted variants are indicated in the following headnotes for each poem.

Editions Cited

Editions are identified by date, serial versions by initials. No date after a variant indicates that it first appeared in *1881* and remained in all subsequent editions. Unless *1889* is followed by *only*, the variant also appeared in *1900*.

1872	*Betsy Lee. A Fo'c's'le Yarn.* Cockermouth: I. Evening [1871 or more probably 1872]. The poem was published anonymously, as were all the yarns until *The Doctor and Other Poems* was published in London by Swan Sonnenschein, Lowry, and Company in 1887.
1873	*Betsy Lee, A Fo'c's'le Yarn.* London: Macmillan, 1873.
MM	*Betsy Lee, A Fo'c's'le Yarn. Macmillan's Magazine* 27 (April 1873): 441-57; 28 (May 1873): 1-18.
IMT	*Betsy Lee, A Fo'c's'le Yarn. Isle of Man Times*, 5 April–26 July 1873.
1873	*Christmas Rose.* Cockermouth: I. Evening, 1873.
1878	*Captain Hugh and Captain Tom: A Manx Story in Verse.* Reprinted from "The Isle of Man Times" [15 December 1877–12 January 1878]. By the Author of "Betsy Lee," "The Doctor," &c., &c. Douglas: James Brown and Son [1878]. Following the text is "Clifton, Dec. 7, 1873." The poem also appeared in *The Isle of Man Times*, 15 December 1877–12 January 1878.
1880	*Tommy Big-Eyes.* By the Author of "Betsy Lee," "The Doctor," "Captain Tom and Captain Hugh," &c., &c. Douglas: James Brown & Son, [1880]. Following the text is "Clifton. T.E.B." The poem also appeared in the *Isle of Man Times*, 22 November 1879–10 April 1880.
1881	*Fo'c's'le Yarns, including Betsy Lee and Other Poems.* London: Macmillan & Co., 1881.
1889	————————New edition, 1889.
1900	*The Collected Poems of T. E. Brown.* Ed. H. F. Brown, H. G. Dakyns, and W. E. Henley. London: Macmillan & Co., 1900. The second edition (1901) has an introduction by W. E. Henley.

St. Matthew's Church, Douglas
Frank Cowin Library

Textual Notes: Betsy Lee

The basic text for this edition is *Betsy Lee, A Fo'c's'le Yarn* (London: Macmillan and Co., 1873). It was preceded by a private printing at Cockermouth by I. Evening in 1871 or 1872--identified in the notes as *1872*. Although Brown was reading the manuscript to friends by November 1870, the poem was not finished until January 1871, according to his note in a copy of the 1873 edition. See Simon Nowell-Smith, "Some Uncollected Authors XXXIII: Thomas Edward Brown, 1830-1897," *Book Collector* 9 (1962): 342. (Nowell-Smith also reports that it was reprinted in *Every Saturday* [Boston, Mass.] in May 1873.) The *1873* text with typographical exceptions follows the serial version (*MM*) in *Macmillan's Magazine*, 28 (Part I in April, 1873): 44-57; (Part II in May, 1873): 1-18. Another serial version, copied from *MM*, appeared in five parts in the *Isle of Man Times and General Advertiser*, April 5, 12, 19, May 31, and July 26, 1873--identified as *IMT*. The substantial cuts made in the poem for Macmillan's first collected edition (*1881*) have been preserved in all subsequent editions, with minor exceptions which are noted. In *1872*, *Taylor* is *Nelson*, *childher* is generally *childer*, *divil* is *divel*, *Misther* is *Mister*, and ships' names lack italics. These variants are unlisted. When possible, typographical errors in *1873* have been corrected by using *MM* and other editions.

3	Clerk,] Clerk. *1900*.	58	patchin] patching *1872*.
5	pert,] pert *1900*.		mendin] mending *1872*.
14	divil of divils] divil of divil's *1881 only*.	59	goin] going *1872*.
		64	And a pretty face is] And we always find room for *1872*.
19-26	Omitted.		
20	case] case, *1872*.		
22	regular] reglar *1872*.	66	in,] in *1872*.
23	see,] see? *1872*.	68	speakin] speaking *1872*.
25	perhaps—] perhaps *1872*.	73-84	Omitted.
		78	tellin] telling *1872*.
31	hisn.] hisn, *1872*.	79	he—] he *1872*.
37	slidin] sliding *1872*. slippin] slipping *1872*.	85	Well—as I was a sayin,] That's the way. For
38	makin] making *1872*.	103	blue,] blue *1900*.
41-6	Omitted.	116	feet;] feet: *1900*.
45	somethin] something *1872*.	117	kep childher] *MM*; kep childer *1872*; keep childher *1873*; kept childher *1881*, *1889*.
46	now,] now *1872*.		
47	No ¶ *1872*.		
50	lumps,] lumps	119-24	Omitted.
54	sprat;] sprat, *1900*.	120	goin] going *1872*.

123	You—*ast my pardon?*—] You *ast my pardon? 1872.*	268 272 276	poethry] poetry *1872.* screetch] screech before,] before
128	done;] done: *1900.*	285	good-lookin] good
131	lookin] looking *1872.*		looking *1872.*
133	climbin,] climbin *1900.*	289	No ¶ *1872.*
	breakin] breaking *1872.*	291	shore,] shore *1900.*
	skulls] sculls *1872.*	294	moorins] moorings
141-2	Omitted.		*1872.*
149	bare,] *1872, MM;* bare *1873, 1881, 1889 only.*	311	me;"] me": *1900.*
155	my gough] aw dear.	328	smirk,] smirk:— *1900.*
158	higher;] higher! *1900.*	335	lookin grand] looking
166	pantin] panting *1872.*		grand *1872.*
168	I d—-s his eyes, and I] one for his nob, and	344 349	And—] And, *1900.* swear;] swear *1872.*
169	day] day, *1872, 1889.*	349-50	Omitted.
177	*Terrible—] Terrible,* *1872.*	364 365	thinkin] thinking *1872.* harm;] harm! *1900.*
	yes,] Yes, *1900.*	370	frock.] frock; *1872.*
179	somethin] something *1872.*		*After this line* And the breeze said—
187	well, well,] well, well! *1872;* Well, well, *1900.*		"I'm comin, I'm comin, dear!" / And the little
188	well, well] Well, well *1900.*		waves answered—"She's here, she's here!" / And
195	pretendin] pretending *1872.*		mawther a callin me in to bed! / God bless me—the
196	nothin] nothing *1872.* mendin] mending *1872.*		stuff that comes into my head! *1872*
198	eyin] eyein *1900.*		This was omitted in 1873
203	dungin,] dungin *1900.*		on the recommendation of
206	nimbly] nim'ly *1900.*		Alexander Macmillan,
209	said] said:— *1900.*		who wrote Brown that
210	Now,] Now *1872.*		"The two lines . . . telling
211	riz,] riz:—*1900.*		what the breeze and little
213	door;] door, *1900.*		waves said have a ring of
217	No ¶ *1872.*		some lines in hand. A
221-44	*Replaced with:* Yes, yes! and the cryin when I went, / Aw the Innocent! the Innocent!		very slight change would remove this, and the whole poem is so fresh and original that a small
232	divil] Divil*MM.*		thing of that kind which
236	cuttle-fish] cuttle fish *1872.*		minor critics would fasten on should not be left" (21
245-6	*Replaced with:* Now listen, my lads, and I'll give you the cut / Of what I calls a innocent fut.		Feb. 1873—"Letter Book" Add. 55393[1], Macmillan Collection, British Library). Apparently Macmillan
253	barra] barra, *MM,1889.*		had in mind Tennyson's
258	that can talk] that talk *1872.*		use of the pathetic fallacy in *Maud,* I, 837ff.—

Textual Notes: Betsy Lee

	parodied in 1871 by Lewis Carroll in Chapter II of *Through the Looking-Glass*.	530	a-top] a top *1872*.
		548	In the orchard—and the apple blossoms there
371-8	Omitted.	549	into Betsy's bosom] on Betsy's hair
379	¶.	550	out] off
390	picthurs] picturs *1872*.	557	handkecher] handkercher *1872*.
393	spunky] pert		
407	blows] blows, *1889*.	560	No ¶ *1872*.
410-1	Omitted.	566	kem] came
415	ould] Ould *1872*.	567	And as grand as grand, the two of them— *1881, 1889*; . . . them! *1900*.
432	tits] tits, *1900*.		
433	puzzle:] puzzle; *1900*.		
436	No ¶ *1872*.	568-9	Omitted.
	pat,] pat *1872*.	580	says—] says, *1900*.
437	Ayreshire] Ayrshire		go,] go *1900*.
438	strippin] breedin	582	Aw, Betsy] aw, Betsy *1872*.
443	Tite?] Tite. *1872;* Tite; *1889*.		
		586	No ¶ *1872*.
447	Tight for sure] Tight, for sure	590	she;] she.] *1889*.
		594	tenors] tenors, *1889*.
452-3	Omitted.	601	night.] night, *1872*.
455	and retch and hawk] but an eye like a hawk	602	I.] I, *1872*.
			he.] he, *1872*.
456	And cunning written all over his face—		Good night] Good-night *1900*.
457	farm] place	604	cussed] cussed, *1900*.
458-9	Omitted.	607	if] If *1900*.
460	No ¶ *1872*.		Come,] Come *1872*.
461	turmits,] turmits *1900*.	608	have] Have *1872, 1900*.
474	lookin higher] looking higher *1872*.		out,] out *1872*.
		611	have] Have *1872, 1900*.
483	hot,] hot *1889*.	615	no] No *1872*.
490	hopes, Misther Tite,] *1900;* hope's Mister Tite *1872;* hope's Misther Tite *1873, MM, 1881, 1889*.	616	the seat] him straight
		617-8	Replaced with: And sends him flyin over a gate, /And gives a look, and nothin stirred.
494	umble] 'umble *1900*.		
495	Misther] Mr. *1900*.	625	clerk] Clark *1872*.
496	myself—] myself, *1900*.	634	seine] seine, *1872*.
500	day,] day *1900*.	662-9	Omitted.
502	all right! all right!] All right! all right! *1900*.	665	say,] *MM, 1881, 1889;* say? *1873 only;* say! *1872 only.*
511	swilsh] swish *1900*.		
	tantaran] tăntărăn	668	No ¶ *1872*.
520	pressin] *1889;* pressin, *MM, 1872, 1873, 1881*	670	¶. And Betsy speakin so soft and low,
524	No ¶ *1872*. sing] sing, *1900*.	673	"Gentle Jesus"] Gentle Jesus *1900*.
		675	tight—] tight. *1900*.
527	and bless me] and, bless me, *1889*.	676	darlin] darling *1872*.
		680	all] quite *1872*.

684	shever] shiver		the beggarly breed] *the beggarly breed 1881 only.*
687	I] I've		
691	steer!] *1872, MM;* steer *1873;* steer. *1881, 1889.*	744	The lot of us was,] *The lot of us was; 1881 only.*
700	goin] going *1872.*		and—] and *1872.*
704	herrins] herrings *1872.*		how] How *1900.*
706	rent?] rent?— *1900.*	746-9	*Replaced with:*
708	No ¶ *1872.*		And *Jenny, and the proofs she'd got, / And I'd have to marry her, whether or not; / And— Taylor had taken up the case; / And how did I dar to look in his face? / "Taylor!" I says; "then let him take warnin! / For I'll have his blood before the mornin." 1881 only.*
715	quiet] quite *1872, 1881, 1889.*		
718	way,] way; *1900.*		
725	legs,] legs— *1900.*		
728-42	*Replaced with:* And says he, "I thought it was you," he says; / Now go your ways! just go your ways!" / "What is it?" says I. "That will do," says he. / "What is it?" I says. "Don't spake to me!" / He says; "and it's gettin rather could"— / And—*Misther Taylor— and what he was tould—* / *Yes—Misther Taylor.—* "Misther Taylor!" says I— / And then he out with it all, and the why / And the wherefore— and *Jenny Magee, indeed! 1881 only.*		
		746	says;] says. *1889.*
			no] No *1872.*
		750	"Oh!"] "Oh *1872.*
		751	and—*Could I expec'?*—] *and I could expec'— 1872;* and—Could I expec'?— *1889.*
		752	And—] And *1872.*
			did] Did *1900.*
		754	No ¶ *1872.* enough,] enough. *1872.*
		757	come] came
			and] *Not in 1872.*
		769	died;] died *1889;* died, *1900.*
		770	So help me God, sir] It is, sir, it is
728	very] verry *1872.*	773	Misthress] Mistress *1872.*
730	says;] says, *1889.* Oh] oh *1872.*	774	Betsy!] *1872, MM, 1889;* Betsy? *1873, 1881.*
733	"Oh raely,"] "Oh raely! *1872;* "Oh raely!" *1889.*		she'll] She'll *1900.*
734	it's] It's *1900.* in—] in *1872.*	779	houldin] holding *1889.*
		784	No ¶ *1872.*
736	Sin,] Sin *1872.*	795	found.] found, *1873 only.*
737	this!] this? *1889.* who] Who *1900.*	798	nothing] nothin
738	says;] *MM, 1889;* says, *1873.*	799	mornin] morning *1872.*
	I,] *1889;* I; *1873.*	800	Well,] *MM;* Well *1873.*
739	then he tould me why] Then he tould me the why *1889.*	800ff.	*villyan* —] villyan, *1872.*
743	And—] And *1872, 1881 only.* who] Who *1900.* I?] I? — *1889.*	812-21	*Omitted.*
		822	No ¶ *1872.*

834	'spec] spec *1872*.	973	twisses,] twisses *1872*.
837	was,] was *1872*.	981	Aldebarn] Aldebar'n
839	do?] do?" *1881, 1889 only*.	982	Orion] O r i̇ o n
		990	And—] And *1872*.
840	and—] and *1872*. fishin?"] *1872, MM, 1900;* fishin? *1873, 1881, 1889*.	992	And—] And *1872*.
		994	Good night,] Good night! *1872;* Good-night, *1889*.
		995	sir] Sir *1872*.
842	and—"How's] and How's *1872*.	996	Good night] good night *1872;* Good-night *1889*. good night] good-night *1889*.
851	smookin] smookin, *1900*.		
857	paunch!] paunch: *1872*.	997	all] All *1872*.
861	wire.] wire! *1900*.	998	No ¶ *1872*.
862	No ¶ *1872*.	999	What's] What
882-91	*Omitted*.	1003	and "What] and, "What *1900*.
891	roarin] *1872, MM;* roaring *1873*.	1009	And] And, *1900*.
892	quiet] quite *1872*.	1010	skutched] scutched *1872*.
892-3	*Replaced with:* Quiet he was, but you couldn doubt / The Pazon was knowin what was he about.	1013	be,] be *1872*.
		1017	toor] tore
		1021	aw,] Aw, *1900*.
		1023	young,] young *1900*.
		1035	cried—] cried *1900*.
898	No ¶ *1872*.	1036	out,] out *1872*.
909	nothing] nothin *1872*.	1039	sperrits] sperits *1872*.
916	No ¶ *1872*.	1040	Baynes] Baynes, *1900*.
918	Backwards] backards *1872, 1881, 1889*.	1041	aw,] Aw, *1900,* hard.] hard! *1900*.
924	said,] said: *1900*.	1047	The woman's-juice] The juice of her life
927	is] Is *1900*.		
928	No it isn!] No, it isn? *MM, IMT*.	1054	He] he *1872*.
		1061	death—] death. *1900*.
931	he,] he *1872;* he: *1900*.	1063	it] *1873, 1881, 1889;* it—*1872, MM;* it: *1900*.
933	he,] he: *1900*.		
937	Misthress] Mistress *1872*.	1066	did,] did; *1900*.
		1074	And who] and who *1872*.
943	spiteful] spiteful, *1889*.	1079	d——d] stupid
944	No ¶ *1872*.	1080-91	*Omitted*.
945	he says,] says he—*1872;* he says: *1900*.	1091	skum] scum *1872*.
		1092	No ¶ *1872, 1881*. "And] And
950	talkin] spakin		
955	home—"*in-tel-li-gent*"—] home, "*in-tel-li-gent,*" *1872*.	1094	And—*Misses Baynes!*] And *Misses Baynes 1872*.
		1095	got—and] got! and *1872*.
957	Pazons just] pazon's just *1872;* pazons is just.	1102	Misthress] Mistress *1872*.
958	talkin] talking *1889*. aw,] aw *1872*.	1103	people!—] people! *1872*.
		1108-13	*Replaced with:* And what was the matter with Jinny Magee?
959	Dan] *Dan*		
971	study] studdy		
972	wouldn't] wouldn *1872*.		

	/ Your wife! your wife! and why shouldn she be?	1202	my God] aw then *1881;* Aw then *1900.*
1114	And] She was	1205	ghoses] ghos'es *1889.*
After 1115	Bring home my bychild! bring home my w—e! / She'd never turn them away from the door. *1872*	1209	aren't] aren
		1210	kiss:] kiss:— *1900.*
		1212	Aw, Christ,] The look!
		1213	the] The *1900.*
		1226	child,] child; *1900.*
1117	Aw, she was raely quite ondacent to hear her. *1872.*	1227	villian] villain *1889* (*"villian" is not a typographical error, but is another spelling of the Manx form "villyan" used in 800ff.*).
1118	No ¶ *1872.*		
1124	strent',] strent' *1900.*		
1130	No ¶ *1872.*		
1134	d—- the shame] then I begun	1229	go,] go: *1900.*
1135	*Omitted.*	1230	owners] owners, *1872.*
1136	To think of yandhar Absalun, Absalun,] Absalun *1872.*	1231	Lloyd's] Lloyds *1872.* immadient] immedient *1872.*
1137	cryin] cryin: *1900.*	1237	But] But:— *1900.*
1141	hide:] hide; *1900.*	1248	No ¶ *1872.*
1145	free.] free, *1889.*	1253	Bell—] Bell. *1872.*
1154	her,] her *1872.* stirred;] stirred. *1872.*	1260	say] say:— *1900.*
		1266	Excep] Excep'
1155	word,] word. *1872.*	1272	the] they *1873 only.*
1161	aye] Aye *1900.* her.] her *1881;* her, *1889;* her: *1900.*	1278	And "he'd come again another day," *1872.*
		1279	glass] glass, *1889*
1176	"And surely hadn I heard] *And surely hadn I heard 1900.*	1280	No ¶ *1872.*
		1282	mornin] morning *1872.*
		1297	bleat!] bleat— *1872.*
	heard] herd *1872.*	1303	strange?—You didn—] strange? "You didn," *1872.*
1177	From nobody?"] *From nobody? 1900.*		
	divil a word] not a word	1304	d—n it] what
1178	No ¶ *1872.*	1306	Well,] So
1181	burnin] burning *1872.*	1323	Tom;] Tom, *1872.*
1183	pane] pain *1872.* half-hidden] half hidden *1872.*	1325	sea!] sea? *1872.*
		1330	betwix] betwixt
		1339	I:] I; *1900.*
1184	arm-cheer] arm-chair	1342	hesn] hasn't
1185	speer!] speer; *1872;* spare!	1343	heaven] Heaven *1872.*
		1344	him] Him *1889.*
1187	knee,] knee: *1900.*	1345	be G—] he'll die!
1190	tracks] track's *1872.*	1346	Thomas,] Thomas *1872.*
1197	God's!] God's? *1872.*	1348	and "wouldn] and "wouldn *1872;* and: "Wouldn *1900.*
1198	"But how about Betsy?" well] *But how about Betsy? Well 1900.*		
		1349	letter,] letter—
		1350-56	*Omitted.*
1199	aye] Aye, *1900.*	1355	villian] *Omitted in 1872; there is simply a blank*
1201	goes,] goes. *1889.*		

	space, which may suggest that Brown had originally used a stronger word which the printer saw fit to remove.	1530-2	So I took him up, and— "His name?" "It's Simmy:"
1356	Will you go to the Pazon?" says she; I laughed—	1531	Omitted.
		1536	Him] him *1872.*
		1537	ever—] ever,
		1546	No ¶ *1872.*
1357	craft,] craft; *1872.*	1551	going] goin *1872, 1881.*
1358	says;] says, *1872.*	1552	says I,] says I *1872.*
1359	Would I] Will you	1555-6	No italics *1872.*
1360	that] that,	1564	cowards;] cowards! *1872.*
1373	true.] true! *1900.*	1566	No ¶ *1872.*
1374	No ¶ *1872.*	1573	nathur] natur *1872.*
1381	mawther—] Mawther— *1881;* mawther:— *1900.*	1574	him,] him *1872.*
		1578	No ¶ *1872.*
1385	he;] he. *1872.*	1588-91	These lines do not appear in 1872, but were added in 1873 and included in all subsequent editions.
1386	"What wreck?" I said, "there wasn no wreck— /		
1387	Just Taylor's lies!" and I cussed him lek.		
		1590	logger] lugger
1388	stud.] stud, *1872.*	1600	Hungry!] "Hungry!" *1889.*
1397	'scuse] scuse *1872.*		
1406	No ¶ *1872.*	1612	No ¶ *1872.*
1414	right!] right *1872.*	1612-25	These lines do not appear in 1872, but were added in 1873 and included in all subsequent editions.
1416	Now,] Now		
	says,] says *1872.*		
1419	smilin] smiling *1872.*		
1420	*A son of ould Dan's!*— aye,] "A son of ould Dan's!" aye *1872.*	1614	Map] *Map*
		1618	—well! well! good Lord!"] too—my word!"
1421	*A son of ould Dan's!*—] "A son of ould Dan's!" *1872.*	1625	couldn] could *1873 only.*
		1626	And you] You *1872.*
		1632	No ¶ *1872.*
1429	then,] then *1872.*	1641	long,] long *1872.*
1436	No ¶ *1872.*	1647	sonny?] sonny, *1872;* sonny— *1889.*
1441	luck!] luck *1872.*		
1444	lodgins] lodgings *1872.*	1649	laughin,] laughin; *1889.*
1465	thinkin—] thinkin, *1900.*	1656	middling] middlin *1872.*
		1658	sky;] sky, *1872.*
1484	No ¶ *1872.*	After 1658	And "Awake my soul," and then down! down! / And takin the road for Castletown, / And the bright the sun was shinin then— / And the church peepin up at the end of the glen, / And the vane like a spark of gold, and below— / The stones— and—well, you know! you know! *1872.*
1490	childer] childher		
1496	I;] I, *1872.*		
	dying] dyin *1872, 1881.*		
1503	And] And: *1900.*		
1510	No ¶ *1872.*		
1522	ye!—Yes!"] ye? Yes!"— *1872.*		
1529	and, my God!] and she smiled!		
		1662	well,] well—

Textual Notes: Betsy Lee — 275

1663	*No ¶ 1872.*	
1672	all] all, *MM*.	
1686	ye,] ye! *1872.*	
1687	*No ¶ 1872.*	
1692	bending] bendin *1872.*	
1697-99	*These lines first appear in 1873.*	
1699	There at her grave! at her grave! at her grave! *1872.*	
1705	murderer's] murderers *1872.*	

Textual Notes: Christmas Rose

The basic text for this edition is the privately printed *Christmas Rose* (Cockermouth: I. Evening [1873]). There is no serial version of the poem. It was substantially cut and revised for the Macmillan edition of 1881. Except for the rare *amn'* (*am not*), variants in the use of apostrophes after contractions have not been listed. *Betsey* (spelled thus everywhere but 2336 in *1873*) has been changed to *Betsy* as in *Betsy Lee* and in *1889* and *1900*.

1	the Pazon!" says you—] just stop a bit!	187	bresses] breasts
2-51	*Omitted.*	195	¶.
53	gorrit. . . gorrit! It's lek] got it. . . got it? It's like *1881;* got it! *1889.*	196	do] do,
		198	rolled him] rolled him,
		207	handkercher] handkecher
		208	looked,] looked
59	practisin] practīsin,	211	ther] their
67	shore] shore,	218	espec'] expec'
78	bame] beam	225	manifess] manifess,
80	mawther!] Mawther! *1889.*	228	Hidalgar] *Hidalgur 1900*
		229	home at the Pazon] up to the church
83-4	*Omitted.*		
85	And cuttin like mad;] And this way, that way,	230-8	*Replaced with:* And next day the Pazon come down to search / For a nuss, and got an aunt of mine— / Just the woman! in the washin line— / And shuited capital—aw the best / Of characters— aye—and no sort of address, / No sign, nor marks, except on its shirt / An I, and a D, and a thing like a sort / Of a haythen God, or some of these charms— / I think they called it a *coat-of-arms*;
95-7	*Replaced with:* Wasn I after him? knowin his ways,/ And a hold of his arm, and we saw the blaze / Of a rocket go		
105-48	*Omitted.*		
149	¶. Not on the point,] Ashore, but not		
152	shoals] shoal's *1873 only.*		
161	D—— ye! drop it now!] Well look here now! drop it,		
168	back;] back?		
169	lef'] lift	249	vess] verse
170	adref'] adrift	250	fess] first

277

253	fuss-rate] stunnin		I'd miss my stroke for lookin—yes! / Aw, I couldn take no rest.
259	soopil] soople		
262	darkie] darkey *1900*.		
273	tould] told	417	¶.
275	no-ways] noways *1900*	433	Ghos'] Ghost
278	you] you,	436	That 'd. . . brek] That would . . . break
279	but] But *1900*.		
281-4	*Omitted.*	437	waking] wakin
287-90	*Omitted.*	438	enough . . . shaking] enough, . . . shakin
295-306	*Omitted.*		
312	upon my sowl] that's the way I'm tould—	440	drame.] *1881;* drame *1873*.
317-8	*Replaced with:* The time she took Hagar, that was imperint to her, / And jawed her, and put her to the door.	441	¶.
		443	us] us,
		446	judgement] judgment
		449	doesn] doesn't
		452	gloriously.] gloriously?
323	aw d——] ah, dart	455-6	*Omitted.*
324	brek] break	457	And bless ye! keeping] Bless ye! keepin
328	yit] yet		
332	snotty noses] big round eyes	461	kind] kind, *1889*.
		462	la'] la *1881, 1889 only*.
337	aburrit] middlin free	469	yis] yes
338-9	*Replaced with:* "Now 'Tilder," he says, "don't worry me / About the lek; for, I tell ye, 'Tilder—	474	fet] fit
		483	imprince] imperince
		495	sorras] sorrows
		496	sporras—?] sparrows?—
		500	'a] have
354	spunk] go	504	thes] this
355	trees] trees,	512	it] it,
360	ger] get	527	behin'] behind
361	Bless me the emps] Bless me! the imps	535-42	*Omitted.*
		543	Me] And me
363-4	then they were jus' / Soft innocent baby things, I suppuss:] then, no doubt, / They were innocent baby things, runnin about,	545-6	*Omitted.*
		555	art] art,
		559-60	*Omitted.*
		563	scandalous] scand'lous
		568	curley] curly
367	come] grew	569	wenches] wench's *1900*.
	lumps] lumps, *1900*.	583-5	*Replaced with:* Comin off her skin, like it's sayin about Moses
369-400	*Omitted.*		
401	That's it—aye!] And me of them,	592	Ger] Get
		596	red] red,
403	sense] sense, *1900*.	602	drem] dream
406	nine] mine,	603	drem] dream
407-9	the brave. . . of them] *Omitted.*	605	¶.
		612	lep] lip
411	strong] strong,	627	when jig-a-maree!] when—what was the spree
413-6	*Replaced with:*		
		628	Her] But her
		633	wase] waist

634	aw it was a race] it was just a race	735	d——d your eyes] cussed ye,
638	asund'rin] a'sund'rin *1873 only*.	744	that—eh? What cheer?] —Ah Betsy, dear!
639	and] and,	745-67	*Replaced with:* Yes, yes, yes, yes! the difference! / I know, I know! and taken hence— / That's it—we must— and—Come, come, come!
644-5	dar] dare		
647-50	*Replaced with:* And never stopped for gate or stile, / Till I'd done the bettermost part of a mile. / But that same night I couldn sleep, / And back to the place, and I made a sweep		
		774	singin,] singin— *1889*.
		782	And] And, *1889*.
			me] me, *1889*.
653	queck] quick	786	dirt;] dirt! *1900*.
658	d——] despard	787-8	*Omitted.*
662	they] they,	790	but] but, *1900*.
667	stud] should	793	this stuff!] then!
673-4	*Omitted.*	794	d—— the clothes!] and—clothes! is it clothes?
675	And] But		
682	imprint] imperint		
685	My gough] Aye!	795	d—— the lot!] Aw blow the lot!
687-8	*Omitted.*		
689	*wasn I ouldher*] wasn I ouldher *1873 only*.	815	bruk. . . henges] broke. . . .hinges
		825	sparra] sparrow
691	talkin,] talkin *1873 only*.		drops] drops
		836	ha'] ha *1881, 1889 only*.
707	come forrit!] draw near!	845	Yes] yes, *1889*.
708	I hadn gor it] it didn appear	847	kep] kept
		848	A purpose . . . swep] O' purpose. . . swept
709	No not a bit] I had it at all		
711-2	a mixture / At them and at me—that's the way I fixed her] and them / And me betwixt us, and—*Miss* and *Mem!*	870-3	gunwhale] gunwale *1889*.
		877	No! d—— it] No! no
		879	my gough] dear heart
		880	Come] That come
		882	her] her
714	up's *in all editions*.	884	urr o'] out o' (*x2*).
715-6	gives . . . God] says—"I forgive his rudeness;" / And "He has his pardon"—his pardon! My goodness!	886	strenth] strength
		888	lightnin] lightnin,
		899	faintin,] faintin *1873 only*.
		904	bit] bit,
718	at me straight] to lift me	906	Lek it 'd . . . tong] Like it would . . . tongue
720	*nacassary*] *necessary*		
721	I'd bathar] *That was it!*	908	dreft] drift
722	rather] a bit	909	coorse] course
723	¶.	910	oors] oars
727	and in] and the in	912	nothing] nothin
731	me that was in] me, aw it was	915	my God] yes, yes
		916	O Christ] the wild
732	houldt] held	919	yit] yet
		921	¶.

924	the divil itself] despard though	1077	My gough!] Aw dear *1881, 1889;* Aw dear! *1900.*
928	And d—— it all!] Three strokes, and	1080	picthar] picthur *1889.*
941-2	*Omitted.*	1083	D—— it all] Aw, I tell you what
943	Or] To	1085-90	*Omitted.*
952	urr ov] out of	1102	he says, "what are you at?] says he, "what stuff have you got?
955	Ger out] Get along		
963	hevn] haven't		
965-6	hise] heise	1103	the lot of us] the three of us
976	And . . . do!] White as the dead! huroo! hurroo!	1104	God d—— it!" he said,] And he out with a cuss—
977	shadder] all		
978	Wavin . . . feddhar] Like a tree when it doesn't know which way to fall	1105	when he said that though] aw as free as free
		1106	And . . . know] Just a little cuss, you see,
981	clothes] lap		
983	well lerrit! lerrit!] but it's likely not—	1126	couldn't] couldn
		1135	doubt;] doubt:
984	what. . . sperrit] still now? was it the sperrit— what?	1137	and 'll try] and she'll try
		1139	by this and by that—] —"Aw," I says, "Masther James,
989-94	*Omitted.*		
995	Navar mind!] And	1140-1	*Omitted.*
997	then] then?	1148	nussed] nursed
999	is."] *1881;* is" *1873.*	1149	wouldn't] wouldn
1003	to mother;] with us straight,	1150	sek] sake
		1151	quite] quiet
1004-5	And. . . not—] And mawther there, and gettin a light, / And grumblin (I heard her; but lettin on not)	1155	d'ye see?] so he says
		1156-7	*Omitted.*
		1158	*Parentheses.*
		1167	at us] betwixt us
		1170	hot:] hot;
1010	"Masthar] Masthar *1873 only.*	1172	wrong.] wrong *1881 only.*
1014	freckened] afraid	1173	comin. . . ragin,] aye fits! and him I'd known
1019	seck] sick		
1026	th' tell] to tell	1174-6	*Omitted.*
1029	not much of a light] and lost no time	1177	Aw dear! aw dear!] *Omitted.*
1030	but aw! he turned white] but turned like lime	1179	well the Lord he] well the Lord He *1889;* Well, the Lord He *1900.*
1035	handhar] hinder		
1036	wandhar] winder	1187-8	*Omitted.*
1046	My God!] Aw dear!	1189	About] And
1053	¶. yes] Yes *1900.*	1195	he says, and he grips] he says; aw dear!
1057	My gough! . . . the fur] Well now!. . . what at	1196-7	*Replaced with:* What would he do? and his eye that clear / And
1058	like her] like that		
1059	And upon my soul] And, it's no use o' talkin,		

	strong! and all that proud and keen,	1426	head] head;
1204	bye-and-bye] by-and-by	1437-9	*Replaced with:* Does it float about everywhere like a mesh / So fine you can't see't? is it blast? is it blight? / Is it fire? is it fever? is it wrong? is it right?
1207	know] know—"		
1208-11	*Omitted.*		
1212	But them so young] Aisy, Billy!		
1213	Strange!] *Strange!*		
1233	rainin] rainin,		
1247	tippin] tippen *1873 only.*	1451	by G—— he sees us!] ah! He sees us!
1251	clothes—aw the holy father!] clothes; he beat me clane,	1455	the houldt and the grep] the hold and the grip
		1464	"he loves her! he does!] "he loves her true;
1252-3	*Omitted.*	1465	*Replaced with:* And what am I to do? what am I to do?
1256	what—] what *1881, 1889;* what, *1900.*		
1267-74	*Omitted.*	1478	D—— it!] By Jove!
1280	"My God!"] The hard!	1480	You! by ——,] You then, you!
1291-2	*Omitted.*		
1293	And love] Love	1489	d—— ye!] will ye?
1295	said] said, *1889.*	1496	you must ha' knowed;] and knowin what you knows—
1296	and big d—s] and the cusses		
1299-1304	*Omitted.*	1497-9	*Replaced with:* Me! me, did ye say? for the Christmas Rose!
1305	But on and on] And cusses again		
1309	and put] and then	1504	here I am!] that's it! that's it!
1310-4	*Omitted.*		
1316-8	*Replaced with:* Three times she said it—"and the eyes lookin down,	1505	a d——] a spit
		1510	and] and, *1900.*
		1517	troubles] troubles,
1333	says] says, *1889.*	1533	When the wind's bruk at him] When his wind is broke
1341	might] *might*		
1342	yit] yet	1534	In his belly] That bad
1353	bress] breast	1537	d—— it all!] bless my heart!
1356-71	*Omitted.*		
1372	And *How was she there?*] And *What had happened?*	1539	force] foorce
		1542	my gough! Well] My goodness! Well *1881;* . . . Well, *1900.*
1377	studdy] steady		
1378	He was at her again; and] He stooped, and he kissed her;		
		1544	d——d] nasty
		1546	bruck] broke
1380	To her bress—] To hear—	1548	blast] dart
1390	—aw scandalous!] — aw dear! if they'd seen us.	1550	¶.
		1553	what the divil] I'll tell ye what
1391	at us] between us		
1392	wake, and treigh] weak and slack	1573	fiss] fist
		1574	my gough! the smash] aw dear! the smash!
1422	my God! they're about] I say!—they're about		
1424	¶.		

1578	No by ——] No, George Gale	1697	guess—] what?
1582	could,] could *1873 only.*	1698	Women eh?] Women, aye!
1584	yis! yis,] yis! yis *1873;* yes! yes! *1881;* yes! yes, *1889.*	1702	D——] Avast
		1703	all that sort] every sort
		1714	d—— it] I'll tell ye
1587	agin] against	1719	lekly] likely
1590-1	Omitted.	1723	bress] breast
1593	"take] take *1873 only.* blow] blow, *1873, 1881 only.*	1728	¶.
		1730	screp] scrape
		1737	hoss] horse
1594	pipe"] pipe *1873, 1881 only.*	1740	hent] hint
		1748	yis] yes
1598	¶.	1752	Harvis] harvest
1604-7	Omitted.	1768	My gough] Aw dear
1608	whether—"] whether— *1873, 1881 only.*	1769	spec] speck
		1771	hould the handkercher] hold the handkecher
1611	He had though for all— "Now ger] He had, you know——"Now get	1776	¶. I felt] So I felt
		1778	d——d. . . keer] boostly. . . care
1613	I gor it] I've got it	1779	feer] fair
1623	And childer to foller] And as happy as happy	1780	gor] got
		1791	then] then,
1627	till] than	1796	your] *your*
1642	queen] Queen *1881 only.*	1797	*I've*] I've
1645	d—— nonsense] nonsense	1799	*Strong-hearted,]* Strong-hearted
1652	now—hurroo] now hurroo *1881, 1889;* now, hurroo *1900.*	1806	juss] just
		1813	them'll] them will
1654	¶.	1833	¶.
1656-70	Replaced with: It's like lovin God: for it's seemin to me, / When you're lovin the loveliest things you see, / It's lovin God that made the things—	1842	b'live] believe
		1847	Queen] queen *1900.*
		1854	and a rippin her bresses bare] aye, aye, and her neck all bare
		1862	What 'd ye do] What would ye do
1664	everything!"] everything "*1873 (space for punctuation).*	1863	¶.
		1883	ups] *1900;* up's *1873, 1881, 1889 .*
1671	That God has made:] That made them—eh?	1900	harvis] harvest
		1909	wanting] wantin
1675	hoss] horse	1911	quite] quiet
1676	whan] when	1921	Quite—tervil quite] Terrible quiet
1677	his. . . avar] His. . . ever		
1679	heises] lifts	1922	And a sort of a choke at him, and] And—what to do? and,
1680	Till] Than		
1681	for you la! not for you.] *period added 1889;* for you man, not for you	1924	Dodgin] dodgin
		1926	and dear! aw dear!] aw dear! aw dear! *1889.*
1696	hess] has got		

1933	miserble] miser'ble	2175	He] *He*
1944	plain eh?] plain, eh *1889.*	2193-2212	*Omitted.*
		2217	yit] yet
1956	Queen] queen *1889.*	2225	punch and judy] Punch-and-judy *1881;* Punch-and-Judy *1889.*
1967	bress] breast		
1968	Aye] Aye, *1889.*		
1979	Rose!] Rose; *1873 only.*	2229	beggar] begar *1873 only.*
1984	Queen] queen *1889.*	2237-42	*Omitted.*
1988	navar 'll] never will	2257	no no! not he!] no! no not he! *1873 only.*
2004	And] Aw *1889.*		
2017	stell] still	2265	come home—aw then the work] was home again—aw the work
2023	¶.		
2025	why . . . fran] *why not have a spree when you can*		
		2275	¶.
2029	and *yandhar fellas*] and blow the fellows	2290	closs] close
		2307	and *scoffers*] *and scoffers*
2031	chaps 'd] chaps would	2321-4	*Replaced with:*
2034	leks] likes		And to think a woman that locked away / Her soul in a safe, and hid the key
2041	¶.		
2052	baiting] baitin		
2056	keer] care		
2070	gone down, and] gone and	2333	ye see,] I heard
		2334-5	*Replaced with:*
2073	piller. . . heer] pillar. . . hair		From ould Peggy long after—aw every word. / Of coorse! of coorse! But the very next day—
2075	tobacco dust] tobacco-dust		
2076	heise] rise		
2081	¶.	2342	scess] skess
2081-2	*Replaced with:* But the first sign of day, we'd be down to the boat, / And him rather heavy and stupid to 't,	2349	middin] midden
		2355	what] *What*
		2357	Manin] Meanin
		2368	"Oh] Oh *1873, 1881 only.*
2099	it Tom] it, Tom *1889.*	2369	¶.
2106	knowin?] knowin *1900 only.*	2370	brest] breast
		2378	one *one*] one, *one*
2115	¶.	2389	Love me mother. . . Misthress'] Love me, mother. . . Misthress's
2117	Mawther . . . *aweer*] mawther. . . *aware*		
2122	and] and *1881, 1889 only.*	2393	¶.
		2422	anger] anger,
2125	told] tould	2432	my Queen! my Queen!] my Queen—my Queen! *1881;* my queen—my queen! *1889;* My queen—my queen! *1900.*
2129	chatt'rin] chatter'n		
2130	pattrin] pattern		
2144	couldnt] couldn		
2169	¶.	2433	¶.
2171	furder from him he drev her] furder, and sick and sore	2436	mane] mean
		2447	surt] sort
		2460	Till. . . duss] Than. . . dust
2172	than ever.] and more, *1881;* and more. *1900.*		

2468	ham,] ham *1873, 1881 only.*
2479	man's,] man's *1873 only.*
2489	down on a big ould stone] down, like for him to be goin
2490	like] wish
2495	star] stare
2501	¶.
2505	feer] fair
2506	Lancashire] Lancasheer
2508	aw well well well] aw well, well, well! *1889.*
2514	Australia] Austrilia
2529	her] *her*
	I know] I know—
2532	men!)] men!)—
2535	Half-a—d—— it then!] Half-a—half-a——Well,
2540	home] home,
2543	bay] bay *1873 only.*
2546	its] it's *1873;* the *1881, 1889, 1900.*
2556	back suck] back-suck
2562	crag?] crag
2563	*Replaced with:* I couldn tell, and wondhering,
2575	shouted—] shouted. . .
2577	lek,] lek

Textual Notes: Captain Tom and Captain Hugh

The basic text for this edition is *Captain Tom and Captain Hugh: A Manx Story in Verse* (Douglas: Brown & Son [1878]), reprinted from the *Isle of Man Times* (*IMT*), 15 December 1877 through 12 January 1878. This text (*1878*) was severely cut for the Macmillan edition of *Fo'c's'le Yarns* (*1881*). Subsequent editions, *1889*, *1900*, substantially reproduce the *1881* text, with variants only in punctuation and spelling. Ships' names were first italicized in *1889*, and this change is not marked. When possible, misprints in *1878* have been corrected by using later editions.

15	divilment] fun that was goin	183	father 'd. . . owner 'd] father would. . . owner would
16	other 'd] other would		
35	kem] came	184	rascal 'd] rascal would
37	hem] him	208	No ¶.
46	keer] care	225	much] much,
51	'ill] will	226	plaise] plaze
55	aw] bless ye!	244	nearer] nearer,
56	No ¶.	251	hawk] hawk, *1889*.
58-9	Omitted.	256	doesn] *1881;* does'n *1878 only.*
69	look 'd] look would		
70	own] own, *1889*.	262	gev] gove
82	ded] did	268	aqual] aequal
86	husbands 'd] husbands would	276	know the odds] throw the odds *1878 only.*
87	may be] maybe *1889*.	279	dog 'd] dog would
94	evenin] everin	282	No ¶.
95	though] though,	298	lek 'll] lek will
104	good nathured. . . and 'd] good-nathured. . . and would	314	No ¶.
		319	By gogh I'd ha'] Aw deed! I'd have
110	shoors] shores	326-36	*Replaced with:* So they fell in love like birds in the spring,
111	coorse] course		
129	Hugh] Hugh,		
139	another,] another.	337	Till] And
140-63	Omitted.	340	collogin] colloguin
174	th'd] tha'd	352-3	Omitted.
		354	And] But

Fo'c's'le Yarns

356-7	Omitted.	596	hommer] hammer
360-1	Omitted.	598	¶.
362	No ¶.	604	Hugh!] Hugh;
364	Again] Against	607	they were on deffrin floors] *they were on diff'rin floors*
375	Their] *Their*		
380	linking] linkin		
381	thinking] thinkin	609	compar] *compare*
398	No ¶.	611	my gough] look here
400	bezniss. . . some 'll] business. . . some will	614	agin] against
		616	New-street] New Street
401	my gough. . . tember] dear heart. . . timber	617	Malew-street] Malew Street
404	fust] first	621	cheer] chair
415	No ¶.	622	considhern] consider'n
417	together—] together *1878 only.*	623	had] have *1889.*
		632	skallions] a smell
421	druv] drove	633	lek these chaps with stallions] lek something to sell
422	hoss 'd] hoss would		
425	Now,] Now *1889.*		
430	Castletown 'd] Castletown would	654	gor] *got*
		664	saying] sayin
433	No ¶ *1881, 1889 only;* thigh] thigh,	671	mainin] meanin
		677	ha'] ha *1889 only.*
441	somewhers] somewhere	679	quevers] quivers
442	says, "ha!] says, ha! *1881 only.*	680	I muss I muss] I must, I must
443	may be] maybe *1889.*	681	buss] bust
449	Tom. There's] Tom—there's *IMT*.	688	maenin] meanin
		689	gone?"] *1889;* gone? *1878.*
451	differin.] differin--	704	"Aw] *1889;* Aw *1878, 1881 only.*
457	agin] against		
458	The. . . Deed. . . Hughie] the. . . 'Deed. . . Hughie,	705	batthar] better
		709	"Ruch] Ruch *1878 only.*
462	semple] simple	716	the rale ould blood;] who was he?
473	gor] got about—] about *1878 only.*		
		729	them!] *1900;* them? *1878, 1881, 1889.*
474	roor] roar		
476	agin] aginst	736	flent] flint
502	[God bless me!] *Omitted.*	763	uncle] Uncle
512-4	Replaced with: Or—well, ye see, what you're knowin, you're knowin;	764	things!] things? *1881 only.*
		767	clapsin] claspin
545	urro] out of	772	Deed] 'Deed *1900.*
546	and 'd] and would	792	mane] mean
572	man] man, *1889.*	804	deed] 'deed
578	¶. gor] got	805	good!] good.
580	sundhar] sundher	811	my gough] my word
593	Ned] Ned,	812	dart] dart,
595	there] *1889;* their *1878, 1881 only;* tay—] tay, *1889.*	822	agin] aginst
		873	study] steady
		878	whataver] whatever

881	Clypse] Clyps	1302-61	*Replaced with:*
882	By gough] Why, bless ye		And poor Annie, you know, the fond she was / Of Uncle Hugh; but lost is lost, / And that's a fact, and, do what you will, / The world must go on, and its good and its ill--
889	sleppy] slippy		
891	They] There *1878, 1881 only.*		
894	ould] ould, *1889.*		
896	¶.		
910	Tom 'd hav'] Tom would have	1362	And married him] So married the chap
911	well, you see] well, now		
920	Hould] hould		
945	Hugh; so says he] Hugh: so says he,		
959	silen'] silen *1881 only.*		
966	movemen'] movemen *1881 only.*		
967	improvemen'] improvemen *1881 only.*		
974	Aw, very] Very		
999	lent] leant *1889.*		
1000	agen] against		
1008	brek] break		
1011	gor] got		
1024	they 'll] *1900;* they 'all *1878, 1881, 1889.*		
1025	breathin] beathin *in all editions.*		
1027	still.] still,		
1028-9	*Omitted.*		
1030	"Coortin] Coortin		
1033	talk 'd] talk would		
1040	listen,] listen. *1878 only.*		
1045	bough] bogh		
1056	side!] side:		
1066	by gough] indeed		
1084-1127	*Omitted.*		
1135	by gough] off		
1166	urro] out of		
1193	twisses] twists		
1214	canvass] canvas *1889.*		
1231	Clypse] *Clyps 1889.*		
1240	afterwards] you know,		
1241-3	*Replaced with:* That the Captain tould him to go below.		
1252	outs] *1900;* out's *1878, 1881, 1889.*		
1253	life,] *1889;* life *1878, 1881.*		
1285	studdy!"] *1889;* studdy! *1878.*		

Peel Bay and Town, published by T. Carran c. 1850
Rodney Quayle Collection

Textual Notes: Tommy Big-Eyes

The basic text for this edition is *Tommy Big-Eyes* (Douglas: James Brown & Son [1880]). The poem first appeared in the *Isle of Man Times* (*IMT*) from 22 November 1879 through 10 April 1880. It was substantially cut for the first Macmillan edition (*1881*); major restorations appear in *1889*; these remain in *1900*. Unmarked changes include the use of periods after *Mr* and *Mrs*, which started with *1881*. The different forms of *misthress* in *1880* have been regularized according to *1889*; *terible* has been given the standard spelling. When possible, misprints in *1880* have been corrected by using later editions. One correction has been made on the basis of the single known page of surviving manuscript (MS. 1301c. in the Manx Museum Library).

The dedicatory poem that introduced this yarn in the 1880 edition was also printed in the first installment in the *Isle of Man Times* (22 November 1879).

5	Now,] Now *1889*.	493	Being] Bein
17	*No ¶*.	494	bad,] bad.
37	Then,] Then *1889*.	495-516	*Omitted*.
148	May—] May *IMT*.	540	Bellies like] As round as
168	And "Aw, my gough!] "And listen, Tommy!	547	evenin, an'] everin, and
169	slow] slow, *1889*.	566	despard] desp'rate
179	duck"; . . . dove";] duck;" . . . dove;"	603-16	*Omitted*.
180	love";] love;"	653-79	*Omitted. New ¶ begins* So that'll do—all right! all right!
205	master;] master then;	669	scowlin,] scowlin *1880*.
345	way—] way;—	685	*No ¶*. wasn't] was'nt *IMT, 1880;* wasn
348	"My gough] "Dear heart		
349	Turn] Turn,	688	evenin] everin
357	Tommy,] Tommy	689	getting] gettin
369-70	*Omitted*.	700	misthress] Misthress *1880, with erratic spelling and capitalization; this text follows 1889 by keeping the h and capitalizing the word only in direct address or when it precedes a proper name.*
430	me!] *1900;* me *1880;* me. *1881, 1889*.		
462	Pa'sons] Pazons		
477	"Nelly!"—certingly! Nelly!] "Nelly!"—certainly! Nelly! *IMT;* "Nelly! Nelly!"—certainly!		
489	Must,] Must *IMT*.	714	Crusa—] Crusoe.

289

751	*wasn't*] wasn		A piece with him, just for a trial / How the piano would work with the viol
755-88	*Omitted.*		
811-32	*Omitted.*		
841	¶.	1068-71	*Replaced with:*
845	right over him, a way he had,] far off—"Now, gifts, my friend,		"It's—a very unsatisfactory sperrit;" / Says Cain, "but, however, lerrit! lerrit!
846-53	*Omitted.*		
849	said. He] said, he *IMT*.	1068	carnel;"] carnel" *IMT*.
873-4	*Omitted.*	1072	*Lerrit*] Lerrit"
881-2	*Omitted.*	1075	Was] Wos *1880 only*.
883	That time at all.] "Who asked your opinion?	1092	man] men
		1104	No ¶.
889-92	*Omitted.*	1129	Excellent] Excellent,
893	Very holy and] And then he got as	1130	these] them
		1168	¶.
894	now] *Omitted.*	1190-1	*Replaced with:*
959-60	scrubs . . . molligrugs] scrowls, / But a sort of booin you'll hear at these owls.		Take the viol from him! fall him! / Lick him! kick him! smash him! maul him!"
976	tenor] tannor	1192-1207	*Omitted.*
978-9	*Replaced with:*	1208	But Tommy? Tommy!] Poor Tommy! poor Tommy!
	And ript and rapt, and tagged and tore, / And nothin—but now it was different,		
		1212	didn't] didn
		1223	*hedn!*] hedn?
984-7	*Replaced with:*	1224	No ¶. And put to the door, and black in the face
	Like butter, the soft you'll observe, he was playin— / Like butter— Aw he worked it grand!	1228-9	*Replaced with:*
			And that would do. But, whether or not, / A servant like Tommy
991	'll] will		
993	yondhar] yandhar	1265	to'm] *IMT, 1881;* to'em *1880.*
996	No ¶.		
998-9	*Replaced with:*	1267	skin—] skin.
	And the boys to the door, and begun to push, / And shout, and kick: but the gels said—*hush!* / Hush! they said,	1268-73	*Omitted.*
		1279	good] good,
		1283	tongue] tongue.
		1284-5	*Omitted.*
1015	a'] a	1293	Aye,] Aye *1880 only*.
1016	tenor] tannor	1296	can't] can *1881, 1889 only*.
1018	*Not indented 1881; indented 1889.*		
		1303	was—now] *1889;* was. Now *1880, 1881.*
1025-7	But . . *At a leap,*] "But . . . At a leap,"		
		1322-3	*Replaced with:*
1027	may be] maybe *1889*.		"Look up!" and he did, and he saw the dressed, / And the grew and all, and he looked around.
1054-6	*Replaced with:* Them gifts, and *remindin him of Paul,*		
		1329	¶.
1066-7	*Replaced with:*		

Textual Notes: Tommy Big-Eyes 291

1346	Aw, by gough!] I'll tell ye what!	1762-7	*Omitted.*
1378	stock;] stock.	1789	*And her with him?* Well, never say die!] die? *1880;* And her with him. All right! all right! *1881.*
1379-80	*Omitted.*		
1390	gold] gool		
1391	stallions] hosses	1790-7	*Omitted.*
1412	pazon 'd be] pazon would be	1801	my gough!] you know!
		1802	you know:] — the very!
1419	my gough!] is it fun?	After 1807	Moores! it couldn't! don't ye see?
1441	sooryin with their chaps] there they'd wait and watch	1808-19	*But... all] Omitted.*
		1819	But] And
1442-83	*Omitted.*	1826-7	And he'd ... weddin,] (He'd ... weddin),
1488	divil] mortal		
1491	Soup and blankets] Out in the cowld	1871	my gough!] aw dear!
		1905	God 'll] God will
1502	own] *own*	1907-16	*Omitted.*
1504	Agen] Against	1925-40	*Omitted.*
1517	coming] comin	1950	tould] *tould*
1528	bye and bye] by and by	1951-9	Now. ... And] *Omitted.*
1530	verse] vess	1959	¶. But the pride of the man! the pride of the man!
1545-9	The stores... offended] *Omitted.*		
		1963	Make! make! make?] Make? make? make!
1545	And stores and stores; and so, if ye plaze	1972	God bless your soul!] Make what you like!
1550	And] He		
1557	evenin] everin	1973-7	*Omitted.*
1561	¶. happy for all] happy though, for all	1978	fair,] fair? *1889.*
		After 1978	That's it! that's it! I have you there—
1564	And] *And*		
1599-606	*Omitted.*	1995	my gough!] you're foolish!
1608	my gough!] dear bless ye!		
1640	quiet] quite	After 1996	*Simmy repeats:—*
1659	Breast to breast!] Yes, yes!	2011-87	*Omitted.*
		2088	*No ¶.*
1669	*oh! and oh!*] "She's lost! she's lost!"	2089	Like ... hell] To Tommy there—aw well, well, well!
1670-3	Would... he said] *Omitted.*		
		2090-1	*Omitted.*
1679	*¶.*	2120	My gough!] Dear me!
1696	isn!] isn? *IMT.*	2125	My gough!] Ah!
1710	Dear me!] *1881;* Dear me? *1880 only.*	2129-31	*Replaced with:* And no mistake about this gel,
1728	betwixt—] betwix *IMT.*	2132	All... just] No mistake! and
1738	misthress. Would] Misthress would *1881;* misthress would *1889;* misthress: would *1900.*	2136	bould] bold *1900.*
		2150	raal] rael
		2174	took her bonnet off] caught her round the neck
1744	tunes] times *1880.*	2175-6	*Omitted.*
1761	the confidence—what bother!] what was it she wouldn dar?	2178	towld] tould *1900.*
		2190	my gough!] just so!

2209	my gough!] you know,	2746	ar'n] *MS;* ar'n' *1880*
2210	*No ¶.* quiet as quiet,] quite as quite	2748	*No ¶. MS.*
2230	*No ¶.*	2750	Is it leeks—is it—what is it now?] *MS;* Is it leeks. Is it? What is it now *1880.*
2238-9	*Omitted.*		
2264	*No ¶.*		
2266	jack-daw] jackdaw	2753	rhino of—] rhino of; *MS.*
2268	*¶.*	2754	heart, as] heart—as *MS:* heart, As *1880.*
2282	evenin] everin		
2288	nat'ral] nathral	2762	d'ye] do you *MS.*
2302	speaking] speakin	2768	didn't] don't *MS.*
2307	canvass] canvas	2770	*No ¶.*
2309	theere] theer	2772	my gough!] ah dear!
2314	My gough! the drippin!] And wet to the skin,	2788-9	*Omitted.*
		2795	sore that sucked] wheel that spun
2334	bruk] broke		
2357	Betwixt] betwix	2796-834	*Omitted 1881; restored 1889.*
2359	tide 'd] tide would		
2361	My gough!] Bless ye!	2810	ifs] if 's *1900.*
2373	'll] Will	After 2834	And a thing like that, you know, couldn be hidden; / And others saw it, but Nelly didn— *1881.*
After 2373	Are you wantin to get drowned?" says I.		
2374-6	*Omitted.*		
2382	by gough] I tell ye	2843-54	*Omitted.*
2398	my gough] my eye	2855-906	*Omitted 1881; restored with minor changes 1889.*
2399	I swear I thought] I raelly thought		
2400	divils] chaps	2899	*¶. 1889.*
2421	my gough] aw dear	2906	go on] *1881;* go go on *1880.*
2432	*¶.*		
After 2473	Aw very bad! very bad!	2907-14	*Omitted.*
2474-6	*Omitted.*	2915-3403	*Omitted 1881; restored with minor changes 1889.*
2488	as if her neck]—so we done our endeavour		
2489-92	*Omitted through* Cain, sure enough	2929	*¶. 1889.*
		2942	My gough!] Good grayshers! *1889.*
2513	exac] exac'		
2568-71	*Omitted.*	2982	seen] see *1900.*
2572	Nor the nothin them times—] Poor thing! poor thing!	2997	sea,] sea. *1889.*
		2998	*¶. 1889.*
		3002	Isn] Is'n *1880, 1889.*
2573	mane] mean	3015	O God] O God, *1889.*
2584	as] of	3057	My gough!] I don't know what! *1889.*
2633	bother] butter		
2642	evenin] everin	3059	times, sittin] times, though, sittin *1889.*
2645	arm cheer] arm-chair		
2650-83	*Omitted 1881; restored 1889.*	3204	round] around *1889.*
		3228	Cain;] *1889;* Cain *1880.*
2673	My gough!] Aw dear! *1889.*	3252	fax] fac's *1889.*
		3253	ax.] ax? *1889.*
2717	else 'll] else will		
2718-69	*Omitted.*		

3283	'the ... Jerusalem'] "the ... Jerusalem" *1880, 1889 only.*	3514	*He shouted]* And he shouted
3296	his] His *1889.*	3543	*particuler]* particular
3316	arrit] *1889;* arrit! *1880.*	3545	Aw, by gough!] Yes, indeed!
3339	Committee] Cōmĭttēē *1889.*	3553	holiest] holiest?
3352	¶ *after* door. *1889.*	3554-5	*Omitted.*
3355	"Aisy!"] *1889;* Aisy! *1880.* Shuperintendan] Shuperintandan *1880.*	3563	my gough!] bless me!
		3577	divil] fella
		3604	nothing] nothin
		3613	looking] lookin
		3617	case 'll] case will
3356	"Aisy] *1889;* Aisy *1880.*	3632	childar] chidhar *1880 only;* childher
3358	Aisy!] Aisy! *1889.* Gellin.] *1889;* Gellin! *1880.*	3644	By gough] Aw bless ye
		3682	sir] Sir *1880 only.*
3360	tellin;] *1889;* tellin *1880.*	3686	As the Divil] As keen
3367	wasn] was'n *1880, 1889 only.*	3694	pison.] pison, *1880 only.*
3371	*mortgages]* Mortages IMT.	3704	raison.] raison." *1880 only.*
3391	Shuperintendan] Shuperintandin *1880.*	3710	law 'll] law will
		3728	by gough ... fact] aye! ...fac'
3401	knees,] knees *1889.*	3732	By gough] Indeed
3404	So ... Sunday] So one Sunday though	3735	divil] villyan
		3740	kep] kept *1889.*
3413	understand] understan'	3741	villain] rascal
3414	mayve a manner] maybe a way	3751	by gough] bless ye!
		3760	Nelly very pale—] Nelly, and the people expectin
3415	oh Susannar!] but as good as a play		
3416	*Omitted.*	3761	*Omitted.*
3417	looked another way] lookin rather glum	3763	She'd] Lek she'd
		3781	aw faith] aw 'deed
3418	*Omitted.*		
3428	My gough! what would] Ah, think! what *would*		
3436	*misthresses]* misthress'		
3444	My gough] Ah dear		
3478	That ... Nelly.] Nelly! Nelly!		
3481	*won't ... won't]* won't ... won't		
3482-4	*I'm]* I'm		
3494	No ¶.		
3504	Cain] Caine *1880 only.*		
3502	staggering] staggerin		
3512	my gough! what *iss]* aw dear! what is		
3513	The d——] And the		

Castle Rushen and Harbour by G. Pickering, 1832
Rodney Quayle Collection

Selected Bibliography

Broderick, George. "Manx," in *The Celtic Languages*, ed. Martin J. Ball with James Fife. London: Routledge, 1993.

Brown, T. E. "Christ Church Servitors in 1852: By One of Them." *Macmillan's Magazine* 19 (November 1868): 49-54.

———. *The Complete Poems of T. E. Brown*. Introduction by W. E. Henley. London: Macmillan, 1901.

———. *Letters of Thomas Edward Brown*. Edited with an Introductory Memoir by Sidney T. Irwin. 2 vols. Westminster: Constable, 1900.

———. *Poems of T. E. Brown*. Introductory Memoir by Sir Arthur Quiller-Couch. 2 vols. Liverpool: University Press of Liverpool, 1952.

———. *T. E. Brown: An Anthology*. Selected and introduced by Dollin Kelly; illustrated by Catherine James. Douglas: Mannin Printing for the Manx Heritage Foundation, 1997.

Caine, W. S., ed. *Hugh Stowell Brown: His Autobiography, His Commonplace Book, and Extracts from His Sermons and Addresses*. London: George Routledge and Sons, 1887.

Conrad, Joseph. *The Nigger of the "Narcissuss."* Ed. Robert Kimbrough. New York: W. W. Norton, 1979.

Cookson, Elizabeth. *Poems from Manxland, with Legends and Translations from the Manx and German*. London: Eliot Stock, 1868.

Cregeen, Archibald. *A Dictionary of the Manks Language*. 1835. Ilkley: Moxon Press, 1984.

Cringle, Terry, R. E. Forster, and G. N. Kniveton. *Here is the News: An Illustrated Manx History*. Douglas: The Manx Experience, 1992.

Cubbon, William. "Thomas Edward Brown." *A Bibliographical Account of Works Relating to the Isle of Man*, 2. Oxford: Oxford University Press, 1939.

Gill, W. Walter. *Manx Dialect: Words and Phrases*. London: Arrowsmith, 1934.

Godman, Maureen E. "An Edition of *Christmas Rose*: The Second of T. E. Brown's *Fo'c's'le Yarns*." M.A. thesis, University of Kansas, 1990.

Hughes, Arthur, and Peter Trudgill. *English Accents and Dialects*. Second edition; London: Edward Arnold, 1987.

Kennedy, Peter, ed. *Folksongs of Britain and Ireland*. New York: Shirmer Books, 1975.

Killip, Margaret. *The Folklore of the Isle of Man*. London: Batsford, 1975.

Kneen, J. J. *The Place-Names of the Isle of Man, with their Origins and History*. Douglas: The Manx Society, 1925-6.

Manx Sea Fishing, 1600-1990's: Resource Book. Douglas: Manx Heritage Foundation, 1991.

Moore, A. W., with Sophia Morrison and Edmund Goodwin. *A Vocabulary of the Anglo-Manx Dialect*. London: Oxford University Press, 1924.
Moore, A. W., ed. and trans. *Manx Ballads and Music*. Preface by T. E. Brown. Douglas: G. & R. Johnson, 1896.
Morrison, Sophia, and C. Roeder. *Manx Proverbs and Sayings*. Douglas: S. K. Broadbent, 1905.
Nowell-Smith, Simon, ed. *Letters to Macmillan*. London: Macmillan, 1967.
―――. "Some Uncollected Authors XXXIII: Thomas Edward Brown, 1830-1897." *Book Collector* 9 (1962): 338-44.
Oxford English Dictionary. 2nd ed. prepared by J. A. Simpson and E. S. C. Weiner. 20 vols. Oxford: Clarendon Press, 1989.
Paton, C. I. *Manx Calendar Customs*. Publications of the Folk-Lore Society 110. London: W. Glaisher, 1939.
Quiller-Couch, Arthur et al. *Thomas Edward Brown: A Memorial Volume. 1830-1930*. Intro. by Ramsey B. Moore. Cambridge: at the University Press on behalf of The Isle of Man Centenary Committee, 1930.
Raban, Jonathan. *Coasting*. New York: Simon and Schuster, 1989.
Robinson, Vaughan, and Danny McCarroll, eds. *The Isle of Man: Celebrating a Sense of Place*. Liverpool: Liverpool University Press, 1990.
Shimmin, N. L. "The Making of a Manx Literature: Regional Identity in the Writings of Hall Caine and T. E. Brown." Ph.D. diss., University of Lancaster, 1988.
―――. "Nostalgia and Cultural Development--Manx Identity in T. E. Brown's Fo'c's'le Yarns." *Literature of Region and Nation* 1 (July 1989): 3-14.
Shore, Charles John, Lord Teignmouth. *Sketches of the Coasts and Islands of Scotland and of the Isle of Man,* 2 vols. London: John W. Parker, 1836.
Simpson, Selwyn G. *Thomas Edward Brown, the Manx Poet: An Appreciation*. London: Walter Scott Publishing Company, 1906.
Stenning, E. H. *Isle of Man*. London: Robert Hale, 1950.
Sutton, Max Keith. *The Drama of Storytelling in T. E. Brown's Manx Yarns*. Newark: University of Delaware Press, 1991.
Tobias, Richard. *T. E. Brown*. Boston: Twayne Publishers, 1978.
Wright, Joseph. *The English Dialect Dictionary*. 6 vols. 1898-1905. London: Oxford University Press, 1961.

About the Editors

Max Keith Sutton received his B.A. from the University of Arkansas and his M.A. and Ph.D. from Duke University. He is a professor of English at the University of Kansas.

Maureen E. Godman received her B.A. from the University of Leicester and her M.A. and Ph.D. from the University of Kansas, where she is assistant director of Freshman-Sophomore English.

Nicholas L. Shimmin received his B.A. from the University of Sidney and his Ph.D. from the University of Lancaster. He works for Cambridge University Press in Sidney.

Gannet